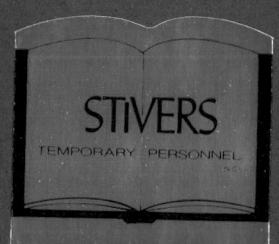

Strauss and Sayles's Behavioral Strategies for Managers

GEORGE STRAUSS

Professor, School of Business Administration and
Associate Director, Institute of Industrial Relations
University of California, Berkeley

LEONARD R. SAYLES

Professor of Business
Graduate School of Business
Columbia University

PRENTICE-HALL, INC.   Englewood Cliffs, New Jersey 07632

Strauss and Sayles's Behavioral Strategies for Managers

Library of Congress Cataloging in Publication Data

STRAUSS, GEORGE.
 Strauss and Sayles's behavioral strategies for managers.

 Includes bibliographical references and index.
 1. Organizational behavior. 2. Management.
3. Supervision of employees. I. Sayles,
Leonard R., joint author. II. Title.
HD58.7.S76   658.3   80–11533
ISBN 0-13-851287-6

Strauss and Sayles's Behavioral Strategies for Managers
George Strauss and Leonard R. Sayles

© 1980 by Prentice-Hall, Inc., Englewood Cliffs, N.J. 07632

All rights reserved. No part of this book may be reproduced in any form or by any means without permission in writing from the publisher.

Printed in the United States of America

10 9 8 7 6 5 4 3 2 1

Editorial/production supervision by Ann Marie McCarthy
Interior design by Maurine Lewis
Cover design by Wanda Lubelska Design
Manufacturing buyer: Gordon Osbourne

PRENTICE-HALL INTERNATIONAL, INC., London
PRENTICE-HALL OF AUSTRALIA PTY. LIMITED, Sydney
PRENTICE-HALL OF CANADA, LTD., Toronto
PRENTICE-HALL OF INDIA PRIVATE LIMITED, New Delhi
PRENTICE-HALL OF JAPAN, INC., Tokyo
PRENTICE-HALL OF SOUTHEAST ASIA PTE. LTD., Singapore
WHITEHALL BOOKS LIMITED, Wellington, New Zealand

contents

preface ix

1 *the meaning of work: employee needs and satisfactions* 2

Impact of the industrial revolution, 3 Needs satisfied by working, 5
Primarily physical and security needs, 6 Primarily social needs, 9
Primarily egoistic needs, 9 Relative importance of various needs, 13
Determinants of job satisfaction, 17
How important is satisfying work? 18 Conclusion, 25

2 *motivating people to work* 27

The traditional approach, 28 Human relations, 32
Implicit bargaining, 36 Competition, 38 Internalized motivation, 39
Expectancy theory, 42 Conclusion, 45

3 *innovations in job design and scheduling* 47

The nature of mass production work, 49 Job redesign, 54
Goal-setting, 63 New work schedules, 66 Conclusion, 71

4 *supervisory behavior: balancing structure and support* 73

Blind alleys, 74 Structure, 80 Support, 82
Structure and support: when to use them, 86 Conclusion, 91

5 *group behavior: organization consequences* 93

Why groups are formed, 93 How work groups are formed, 96
Group commitment creates problems, 101 Status systems, 103
Emergence of functional roles and informal leadership, 107
Group cohesiveness, 108 Conclusion, 110

6 the supervisor as group leader 111

Legitimacy, 112   Building a work team, 117   Developing group participation, 119   Working through the informal organization, 127

7 communications: the information transmission process 130

The communication process; the sender's world, 131
The world of the receiver, 134   Improving communication, 139

8 communications: the problem-solving process 147

The use of the nondirective approach, 152
Listening techniques, 153   Things to avoid, 157

9 introducing change: the managerial issues 160

Types of resistance to change, 160
What causes resistance to change? 161   Reducing resistance to change, 169

10 using discipline for effective performance 180

Avoiding discipline, 181   Types of discipline, 182
The red-hot-stove rule, 183   The role of the union, 191
Government imposed standards, 193   Conclusion, 195

11 decision making and organization levels 196

The nature of hierarchies, 196   Hierarchies create managers in the middle, 200
Delegation, 203   Span of control, 213   Conclusion, 215

12 organization design: alternative structures 217

Lateral relationships, 217   The role of structure, 218   Designing the major subdivisions of the organization, 220   Building work-flow teams, 231
Interdependence among units, 236   Integration mechanisms, 238
Understanding service and advisory relationships, 242   Conclusion, 246

13 organization development and management training 248

Management training, 248   Requirements for effective training, 249   Conventional training techniques, 253   T-group training, 255   Organization development, 258
Evaluating training and OD effectiveness, 267

14 *performance appraisal and management by objectives* 269

Traditional performance rating, 270   Alternate rating methods, 274
The evaluation interview, 277   Management by objectives, 280

index 287

preface

Over the past forty years there has been a virtual explosion of new knowledge about managing people in organizations. Unfortunately, much of this behavioral research is locked in abstruse journals. Many of the textbooks that have sought to summarize these findings are both discouraging and difficult. They emphasize jargon, complex definitions, and oftentimes, rather academic arguments about the intellectual relationship of Professor X's work to that of Professor Y's.

In contrast we have sought to write a book for managers and aspiring managers, in jargon-free English, to emphasize how actual people react to typical organizational and managerial situations. While we have absorbed the relevant literature, we have also spent our entire professional careers studying real organizations. We can be realistic about what is most useful and likely to make a difference in improving managerial effectiveness.

Successful, effective managers have no doubts about the importance of behavioral skills. No matter how technical the field, influencing, supervising and motivating people are at the very heart of the manager's job. First-rate managers are, above all, men and women of action who can develop loyalty and commitment from subordinates as well as from peers. They have learned a variety of organizational and human behavioral skills that enable them to cope with an endless array of challenges and frustrations. Each day will bring new problems, but the managers, who understand how modern organizations function and what motivates people, approach their jobs with confidence that they can correctly analyze the problem and handle the solution.

Managers are attracted to "buzz words" and the latest fads. Although many of these do have real value, we think any "solution"—whether it be MBO, job enrichment, a matrix, organization development, flex-time, behavior mod, and many more—needs to be understood in the context of how individuals, groups, and larger structures function under the pressures of time and day-to-day problems. In this field, as in every other, there are tough trade-offs to be made and difficult choices for the manager who must satisfy a variety of groups and objectives.

Our work is equally balanced between individual and small group problems of motivation and communication and the demands of the larger organization. While we seek to be down-to-earth and practical, our ideas are grounded in the findings of the behavioral sciences.

Both the ideas and the mode of presentation have been tested in hundreds of groups of managers and students, and we have sought to find examples from our own field work to capture the reality and challenge of the issues.

Managers occupy one of the most critical roles in our society; here are the strategies, the concepts, and skills for handling the tough human problems that absorb most of their time and energy.

Strauss and Sayles's Behavioral Strategies for Managers

the meaning of work: employee needs and satisfactions

It's hard to imagine the changes in human life that have come about in western civilization over the past two centuries. For thousands of years the material conditions of our existence (the way food, clothing, and shelter were produced) remained relatively unchanged. And then, since 1800, at an ever faster pace, we have had steam engines, locomotives, the telegraph, automobiles, airplanes, radio, atomic energy, and space exploration. Our way of life has changed unbelievably—but perhaps in no area has the change been greater than in the way people earn their living.

Let us look for a moment at the "industrial relations" of yesteryear—for only by examining the past can we bring into focus the problems of today. Back in 1800, 90 percent of the American people lived on farms, and the percentage was not much lower in Europe. Although there were large plantations in some sections of the country, most farmers owned and worked their own land, receiving aid at harvest time when neighbor helped neighbor. The family was the basic economic unit. Father worked in the fields. Mother processed the food (in a way housewives rarely do in this age of supermarkets), cooked the meals, spun the wool, made the clothes, and did the household chores. Brother and sister were assigned simple tasks almost as soon as they could walk. Labor relations and family relations were the same.

**CHAPTER 1
the meaning of work**

Economically, the farm was almost self-sufficient. A man was his own boss. No one could tell him when to plant or harvest, or could give him a written warning if he started work three minutes late. True, nature and the weather might prove more tyrannical than any foreman, but what a man produced was his own. His motivation was clear: If he was lazy, his own family suffered.

Furthermore (in contrast to what prevails in many jobs today) his efforts brought tangible fruit. Looking at his growing fields, he could say with real satisfaction, "Look what *I* have created." He, his family, his life, and his job were all tied together in a rich oneness that many look back on with nostalgia. (Few farmers today, however, would give up the benefits of tractors or electricity, nor would their wives long enjoy dipping candles and spinning wool. The earlier farmer's hours were long and his frustrations many. The continuing exodus from farm to city over the last century indicates that, for all its disadvantages, many prefer our urban civilization to the simple country life.)

Even in earlier days, the farmer might have had a younger brother who worked in the city as a journeyman wagon maker. He was a wage earner, not his own boss. And yet, how different the meaning of his job was to him than to his great-great-grandchild who tightens bolts on the final line of Chevy No. 3! He knew he would not be a journeyman for long. If he saved his money, he might expect to set himself up in business within a few years. Relations between himself and his boss were simple and easy—at times almost like the relations between father and son. The older man taught the younger what he knew and together they performed the same job. The work was creative and satisfying. Building a wagon required skill, and when the job was finished the worker could see what he had done. He could be proud of his craftsmanship and sure of his place in the world.

Such was the way some people earned their living not so many years ago—even though our picture is admittedly somewhat idyllic. After all, a slave on a plantation or a peasant in Europe was often just a working beast, and few wage earners had the sense of skill enjoyed by our journeyman wagonmaker. In fact, contemporary society may offer far more scope for skills than did any previous society.

Impact of the industrial revolution

The last two centuries have brought a dramatic revolution, not only in what we make, but in how we make it. The industrial revolution has been a revolution not only in technology but also in human relations. As technology grew more and more complex, people became more dependent on one another and the problems of working together became more troublesome. Today, typically, Americans are no longer their own bosses; they are not farmers, but city dwellers. Furthermore, the industrial revolution has brought major changes in what it means to be an employee.

The journeyman wagon-maker did a whole job from beginning to end. But one of the distinguishing marks of the industrial revolution is specialization.

Specialization

Here is Adam Smith's famous description of changes that were taking place in pinmaking two centuries ago, in England:

A workman not educated to this business . . . could scarce, perhaps, with utmost industry, make one pin a day, and certainly not make twenty. But in the way in which this business is now carried on . . . one man draws out the wire, another straightens it, a third cuts it, a fourth points it, a fifth grinds it at the top for receiving the head; to make the head requires two or three distinct operations; to put it on is a peculiar business. . . . I have seen a small manufactory of this sort where ten men only were employed and where some of them consequently performed two or three distinct operations. But though they were very poor, and therefore but indifferently accommodated with the necessary machinery, they could, when they exerted themselves, make upwards of forty-eight thousand pins in a day.[1]

Economically, specialization has brought great advantages. But it has brought many disadvantages as well: boredom and the loss of a sense of individual importance, of accomplishment, of pride in work. How much satisfaction can a worker obtain from spending the entire day pointing pins?

Further, workers feel that they are shackled to work processes they have had no hand in developing. The Industrial Engineering Department frequently determines every detail of the job, depriving the individual of any chance to show initiative or originality. Specialization has sharpened the dividing line between workers and management.

Specialization has also developed within management. Instead of a single owner-manager with complete control over the plant, or a foreman with complete control over a department, we have staff departments such as engineering, production scheduling, purchasing, and personnel. No person performs more than a small part of the whole job or has significant control over what he or she does. A dozen staff agencies may be involved in making a simple decision, and the worker is at the very bottom: "Everybody gets consulted but me. I just carry out their orders."

Opportunity to get ahead

To make the industrial revolution possible, elaborate machinery was necessary—and machinery requires money. The journeyman craftsman needed little more than his own tools to set himself up in business, but the worker on the automobile assembly line cannot hope to compete with General Motors. Unless he or she wants to operate a small store or a gas station, the modern worker has far less chance to own his own business than did his great-grandfather.

Even after the average person's chance to become an *independent* industrialist had vanished, the avenue of promotion within a company remained wide open for many years. Fifty years ago an able and ambitious man might conceivably work himself up from sweeper to president. Today, as our technology and business life become more and more complicated, opportunities for noncollege people become increasingly limited. Sociologists call this phenomenon *blocked mobility.* People can still get ahead through hard work, but without a college degree it is a much more arduous task than it used to be.

[1] *The Wealth of Nations* (New York: Modern Library, 1937), p. 4.

Organizational growth

The industrial revolution has made business organizations larger and the boss more remote. The journeyman wagon-maker had no trouble talking to his boss; communication was easy. Today, however, an employee may spend a lifetime in a steel mill and never talk to the plant manager, let alone the president.

The owner of a wagon shop could easily supervise all phases of manufacture. In a business like AT&T, supervision and coordination require the services of thousands of executives. All this leads to the process of bureaucratization, the making of rules that restrict individual discretion even to the point where top executives find themselves tied down.

Constant change

In the simple society of the early 1800s, changes were rare. Behavior was governed by tradition: there was no need to tell a man what to do—all he had to do was follow the patterns laid down by his ancestors.

Modern industry is subject to constant change. That very fact creates two types of problem: (1) Less can be left to routine; careful planning, deliberate orders, and elaborate communications are essential. Since personal experience and tradition are less valued, there is a correspondingly greater need for rules and regulations. (2) Motivating people to work together has become more complex. People often resist change, particularly when it is imposed upon them; consequently, they must be convinced that the new way is better.

In short, the industrial revolution has done wonders to make life easier for all of us, but at a serious cost in terms of the rewards and enjoyments that individuals derive from their jobs.

The rest of this chapter will be concerned mainly with three questions. What sorts of needs are satisfied through work?[2] How can these needs be ranked in relative importance? And how important as a source of satisfaction is one's *job* compared with other means of satisfaction available in life?

Needs satisfied by working

Although the authors recognize that all attempts to categorize needs are somewhat artificial, we shall speak of three forms of need satisfaction.[3]

1. *Physical and security needs.* These relate to the satisfaction of bodily desires, such as hunger, thirst, shelter, and the like, as well as the need to be secure in the enjoyment of these.

2. *Social needs.* Since human beings are dependent on each other, some needs can be satisfied only when the individual is helped or recognized by other people.

---

[2] The concept of needs has been criticized by two schools of thought. The oldest, the Skinnerians, argue that behavior should be studied in terms of *what* people actually do rather than through seeking to determine a *why* in terms of felt need or purpose. B. F. Skinner, *Science and Human Behavior* (New York: Appleton-Century-Crofts, 1957). A second, newer approach denies that needs are fixed or stable and argues instead that felt needs in any given situation depend on factors such as expectations, commitments, and social forces. Gerald Salancik and Jeffrey Pfeffer, "A Social Information Processing Approach to Job Attitudes and Task Design," *Administrative Science Quarterly*, 23, No. 2 (June 1978), 224–53.

[3] We are indebted to our teacher, Douglas McGregor, for many of the concepts discussed in this chapter. McGregor, in turn, adopted these from Abraham Maslow, "A Theory of Motivation," *Psychological Bulletin*, 50 (July 1943), 370–96.

3. *Egoistic needs.* These relate to the desire to be independent, to do things on one's own and to sense accomplishment.

Another way of categorizing needs is in terms of the means by which they are satisfied. Some forms of satisfaction are enjoyed *off the job*—paychecks are usually spent after work, away from the job. Other needs are satisfied through having a happy, satisfying work environment *around the job*. A third form of satisfaction can be obtained only through the process of working and so can be called intrinsic or *through-the-job* satisfaction. As we shall see in later chapters, this three-way distinction is critical for the motivation of employees. When management emphasizes off-the-job satisfactions, it assumes, in effect, that work is a punishment that employees endure in exchange for rewards to be enjoyed after work. Managers who stress around-the-job satisfactions seek to make the work environment a pleasant one, but do not provide direct, positive motivation for people to work harder. To the extent that through-the-job satisfactions are provided, employees work hard; the harder they work the greater their satisfaction.

As will be seen, both categories—the needs and ways in which these needs are satisfied—overlap a bit, and many needs can be placed in more than one category. Nor is there any hard-and-fast relationship between the sets of categories. To a considerable extent, however, physical needs are satisfied off the job, social needs are satisfied through personal contacts around the job, whereas egoistic needs are chiefly satisfied through the job. There are, of course, many exceptions: Safe working conditions satisfy an important physical need, yet they are enjoyed on the job; status is a social need, yet the status derived from holding an important position is enjoyed away from work as much as on the job; praise is another social need, yet praise from one's boss is often best obtained through doing one's job well; a salesclerk may satisfy social needs through work—the more sales he makes, the greater his opportunity to meet people.

With the above warnings in mind, let us now look at the various forms of need satisfaction obtained from work, starting with physical and security needs.

Primarily physical and security needs

Ask people why they work, and chances are they will tell you, "to make money." Certainly the need to earn a living is the most powerful single reason for working, though, as we shall see, nonmonetary incentives are also important.

Money

Money satisfies all types of needs. Its principal use may be to provide the physical necessities of life as well as security; however, social status in our society depends largely on the size of one's earnings; and earning a good income provides many people with an egoistic sense of accomplishment.

The first demand most people make of a job, then, is that it provide them with enough to enjoy a "proper" standard of living. But what we accept

CHAPTER 1
the meaning of work

as "proper" tends to rise over time. Today we consider a house substandard if it lacks running water or central heating; this was not so a hundred years ago. To many people today, an automobile and a TV set are among the essentials of life. Moreover, our concept of the proper standard of living depends a good bit on what our neighbors have. If the family next door buys a shiny new Buick, our five-year-old Chevy becomes less adequate.

This tremendous interest in material goods is not a natural characteristic of man but a special trait of our own culture. Many other societies ascribe far less importance to material goods than to holiness or physical or military power. The individual's place in society may be determined purely by who his or her ancestors were; displays of wealth may be regarded as poor taste. Among certain tribes competitiveness is socially tabu; when the missionaries taught these people how to run races, they insisted that every race must end in a dead heat.

Even in our own culture, money is ordinarily more important to the salesman than to the teacher or the minister. Some people refuse a promotion with a higher salary simply because it involves "too much responsibility." And today there is an entire "counter culture" that has "dropped out of the rat race" and has rejected money as a standard of value or achievement.

Although in the larger community income may be only a rough measure of status, within an organization it measures very precisely the importance of a job. Even the difference of a cent in hourly rates may assume great significance. If one job pays $9.62 an hour and another $9.63, employees feel that (a) the $9.63 job is more important or (b) the $9.62 job should be higher paid. Thus wage and salary administration become critical for motivation and morale.

Security

Job security is a fundamental human need; for many people it is more important than either pay or advancement. The forces driving toward unionism, the most serious problems of superior-subordinate relations, the fears surrounding changing technology—all revolve around the need for security.

It is not enough for people to have their physical needs satisfied from day to day; they want to make sure their needs will continue to be satisfied in the future. In some cases, seniority offers the unskilled worker a sense of security akin to that of the farmer who owns his property or the craftsman who possesses special skills. In recent years, however, automation and other economic changes have brought unemployment to many who once thought their jobs secure. Older workers, members of minority groups, and those with limited education or outmoded skills find it extremely hard to find steady work. As a consequence, losing a job can be a catastrophe, both physically and psychologically. No wonder workers' desires to hold on to their "property rights" to their jobs have led to labor-management disputes over working rules and featherbedding, particularly in industries with declining employment.

Illness and old age provide similar threats to security. Understandably, many companies and unions now seek to provide employees with "total" or "employment-to-grave" security against all forms of income interruption.

Advancement

The urge to advance, "to get ahead," is particularly strong in America. In many other societies a man is born to a rigidly defined class and follows his father's occupation without question; bootblack or king, he fulfills as best he can "the station to which God has called him."

Deep in the heart of every "true" American lies the Horatio Alger dream of unlimited occupational mobility, the belief that every man and woman, no matter how humble their birth, can rise to the highest positions in the land. Indeed, our fondest stories concern men like Abe Lincoln who through honesty and hard work make their way from log cabin to White House. "Your future is strictly up to you," said a National Association of Manufacturers pamphlet in 1951. "Your opportunities will be limited only by your vision of what your future may become, your abilities and how you use them, your character and your determination." At one time it was believed that poverty was largely due to moral weakness, that failure was the fault, not of the system, but of personal character.

Historians and sociologists are finding increasing evidence that the "sweeper-to-president" phenomenon has always been something of a myth. Even a century ago opportunities to get ahead were considerably limited. Yet for a long time this myth of unlimited opportunities for "upward mobility" was generally believed and provided hopes for millions. Today this dream may be fading. The average blue-collar worker without college education has little opportunity to advance much beyond the rank of foreman; further, as the numbers of white-collar workers and junior executives increase, the chance for any given individual to reach top management has declined. A college education is no longer a sure road to success. Despite these declining opportunities, people still have a strong need to feel they are getting ahead. So, if prospects for promotion are few, the employee may redefine the meaning of "advancement."

1. A pay or salary increase is a sign of progress, even though everyone in one's group gets the same increase, and even if the increase may well be eaten away by inflation.

2. Over the years many employees have come to regard seniority as a way of getting ahead. After all, unions emphasize seniority as a determinant in layoffs and fringe benefits (such as length of vacations); and management concurs, with such symbols as long-service pins and testimonial dinners. Greater seniority normally means greater security.

3. Many workers feel they are advancing when they move to a job that may not be better paying but that seems "better" in the sense that the work is more responsible, the pace is slower, or the opportunities for discretion are greater.

4. Finally, many people interpret "getting ahead" in terms of security and material possessions. As one person put it, "If you've got security, if you've got something to fall back on, you're getting ahead." People may measure success not in terms of what they do, but in terms of what they own, a bigger car or a fancier tape deck.

Ambitions for advancement vary greatly among people, in part depending on factors such as personality and expectations. If everyone else "gets ahead," regardless of how this is defined, few want to be left behind; but if nobody makes much progress, even the potentially ambitious are less active. In any case, the opportunities for advancement which organizations make available greatly affect individual behavior and commitment to the organization. For example, too much emphasis on promotions may lead managers to engage in cutthroat competition; too little may engender apathy.

Primarily social needs   People are social animals. They crave friendship, are unhappy when left alone for too long, and often associate with their fellows just because they are hungry for companionship. Two of their basic social needs are for *belongingness* and *support*.

Contacts with others make many jobs bearable, especially uninteresting ones. In the social life of the plant or office, workers can demonstrate the skill and initiative denied them on the job. If there is nothing more constructive to talk about, small issues can be magnified and boredom can be relieved through circulating rumors. Even the work itself can be socially rewarding for some employees, such as salesclerks and receptionists who gain satisfaction from talking to customers.

Belongingness

Beyond this, membership in a clique provides employees a sense of identification and belonging, and they insist on forming informal groups even in the face of management opposition. Indeed there is evidence that workers who belong to small, integrated work groups have higher morale than those who work either alone or among large masses of workers with whom they have no social ties. And for employees who have an unsatisfactory home life the job provides a large part of their social need satisfaction.

Aside from social contacts, people need support from others. They want to feel valued and important; also they want to feel they will receive help when needed. Support needs can be satisfied by praise, recognition, or merely by acceptance. The source of support may be fellow workers, superiors, or even subordinates. As we shall see later, one of the supervisor's most important functions is the establishment of a supportive atmosphere.

Support

Primarily egoistic needs   "The trouble with this work is that I don't have a sense of achievement. I'm just nobody, doing nothing, getting nowhere. I'm just a cog, so small I'd never be missed." So one worker complained, even though the disliked job was one of the highest-paying in the organization.

Achievement

One of the strongest of human needs is the need for achievement, for the feeling that we are getting something done, that our work is of importance. How is a sense of achievement obtained?

Task significance.   Work that seems pointless is bound to lead to frustration. One of the most unpleasant forms of punishment used by the military is to have soldiers dig holes and fill them in again. Compare this to the rich reward that some people get by performing such menial tasks as serving bed trays in hospitals.

In one of the first reports of this sort, two English researchers found that the greatest dissatisfaction in a candy factory centered in a small work group whose job consisted of unwrapping defective chocolates as part of a salvage operation.[4] The workers felt that their job was not very useful. Telephone supervisors report that production and morale are usually higher during an emergency. As one said, "It's amazing. An operator may be a slow producer, and often tardy and absent, but come a blizzard when highways are closed, she will walk great distances to come to work." The various forms that this sense of task significance can take are suggested by the following:

Responsibility for the welfare of others: "I take pride in what I do because I test and inspect the equipment. I prevent a lot of accidents—even fatalities—by keeping my eyes open."—*Elevator inspector.*

Service to others: "There is a lot of satisfaction in knowing that the guy whose car you fixed is going to drive better and safer."—*Auto mechanic.*

Satisfaction in product: "When you sell sterling silver you are putting something into people's lives. Fine silver is a central part of family life, and it is passed on for generations."—*Salesclerk.*

The elevator operator, the janitor, and the groundskeeper—all *want* to feel that their job is important, and good management can do much to enhance their sense of achievement and self-respect.

Studies suggest that there is a close correlation between an occupation's prestige and the satisfaction people get from working at it. People like jobs that the general public views as prestigious, even though many aspects of the work may be dull or distasteful; conversely they dislike low-status jobs. Thus, one way to make a job better is to change how the outside world sees it. There are some experts who believe that the satisfaction of blue-collar workers has declined largely because blue-collar workers have lost status.

Skill. All of us enjoy the sense of skill that springs from doing something well, from being on top of our jobs. The chef takes pride in cleanliness or good shortbread; the safecracker, in sensitive fingers; the professor, in brilliant lectures or searching questions.

We also like to imagine that our job requires unusual skill, and as a consequence we tend to exaggerate its importance. Every machine seems to have special quirks in the eyes of its operator. Every trade has its tricks which require skill, ingenuity, and expertise. The janitor feels he has developed a number of special techniques (knowing that Executive A likes his desk dusted, but that Executive B never wants her desk touched) that raise him above the level of unskilled labor. "The bricklayer as a rule is more than a workman. He is a craftsman," says the Bricklayers' Union journal.[5] "His work endures

---

[4] S. Wyatt and J. N. Landon, *Fatigue and Boredom in Repetitive Work*, Industrial Health Research Council, Report No. 77 (London: H.M. Stationery Office, 1938).

[5] *The Bricklayer, Mason and Plasterer*, Vol. 30 (May 1927), 134.

and stands the gaff of years . . . I have worked with a certain bricklayer who takes great pride in telling you one of his ancestors used to take his son to Buckingham Palace and point out some of the stately arches which he himself had built. . . . When a bricklayer has finished with a day's work there is something real to compensate for it. He can go home feeling that he has created something that will last longer than he will."

Employees resent any implication that they can be easily replaced by untrained workers. Partly, of course, such an implication threatens their job security. But there is more to it than that: If anybody can do your job, what can you say that you have accomplished in your working life? What more significant sign of failure?

For the skilled craftsman, the feeling of skill is particularly important. Many companies have discovered that it is harder to get employees to lower their standards of quality than to raise them. When management decides that customers will accept lower quality, and that looser tolerances can be maintained, skilled workers stubbornly resist the consequent reduction in skill required. Looser standards mean less sense of accomplishment.

It is for this reason that many companies are plagued by running battles between engineers and top management. The engineers insist on close tolerances and top quality; they try to delay a new model from being put into production until all the "bugs" have been eliminated. Top management regards this desire for perfection as financially ruinous.

Productiveness. Perhaps all that we have been saying adds up to one point: most people have a genuine desire to be productive, to keep busy. Certainly our observations cast doubt on the common assumption that most people prefer to "goldbrick" than to work. In fact, it is harder to look busy than to work. Time passes more quickly when a worker is absorbed in what he or she is doing than when trying to avoid work. In our society, a healthy individual feels lost without some sort of job or hobby. Normally, expending mental and physical energy is a pleasant, not a painful, experience.

But if all this is true, how can we explain why people often do loaf on the job and go to extraordinary extremes to avoid work? Often such behavior is a sign of dissatisfaction with the job, with supervision, or with the company as a whole. Workers who feel that they have been treated unfairly direct their energies toward beating the system and show high skill in doing as little work as possible. This response, however, is a sure sign that the organization is beset with severe problems.

The sense of productivity and achievement is particularly important to business executives who typically consider themselves hardworking people who must constantly be producing in order to be happy. Many executives feel a need to be constantly challenged, to be forever busy doing and creating.

Autonomy

"You know, it's a funny thing. I work all day at the plant and then I come home and what do I do? I work some more—I mean in the shop in the basement. I love to do things with my hands. Funny, that's what I do at work—only it's different.

"You see at work I don't have any freedom. That's the difference. The company tells me when to start working, when I get time to go to the john, when I get my lunch and how long (I get .7 hours—that's 42 minutes for anyone who isn't an engineer). They tell me how fast to work and exactly what motions to make. About the only thing I'm free to do is to think how damn lousy the job is.

"Now, at home I'm my own boss—and believe me, that's a wonderful feeling."

—*Autoworker.*

Most people like being their own boss. Yet in modern industry only a few employees really have this feeling. The process of specialization has deprived the individual workers of their freedom to plan and organize their own jobs and has transferred initiative and responsibility to management. The effect of this approach has been to strip many jobs of every opportunity for spontaneity and creativity.

Sometimes the tall stories told by workers are indicative of their hidden desires to do things in their own way. For instance, there is the tale of the assembly-line workers who fixed their cars so that when the customer stepped on the accelerator the windshield wipers started flapping and the horn blew. Then there is the story about the skilled glass blower who for years had been making glass rabbits with straight ears. One day he decided to let the ears droop. "I thought it would be a nice change," he told an amazed management.

Initiative and imagination are essential to any sense of autonomy; yet too often management fails to use its employees' creative abilities. As a consequence they display their initiative and imagination in such activities as sabotage, union activity, and horseplay. Even among managers the creative individual is often considered a troublemaker.

We must not paint too dark a picture, however, for on many jobs workers do have a great deal of freedom. We have all seen janitors who really felt that they were kings of all they surveyed—and behaved accordingly. Skilled workers, guards, inspectors, and many secretaries frequently have this same feeling of independence.

How people feel about their jobs depends in part on how they are supervised. Mineworkers, truckdrivers, and railroaders all have above-average job satisfaction. What do these jobs have in common? Constant travel, which makes close supervision difficult. Of course, no one can have complete freedom from supervision, but within limits an employee can feel that he is his own boss. This is particularly true if he can feel that what he does is determined by the objective requirements of the situation rather than by human orders. (From an objective point of view, the utility operator has almost no freedom; he must make constant adjustments to meet the changing demand for power. Yet he feels independent since the orders come from dials rather than from people.)

Many jobs demand such a high degree of teamwork that the individual worker has little opportunity to make decisions alone. Under such circumstances group decision making may serve as a substitute for individual autonomy.

Knowledge

The desire for knowledge is a basic human need. People like to know not only *what* is happening to them but *why*. They want to understand the present and predict the future. Arbitrariness, caprice, and unexpected events all make it hard for us to fashion an orderly, reasonable explanation of the events that shape our lives. To be at the mercy of people and forces that we can neither understand nor control is a serious threat to our security. Take, for example, the unrest that prevails in an office after a familiar, well-known supervisor is replaced by someone new, with unknown preferences, attitudes, and idiosyncracies.

People want to know about things that are directly important to them, and also about those that are not. Satisfying idle curiosity is also a way of spending one's time. The village busybody and the bored receptionist have nothing better to do than to pry into other people's business. The desire for information is so strong that if the truth is not available, appropriate substitutes will be fashioned.

The quest for knowledge has more constructive elements as well. Many people find that learning gives them a sense of achievement. Being an expert on something—whether it is baseball, trout flies, the fine points of one's job, or the ramifications of union politics—gives the individual a sense of uniqueness and progress.

Relative importance of various needs

Obviously, all the previously mentioned needs are important, but which is most important? Which can be used most effectively to motivate employees to work for organizational objectives?

This question has been the subject of extensive research. The answer has been found to vary with the individual concerned, the job, the general economic climate, and a host of other factors. Several generalizations seem to be at least partly valid, however, as we shall discuss below.

Maslow. According to the well-known Maslow "needs hypothesis," human needs can be ordered into a hierarchy, with physical needs being the "lowest" and most basic, followed in ascending order by what we have called security, social, and egoistic needs—and finally "self-actualization."[6] In this hierarchy a higher, less basic need does not provide motivation unless all lower, more basic needs are "largely" satisfied; but once a lower-level need is largely satisfied it no longer motivates.

Thus, once physical needs for food, clothing, and shelter are reasonably well satisfied, individuals become relatively more concerned with other needs. First, they seek to satisfy their safety or security needs for protection against danger, threats, and deprivation. (As we have seen, physical and security needs are usually satisfied through pay, seniority, fringe benefits, and the like.) When the standard of living rises so that security is assured, then social needs take first priority, followed by egoistic needs. Finally, according to this hypothesis, only when most of the less pressing needs are satisfied will individuals turn to the ultimate form of accomplishment, self-actualization, which has been

[6] The terms Maslow actually used were *physiological* (equivalent to our physical), *safety* (our security), *love* (our affiliation), *esteem* (which includes part of our ego needs), and *self-actualization*. In our previous discussion, we have not considered self-actualization as a separate need, largely because we find it difficult to distinguish this need from such egoistic needs as accomplishment.

described as "the desire to become . . . everything that one is capable of becoming," to make the very most of one's potentialities.[7]

The message for management in this hypothesis is that as long as employees' lower-order needs are unsatisfied, higher order needs will not motivate them. But once these lower-order needs *are* reasonably well satisfied, only higher needs will provide continued motivation. Thus a hundred years ago, when our standard of living was lower, motivational techniques emphasizing physical and security needs may have been appropriate. Today demand for ego-satisfying jobs is growing (although the extent of this demand is sometimes exaggerated).

There is some evidence consistent with this theory. For example, during the 1940s (with the memory of the Great Depression in mind), employees generally ranked *job security* as the most important thing they wanted from their jobs. In recent years this has changed. By 1969 in a nationwide survey, the average of all workers placed *interesting work* first, with *pay* fourth, *friendly coworkers* sixth, and *job security* eighth.[8] Nevertheless, the Maslow hypothesis has been subject to much criticism.[9] The most telling points are the following:

- People differ greatly in the extent to which a need must be satisfied before they move on to a higher level. For some people egoistic needs may be more basic than social needs. Scientists' physical needs, for example, may be very easily satisfied, their social needs may be minimal, and their consuming passion for research may involve egoistic and self-actualizing needs. By forcing the facts, one might say that the scientists conform to the needs hierarchy, but this does not help us understand their behavior.
- Research indicates that the vast range of human needs do not clearly separate themselves into Maslow's five distinct categories (or our three). Money, for example, is perhaps the most important single source of need satisfaction; yet, depending on the circumstances, it may satisfy any of the needs listed.
- One form of satisfaction may make up for another. Thus workers whose jobs permit little sense of achievement sometimes compensate for this loss (at least in part) by giving greater attention to social needs. In effect the felt need (demand) for satisfactions adjusts itself to their supply.

For these reasons, it is hard to put this hypothesis in operational form and to test whether it is true. Yet, despite its limitations the hypothesis does

---

[7] Maslow, "A Theory of Motivation," p. 372.

[8] Mitchell Fein, "The Real Needs and Goals of Blue Collar Workers," *Conference Board Record* (February 1973), 28. Maslow's hypothesis is consistent with economic theory, which would lead us to predict that as jobs become better rewarded and provide more security, the marginal utility of additional income will decline, and the relative marginal utility of noneconomic benefits (which satisfy higher order needs) increase.

[9] For example, Mahmoud A. Wahba and Lawrence G. Bridwell, "Maslow Reconsidered: A Review of Research on the Need Hierarchy Theory," *Organizational Behavior and Human Performance*, Vol. 15 (1976), 212–40. It should be noted that Maslow himself recognized that his theory was not equally applicable to all people. For research that suggests the existence of three sorts of needs, existence (or physical and security), relatedness (social), and growth (egoistic) without the last two being ranked in any necessary hierarchy, see Clayton Alderfer, *Human Needs in Organizational Settings* (New York: Free Press, 1972).

present some useful insights into human behavior. Other factors must be considered, however.

McClelland. In recent years a theory of human needs has come into prominence that both recognizes the existence of personality differences and challenges the place of the Maslow hypothesis in organizational thought. According to this theory, developed by McClelland and his associates, there are at least three major positive needs related to employee behavior in organizations: the need for *achievement*, the need for *power* (having control and influence over people), and the need for *affiliation* (to be accepted by others). There is also a negative need, the need to avoid *failure*.[10]

In contrast to Maslow's theory, the McClelland hypothesis makes no provision for a *hierarchy* of needs. People's needs differ in strength, and these differences are largely determined by the environment in which they have grown up. Only those with a high need for achievement will obtain a great deal of satisfaction from jobs that provide a feeling of accomplishment. Those with a high need for affiliation will prefer jobs that involve a strong sense of community.

The most extensive research has dealt with need for achievement (often shortened to *n Ach*). According to this research *n Ach* is closely related to the entrepreneurial spirit; successful managers the world over score higher on *n Ach* than do professionals and specialists.[11] Economic progress has been most rapid in countries and periods of history that have been characterized by high *n Ach*. "What accounts for the rise of civilization? Not external resources (i.e., markets, minerals, trade routes or factories), but the entrepreneurial spirit which exploits these resources." [12]

N Ach is closely related to the propensity to take moderate but realistic risks. High-need achievers seek challenging tasks with some risk of failure, but not jobs so difficult that success is almost impossible. They are realists, not romanticists.

High-need achievers also need concrete feedback as to the success of their *own* efforts. They avoid tasks on which progress cannot be measured or in which success is related to luck or the efforts of others. Similarly they prefer to be held personally responsible for assignments rather than have credit (or blame) for achievement divided among a committee. Finally, they like tasks that provide relatively quick feedback, for instance in which success or failure can be determined within a year. On long-range tasks the sense of accomplishment is deferred too long for high-need achievers.

---

[10] For example, see David McClelland, *The Achieving Society* (Princeton: Van Nostrand, 1961). As defined, the needs for achievement and affiliation bear some resemblence to egoistic and social needs, while need for power relates to esteem needs, but the correspondence is not close. McClelland recognizes that physical and security needs are more basic than his three higher level ones; however, he gives these lower level needs little attention.

[11] J. W. Atkinson and J. O. Raynor, *Motivation and Achievement* (Washington: Winston, 1974) and J. B. Miner, *Motivation to Manage* (Atlanta: Organizational Measurement Systems Press, 1977).

[12] David C. McClelland, "Business Drive and National Achievement," *Harvard Business Review*, 40, No. 4 (July 1962), 99.

N Ach is learned largely from one's family. Parents of high-need achievers set high, realistic goals for their children, encourage their efforts, but do not direct them in detail. On the other hand, McClelland reports considerable success in training managers in underdeveloped countries to raise their *n Ach*.[13]

Substitution of one satisfaction for another. To some extent people will give up one source of satisfaction for another. On the typical automobile assembly line, one will find many workers who have enjoyed social and egoistic satisfactions in low paying jobs, but gave them up for the substantially better pay associated with assembly work. Conversely, there are other workers who will accept lower wages in return for jobs with greater challenge and freedom. As one such individual put it:

> "Sure this job doesn't pay much. But nobody pushes you and you are your own boss. I could get more in the mills, but I would hate myself doing it: push, push, and bosses. Life is too short. I like the guys here."

And Vermont and the Mendocino coast are heavily populated by ex-managers who have given up the "rat race" for less rewarding and presumably less demanding jobs of running craft or antique shops.

Role of money. Management is sometimes deceived by workers' demands for money, because money has many meanings in terms of need satisfaction. If we looked solely at union demands on management and at the overt causes of strikes, we might well conclude that workers were interested in money alone. Yet, as we have seen, this is not the whole picture.

There are two reasons for this overemphasis. In the first place, workers may regard higher earnings as a partial compensation for the lack of other forms of need satisfaction. Second, money has a symbolic value. Money earnings are tangible; psychic earnings are not. If one is going to gripe, one seizes on something tangible to gripe about. Dissatisfaction with the job in general is often semiconscious and hard to put into words. If workers went to the boss demanding that he provide them with more interesting work, they would feel foolish; but a demand for an increase of 50 cents an hour can be put in writing.

From the union's point of view, of course, the size of the paycheck is a measure of the union's strength and the officers' bargaining skill. Wage improvements can be obtained for everyone at one fell swoop around the bargaining table, but the union can improve human relations only piecemeal through the grievance procedure.

As mentioned earlier, money provides more than merely physical needs.

---

[13] David McClelland and D. G. Winter, *Motivating Economic Achievement* (New York: Free Press, 1969). See also Douglas Durand, "Effects of Achievement Motivation and Skill Training on the Entrepreneurial Behavior of Black Businessmen," *Organizational Behavior and Human Performance*, 14, No. 1 (August 1975), 76–90. For a critical review of the relevant literature, see Gerald D. Barrett and Bernard M. Bass, "Cross Cultural Issues in Industrial and Organizational Psychology," in Marvin Dunnette, *Handbook of Industrial and Organizational Psychology* (Chicago: Rand McNally, 1976).

For the high-need-achieving manager, the size of the paycheck provides concrete feedback as to the extent of his or her success.

Determinants of job satisfaction

When is a job satisfying? At one time social scientists thought the answer was obvious: a job was satisfying when there was a match between the characteristics of the job and the needs of the individual. Recent research suggests the determinants of satisfaction are more complicated than this.[14] To be sure people and their jobs are the basic elements involved, but it is clear that there are numerous variables between people and their jobs that help determine whether the relationship is satisfying. Whether I am satisfied on my job depends on:

- *Expectations.* If I expect the job to be challenging (or well-paying), and it is not, then I am dissatisfied. But if I expect it to be dull (or low paying), and it turns out that way, my frustration might be minimal. An example of the expectation process at work: reported job satisfaction of black workers dropped sharply during the mid-1960s, probably not because objective job conditions had changed, but because the Civil Rights Movement engendered higher expectations.
- *Self-evaluation.* If I look upon myself as a generally satisfied person (or a person who can cope well), I will be unwilling to admit the job can get me down. If I have a generally sunny disposition, this may be reflected in my attitude toward the job.
- *Social norms.* If other people, particularly people I respect, see my job as a good one—or as one on which I *should* be satisfied—or if people tell me that what I do is important, then I am more likely to be satisfied.
- *Social comparisons.* If all my friends have more challenging jobs than I have, I will be more dissatisfied than if we all are in the same boat.
- *Input/output relations.* My satisfaction with my job depends on how I perceive the relationship between what I bring or put into the job *(input)* and what I get out of it *(output).*[15] If I work hard (input) and fail to finish what I sought to accomplish (output) I will be less satisfied than if I merely put in a halfhearted effort. Similarly if I have trained for years to qualify for a job that then pays me very little, I will be less satisfied than if I had very little training.
- *Commitment.* If after careful thought I pick one job from a choice of opportunities, I make a free commitment to it. If so, I'll be reluctant to admit that my job is not rewarding, for I would be conceding that my ability to make a sound choice is defective. My sense of commitment (and resulting satisfaction) may be particularly strong if my decision is well known among my friends.
- *Priming.* If there is a lot of talk about pay among my companions, I'm likely to think pay important. If management publicizes its job enrichment program, I'm likely to think *that* important—and to be upset when the program fails to live up to its billing.

[14] Salancik and Pfeffer, "An Examination of Need Satisfaction Models . . . ," Barry Staw, "Motivation in Organizations: Toward Synthesis and Redirection," in Barry Staw and Gerald Salancik, eds., *New Directions in Organizational Behavior* (Chicago: St. Clair, 1977); Abraham Korman, *Industrial and Organizational Psychology* (Englewood Cliffs, N.J.: Prentice-Hall, 1971).

[15] Actually, it may be even more complicated than this. My evaluation of my own input/output ratio may depend on my evaluation of other people's input/output ratios. If theirs is more favorable than mine, I will be dissatisfied. See J. Stacy Adams, "Inequity in Social Exchange," in L. Berkowitz, ed., *Advances in Experimental Social Psychology*, Vol. 2 (New York: Academic Press, 1965), 267–300.

All of the above factors suggest that job satisfaction is an elusive concept. It is related to the context in which the question is raised, reminding us of the old vaudeville routine. "How's your wife (husband)?" A: "Compared to what?" But it is also related to the meaning of work, and even to the meaning of life itself.

How important is satisfying work?

Recent years have seen a hot debate as to whether American society is undergoing a "revolt against work."[16] The debate raises important questions as to the importance of job satisfaction—especially having a challenging job—to American workers. Related to this question there are other, perhaps even more difficult ones: (1) what is the relationship between work and leisure? and (2) how do people differ in their orientations and adjustments to work?

The need for challenge

The question of what role work—especially challenging work—plays in human life is of concern not just to management; it is a psychological, moral, and even theological question about which scholars are in considerable disagreement. There is no clear answer, but let us state some of the issues in terms of debate, returning to others later.

The case for challenging work being very important. One group argues that mature human beings require high levels of egoistic and self-actualization need-satisfaction from their jobs.[17] The process of growing up involves accepting increasing challenge and experiencing greater autonomy and independence. Those who do not have these opportunities (in particular, those who are unable to express themselves meaningfully through work) never reach psychological maturity. Since the average worker spends nearly a third of his or her waking hours on the job, if the job does not provide challenge and autonomy he may suffer severe frustration, with results that are costly both to himself and his employer.

The existence of the Peace Corps suggests that many seek meaning in their work and, indeed, through their work seek a meaning in life. The importance of work is also indicated by the deleterious impact of unemployment and retirement on people who have been active and productive for decades. Workers on unskilled (and presumably boring) jobs are more likely to suffer from personality disturbances (as measured by interviews) and psychosomatic illnesses (as measured by dispensary visits) than are skilled workers.[18] Individu-

---

[16] For various points of view, see *Work in America,* Report of a Special Task Force to the Secretary of Health, Education, and Welfare (Cambridge, Mass.: MIT Press, 1973); Jerome Rosow, ed., *The Worker and the Job* (Englewood Cliffs, N.J.: Prentice-Hall, 1974); Roy P. Fairfield, ed., *Humanizing the Work Place* (Buffalo, N.Y.: Prometheus Books, 1974).

[17] For a classical statement of this point of view, see Chris Argyris, *Personality and Organization* (New York: Harper, 1957); see also Chris Argyris, "Personality and Organization Theory Revisited," *Administrative Science Quarterly,* 18, No. 2 (June 1973), 141–67.

[18] Arthur Kornhauser and Otto Reid, *Mental Health of the Industrial Worker* (New York: Wiley, 1965). John R. P. French and others, eds., "Work, Health and Satisfaction," *Journal of Social Issues,* 18, No. 2 (July 1962). For opposite evidence, see Iradj Siassi and others, "Loneliness and Dissatisfaction in a Blue Collar Population," *Archives of General Psychiatry,* Vol. 30 (February 1974), 261–65.

als who move from unskilled to skilled work tend to become better adjusted after the move, and vice versa. Study after study indicates that job challenge and job satisfaction are inversely related to turnover and absenteeism. People display little commitment to dissatisfying, challengeless jobs.

In addition, as we shall discuss in later chapters, low morale and poor motivation may lead to inefficiency and low productivity. In sum, so the argument runs, the existence of unrewarding jobs creates an unhealthy situation that is harmful to the individual, to the organization, and to society generally.

The case for challenging work not being important. The opposing argument is that many people adjust easily to dull work. They center life away from the job, expect relatively few satisfactions from it, and are not disappointed when it offers them little challenge or sense of creativity. Indeed, it is argued, many people would not want a high level of challenge and autonomy on the job, even were it available. Possibly they are immature, but their immaturity is due far more to family environment than to the job; they have learned to be dependent in childhood and are unlikely to change this in later life.

According to some studies, retirement in itself does not bring on the rapid deterioration of physical and mental health as was once supposed; health tends to improve immediately after retirement. Further, evidence of the impact of unskilled work on mental health is inconclusive. Apparently, not everyone suffers equally from unskilled work and some adjust to it more easily than others. And it is also not clear whether mental ill health results from the intrinsic nature of unskilled work or from the poor pay and low status that accompany such work. Insofar as mental disturbances are caused by economic and social pressures at home, higher wages may be a better solution than improved satisfaction on the job.

It is claimed that most of the evidence designed to show the importance of need satisfaction is misleading, showing in fact that in our culture people want *some* sort of job (and preferably one with high pay), but that it is not necessary for the job to provide higher orders of need-satisfaction. The results reported in the table (p. 20) are typical of most studies of job satisfaction. Even though few jobs are ideal, most workers report themselves satisfied (and even very satisfied) with what they have; they would take the same job again and would recommend this job to a friend. Even among factory workers, roughly 40 per cent report themselves "very satisfied." [19]

This suggests that workers do adjust rather easily to presumably boring jobs. Of course, it *might* be better if every job offered at least a chance of self-actualization. Possibly job satisfaction would be greater if we were to return to the idyllic preindustrial conditions pictured at the beginning of the chapter— if, for example, cars were made on a handicraft basis rather than on an assembly

---

[19] Argyris would argue that reported satisfaction means little in this context, since unskilled workers compare their jobs against the limited alternatives available to them. To Argyris, the very fact that a worker reports satisfaction with an objectively unchallenging job may mean that this worker has become "psychologically impoverished" and his expectations have dropped. He has become resigned to his fate.

line. But the cost of so doing would include abandoning our modern technological efficiency and substantially reducing our standard of living. Few would be willing to pay the price. So the argument goes.

Work and leisure

Perhaps the issues will seem less confused if we step back and examine them from both a historical and cultural point of view. Remember that our present attitude toward work is culturally based. Work has not always been so important as it is today; it might not be considered so important in the future. In past centuries, particularly when civilization was flourishing in Greece and Rome, work did not occupy an exalted position. In fact, those of higher social status did not expect to work, for work was primarily restricted to slaves and free citizens who lacked independent resources.

During the Protestant Reformation, work took on religious connotations. It was clearly a duty to fulfill one's predestined "calling." It was also regarded as an ordained punishment for one's sins. Failure to work was immoral. Our traditional feeling about the idle—that they somehow are not behaving morally—is a reflection of this religious emphasis. To maintain respect in our society, even the rich must work.

Most Americans today seem to feel that work is a necessity, regardless of material needs. When asked what they would do if they were to get enough money so they could live comfortably for the rest of their lives, most workers respond, perhaps surprisingly, that they would *continue* working. But why would these workers continue to work? Here an interesting phenomenon oc-

Results of a nationwide study of job attitudes

Question	Response	%
All in all, how satisfied would you say you are with your job?	Very satisfied	46.7%
	Somewhat satisfied	41.7
	Not too satisfied	8.9
	Not at all satisfied	2.7
Knowing what you do now, if you had to decide all over again whether to take the job you now have, what would you decide?	Decide without hesitation to take same job	63.9
	Have some second thoughts	28.3
	Decide definitely not to take the same job	7.8
If a good friend of yours was interested in working in a job like yours for your employer, what would you tell him or her?	Strongly recommend it	61.8
	Have doubts about recommending it	29.7
	Advise friend against it	8.6
If you were to get enough money to live as comfortably as you'd like for the rest of your life, would you continue to work?	Would continue to work	71.5
	Would not continue to work	28.5

Source: Robert P. Quinn and Graham Staines, *1977 Quality of Employment Survey* (Ann Arbor, Michigan: Institute of Social Research, University of Michigan, 1978), Tables 13.1 and 14.6.

curs. As expected, the main reason why middle-class workers would continue working was for "interest and accomplishment"; but for blue-collar workers the most frequently mentioned reason was "to keep occupied." [20] This latter group would rather work than not work, even though working involves just filling time.

This may be a depressing commentary on the meaninglessness of life off the job, but it suggests the centrality of having a job—any job—to the average male (and increasingly for females) as a source of identity, status, self-respect, and for social interaction.

On the other hand, the differences in response between middle-class and blue-collar workers indicates that attitudes toward work differ greatly among occupational groups. For some, "work has now become the main business of life." [21] Certainly many professionals and executives feel this way, and some corporations require their executives to be *Organization Men* 24 hours a day.

But for others the central focus of life is not the job (which is merely a way of making a living).[22] Such people find a large measure of challenge, creativity, and autonomy in raising a family, pursuing a hobby, or taking part in community affairs.

In many occupations people spend less time on the job today than they did in the past. Sixty years ago the 6-day week (for, in some instances 10 to 12 hours a day) was the rule, and vacations and holidays were far from common. Today few people work more than 5 days a week, and the average worker has at least 3-weeks' vacation and 12 paid holidays a year. Not far over the horizon is the 30-hour, 4-day week (the New York City electricians' contract calls for a 25-hour week), while more and more women seek part-time work.[23] In addition, our life span grows longer and the average age of retirement is decreasing. All these influences are eroding the key position held by work in our daily lives.

It has been predicted that work will become increasingly routine and provide fewer and fewer opportunities for creativity and discretion. On the other hand, as working hours grow shorter, there will be "a new dedication to diversity and individualism off the job. . . . Leisure will be the happy hunting ground of the independent spirit.[24]

From such predictions, some conclude that perhaps the best use of our resources is to accelerate automation, shorten the workweek as quickly as

---

[20] The original study was reported in Nancy Morse and Robert S. Weiss, "The Function and Meanings of Work and the Job," *American Sociological Review*, Vol. 20 (April 1955), 191–98. The question continues to be asked, as the preceding table indicates.

[21] Charles R. Walker, *Modern Technology and Civilization* (New York: McGraw-Hill, 1962), p. 439.

[22] There are also important differences among cultural groups. The attitudes of U.S. factory workers may be very different from those in a Japanese factory or the Israeli kibbutz. Further (as we discuss below) attitudes of rural workers in the U.S. may differ considerably from those of urban workers.

[23] On the other hand, to large numbers of moonlighters, work and its monetary rewards are preferable to leisure.

[24] Clark Kerr, John T. Dunlop, Frederick H. Harbison, and Charles A. Myers, *Industrialism and Industrial Man* (New York: Oxford, 1964), pp. 237–38.

Summary of the argument

Job satisfaction important	Job satisfaction unimportant
People want self-actualization.	Some people prefer unchallenging work.
Those who don't obtain job satisfaction never reach psychological maturity.	Individual personality becomes fixed before people start working. Work is not to blame.
Those who fail to obtain job satisfaction become frustrated.	Most people have relatively low levels of aspiration for job satisfaction and expect only routine work.
The job is central to man's life.	This is a professor's value. Many people focus their lives on family and community.
Those without work are unhappy. People want to work even when they don't have to.	Even though there are social pressures to have a job, this does not mean the job must be challenging, etc.
Lack of challenging work leads to low mental health.	Poor mental health may be due to low income or low status of routine jobs. Anyway, research findings are not conclusive.
Work and leisure patterns spill into each other. Those with uncreative jobs engage in uncreative recreation.	A new Bohemianism off the job will make up for increasing boredom at work.
Lack of job satisfaction and alienation from work leads to lower productivity and an unhealthy society.	We can provide challenging work for everybody only at the cost of eliminating our mass production technology and high standard of living—and society is unwilling to pay this price.

possible, forget about on-the-job satisfactions, and concentrate our energies on making leisure more meaningful. Certainly there are dropouts from our society who believe that there must be more "relevant" and "meaningful" things to do with one's life than to spend eight hours a day in a factory or office.

Others argue that it is impossible to compartmentalize work and leisure activities and that expanded leisure activities will never substitute for what is missing on the job. One view is that work routines spill over into leisure routines, and that those who have routine jobs tend to engage in passive, routine types of recreation.[25]

Nevertheless, the line between work and nonwork activities is drawn much sharper today than it ever was in the past. Prior to large-scale commuting, people lived and played with the same people they worked with, and a whole series of ceremonies and other social activities tended to integrate work, family, and community life into a seamless web. In those days, people felt little need to "get away" from work (and had less opportunity to do so). Today, since work and play occupy separate spheres in our lives, we feel under pressure to decide which is most important.

[25] Martin Meissner, "The Long Hand of the Job: A Study of Work and Leisure," *Industrial Relations*, 10, No. 3 (October 1971), 23–60.

Differing orientations toward work

As the foregoing makes clear, there are substantial differences in the meaning people give to work. Research suggests the usefulness of distinguishing between expectations work in terms of *instrumental* and *expressive* "orientations." Those with instrumental orientations look upon work as merely a means (an instrument) of obtaining financial resources to pursue their real interests, and these real interests typically lie in nonwork settings—family life, recreation, or community activity—although occasionally they may lie in around-the-job socializing (for instance, coffee breaks). By contrast, those with expressive orientations view work as an end in itself (a form of expression) and typically tend to rank high in terms of n Ach and desire for ego satisfaction on the job.[26]

The orientation of many unskilled workers is instrumental: their main goal is to earn more money, to obtain greater job security, and to enjoy more leisure. Their need for job challenge is limited. For some women (and an increasing number of men) commitment to work is secondary to commitment to family and home; this is especially so when the work is routine and poorly paid. There is evidence that suggests that city (as opposed to country) blue-collar workers and those with low ego needs settle relatively easily for unchallenging jobs that provide plenty of social interaction and high rates of pay.[27]

Workers who adopt an instrumental orientation toward work are not totally unconcerned about whether the job provides intrinsic interest or challenge. However, such workers tend to prefer jobs which are high paid to those which are interesting.[28] Neither does an instrumental orientation mean that the worker prefers not to work at all. As reported above, blue-collar workers say they would prefer to work (even if they didn't have to), but primarily "to keep occupied." As a study of auto workers put it, these workers "would rather stay on the job, not out of a sense of duty (to satisfy the moralists) or to get their quota of sociability (to satisfy social scientists), but rather because working provides organizational cement to their lives."[29] On the other hand, those with an expressive orientation require more than "organizational cement"; they want "interest and accomplishment."

The adjustment process. Just as we can divide workers into those with instrumental and those with expressive orientations, so, in a similar oversimpli-

---

[26] Naturally, this distinction is a bit oversimplified. Most workers have both forms of orientation; indeed, some may be very high on both scales; other, apathetic individuals can be low on both.

[27] For a summary of the evidence, see J. Richard Hackman and J. Lloyd Suttle, *Improving Life at Work* (Santa Monica, Calif.: Goodyear, 1977), p. 118. The evidence suggests that the key variable here is importance to ego needs rather than whether the job is located in a city as opposed to the country. Country workers tend to have higher ego needs and therefore react more favorably to challenging work. For a different view, see J. Kenneth White, "Individual Differences and Job Quality," *Academy of Management Review*, Vol. 3 (April 1978), 267–80.

[28] Among the relevent studies are John H. Goldthorpe, David Lockwood, Frank Bechofer, and Jennifer Platt, *The Affluent Worker: Industrial Attitudes and Behavior* (Cambridge: Cambridge University Press, 1968); Stephen Cotgrove, "Alienation and Automation," *British Journal of Sociology*, Vol. 23 (December 1972), 437–71; and H. Benyon and R. M. Blackburn, *Perceptions of Work* (Cambridge: Cambridge University Press, 1972).

[29] William H. Form, "Autoworkers and Their Machines: A Study of Work, Factory, and Job Satisfaction in Four Countries." *Social Forces*, Vol. 52 (September 1974), 13.

fied manner, we can divide work into that which is challenging and that which is not (using the term *challenge* to cover factors such as autonomy, variety, opportunity to participate, and the like—factors that are far from perfectly correlated with each other). With these two sets of arbitrary distinctions, we can construct the following matrix:

		Type of work	
		Nonchallenging	Challenging
Employee orientation	Expressive	3	1
	Instrumental	4	2

By middle-class standards, those who fall into Cell 1 are the lucky ones. They are the professors, managers, and others who seek self-fulfillment on the job and are fortunate enough to find jobs that make this possible.

Those in Cell 2 are less happy. They are faced with more challenge than they want—perhaps because the job is beyond their abilities, because they are low in need achievement, or because they prefer to center their lives off the job. Perhaps, through proper training they could learn to enjoy greater responsibility and to change their orientation. Alternatively, they could reject their responsibilities outright or perform them in the most routine, bureaucratic manner possible. However approached, Cell 2 represents an unstable situation. People placed within Cell 2 tend to change their orientation from instrumental to expressive (and thus move to Cell 1) or to change the nature of the job (and move to Cell 4). Those who can do neither report themselves overloaded and dissatisfied.

Cell 3 is also unstable. It encompasses those who seek ego satisfactions on the job and are unable to obtain them. Faced with this predicament, some people simply quit. Others, through sabotage, fantasy, or empire building transform routine work into something challenging (and move to Cell 1), but the most common reaction is to withdraw psychologically from the job, to lower one's expectations, and to change one's orientation from expressive to instrumental (and move to Cell 4). Some people develop a rich social life on the job; others transfer their attention to family or recreational activities. The few who fight fate and refuse to change their orientation are among those likely to report their jobs dissatisfying.

Cell 4 is stable. It consists of those who have withdrawn from an expressive orientation and those who have never developed one. They work for money or for self-respect, but not for the challenge of the job. These people are apathetic and unmotivated to do much more than a "fair day's work." As long as management provides adequate pay, fair supervision, good working conditions, opportunities to chat with other employees, they will not be actively dissatisfied. Finding no alternatives to work, they may respond that they would continue to work in order to "keep occupied," even if they had the money to do otherwise.

To conclude, Cells 2 and 3 are unstable since workers within them either change their expectations or change the nature of their jobs. Thus, most workers have come to terms with their work, psychologically, and therefore may be placed in Cells 1 or 4. They report themselves satisfied: in Cell 1 because their work is challenging, in Cell 4 because they have learned not to expect challenge from work. This means that many workers center their lives away from the job. For some this adjustment comes easily; for others it may come at considerable psychic cost. The nature of the adjustment and the extent of the costs are issues too involved (and controversial) to be discussed at length.[30] It is enough to say that our society has not solved the problem of providing workers with sufficient opportunities for ego satisfaction and personal growth on the job.

Conclusion

Management can do its job only by motivating people to work for management's objectives. But it is impossible to understand motivation without considering what people want and expect from their jobs.

Since people spend about one-third of their waking hours at work, it is not surprising that they should expect work to satisfy many sorts of needs—physical, social and egoistic—and that, further, these needs may be satisfied in a wide variety of ways—off the job, around the job, and through the job. Though there is some evidence that these needs can be ranked in a hierarchy, it is clear that various forms of need satisfaction can be substituted for each other.

There is considerable debate about the importance of satisfaction derived from the job, as opposed to satisfactions achieved generally elsewhere in life. Professors (and they are the ones who do most of the writing in this field) place high value on autonomy, creativity, and the quest for maximum self-development. Their existence is work-oriented; for them creative achievement is an end in itself and requires no further justification. As a consequence, they are inclined to equate true happiness with interesting work, and they assume that everyone should be as work-involved as professors are. Perhaps those professors who find job satisfaction so important are right—but the case is not black-and-white.

The authors of this book hold a middle-of-the-road position. Work is one of the most important (if not the most important) activities in a person's life. Those who do not have satisfying jobs rarely have fully satisfying lives. As we shall discuss in future chapters, dissatisfying work can lead in many (but not all) circumstances to lower production and friction on the job, so that it may be in management's economic interest to reduce such dissatisfaction. But even where this is not true, management has a certain degree of social

[30] See, for example, *Work in America* and chapters by Daniel Yankelovich and George Strauss in Jerome Rosow, ed., *The Worker and the Job* (Englewood Cliffs, N.J.: Prentice-Hall, 1974).

responsibility (as we shall discuss in our concluding chapter) to provide work opportunities that are psychologically meaningful. Regardless, we must bear in mind that work is not a person's only objective, nor is work satisfaction the sole objective of management.

motivating people to work

One of the basic problems in any society is how to motivate people to work. In a modern society this is not an easy task, since many people derive only slight personal satisfaction from their jobs and enjoy little sense of accomplishment or creativity. In large organizations people must work together, follow orders they may neither understand nor approve, and obey instructions from superiors they had no part in selecting and may never see. Few have the opportunity for self-expression or the freedom from control enjoyed by the farmer or the independent business or professional person. How can we create a situation in which employees can satisfy their individual needs while working toward the goals of the organization? In particular, how can one motivate people who have boring jobs, little freedom to make decisions on their own, and the normal human quota of laziness and stubbornness?

In this chapter we shall consider five alternative methods for motivating people: (1) the traditional approach, (2) human relations, (3) implicit bargaining, (4) competition, and (5) internalized motivation.[1] Finally, we shall present a broad overall approach to motivation, expectancy theory, which may help us determine under what conditions any given approach will be best.

[1] We make no claim to have exhausted the list of possible forms of motivation, and in practice most managers use a combination of all five.

The traditional approach

The traditional form of motivation (and the one that seems to come easiest to most managers) emphasizes authority and economic rewards. At its crudest, this method (sometimes called "Be Strong") consists of forcing people to work by threatening to fire them or cut their economic rewards if they don't. The assumptions of this Economic Man model are that the only reason people work is to earn money and that they will work only if driven to it by fear of losing their jobs.

This approach further assumes that since no one likes work, people will try to get away with doing as little as they can.[2] Management must tell every worker exactly what to do every minute of the day, spell out every rule, and give the worker the narrowest possible range for discretion. Often rules are promulgated just "to show who is boss." Individuals are kept busy "to keep them out of trouble."

The traditional approach is often associated with scientific management, especially the division of work into small segments and the careful specification of how the work is to be done.[3] The assumption here is that workers are neither interested nor able to direct their own jobs; in other words, they are hired to work rather than to think. Thus management does the planning and workers the execution.

This approach paid off fairly well in the early days of the industrial revolution when workers were so close to starvation that the physical, off-the-job needs for food, clothing, and shelter were paramount. In recent years, however, people have begun to expect more than sheer punishment from their jobs. As a consequence, the traditional approach has become less effective as a motivating device. There are three major reasons why this approach has become less appropriate.

1. We suggested in Chapter 1 that as our standard of living has risen and our physical needs have become better satisfied, people have begun to look for social and egoistic satisfactions higher up on the need hierarchy. This is particularly true in times of full employment. Or to put it another way, we have used our increased productivity partly to provide ourselves with more material goods, such as bigger houses, better cars, and fancier cuts of meat; partly to increase our leisure time through shorter hours and longer vacations; and partly to improve our work environment by slowing the work pace and eliminating tyrannical supervision.[4]

2. Seventy years ago children were taught, both at home and at school, to show strict obedience to their elders. And so the child-grown-adult found

---

[2] Often we see a self-fulfilling prophecy at work: if management behaves as if it expects workers to do only a minimum of work, workers will, in fact, do as little as they can.

[3] Fredrick W. Taylor is often called the Father of Scientific Management. See his *The Principles of Scientific Management* (New York: Harper, 1911). Taylor, himself, argued for "the training and development of each individual . . . so that he can do . . . the highest class of work for which his abilities fit him." On the other hand, he believed that his approach would work best with workers who were "as phlegmatic as an ox."

[4] Economists might say that as income rises the marginal utility of money declines and preference increases for nonpecuniary rewards.

little difficulty adjusting to stern discipline in the office or factory. Recent years have seen a revolution in the way children are brought up. Freedom and self-expression are encouraged in the home; schools stress spontaneous discussion and individual expression. Youth culture today emphasizes self-expression. As a consequence, the young worker finds it hard to accept autocratic leadership.

3. Basic to the traditional approach is the expectation that if an employee doesn't do what the boss tells him to do, he or she will be fired. Unions, however, have made it more difficult to fire people; in effect, the minimum work standards are lower than before. Civil Service regulations have had the same effect on some government jobs.

Application to white-collar workers

We all know how the bullying foreman uses traditional techniques. But others with authority apply the same policy to executives, supervisors, and white-collar workers. It is common practice for top management to set goals (increased sales, lowered costs, and so forth) for their executives, and then to exert constant pressure to ensure that these goals are met. The penalty for not meeting them is usually the withholding of promotions or salary increases, if not outright discharge. Some companies deliberately set their goals too high. Every time a goal comes close to being met, management raises it even higher, hoping to stir employees to work harder and harder. As one manager remarked, "My philosophy is always give a person more than he can finish. That way you can be sure you are getting the most out of him."

The consequent feeling of frustration is intensified because managers and white-collar employees typically do not have the channels of redress or the opportunities to express aggression that are available to their blue-collar brothers or sisters. With no union to protect them and with a keen interest in advancement, these people can be motivated by the fear of punishment. Their motivation, however, is to engage in apple polishing subservience rather than to be imaginative or to exercise discretion.

Difficulties of the approach

The trouble with the traditional approach is this: it ignores the fact that people are not passive, inert machines and that they often react in ways not intended by management.

• This policy normally provides no incentive to work harder than the minimum required to avoid punishment.[5] The minimum may be fairly low for unionized workers who are promoted on the basis of seniority and who have a union to protect them if they are fired. On the other hand, the minimum may be relatively high if the work is closely programmed and if it is easy to see whether an employee is falling down on the job. (And, as we have seen, it sometimes seems to work with white collar employees, but at a high cost.)

• The essence of the traditional approach is the application of pressure. But when subjected to *too much* pressure, employees fight back. When they

---

[5] Piecework does provide such motivation; but as we discuss elsewhere, the effectiveness of piecework is reduced by group-imposed "bogeys" (output restrictions).

can, they fight through their union. Even if they have no union, they engage in slowdowns, sabotage, and spoilage. As one worker commented, "In my shop there is an undeclared war of nerves. If management won't treat us like humans, we aren't going to show much respect for them."

Part of this "war of nerves" consists of workers' efforts to get away with doing as little as possible; there is no incentive for doing more than the minimum, but there is a great deal of satisfaction in making management look silly. Naturally, management reacts by deciding, "We have to watch these people like hawks to get anything done." Both sides spend a tremendous amount of energy trying to outsmart the other. Efficiency declines and management, in frustration, often strikes back irrationally, perhaps by imposing needless restrictions or by firing alleged ringleaders. Thus, a vicious cycle is set in motion, a cycle of restraints and more evasions.

- To protect themselves from pressure, employees organize groups and cliques. Existing groups draw closer together and take on a new purpose, protecting themselves against management pressure. As we shall see, work groups frequently establish "bogeys" or standards of output that no member is expected to exceed. This policy of self-protection is openly practiced by hourly-paid workers; however, even executives can band together in an implicit alliance to protect themselves against superiors or other departments.

- Probably the most serious trouble with the traditional approach is that it ignores a basic factor in human behavior: When people are put under too much pressure, they become *frustrated.* (Note: we say *too much* pressure. Most of us respond well to some pressure, but all of us have a critical point—which differs from one person to another—beyond which frustration sets in.) [6]

When people become frustated they react in strange ways that tend to reduce the effectiveness of the organization in its main task of getting out work. Often their behavior seems quite irrational, since it cannot be understood in terms of the apparent stimulus.

Superintendent Jones's secretary usually does a fine, conscientious job. Today she forgot to type an unimportant letter. Jones bawled her out unmercifully.

Jones is normally a kind woman. Why did she act this way today? Certainly her behavior would not help get the letter out more quickly or even prevent her secretary from making mistakes in the future. Actually the superintendent had been trying to meet an important deadline with an inadequate staff, and *her* boss had just called to spur her on.

One response to frustration is *aggression,* which expresses itself in many ways. Instead of bawling out her secretary, Jones might have picked a fight with another supervisor, had a hassle with her husband, or whammed a defenseless golf ball around the course. If her frustration became too intense, it might have lead to psychosomatic illnesses, such as high blood pressure or ulcers.

---

[6] Evidence suggests that up to a certain point, anxiety facilitates the performance of all tasks, but that anxiety is more effective with simple than with complicated tasks.

> Once we observed a group of working supervisors who had been strongly pressured to increase production under difficult circumstances with no backing from management. There were nine workers regularly assigned to the day shift. One had a nervous breakdown, another had a fatal heart attack that was generally attributed to overwork and fatigue. Of the remaining seven, five had serious illnesses, and in most cases no organic cause could be determined. All this happened during a period of twelve months. Meanwhile the workers on the night shift, where pressure was much less, had an almost perfect health record.

There are many other reactions to frustration. Some people *repress* their feelings for a long time and then suddenly blow up without notice. Others *regress* to less mature levels of behavior. Everyone is familiar with the three-year-old who reverts to thumb-sucking when a baby sister arrives on the scene. Similarly, adults who are frustrated by excessive pressure may find it difficult to make decisions or react intelligently and may engage in juvenile (and aggressive) activities such as horseplay. Though employees may be dragooned into submission by the traditional approach, the consequent frustration may lead to a serious reduction in the quality of their work and less intelligent behavior. Under extreme frustration, they may simply fall into *resignation* and give up trying altogether.

Frustration may also lead to *scapegoating*—that is, picking on those who are weak and defenseless. It is not accidental, for instance, that racial tensions in plants are higher when times are bad and layoffs are pending. Another response is *fixation*, in which the individual persists in some fruitless activity, such as Lady Macbeth's handwashing, even though it obviously accomplishes nothing. When assigned a difficult problem, some managers spend their time shuffling papers rather than trying to work out a realistic solution.

Finally, there is *sublimation*, in which the individual seeks to satisfy frustrated needs in some more effective fashion. Thus, the executive who has been denied promotion may become active in a social club.

The collective reaction of a group of workers to frustration may have a devastating effect on the entire organization. It may disrupt group solidarity and cooperation, turning departments, groups, and individuals against one another. It may lead to rumor, mistrust, and suspicion. It may result in unexplained wildcat strikes or a general state of snarling irritability. In most cases, the basic objective of the organization—*production*—is bound to suffer.

The value of the traditional approach

Thus, the effectiveness of the traditional technique of motivation is subject to significant limitations: (1) it motivates employees to do only enough work to keep from being fired (except where there are significant opportunities for promotion); (2) it motivates them to get away with as much as possible (often making a game of it), thus leading to a vicious cycle of further management restrictions and employee evasions; (3) it motivates them to band together in self-protection; and (4) it leads to frustration and, in turn, to a whole series of deleterious side reactions that jeopardize production.

And yet, as we shall see, there are times when this approach works fairly well. It works better in the short run than in the long run. It is most effective in nonunionized situations, during depressions, when employees are desperate for work, with members of any group who have difficulty finding work, and in highly programmed work where deviation from rules may be easily spotted. Even in these situations, though, there are undesirable side reactions.

Human relations

By the early 1920s, managers and scholars were pointing to what they believed were signs of rebellion against the excessive regimentation and impersonalization caused by the traditional approach. They argued that organizations had lost sight of the human needs for belonging, social interaction, and feeling important. These early critics of autocratic and bureaucratic organizations were soon augmented by the interpreters of the famous Hawthorne experiments.[7] These developments gave birth to the human relations movement that dominated management thought during the Forties and Fifties.[8]

As a substitute for the traditional approach of work-or-be-fired, human-relations-oriented managers sought to motivate employees chiefly through satisfying their security and social needs (though physical needs for fair pay were not ignored, at least not in theory). Human relations management tried to satisfy security needs through fringe benefits that provided some protection against illness, old age, unemployment, and the vicissitudes of life as well as through managerial policies that treated employees with fairness. The social need for belonging was to be met by various recreational activities and, more significantly, by the development of strong cohesive work groups. Finally, to meet the second main social need—support—supervisors and consultants were trained to listen to, and to show concern for employee problems, to treat each employee with dignity (not as a phlegmatic ox), and in general to display what Chapter 4 calls "consideration." On occasion human relations managers even permitted workers a mild degree of participation in solving trivial problems. Beyond this, human relations management sought to provide a comfortable environment in which to work. To achieve this, it emphasized such amenities as clean attractive work places, safety and health programs, and cafeterias serving good food at reasonable prices.

We may distinguish between two forms of human relations: *paternalism* and *hygienic management.* The argument for paternalism holds that if management is good to employees, they will work harder out of loyalty and gratitude. The argument for hygienic management ignores the question of gratitude; it holds that liberal benefits, good working conditions, and friendly supervision develop satisfied employees, and that satisfied employees work harder.

---

[7] The results of these experiments, conducted at the Hawthorne plant of Western Electric during the late Twenties and early Thirties, were believed to point to the importance of what were then called "irrational" (as opposed to "rational" or economic) needs: the needs for approval, belonging, and group membership. See Elton Mayo, *The Human Problems of an Industrial Civilization* (New York: Macmillan, 1933) and Fritz Roethlisberger and William Dickson, *Management and the Worker* (Cambridge, Mass.: Harvard University Press, 1969).

[8] For our particular use of the term "human relations," we are indebted to Raymond Miles, *Theories of Management* (New York: McGraw-Hill, 1975).

Paternalism

Paternalism is pretty much outdated, having had its heyday in the 1920s. In part, its wide adoption at the time was the result of employers' genuine interest in their employees. In part, too, its popularity was a reaction to the rise of unionism during and immediately after World War I. In any case, under the banner of the "New Industrial Relations," management became interested in a wide variety of projects, varying from cafeterias and recreation programs for employees to cooking classes for their wives. Some of these programs were designed to change the employees' personal lives as well as their on-the-job performance. The Sociology Department of the Ford Motor Company of an earlier day went further than most programs. Headed by a Protestant minister, this department was manned by 30 investigators.

In what amounted to a brief reign of benevolent paternalism, these gentlemen and their house-to-house canvassers imposed . . . a set of rules which blended good sense with Ford whims and Puritan virtues.

On the positive side, the men . . . behaved like the home visitor of the modern public welfare agency. They doubtless helped to "Americanize" Ford's vast body of immigrant workmen. Their charges were encouraged to start savings accounts and to budget their incomes. They were given elementary lessons in hygiene and home mangement. . . .

At worst . . . its agents became, to some extent, collectors of tales and suspicions. . . . Hearsay as well as fact found its way into a card catalogue where a record was kept of every worker's deviations. . . . Frittering away one's evenings "unwisely," taking in male boarders, sending funds to the "old country"—these things came to be regarded as earmarks of "unwholesome living." The use of liquor was forbidden . . . as was marital discord that resulted in a separation or divorce action.[9]

Ford's program was shortlived, but similar patterns of paternalism were developed in other companies. There is little evidence that any of them were particularly successful in eliciting gratitude, in motivating workers to do a better job, or even in staving off the development of unions. In fact, some of the companies with the best-known histories of paternalism later became scenes of bitter labor-management strife.

There are good psychological reasons for believing that if management expects employees to work harder out of gratitude for benefits, then paternalism will fail to accomplish its purpose. What actually happens may be this:

1. Paternalism may engender resentment rather than gratitude. Unearned rewards given out of the kindness of the employer's heart are often regarded as slights to employees' sense of self-esteem.[10] Instances of "biting the hand that feeds one" are common.[11]

2. As time passes, the novelty of being given free handouts wears off, and these benefits are taken for granted.

---

[9] Keith Seward, *The Legend of Henry Ford* (New York: Holt, 1948), p. 59.
[10] In Britain, paternalistic benefits are sometimes called "grace and favor handouts."
[11] In Japan, such paternalism may be less resented. Employees enjoy a real feeling of belonging to a family in which there are reciprocal obligations. The boss's (and the company's) favors are expected to be reciprocated by hard work and loyalty.

3. In most instances, since the rewards are distributed to everyone on the payroll, there is little incentive for the employee to do more work than the minimum required to keep from being fired.

4. Paternalism incorporates the basic assumptions of the traditional approach to motivation. Workers are expected to be docile, in return for their gifts. Work is still regarded as a form of punishment that people undergo only in return for a reward. Moreover, many of the rewards must be enjoyed *off* the job. Little effort is made to make the job itself more rewarding.

Hygienic management

Old-fashioned paternalism is seldom practiced today except in small firms. A more subtle version of human relations is still common, however. The basic assumption is that happy workers work harder. Management provides workers with fringe benefits, good working conditions, considerate supervision, and the like, with the hope that these amenities will raise employees' morale and therefore induce them to produce more. Management that emphasizes these benefits is called *hygienic management* and the factors considered important are called *hygienes* (since they are used to avoid discontent).

The term *morale* has been used in different ways; but if morale means the employees' attitude toward the organization as a whole, there is little evidence that high morale leads to high productivity. Just the reverse may be true. Morale may be low in a concentration camp, yet production very high. Similarly, workers may well be satisfied to "goof off" in a department where the work pace is extremely slow. Indeed, numerous careful psychological studies show that the relationship between productivity and satisfaction is close to zero.

A significant, but controversial, study has given us a new insight into the effectiveness of the human relations approach.[12] In this study, accountants and engineers were asked to "think of a time when you felt exceptionally good and exceptionally bad about your job" and then asked to describe what happened and why they felt as they did. Interestingly, the factors which made people satisfied with their jobs were neither the same as (nor the opposite of) factors that made them dissatisfied. Apparently, the presence of so-called satisfiers would increase an individual's satisfaction, but their absence would not make him actively dissatisfied, only apathetic. Similarly, the presence of so-called dissatisfiers made people feel they had a "bad" job; but the absence of dissatisfiers did not make a "good" job.

[12] Frederick Herzberg, *Work and the Nature of Man* (Cleveland: World, 1966). A number of attempts to replicate this study have had various degrees of success. The research techniques have been subject to quite serious (and we think justifiable) criticism. Victor Vroom suggests that (1) the findings are inconsistent with other evidence, and (2) people are "more likely to attribute the causes of satisfaction to their own achievements and accomplishments on the job. On the other hand, they may be more likely to attribute their dissatisfaction, not to personal inadequacies or deficiencies, but to factors in the work environment." *Work and Motivation* (New York: Wiley, 1964), pp. 127–29. Further, a given reward, such as praise, may be perceived as a motivator in one context and a hygiene factor in another. For a critical evaluation of the research as a whole, see Edwin Locke, "The Nature and Causes of Job Satisfaction," in Marvin Dunnette, ed., *Handbook of Industrial and Organizational Psychology* (Chicago: Rand McNally, 1976), pp. 1309–19. The authors of this present volume feel that despite the drawbacks of the research technique, the Herzberg study does point to a useful way of examining motivation.

What were these satisfiers and dissatisfiers? The satisfiers were: achievement, recognition, work itself, responsibility, and advancement. Note that all these forms of satisfaction arise *out* of the *content* of the work itself. The dissatisfiers were: interpersonal relations (both with one's superiors and peers), the technical ability of the supervisor, company policy and administration, physical working conditions, and the individual's personal life off the job. Note that all these factors relate to the *context* or the *environment* within which the job is performed, but not to the job itself. (Interestingly, salary ranked as both a satisfier and a dissatisfier. In general, when a person indicated that salary helped make his job a bad one, he was referring to the system by which salaries were set; when salary was mentioned as making a job a good one, salary was looked on as a sign of achievement and recognition.)

What is the relationship between these factors and productivity? The evidence is quite tentative, but Herzberg suggests that the presence of satisfiers leads to higher productivity (and for this reason satisfiers have also been called *motivators*). Dissatisfiers, on the other hand, do not lead to lower production nor does their elimination tend to raise it. Their elimination may reduce active resistance to the job, but promote only a passive acceptance of it. This attitude is illustrated by an interview we once held with a blue-collar worker on a routine job. This worker said:

"I got a pretty good job."
Q: "What makes it such a good job?"
A: "Don't get me wrong. I didn't say it is a *good* job. It's an OK job—about as good a job as a guy like me might expect. The foreman leaves me alone and it pays well. But I would never call it a *good* job."

Thus, a policy of hygienic management may provide a pleasant environment in which to work and a considerable amount of around-the-job satisfaction, but little satisfaction *through* the job and little sense of enthusiasm or creativity. The emphasis is on job *context* rather than job *content*.

The value of human relations

We have applied the term human relations to the philosophy that a comfortable environment, good treatment, and other benefits will automatically motivate employees to work harder. And we have suggested that this is an oversimplified theory of human behavior. Does this mean that it is a complete waste of time to make the company a better place to work? Of course not. Properly administered, fringe benefits and employee services are an important part of any personnel program. Such benefits bolster the organization's reputation in the community, attract better workers, and reduce turnover. Further, a feeling of security helps reduce tension among employees and thus, to some extent, contributes to higher productivity.

Hygienic factors are particularly important for workers with an instrumental orientation who do not expect challenge from the job (those in our cells 3 and 4 on p. 24), and for those who work on inherently boring jobs for which motivators, such as sense of achievement, are hard to find. Beyond this, fair, considerate, supportive supervision is required, regardless of the job or the employee's interests.

Put another way, good human relations tend to make the job more tolerable. Without question, efforts to make the company a better place to work do pay off in terms of better workers and more harmonious relations. But they provide little direct motivation for employees to contribute more than a minimum effort. In effect, human relations are a necessary but not sufficient condition for high motivation.

Implicit bargaining   One of the most common forms of motivation today (though some managers may hate to admit it) is bargaining. When using this approach, management encourages workers to put out a *reasonable* amount of work by agreeing to provide *reasonable* supervision in return. The bargain is usually a matter of implicit, unspoken understanding.[13] In a sense management agrees not to use all the pressures at its disposal if the employees will agree not to restrict output unduly. The chief difference between this approach and the forms of motivation already discussed is that the terms of the bargain (namely, what constitutes reasonable supervision and what constitutes reasonable output) are agreed upon more or less voluntarily by the parties.[14]

Thus, in practice, the level of output and the conditions under which people work are not determined unilaterally by the manager, but through unwritten agreement between manager and subordinate. There is an assumption that the parties are more or less equal in power, so that the terms of the "effort bargain" or "psychological contract" are agreed upon voluntarily. Just how favorable the final bargaining is to each of the parties is determined by their respective bargaining power. Let us look for a moment at the weapons the parties possess.

The employees' major weapon is this: they can either display cheerful cooperation and maintain high production or else they can indulge in excessive clumsiness, misunderstanding, or overt slowdowns or strikes.

The managers' most obvious weapon is their power to discipline workers who fail to produce. In practice, in the typical unionized situation, formal discipline is difficult to impose unless the workers' behavior is completely out of line. Still the manager can use a whole arsenal of minor weapons: small but highly prized "plums," minor concessions, and petty but very real punishments. Managers can assign easy jobs or hard ones. They can make concessions in terms of time off and accept obviously false excuses for absenteeism or tardiness—or they can nag employees for minor offenses. They can provide the help that makes a job easier—or they can make work almost impossible (this is a particularly telling weapon where piecework is involved).

Sometimes the bargain involves an informal agreement to relax formal rules. For example, employees may be permitted to leave work before the

---

[13] At times, of course, management and a union do engage in explicit bargaining over production levels and occasionally their agreement is put in writing.

[14] There are other differences, too. The other approaches to motivation view the boss as motivating the subordinate; implicit bargaining assumes that boss and subordinate motivate each other. The other approaches involve conscious or semiconscious management philosophies; implicit bargaining is more a description of actual workplace behavior.

formal quitting time, make personal calls on the company phone, or take home company pencils. In return for this "indulgency pattern" they implicitly agree to work harder. Although such agreements are never put into words, they are tacitly understood by everybody concerned. They become group norms of behavior. As one worker put it:

"Our policy is to live and let live. We give the foreman reasonable production. He protects us from the time-study man who tries to jack up the output rate and looks the other way if we take a smoke. We look out for each other."

These privileges are extended only so long as the supervisor feels that the subordinates are doing a satisfactory job. Otherwise they are withdrawn.

A case in point was the "no-floating around rule" which specified that workers must stay at their workplace, except to go to the washroom or eat. When foremen felt that things were going smoothly in their group, that their men were "doing a day's work" and were friendly and "cooperative," they would allow their workers to "sneak off" for a smoke, and they would make no caustic remarks if they wandered over to talk to a friend. If, however, a man or a group was felt to be "goofing off," or was being "snotty," foremen were more likely to invoke the "no floating" rule.[15]

An analogy may be drawn between the indulgency pattern and bank deposits. Both subordinates and supervisors build up credits by doing favors for the other party, and both expect to draw on their account when they need a favor for themselves.

In many situations this policy of "live and let live" is the most realistic approach available to the supervisor. For all its disadvantages, it does make possible a reasonably satisfactory level of production and reasonably harmonious worker-supervisor and labor-management relations. Employees enjoy a sense of independence that they are denied under the traditional and human relations approaches, even though they are partially motivated by the fear that if the supervisor is dissatisfied with their work, their petty benefits could be withdrawn. Equally important is the feeling that since the supervisor is "fair" to them, it is only proper that they put out a "fair day's work." (In Chapter 6, we shall point out that when supervisors are considered fair, their orders acquire greater legitimacy.)

The picture we get from this point of view is not that of the worker crushed by the organization, but of one who fights it, copes with it, and retains his or her autonomy—making deals that satisfy both the individual and the organization. Yet, unless bargaining is coupled with more positive forms of motivation, it suffers from many of the disadvantages of the traditional and human relations approaches. At best, "fair supervision" is a form of hygienic management. Implicit bargaining provides little egoistic satisfaction (except in the sense of outwitting management). Work is still a punishment that one endures only for the benefits that accrue from abiding by the agreement. From management's point of view, bargaining offers little opportunity to raise production. Since restrictive work practices may become part of the work culture, production is often stabilized at a fairly low level. Furthermore, it

---

[15] Alvin Gouldner, *Patterns of Industrial Bureaucracy* (New York: Free Press, 1954), p. 173.

becomes difficult to introduce change. On the other hand, in some cases this may be the most management can realistically expect.

Competition

Another form of motivation is competition for the pay increases and promotions that accompany outstanding work. Competition furnishes several forms of need satisfaction. The prospect of winning a promotion or a pay increase provides a meaningful goal. Actually attaining the goal means that the employee enjoys an economic reward, as well as a sense of accomplishment and completion, a sense of progress, and added social prestige. Less supervision is required on jobs where competition provides a reasonably satisfactory source of motivation, since each person is on his own to do the best job he can. There is no need to push him.

Competition is not particularly successful as a motivating device among factory workers, however. In union plants the principle of seniority substantially decreases the possibility of winning a promotion on the basis of hard work alone. The trend to reserve foremen's jobs for college-graduates has further reduced the factory worker's chance of rising into management. In theory, the incentive (piecework) system does provide an opportunity for workers to compete with one another. In practice, however, they usually cooperate to restrict output and prevent competition.

Among blue-collar workers (or white-collar workers in mass-production offices), competition is often more effective among *groups* than it is among *individuals.* We have observed numerous incidents where competition has arisen almost spontaneously between groups to see who will put out the most work, make the biggest reductions in scrap losses, and so forth. Workers seem to enjoy the increased sense of group belonging, the excitement of the game, and the thrill of winning.

Competition among individuals is much more widely accepted on the white-collar and managerial levels, particularly among salesmen. Yet even among nonfactory employees competition as a means of motivation suffers certain limitations and undesirable side-effects:

1. Not everybody is equally interested in advancement. Some people are highly ambitious, but others—who may be just as competent and hardworking—seek to avoid situations where they have to "cut the other man's throat" to get ahead. And many people, reasonably satisfied with their present jobs and earnings, do not want to expend the extra effort necessary to win a promotion.

Many engineers and scientists are more interested in professional advancement than in promotions, particularly if the higher-rated job takes them from their laboratory and saddles them with administrative chores. In a sense, these professionals are competing, but they are competing for professional recognition rather than for the goals management has set for them.

2. Excessive competition has been known to disrupt entire organizations. Competition between organizations is often healthy; competition within an organization can be dangerous. As modern organizations become more specialized, activities such as credit, sales, engineering, and product development

cannot be carried out without continuous cooperation from people who are performing other activities. There are fewer and fewer one-person operations, particularly at the higher levels of management. As a consequence cooperation at the managerial level is vital to sustained efficiency.

3. In many fields it is difficult to measure each employee's output and, consequently, to determine who has been most successful. Yet, unless there is some purely objective way to determine who should receive promotions and rewards, competition could make subordinates overly dependent on their boss. They may be more anxious to look good than to do a good job.

4. Efforts to encourage competition are often regarded as pressure, and as we have seen, excessive pressure is frustrating. Aggression and regression are common by-products of the contests conducted by sales organizations. *Time* magazine writes:

> Many firms have . . . enlisted salesmen's families in ulcer-building campaigns to spur the breadwinner on. One company regularly sends cards to the home showing the salesman's standing in the current company contest, gives wives tags to hang on furniture around the house to remind their husbands of the furnishings they can earn. Some firms have even sent buzzers and shrill whistles to salesmen's children; when dad asks what the noise is all about, the kids are instructed to tell him it's only a reminder to straighten up and sell harder. . . . Such constant pressure from home and office is bound to take its toll on even the strongest salesman. . . . "You can carry this business of pounding away at a salesman too far," says Republic Steel's General Sales Manager L. S. Hamaker. "It can be too demoralizing." [16]

Excessive emphasis on competition is particularly frustrating to the loser. Since most promotional hierarchies are shaped like a pyramid, with fewer jobs at the top than at the bottom, there are always more losers than winners.

Many work groups actually band together to protect themselves from attempts to encourage competition, either by formulating group standards of "fair competition" or by banning competitive practices altogether. (For examples, see Chap. 5.) This response is most common among hourly-paid workers, but employees at all levels apply pressure on the "eager beaver."

In conclusion, excessive competition may do more harm than good. In its pure form, the philosophy of competition as a motivating device seems to assume that work is itself uninteresting. When used in moderation, however, and in conjunction with other forms of motivation, competition among individuals may be useful, particularly with certain groups (salesmen, for example), and in situations where teamwork is not essential.

Internalized motivation

A fifth approach to the problem of motivation is to provide opportunities for need satisfaction *through doing the job itself,* and thus to internalize motivation so that people will enjoy doing good work.[17] This approach makes use of Herzberg's "motivators." It requires that management accept the responsibility to create conditions under which employees "will willingly

---

[16] *Time*, Vol. 72, No. 2 (July 14, 1958), pp. 75–76. For a good discussion of the disruptive consequences of excess competition, see Rosabeth Kanter, *Men and Women of the Corporation* (New York: Basic Books, 1977).

[17] This approach to motivation has been called by various authors "spontaneous cooperation," "Theory Y," and "Human Resources."

and voluntarily work toward organizational objectives"[18]—because they enjoy the *work* (not just the work place) and feel it important to do a good job. It requires management to discard the assumption that work must be objectionable. It also de-emphasizes economic motivation and instead stresses ego needs. And above all, it looks upon workers as having untapped creative abilities, which if unleashed, could be directed towards achieving managerial objectives.

Note how this approach differs from human relations. If management uses the human relations approach, the employees are given rewards, usually just for doing the bare minimum of work; using internalized motivation, employees obtain satisfaction *through the work itself.* In the human relations approach, it is assumed that greater satisfaction leads to harder work. In the internalized motivation approach, the relationship is reversed: it is assumed that harder work is the element that leads to greater satisfaction.

Later chapters will provide greater detail about how internalized motivation may be provided. Here we shall list only a few major themes.

- *Job redesign.* Intrinsic job satisfaction can be increased through redesigning the job, and especially through job enrichment (see Chap. 3).
- *Participation.* Opportunities can be provided to work together as a team. When members of a group participate in solving work problems, they become more involved in the job so that their productivity often rises. By contrast with the human-relations type participation, which is normally confined to unessential matters, for internalized motivation to work employees should be allowed to participate with regard to important problems.
- *General supervision.* Equally important is management's style of leadership. Employees may be given an opportunity to be their own boss as much as possible. Under such circumstances supervisors consider their job to be a means of helping rather than pushing their subordinates.
- *Commitment to superordinate goals.* During times of war and crisis individuals often subordinate their personal interests to the superordinate goals of the organization as a whole. This is the technique used by the leaders of totalitarian countries, by successful football coaches, and by many leaders of scientific and exploration groups in which the excitement of working toward common objectives transcends individual self-interest.
- *Open-system career paths.* Instead of rigid career paths, in which the jobs employees do and their opportunities for promotion are determined exclusively by management or in accordance with seniority rules, some organizations now permit employees (especially professionals and managers) considerable freedom to select the kinds of training they wish and the kinds of jobs they would like to perform.

The limits of internalized motivation

For all its merits, internalized motivation is not a panacea, though some observers are more optimistic about it than the authors are. To our minds, those who unreservedly praise internalized motivation tend to overestimate the possible gains from its use and to underestimate the costs involved in making it work.

We have just discussed why the traditional, human relations, and implicit bargaining approaches provide little motivation to produce more than a minimum amount of work. Yet on many routine jobs this minimum may be enough, since management may have no need for outstanding performance. What is outstanding performance in the case of the assembly-line worker? Working

[18] Douglas McGregor, *The Supervisor's Job*, mimeographed, undated.

faster than the line? Showing creativity and imagination on the job? Management needs none of these. *Adequate* performance (as set by implicit bargaining, perhaps) is all that can be used on the assembly line and on many other jobs in our society. Here the conforming, dependent worker (who is not *dis*satisfied) may well be the best.

Further, as we have seen in Chapter 1, many people center their lives off the job and have little desire for the challenge internalized motivation provides. In fact, challenge may merely make them anxious. There are those who argue that such people are immature and that they have adjusted to techniques such as hygienic supervision by becoming apathetic and dependent: were the organization environment healthy, were internalized motivation available, the argument goes on, these people would react differently. But in many cases, these people's limitations stem from childhood or from the general culture. Even if the argument is valid, such persons may be too far gone to react well to internalized motivation, and their attitude is not likely to be changed short of intensive psychotherapy.

In addition, the reliance on internalized motivation can be quite costly to the organization. To increase intrinsic job satisfaction may require the use of job processes that are technologically inefficient. Increased teamwork may not be useful to the organization if employers unite to keep production low. To make general supervision work, many of the old-time autocratic supervisors must be retrained or replaced; this is an expensive process that could result in the demoralization and elimination of the organization's technically most competent employees. And only in very unusual circumstances are people prepared to sacrifice their own interests for the good of the organization as a whole—chiefly in times of great national danger or after being brainwashed.

Since it is extremely difficult to develop internalized motivation on many routine jobs, once the traditional, external sanctions (implicit bargaining, fear of discharge, and so forth) are removed, *net* motivation may fall. Freedom may result merely in workers "goofing off."

Furthermore, it is fairly meaningless to talk of permitting assembly-line workers or punch-card operators to exercise discretion; the very nature of these jobs requires that all essential decisions be centrally programmed. There are those who suggest that such programmed jobs should be redesigned to permit job enlargement, and thus greater challenge and discretion. Yet, such technological changes can be made only at a substantial cost in terms of productivity.

Thus internalized motivation works best when the nature of the job permits the employee to enjoy autonomy (there may be little opportunity for it on the assembly line, but a good deal in professional work); with employees who accept the organization's objectives (it might work better with managerial than blue-collar employees); and among those who make the job their central life focus.

In any case, the philosophy of internalized motivation is somewhat idealistic. It assumes that somehow the needs of the organization and needs of the individual can be simultaneously maximized, so that what is good for one will be good for the other. Rarely if ever is this the case. Normally there must be some sort of trade-off: if organizational needs are to come first, the individual will suffer to some extent, and vice versa. The most the manager can expect to provide is a reasonably satisfactory level of satisfaction for both parties. Conflicts of interest will continue to exist. Employees always want more satisfaction, management always wants more production. Where the balance is to be poised between the two "is a matter to be solved by bargaining, not by scientific evidence." [19]

Expectancy theory   A new approach helps put the previous discussion in context.[20] Called expectancy theory (or sometimes path-goals analysis), it suggests that employees will be motivated to produce only if they *expect* that productivity will lead to (or is a *path* toward) a *goal* they value.[21] More explicitly, increased *effort* will lead to increased *performance* (productivity), and increased performance will lead in turn to *rewards* that provide *satisfaction* of important employee needs. A final requirement is that the satisfaction resulting from this initial effort be sufficiently great *(equitable)* to make the effort worthwhile. Though there are various versions of the relationship, the one we will utilize here is diagrammed here. Let us more closely examine this approach.

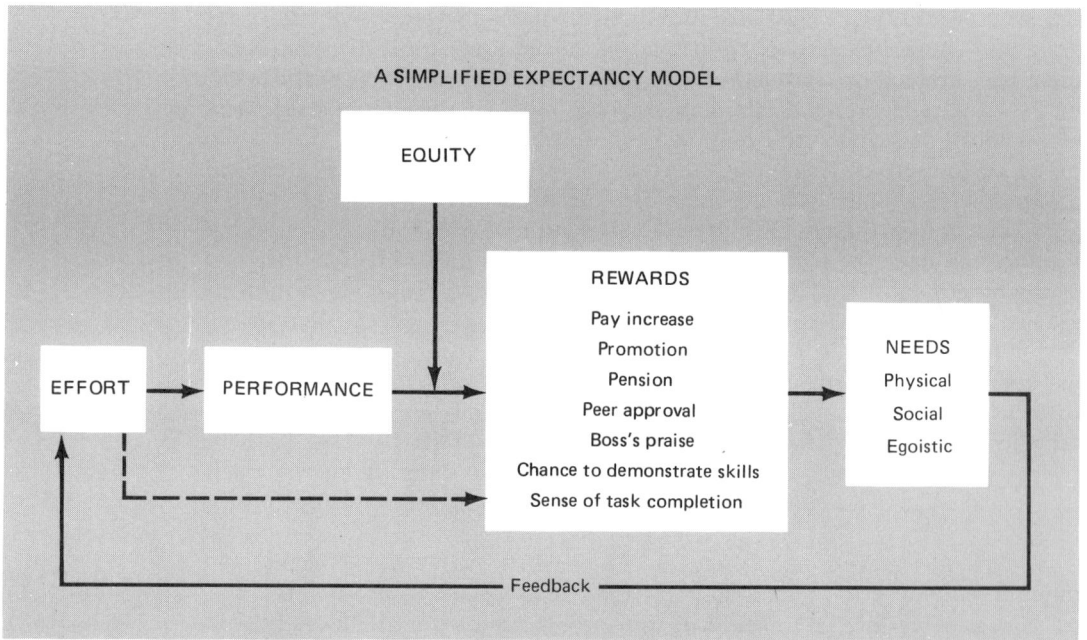

[19] Herbert A. Simon, "Authority," in Conrad Arensberg and others, eds., *Research in Industrial Human Relations* (New York: Harper, 1957), p. 114.

[20] Expectancy theory is not so much a sixth form of motivation as a means of analyzing various forms of motivation, including the five we have just discussed.

[21] For early statements of the theory, see Vroom, *Work and Motivation,* and Lyman Porter and Edward Lawler, *Managerial Attitudes and Performance* (Homewood: Irwin, 1968). For a recent and more complex statement, see Barry Staw, "Motivation in Organizations," in Barry Staw and Gerald Salancik, eds., *New Directions in Organizational Behavior* (Chicago: St. Clair, 1977).

1. Let us start with effort. Greater effort must be expected to lead to performance.[22] Normally it does. But if the job is such (as on some assembly lines) that effort is perceived as unrelated to production (or some other organizational goal) then expectancy theory (and common sense) tells us the employee will not exert effort.[23]

2. Performance must be expected to lead to some sort of reward (or set of rewards). The expectancy model shows some possible rewards, but obviously not an all-inclusive list. Note that the "expectancy" that effort will lead to a specific reward varies from reward to reward. Thus, in a given case there may be low expectancy that hard work will be rewarded by promotion (since promotions are by seniority), but a high expectancy that it will be rewarded by the boss's praise.

The performance-reward relationship is often the critical link in the motivational chain. Too often employees believe that doing a good job is not rewarded. This may be because they are not rewarded in fact or because management has not adequately explained the reward system.

3. The reward must satisfy needs that are important to the employee. The reward may be peer approval; but if the employee wants money, peer approval will be less motivating. Naturally, at this point personality variables come into play. Praise, for example, may not be motivating unless the employee has a fairly high need for approval. Similarly, the shoe salesman, whose main interest is not related to his job (perhaps he composes music in his spare time), may not be motivated when customers praise his care in selecting shoes.

4. The satisfaction gained from effort must be enough to make the effort worthwhile. Employees often have strongly held concepts of *equity*, which relate to how much they should be rewarded for their efforts.[24] If the reward and the resulting satisfaction from effort are judged to be inequitably low, employees are unlikely to exert themselves. Often their concepts of "fair reward" are the result of implicit bargaining. In addition, they are heavily influenced by the attitudes of fellow workers and by comparisons made between one's own rewards and the rewards others receive for the same effort.

5. Finally, there must be feedback: motivation is likely to decline if employees are uncertain whether their efforts will lead to payoff. Psychological theory suggests that motivation is greater when the payoff immediately follows the effort; thus, if the payoff is long delayed, motivation will suffer.

How does expectancy theory help us understand individual situations? Let us look at a few examples.

---

[22] Expectancy theorists state their expectations in terms of probabilities, for example, that a unit of effort (however measured) will have, say, a .75 chance of leading to a unit of performance.

[23] On occasion, just engaging in effort may be rewarding in and of itself, and the reward comes from the effort, not the performance (see the broken line in the expectancy model). For example, just doing research may be satisfying for a scientist, though successful research, of course, may be even more satisfying.

[24] The voluminous research on equity is summarized in Campbell and Pritchard, "Motivation Theory," in Dunnette, *Handbook of Industrial and Organizational Psychology.*

Assembly-line workers. Here effort has relatively little impact on production, since production is largely determined by the speed of the line. In the typical case it is difficult to reward higher production economically, since wages are uniform for everyone on the job, and promotions are determined by seniority. The foreman may praise a good worker (social reward), but the worker may not value this praise highly, at least not highly enough to induce him to put out extra effort. The job is boring, and it permits little sense of accomplishment; therefore, egoistic satisfactions are not forthcoming.

Thus the job provides little positive motivation. As long as the foreman engages in hygienic supervision, however (for example, he gives the worker as much relief as he can), the worker's concept of equity may make him feel that he should put in a "fair day's" work—which might mean keeping up with the line but not making any special effort to maintain quality.

Piece-rate workers. Presumably, here effort does lead to higher productivity, and high productivity leads to economic rewards in the form of piece-rate earnings. The motivational impact of piecework, however, may be reduced by other factors: (1) the worker may believe that if he increases his output, his piece rate will be cut (that is, he will be paid less money per item produced), and so his total earnings will be reduced; (2) by increasing output he may violate group standards (see Chap. 5) and thus be stigmatized as a "bogey breaker." If he has what McClelland calls high need for affiliation, group approval may be a more valuable reward for him than the somewhat uncertain possibility of higher earnings. Thus the limited satisfaction to be gained from working harder may not be viewed as worth the effort.

Increased production that results from a worker's efforts may give him an egoistic sense of accomplishment, but he will value the feeling only if he has a high need for achievement. He may gain an even greater sense of accomplishment by restricting output.)

Underprivileged workers. Workers who have grown up in poverty areas may have "learned"—either from their own experience or from the experience of people they know—that hard work does *not* pay off. No one they know has ever been rewarded for his or her efforts, and as far as they are concerned the system is rigged against them. Such workers are unlikely to be motivated unless their perceived expectancies are changed.

Managers. In contrast to assembly line workers, there is usually a direct relationship between how hard a manager works and his or her performance. Presumably, too, better performance is rewarded through promotions, salary increases, and bonuses. In practice, however, the effectiveness of an organizational unit is a function of many factors other than its manager's effort. Further, managerial compensation schemes are often poorly designed; as a consequence pay is often vaguely related to performance. Indeed there is reason to believe that often the most effective motivator for management is egoistic—the sense of achievement derived from having one's own decisions (efforts) lead to improved performance, thereby demonstrating one's skills as a manager. By and large, egoistic motivation works better for managers than for blue-collar workers, because the managerial job provides a greater sense of discretion and because, in general, managers are strongly achievement-oriented.

We should note that expectancy theory has been subject to considerable criticism, especially in the following areas:[25]

Criticisms of expectancy theory

- The key variables are hard to conceptualize and measure, thus making research difficult.
- The theory mistakenly assumes that workers make decisions on the basis of careful rational calculations; in practice, people often follow routine, act on impulse, copy their friends, and make decisions on the basis of limited information.
- The theory mistakenly assumes that the satisfaction gained from rewards are additive. For example, upon finishing a task a worker may gain both a feeling of completion (satisfying ego needs) and a cash bonus (satisfying physical needs). The theory suggests that the worker will add up the two forms of satisfaction. Recent research suggests that under some circumstances, the fact that the job provides an *extrinsic* reward (here the bonus) may actually reduce the satisfaction gained from the *intrinsic* reward.

Despite these criticisms the expectancy theory framework can be used to analyze a variety of motivational techniques. The theory is relevant for job redesign (Chap. 3), management by objectives, salary administration, and fringe benefits.

Conclusion

The table on page 46 summarizes three forms of motivation discussed in this chapter; implicit bargaining and competition are too complex to summarize this easily.[26] With the growth of unions, our rising standard of living, and the changing patterns of discipline in home and school, the traditional approach has become less effective. It motivates people to produce only the minimum necessary to keep their job (though in some cases this minimum may be adequate). Moreover, it creates frustration and other undesirable side effects. In practice it is often tempered with large doses of implicit bargaining.

The human relations approach removes some of the traditional approach's harshness. It may help recruit employees and make the job setting more tolerable. But human relations alone provides little motivation to do more than the minimum amount of work to avoid being discharged.

Implicit bargaining is dependent on hygienic management. At times it is the most realistic approach, particularly where there is a union. It provides an atmosphere of live-and-let-live, but it rarely furnishes any motivation to *increase* production.

Competition has only limited effectiveness as a motivating device on

---

[25] Critical reviews of expectancy theory include Campbell and Pritchard, "Motivation Theory," in Dunnette, *Handbook of Individual and Organizational Psychology*; M. Wahbe and Robert J. House, "Expectancy Theory in Work and Motivation," *Human Relations*, Vol. 27, No. 2 (February 1974), 121–47; Terrance Mitchell, "Expectancy Models of Job Satisfaction," *Psychological Bulletin*, Vol. 81 (1974), 457–80; and Barry Staw, *Intrinsic and Extrinsic Motivation* (Morristown, N.J.: General Learning Press, 1976).

[26] The table is adapted from a slightly different one appearing in Miles, *Theories of Management*.

jobs where there is little opportunity for promotion or where seniority prevails. Excessive competition may actually disrupt teamwork and lead to frustration and a host of undesirable side effects.

From many points of view, internalized motivation is the best form of motivation, since it provides the greatest opportunity for individuals to satisfy their needs and to develop their personalities. As expectancy theory suggests, internalized motivation is considerably more appropriate with some sorts of people and jobs (for example, jobs that require individual discretion and commitment) than it is with others.

In practice, most managers use a combination of approaches. If bullying is avoided, the external pressures and economic rewards of "the traditional approach" may reinforce the internal pressures and egoistic rewards of internalized motivation. Hygienic management emphasizes job context; internalized motivation emphasizes job content; but the two approaches can be used in tandem. Only one thing seems sure: there is no simple all-purpose answer to the problems of motivation.

Three forms of motivation

	Traditional	Human relations	Internalized motivation
Managerial assumptions	People dislike work, work only for money, are incapable of self-direction, will "goof off" if given a chance.	People want to work in a secure, comfortable work environment, with a fair, understanding boss; happy workers will work harder.	People want to do meaningful work, are capable of broad self-direction and self-control, represent untapped resources.
Primary rewards	Off-the-job or economic, especially pay.	Around-the-job or extrinsic, including peer approval, praise from boss, comfortable working conditions. Also fair pay, security, and fringe benefits.	Through-the-job or intrinsic, including achievement, exercise of skills, personal growth.
Principal mechanisms for insuring that rewards motivate	Well-designed pay system (including piecework); simple jobs, clear instructions; close supervision.	Hygienic management: fair company policies and fringe benefits, supportive, considerate supervisors (good listeners), encouragement of cohesive groups.	Job redesign, goal setting, autonomy, general supervision, open system career policies.
Primary needs satisfied	Physical.	Security and social.	Egoistic.
Role of satisfaction	Irrelevant. Jobs are inherently dissatisfying.	Satisfaction causes productivity.	Productivity *can* cause satisfaction.
Role of participation	Management knows best.	Participation with regard to minor matters to raise morale.	Participation with regard to major matters to gain useful suggestions.

innovations in job design and scheduling

Recent years have seen a great deal of concern with the nature of work, occasioned in part by reports of a revolt against work and a sharp decline in productivity growth in both the United States and Canada. It is widely believed that job satisfaction and motivation have declined, and to counteract these trends managements are trying a variety of new approaches. Two of the most notable are job redesign and goal setting. Each of these is designed to provide internalized motivation and to restore challenge and meaning to work. The thrust of these techniques is to change the job itself.

Another movement proposes to give employees greater freedom to choose the hours they work. This movement for new work schedules is supported strongly by those women who view it as a means of combining work careers with raising a family. Men who wish to share more fully in family raising also endorse it, as do workers regardless of sex who prefer not to be tied down to the conventional 9 to 5 Monday-Friday schedule.

At first glance the two approaches' solutions to workplace discontent appear radically different. The first approach seeks to make jobs more challenging. The second approach ignores the job itself but makes it easier for workers to leave it. Nevertheless, the two approaches share a common interest in increasing workers' discretion and self-control.

The extent of workplace dissatisfaction

The discussion which follows will give us a chance to apply some of the principles we learned in the first two chapters, especially expectancy theory. It also illustrates other principles which will receive increasing attention in later chapters, for example the problems of introducing changes and the need to integrate compensation policy with other aspects of organizational life.

Many observers have noted that workers are becoming increasingly dissatisfied with their jobs. Although not all scholars agree, some believe our cultural values are undergoing a massive change, particularly among younger workers. They argue that the generation brought up during the campus revolts of the 1960s is particularly resistant to authority. Well educated, relatively secure in their jobs, and interested in doing their own things, these workers resist accepting the boring, challengeless jobs that their elders saw as inevitable.

Evidence as to whether there is, in fact, a growing dissatisfaction with work is somewhat mixed. Earlier we learned that some 80 or 90 percent of employed workers regularly report themselves either satisfied or very satisfied with their jobs. As the following table indicates, these figures have changed very little in recent years. On the other hand, satisfaction with particular aspects of the job has lessened considerably.

Question: "How true . . . is this of your job?"

	Percent answering "very true"		
	1969	1973	1977
The pay is good.	40	41	27
The job security is good.	55	53	42
My fringe benefits are good.	42	44	33
The hours are good.	57	51	43
The work is interesting.	63	61	53
I am given a chance to do the things I can do best.	45	41	31
I am not asked to do excessive amounts of work.	43	34	28
My supervisor is very concerned about the welfare of those under (him/her).	45	41	34

Question: All in all, how satisfied would you say you are with your job?

	Percent responding:		
Response category	1969	1973	1977
Very satisfied	46	52	47
Somewhat satisfied	39	38	42
Not too satisfied	11	8	9
Not at all satisfied	3	2	3

Source: Robert P. Quinn and Graham Staines, *1977 Quality of Employment Survey* (Ann Arbor, Michigan: Institute of Social Research, University of Michigan, 1978), Table 13.1. Percentages rounded.

Why has one measure of satisfaction remained stable while the other has dropped? Psychologists are far from certain. Perhaps it means merely that despite declining satisfaction with specific aspects of the job, the decline has not proceeded far enough so that workers are willing to protest actively. (Saying that one is satisfied with one's job may be like responding, "Fine, thanks," to the question "how are you today?" Unless one wants to complain actively, one gives the conventional, expected answer.) In any case the evidence does not suggest a revolt against *work* itself. Far more workers think their work is interesting than think their pay is good.

Perhaps the question of whether dissatisfaction has *increased* is irrelevant. What may be more relevant is the number of jobs that provide little challenge and are insufficiently motivating. Even if workers are resigned to these jobs, their abilities are inefficiently utilized.

The nature of mass production work

New approaches to motivation in mass production work have been concerned chiefly with semi-skilled work in manufacturing, especially machine tending and assembly line jobs. Such jobs are not unique, however, in their lack of obvious challenge. Many offices today can best be described as white-collar factories, with acres of desks and work tables stretching as far as the eye can see. Minutely described, mechanized short-cycle jobs, requiring such tools as card punchers or typewriters, are performed by clerical personnel, few of whom receive much sense of achievement from their work. Many service workers, telephone operators and dishwashers, for example, have equally routine jobs.

Task characteristics

The way mass production jobs have traditionally been designed has been heavily influenced by the scientific management movement, whose founder was Frederick W. Taylor.[1] Taylor believed in (1) high specialization (breaking down jobs into very small parts) and (2) in specifying exactly how each part should be done (separating the physical work from thinking). In analyzing mass production work scholars have concentrated on eight main characteristics. We shall call these autonomy, skill, significance, identity, feedback, variety, attention, and social relations.[2]

Autonomy. Mass production jobs are designed to eliminate all employee discretion. As Taylor put it:

---

[1] Taylor (1856–1915) was the world's first well-known industrial engineer. His studies of work place and job design influenced the development of mass production work throughout the world, even in Russia. Consistent with the traditional approach to management (as discussed in Chapter 2) and his own view that it was largely useless to try to make work enjoyable, Taylor believed that the best way to motivate people was through payment by result or piecework.

[2] The term *task characteristic* refers to the intrinsic characteristics of the task *itself*, as opposed to the wider environment in which the job is performed. Our list of characteristics is adopted from the work of J. Richard Hackman and Edward E. Lawler III. See Hackman's "Work Design," in J. Richard Hackman and J. Lloyd Suttle, eds., *Improving Life at Work* (Santa Monica, Cal.: Goodyear, 1977).

Each man must learn to give up his particular way of doing things, adapt his methods to the many new standards, and grow accustomed to receiving and obeying directions covering details, large and small, which in the past have been left to individual judgment.[3]

Following Taylor's principles, management engages in engineering studies, which carefully predetermine the exact motions and pace for each employee. Workers are confined to a fixed work position and are permitted to leave it only with permission. In principle, this procedure ensures that the work will be done quickly in a uniform, predictable fashion, and that it will be precisely coordinated with other jobs.

Skill. It goes almost without saying that such highly specialized and programmed jobs deprive the worker of any real sense of skill. Workers who exercise skill take pride in their achievement, but the person who has learned his job in a few hours knows that he can be replaced by almost anyone who happens along. This is one reason why mass-production workers tend to exaggerate the complexity of their jobs: It is too humiliating to admit how simple their work actually is. They may use their ignored skills to process grievances or to sabotage.

Task significance. It is equally obvious that the individual mass production worker's job lacks task significance.[4] Even if the final product is as newsworthy as a space probe to Mars, the individual's contribution may seem trivial (and few products have the significance of a space probe). The meaninglessness of work is accentuated when organizations seem to emphasize quantity over quality. "Why should I do a good job," the typical worker says, "when no one else cares?"

In a largely fruitless effort to instill pride of craftsmenship, some companies have engaged in such public relations activities as a "My Job Contest" in which employees are given rewards for letters describing the meaning of their work. Many companies take new employees on a trip through the plant to show them how their particular jobs fit into the larger picture. In indoctrinating new employees, the telephone company stresses the importance of their jobs in saving lives and helping people in trouble.

The evidence suggests that the impact of such efforts to change job attitudes is likely to wear off quickly. On the other hand, task significance may be increased if workers are permitted direct contact with the people they serve or if the employee is a member of a small work team (provided, of course, that the team as a whole is motivated toward high productivity).

Task identity. Task significance is closely related to task identity, the ability to complete an identifiable task. We all feel that we are accomplishing something when we can break our work down into identifiable units and

---

[3] Frederick W. Taylor, *Shop Management* (New York: Harper, 1919), p. 113.
[4] Task significance has been defined as "the degree to which the job has a substantial impact on the lives and work of other people, whether in the immediate organization or the external environment." Hackman, "Work Design," p. 130.

complete them successfully. If we have two assignments to complete, we breathe a sigh of relief as soon as we finish one. When we are driving a long distance, we break the trip down into sections and feel great satisfaction as we pass by each check point.

Mass-production work characteristically fails to provide this sense of completion, or even a feeling of progress toward a goal. Since each employee does only a small, specialized part of the total job, he rarely has a chance to look at the final product and say, "Mine, all mine." It is more common, instead, to hear, "This job is endless. It just goes on and on. You don't feel that you are getting anywhere."

Even professionals often lack task identity. Physicians in large clinics may complain that they rarely see the same patient twice and so rarely finish what they started. Radiologists who examine hundreds of X-ray films daily, may have little contact with live patients. In some hospitals, nursing duties are so fragmented that twenty or more nurses, nurses' aides, and orderlies deal with the same patient, but none see him or her as a whole person.

Social work suffers from similar problems. Five or six specialists (probation officers, school psychologists, family counselors) may all deal with parts of a single family's problems, but no one is responsible for pulling the pieces together. Engineering work may be similarly specialized. Sometimes draftsmen work on numerous projects, but make an insignificant contribution to each.

Feedback. If we are to have a feeling of accomplishment, we must have some way of measuring progress. We want to know "how we are doing." Only by setting up some goal and knowing that we have reached it can we feel a sense of achievement. Many routine jobs are considered monotonous precisely because they provide no means of checking progress.

Variety. Mass production jobs tend to be tedious and repetitive. An important determinant of job satisfaction is the length of the job cycle: how long it takes to perform a job operation before having to start it all over again. For a college professor, the work cycle may be a semester; for the skilled craftsman, it may be several days or weeks. But for the worker on a machine or assembly line, the work cycle may last less than a minute. If a worker simply tightens one or two bolts over and over again there is deadening lack of variety. As one worker put it:

"The job gets so sickening. Day in and day out I pick two bolts, one with each hand, fasten them in place, and then tighten each in turn. Over and over. Seventy-two times an hour. God knows how many million times a year. I keep doing it in my sleep, only then it is a nightmare."

Furthermore, work pace is rigidly prescribed. Most people like to vary their work rhythms; they may work fast for a while and then gradually slow down as the day wears on. This variety of pace helps to reduce both fatigue and boredom. The typical assembly line, however, makes no provision for the preference of individual workers. More autocratic than any foreman, the assembly line sets a relentless rhythm to which all must adjust.

Fortunately, on most mass-production jobs workers do have a slight opportunity to vary their pace through "building a bank" or "getting into a hole." On some jobs a worker can hurry up a bit and build up a reserve, or "bank," of completed work and then take a break for a few seconds while the work slides by. By pushing 15 seconds ahead and then falling 15 seconds "in a hole," an energetic worker can earn a 30-second break, a small victory at best.

Attention. Another factor affecting workers' satisfaction with their jobs is the amount of attention it requires. Research scientists enjoy their work because it is constantly new and challenging and absorbs all their attention. Jobs like this are said to require *depth attention*. At the other extreme are so-called *no attention* jobs, which are so routine that one's conscious mind is free to wander at will. Dishwashing is an example of such work; so is driving over a straight highway with little traffic.

The least satisfying jobs are those that require *surface attention*. Here one is obliged to perform a routine, unchallenging chore, but at the same time to remain relatively alert. Watching control gauges, inspecting parts, grading exam papers, and adding up columns of figures all require surface attention. They neither provide challenge, interest, or autonomy (as do depth-attention jobs) nor permit daydreaming (as do no-attention jobs).

These classifications, of course, are simply points on a continuum, for there are relatively few purely no-attention jobs. Further, the attention required by a particular job depends largely on the ability of the individual employee. A bright person may find that a job requires only surface attention, while someone who is less able (or less well trained) may find the same job requires depth attention.

Social relations. The physical confinement of many factory jobs reduces the opportunity for social relations. Often employees socialize on the basis of proximity rather than occupational status. Congenial on-the-job relationships reduce boredom and permit workers to express their total personality, especially when the job requires only a small segment of their abilities. Yet, feeling little identification with their occupation, workers on mass production jobs are relatively unlikely to make friendships that carry over after work.

Assembly-line workers are restricted to a very small area and can talk only with those directly on either side or, occasionally, across the line. Machine operators have somewhat more flexibility in making social contacts although a high noise level may make ingenious facial expressions and hand signs necessary as a substitute for words. Of course, work breaks provide an opportunity for social contacts.

Adjusting to mass-production work

How do employees adjust to mass-production work? Many learn to ignore the job by daydreaming, to modify the job, or to play various games at work. Others take more decisive action, either leaving or sabotaging the work.

Daydreaming. Almost all workers regard surface attention jobs as boring, mentally exhausting, and undesirable. (This is true even if the same work might require depth attention from someone else.) But some workers can adjust moderately well to monotonous no-attention jobs. These workers seem to have little need to derive satisfaction from the job itself; they spend their working days daydreaming. One employee told us, "If I thought about the job all the time I'd go nuts. I think about vacation and going hunting. I don't even know I'm working."

Games and high jinks. In spite of its obvious inefficiency, some people like to mow their lawns in fancy figure eights. Making a game out of work provides variety, gives the worker a chance to show creativity, and supplies goals to work toward. Here is a self-description provided by an office worker in a large insurance company.

"As operator I had to complete 720 units in 4 hours with no more than 11 errors. The job was extremely boring. Each pack usually contained 180 account cards. These came in two kinds of forms, a #1 form and a #4 form. Usually each pack had the same number of each type, and I played basketball with #1's vs. the #4's. Punching in the 7 digits of the policyholder account number was my way of dribbling the ball down the floor, and pushing the button that rang up the total was the ball going through the basket. Usually the scores were close, and on a couple of occasions the game went into overtime—that is, it was continued into the next pack."

On jobs that are not tightly machine-paced, the worker may experiment with various speeds. Workers on piecework are particularly likely to set goals for themselves (sometimes called "bogies") and to engage in elaborate calculations to make sure that they produce neither more nor less than the bogey. Although the primary purpose of these calculations is to avoid overproduction (which might lead to a cut in the piece rate), they also provide a diversion from the monotony of work.

Social games also provide a form of diversion. Gambling is common in many workplaces: flipping coins to see who pays for coffee, World Series pools, bookmaking, and numbers games. Horseplay, lunch-time card games, and gossip around the watercooler can provide satisfaction, particularly for those with high social needs. In the context of humdrum routine, human ingenuity is able to extract pleasure from seemingly trivial events.

One guy opens a window, another slams it shut; or someone turns on a ventilating fan, someone snaps it off. They argue, yell, come to blows, and everybody gets excited. "Man this is neat! The best thing that happened all day. Wow, what a fight!". . . In a desparate need for variety, conflict can break up routine.[5]

Modifying the job. Workers can sometimes reduce the monotony of their jobs by introducing variations in their work that are unplanned by management. They may exchange work, modify parts of the job, or avoid some parts altogether. They drag out set-ups, find excuses to pick up parts more

---

[5] Robert Schrank, *Ten Thousand Working Days* (Cambridge, Mass.: MIT Press, 1977), p. 229.

frequently than necessary, and perhaps let the machine break down for a slight change of pace.

Antimanagement activities. In a sense, antimanagement activities are an overt reaction to the frustration of mass-production work. Active union participation, for example, provides an opportunity to release aggression and to enjoy a sense of skill and accomplishment that is denied on the job. Similarly, sabotage and wildcat strikes enable a demoralized work group to let off steam. In Detroit, after long periods of overtime work on boring assembly-line jobs, employees often enjoy the prospect of a strike!

Job redesign

Job redesign is a term describing efforts to restructure jobs to reduce dissatisfaction and increase productivity, especially in mass-production industry. Particularly advanced in some European countries, especially in Sweden, job redesign is viewed as a means of reducing high turnover and absenteeism rates (turnover once averaged 70 percent annually in some Swedish automobile assembly plants and absenteeism was close to 20 percent). There have also been some important experiments with job redesign in North America. Among the approaches tried, in roughly increasing order of complexity, are the following: job rotation, job enlargement, establishment of natural work units, improving feedback, job enrichment, and natural work teams. As we shall see, these techniques overlap considerably and rarely is one technique used alone.

Job rotation. This most simple of workplace reforms permits workers to switch jobs either in terms of a fixed schedule or on an ad hoc basis (to cope with absenteeism or emergencies) without changing the characteristics of the jobs themselves. Thus, workers gain more variety in their work and perhaps in their social relations. It gives them a chance to learn additional skills. Further since jobs are continually exchanged, no one gets stuck with a dirty task permanently. Management also benefits, since workers become able to perform a number of different jobs in the event of an emergency.

Some workers object to being rotated from job to job and jolted out of their routine. Being an "expert" on one particular type of work gives them a feeling of status and importance that they lose when they move around. Our studies suggest that in general, those who oppose job rotation work on no-attention jobs and enjoy daydreaming. On the other hand, workers whose regular job already prevents daydreaming endorse rotation as a relief from monotony.

Job enlargement. This approach combines tasks "horizontally," typically lengthening the work cycle. At times the worker may be permitted to follow a job from beginning to end. At Saab some workers, whose job cycle averaged 1.8 minutes, were given the task of assembling an entire engine, a 30-minute undertaking. Longer job cycles require additional skills and provide a greater sense of variety, task identity, and accomplishment. Job enlargement often allows workers to control the speed of the machines they run and even to turn these off for short breaks.

Some forms of job enlargement merely add together a large number of similar unchallenging tasks: for example, an electronic assembler no longer fastens one tube to a chasis over and over again, now he fastens five. For some people, the additional complications are not intrinsically challenging. For them, job enlargement converts a no-attention job into one requiring surface attention.

Establishing natural work units. Jobs can be rearranged into natural units or batches, so that the employee can gain a feeling of accomplishment every time a batch is finished. The desire to finish a unit has a strong pulling power, thus enhancing motivation. Furthermore, establishing units helps pinpoint job responsibility and measure performance.

The following quotation describes one of the earliest examples of how boring work, telephone central office maintenance, was broken down into natural units:[6]

> There is no challenge to diagnosing trouble, and the job is very confining since a man can work for hours within the space of a few feet. There is never a real experience of progress. When the job is finished the worker starts all over again.
> In one office the frames on which the men worked were subdivided by means of chalk lines. . . . Each block required between one and a half and two hours to complete. The worker made his choice of . . . unit. . . . The benefits of this pattern of work were immediately apparent. . . . Once a man selected a block he worked until it was finished.
> Every time a man completed a unit he took a smoke or a stretch. Even lunch and quitting time found no untagged units. The men liked the plan and the supervisors reported that complaining decreased and the trouble with meeting work schedules was eliminated.

For work that cannot be divided into beginnings and ends, natural units can be created in other ways. Each member of an office typing pool can be made responsible for the work of a given professor, or a telephone installer can provide service in a specific section of town. One caution: assignments of this sort must be made carefully to ensure that the workload is divided fairly.

Feedback. As we stressed earlier, employees like to know how well they are doing. To provide feedback some companies post bar graphs that compare the length of time actually taken to complete jobs as compared to the time planned. A telephone company circulates monthly indices of efficiency, particularly among its white-collar employees.

Research suggests that the more objective and more frequent the feedback, the more motivating it becomes. It is advantageous for the worker to learn about his progress directly, as he does his job, rather than from a supervisor on an occasional basis. Workers may suspect the supervisor's message; on

---

[6] Norman Maier, *Psychology in Industry* (Boston: Houghton Mifflin, 1955), p. 489.

the other hand, they are likely to believe data they have helped gather themselves.

Computers and other automated machines sometimes can be used to provide individuals with data now blocked from them. Many clerical operations, for example, are now programmed on computer consoles. These consoles often can be programmed to provide the clerk with immediate feedback in the form of a CRT display or a printout indicating that an error has been made. Some systems even have been programmed to provide the operator with a positive feedback message when a period of error-free performance has been sustained.[7]

Job enrichment. This approach goes beyond job enlargement in that it adds "vertical" or quasi-managerial elements, especially planning, supply, and inspection. Thus it contributes to workers' sense of autonomy and control over their work. Job enrichment was applied to the work of clerks who assembled telephone directories.

Before the change, directories were assembled on a production line basis. Work was passed from clerk to clerk for a total of 21 steps, many of which were merely for verification. After the change, each clerk was given complete responsibility for assembling either an entire directory or an alphebetical part of one, thus combining 21 jobs into one. Follow up checkers were eliminated because employees were now expected to check their own work for accuracy. The clerks were permitted to talk directly to advertising sales representatives to clear up ambiguity in the ad copy these representatives submitted, thus bypassing their bosses. Finally, they themselves set the deadline dates after which new copy would not be accepted for the next directory issue.[8]

As a result turnover dropped, fewer errors were made, and more work was done with fewer people.

Job enrichment frequently includes the following elements:

- Giving workers whole tasks.
- Introducing new and more difficult tasks not previously handled. *Example:* Operators maintain their own equipment.
- Increasing the accountability of individual workers for their own work. *Examples:* Lab technicians sign their own reports rather than have bosses check them. Production workers inspect their own work and initial the inspection tags.
- Introduce elements of planning and coordination. *Examples:* Maintenance people decide priorities of repair jobs. Operators decide when to order supplies.
- Giving workers additional authority and freedom on their own jobs. *Examples:* Correspondents are allowed to use their own language in answering letters rather than following standard forms. Employees decide when to take their own coffee breaks. Telephone service representatives grant customers credit without consulting their bosses.

---

[7] Richard Hackman, "Job Design," p. 140.
[8] Robert Ford, "Job Enrichment Lesson from AT&T," *Harvard Business Review* (January 1973), 96–106.

- Dealing directly with clients or suppliers. *Example:* Workers "expedite" their own supplies from material control, bypassing their supervisors.

Self-managing work teams. This most advanced form of job redesign involves a group form of job enrichment. Typically, such teams (sometimes called "autonomous work groups") meet periodically to determine job assignments, schedule work breaks, and even decide the rate of production.

At a Philips TV plant in the Netherlands, groups of seven or eight are given total responsibility for assembling sets. The group "not only performs the entire assembly task but also deals directly with staff groups such as procurement, quality, and stores, with no supervisor or foreman to act as intermediary or expeditor. If something is needed from another department or something goes wrong that requires the services of another department, it's the group's responsibility to deal with that department." [9]

At Volvo truck assembly plant, "the production team, a group of 5 to 12 men with a common work assignment, elects its own chargehand, schedules its own output within standards set by higher management, distributes work among its members and is responsible for its own quality control." [10]

The Topeka plant of General Foods, which makes Gaines Dog Food, was set up with work teams of 7 to 14 members. Activities usually handled by separate groups, such as quality control, maintenance, janitorial work, industrial engineering, and even personnel became the responsibility of the group as a whole. Individual jobs were often rotated, but key decisions were made on a group basis. Initially each worker was paid the same rate, with pay increases being given when the group decided that one of its members had picked up additional skills. The group screened new applicants for jobs and apparently even "expelled" (discharged) poor performers.[11]

Work teams have been given responsibility for developing relations with vendors, determining which operations can be handled individually and which by the group as a whole, setting work pace (sometimes fast in the morning, slow in the afternoon), training new employees, and, at one company, even keeping financial records. Sometimes work team members serve in roles normally reserved for staff personnel or supervisors: chairing the plant safety committee, redesigning equipment, or troubleshooting customers' problems.[12] Self-managing work teams are especially appropriate when the nature of the task makes it difficult for an individual to do a whole job alone.

Underlying motivational mechanisms

As we shall discuss in greater detail, job redesign frequently leads to greater satisfaction, higher quality, lower turnover, and (less often) higher productivity. It achieves these objectives, in part, through altering the task

---

[9] William F. Dowling, "Job Redesign on the Assembly Line: Farewell to Blue-Collar Blues?" *Organizational Dynamics* (Autumn 1973), 54.

[10] *Ibid.*, p. 59.

[11] The program apparently no longer works as well as it did at first. See Richard Walton, "Work Innovation at Topeka: After Six Years," *Journal of Applied Behavioral Science*, Vol. 17 (July 1977), 422–33.

[12] The equivalent of self-managing work teams at the managerial level is organization by product or matrix organization.

dimensions. The psychological process at work may be explained by returning to the expectancy model of Chapter 2, a shortened version of which follows: [13]

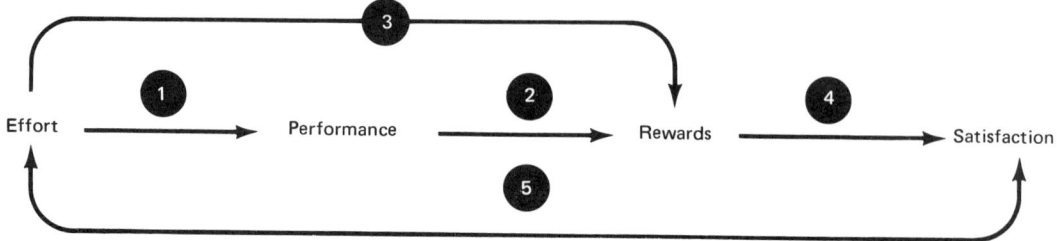

Following the numbered relationships indicated in the diagram, let us analyze what happens when job redesign is successfully introduced (often, of course, it is not).

① Since workers have greater freedom to determine how they do their work, they work more effectively.[14]

② The altered task characteristics provide greater psychological rewards from performance. For example, finishing a natural unit provides a greater sense of completion (or task identity) than does working on an endless task. Similarly, if workers decide *how* a job should be done, actually successfully completing it demonstrates their decision-making and technical skills (both to themselves and to the outside world). Thus workers may be rewarded by both a sense of self-achievement and praise (and higher status) from one's peers.

③ Just working on an enriched job may be psychologically rewarding (perhaps because there is greater variety), regardless of whether one actually finishes it.[15]

④ The sense of skill and accomplishment gained from doing a job helps satisfy ego needs.[16] Praise from one's peers may satisfy social needs.

⑤ Finally, the feedback provided by many forms of job redesign completes the loop.

Yet job redesign will not be equally motivating for everyone. Not everyone wants more responsibility. Some people already obtain all the challenge and stimulation they want, either at home or at work (overstimulation can be even more frustrating than understimulation). The evidence is somewhat mixed, but it suggests that when jobs provide increased opportunity for learning and discretion, people with strong ego needs respond more positively to

---

[13] For a fuller discussion, see Donald Schwab and Lawrence Cummings, "A Theoretical Analysis of the Impact of Scope on Employee Performance," *Academy of Management Review*, Vol. 1 (April 1976).

[14] If the redesigned job is beyond the worker's ability to handle, however, performance may drop.

[15] There is psychological evidence that moderate variety is stimulating and satisfying, regardless of the activity performed.

[16] A much debated question is whether job redesign can change the pattern of needs themselves. According to some researchers, the challenge of redesigned jobs may be so great that workers who have previously centered their lives on satisfying social needs off the job will now place greater weight on satisfying ego needs on the job. In other words, they become more expressive in their orientation, moving from Cell 4 to Cell 1 in the matrix on p. 24.

work than do those with weak ego needs.[17] This doesn't mean that the more challenge the better. Jobs can be made more challenging than even workers with high ego needs *want* or are *able* (two separate points) to handle. The difficult trick is to find the right amount of work stimulation for every worker.

Ego needs are not the only relevant factor. Employees who are satisfied with their "hygienes" (pay, security, supervision) are more likely to react favorably to redesigned work than are those who are dissatisfied.[18] Expectations also play a role: college-trained draftsmen expect more challenging work than do their high-school trained counterparts. Finally, it is reasonable to assume that strength of social needs will influence how people respond to forms of job redesign, such as self-managing work teams, which involve much social interaction.

Sociotechnical change. Job redesign does more than satisfy egoistic needs. New and more effective social and workflow relations are introduced (hence the term *social-technical systems* applied to redesigned jobs by some scholars).[19] Particularly in self-managing work teams the following developments occur:

- Small work groups are established: typically, these groups are considerably smaller (only four to eighteen members) than the large departments they partially replace. Being smaller, they are more cohesive (see Chapter 5). Not only do members participate in group decision-making processes (see Chapter 6), but group pressures force individuals to adhere to these decisions. Opportunities to satisfy social needs are substantially increased.
- Among the drawbacks of the conventional method of having each worker do part of the job is the high cost of maintaining a smooth workflow. Employee *A* must work just as fast as employee *B*, or employee *B* will be slowed down. Each extra person in the work flow increases the number of *interfaces* and makes coordination more difficult. Job enlargement and enrichment reduce the number of such interfaces, and self-managing work groups relieve management of the task of coordinating.[20]
- There are substantial changes in worker-management relations. The work group takes on many of the foreman's responsibilities.

Hygienes. The best-publicized job redesign experiments have also been accompanied by important hygienes. Indeed, some have argued that these hygienes have a more significant impact on job attitudes than do any changes

---

[17] J. Richard Hackman, "Work Design," pp. 118–120. Hackman asks, "What percentage of the workforce actually desires higher order need satisfactions at work and so are likely to respond positively to enriched jobs? Some observers estimate that only 15 percent of rank-and-file employees are so motivated. Others are more optimistic."

[18] Greg Oldham, J. Richard Hackman, and John Pearce, "Conditions Under Which Employees Respond Positively to Enriched Work," *Journal of Applied Psychology*, Vol. 61 (1976), 395–403.

[19] Louis Davis and James Taylor, *Design of Jobs* (Middlesex, England: Penguin, 1972).

[20] *Buffering* is a job redesign technique in itself. *Buffer stocks* are placed between workers at adjacent stages in the work flow. Thus, instead of passing his finished work directly over to employee *B*, employee *A* produces for stock and employee *B* draws from stock as needed. Since the workers are *uncoupled*, each is free to work at his or her own pace; further if employee *A*'s machine breaks down, employee *B* is not likely to be immediately affected.

in job design themselves. These have begun to reduce what a prominent union leader calls

> the double standard that exists between workers and management.... Workers challenge the symbols of elitism typically taken for granted, such as salary payment versus hourly payment; time clocks for blue-collar workers; well-decorated dining rooms for white-collar workers versus plain, Spartan-like cafeterias for blue-collar workers; privileged parking for the elite but catch as you can for workers.[21]

At General Foods' Topeka dog food plant, for instance, there are no reserved parking lots, no time clocks, and no differentiation in decor between management offices and worker lounges. Workers are free to make phone calls on company time (just like management). A number of companies have begun to pay blue-collar workers on a salary basis. Such reductions in status differentials not only tend to reduce dissatisfaction; they also help an atmosphere of trust and confidence to develop between workers and management, and, to some extent, they lead to a covert renegotiation of the "implicit bargain" we discussed in Chapter 2. Thus, a "fair day's work" may mean much more than it previously did.

Wider organizational changes

Organizations are systems, and no one part alone can be changed. Job redesign is unlikely to be effective unless it is accompanied by complementary changes in other aspects of organizational life.

Introducing job redesign. In some companies, higher management or some special staff group draws up the job redesign plan, and the improved jobs are imposed on workers whether they (or their unions) like them or not. In a sense, management uses autocratic techniques to reach participatory objectives. The autocratic approach is consistent with the human relations approach of the Forties and Fifties which gives workers freedom on the assumption that it will make workers happier. Allowing workers to design their jobs themselves is more consistent with the internalized motivation approach. The limited evidence suggests that job restructuring will be more successful if those involved help plan it and retain the freedom to opt out, either individually or as a group. (In some situations, the conventional assembly line has been continued alongside enriched jobs, and workers are permitted to choose between the two kinds of work.)

Impact on other departments. It is difficult to introduce a radically new job redesign program in one department without affecting others. In one coal mine, the freedom granted to a self-managing work team led to much jealousy and friction with other miners; the less favored miners derisively called their colleagues "super-miners." [22] A self-managing work team in a toy factory worked so well that it disrupted the work flow of the factory as a

---

[21] Vice-president Irving Bluestone of the United Automobile Workers, "Comments on Job Enrichment," *Organizational Dynamics* (Winter 1974), 47.

[22] Eric Trust, Gerald Susman, and Grant Brown, "An Experiment in Autonomous Working in an American Underground Coal Mine," *Human Relations*, 30, No. 3 (1977), 201–36.

whole and earned incentives so high that they disrupted the entire plant's social structure. In short, while strengthening relations *within* a work group, job redesign may threaten those *between* groups.

Pay. When workers take on more responsibility, they want more pay. Management argues that increased satisfaction and more interesting work should be reward enough. Often management fears that if it pays one group of workers more, other groups will want similar pay increases, even if their work has not changed. There may be constant disputes as to how the financial gain (if any) from job redesign is to be distributed, and effective resolution of this problem may require some sort of group incentive such as the Scanlon Plan.

Changes in management. For workers one of the main advantages of job redesign is greater freedom to make decisions on their own, rather than having supervisors hover over them. Understandably, this freedom is threatening to supervisors. Sometimes job redesign results in fewer supervisors being needed; in any case those who remain must learn to let subordinates make decisions by themselves.[23]

Equally difficult adjustments must be made by higher management. Among the problems associated with the General Foods' Topeka dog food factory was that

Economically it was a success, but it became a power struggle. It was too threatening to too many people. . . . The problem has not been so much that the workers could not manage their own affairs as that some management and staff personnel saw their own positions threatened because the workers performed too well.[24]

Some of the most successful job redesign programs have been introduced in small, new, plants which are removed from the contaminating influences of the larger and more traditional parent organization. The problems involved in introducing major work structure changes in large organizations are immense. It is equally difficult to extend successful experiments from the small departments in which they started to the larger organization.

The role of the union

In sharp contrast to the situation in Europe, most of the best publicized job redesign changes in North America have taken place in nonunion plants. Unions in the United States and Canada find the issue of job redesign fuzzy and hard to deal with. Despite their dissatisfaction with work, the *expressed* demands of most union members are for higher wages, better fringe benefits, and more job security. Especially during stagflation, such attitudes are understandable, particularly since few workers can imagine alternatives to the traditional ways of doing mass production work.

[23] One reason self-managing work teams were not being used more widely in the TV plant discussed on p. 57 is that foremen in the Netherlands are unionized. Management feared a foremen's strike were the plan extended. Robert Schrank, *Ten Thousand Working Days,* p. 221.
[24] "Stonewalling Plant Democracy," *Business Week,* March 28, 1977, p. 78.

Many union leaders are suspicious of the entire job redesign movement, viewing it as a form of manipulation and speedup as well as an attempt to divert workers' attention from their economic problems. Furthermore, the problem of worker dissatisfaction is difficult to handle through the traditional adversary techniques of collective bargaining. "A union demand is a negotiable demand which, if not satisfied, can be met by a strike," said an AFL-CIO leader. "How do you talk about [job redesign] questions in terms of a negotiable demand and a possible strike?" [25]

Unionists object chiefly to job redesign programs that management introduces unilaterally, without consulting the union. But any such programs, regardless of how introduced, are likely to affect pay, promotional ladders, and job descriptions. (Typically, unions seek to ensure that employees work only within a narrowly defined "job description"; job redesign blurs the boundaries between jobs and even blends worker and supervisory functions.) Unions resist changes in any of these areas unless management makes compensating concessions.

Despite these suspicions, unions and managements have joined together in several instances (notably the United Auto Workers and the major automobile manufacturing firms) to sponsor joint research and experimentation on new ways of doing work. Such a program has been credited with saving General Motors' Tarrytown, New York plant from being closed. Three carefully studied, joint union-management programs came to quite different results.

A joint program among unionized professional engineers at the Tennessee Valley Authority led to substantial changes in design procedures as well as the introduction of more flexible work hours for some employees.

An experiment with self-managing work teams at a unionized coal mine was quite successful for a while but was then partially abandoned in the face of growing union-management hostility in the coal industry generally and the previously mentioned jealousies between "superminers" and those who apparently preferred to work under more conventional arrangements.

An experiment at an auto mirror plant introduced an Earned Idle Time Program, which permitted workers to knock off the job (with full pay) once they had finished their daily work quota. Further gains were not achieved, however, in part because the plan, imposed by top management and top union, gained little grass roots support.

Evaluating job redesign

How successful have job redesign projects been to date? Reports are mixed, and evaluation is difficult. It is hard to separate the results of job redesign from the impact of other developments occurring at the same time. Furthermore, even if one can demonstrate success in one situation, comparisons between situations are difficult to make. "Experimental sites" differ greatly in their technologies, the nature of the work force, and the kinds of changes introduced.

Nevertheless, what do available reports tell us? Turnover, absenteeism, and grievances have generally gone down. Quality has improved, sometimes dramatically, and satisfaction, to the extent it has been measured, has increased.

---

[25] Nat Goldfinger quoted in David Jenkins, *Job Power* (Baltimore: Penguin 1974), p. 317.

About productivity there is more question. Productivity at the automated and job-restructured Topeka dog food plant is much higher than at its traditional counterpart in Kankakee, but Topeka has a much higher capital investment per employee. The European experience suggests that the greatest productivity gains accrue from reducing the rigidity of the assembly line. Since the work force is more flexible (and work flow relations are less complex) a single bottleneck is less likely to disrupt the entire production process. Employees are more likely to handle unexpected problems on their own, technological change is easier to introduce, and costs are saved because fewer first-line supervisors and staff personnel are required. On the other hand, special purpose equipment is used less effectively.

Ironically, although job redesign has been presented as a motivator, in practice it may work like a hygiene. Turnover, absenteeism, and satisfaction improve. But as far as productivity is concerned, the clearest gain seems to be that the workforce is more flexible, not that it is more highly motivated.

A high percentage of job redesign efforts have been abandoned as unsuccessful. The trouble in most cases has been not the particular form of job redesign proposed, but the way the change has been implemented. A new plan may be announced with a blaze of fanfare but quietly dropped because of unanticipated resistance from such interest groups as foremen.

When should job redesign be introduced? The limited research suggests that job redesign is more likely to be successful if the following conditions are met:

- the workers involved should have relatively high ego needs, and, if self-managing work teams are to be introduced, they should also have high social needs. They should be expressive rather than instrumental in their orientations;
- management philosophy generally should be sympathetic to participation;
- lower and middle level managers must be willing to permit their subordinates greater autonomy (perhaps there should be job redesign for management itself);
- the technology should be appropriate for the kind of redesign proposed. When heavy equipment investments have already been made (as in many existing plants) only limited job redesign is possible, except at prohibitive costs.
- management must be willing to share with its workers any financial gains resulting from the redesign program.
- when workers are unionized, the union should be consulted and participate on a fully equal basis.

Finally, management must give careful attention to the way job redesign is implemented. Because of the social tensions it engenders, piecemeal changes may be difficult. Job redesign may work best as part of a wider Organization Development effort.

Goal-setting

Job redesign changes, as we have seen, are more likely to lead to improved satisfaction, quality, and turnover than to productivity. Sales managers have known for years that one

> Much of the research has been done in logging. A typical experiment involved an attempt to increase the productivity of logging crews. Supervisors were trained to set goals, based on average tree-size and other factors. Hard, but not impossible goals were given to ten experimental logging crews but no goals to ten equivalent control crews. The experimental groups were told that the goals represented minimum standards of acceptable performance but that no one would be penalized for not meeting them. Both experimental and control groups were given forms to record their output. The result? The experimental crews' productivity increased significantly, while that of the control crews showed almost no change.
>
> These loggers were on piecework. Other experiments have involved workers paid on an hourly basis, so that increased effort did not lead to increased compensations. In one such experiment, truck drivers met a goal of loading their logging trucks to 92 percent of the legal weight; previously they had averaged 60 percent. In this case, after the goals were set, the truckers began to keep records of their performance and to compete with each other.

of the most effective ways to raise productivity is to set tough, clear-cut goals, but behavioral scientists have begun to study this phenomenon only recently.

By now there is considerable research on goal-setting.[26] This research suggests, first, that people produce more if they are set specific goals rather than merely asked to "work as hard as you can," and, secondly, that the harder the goals, the harder people work. But there is a proviso. For goal setting to be effective, the goals must be *accepted* by the people involved. Goals which are not accepted are not motivating.

What determines whether goals are accepted? Obviously they should be seen as reasonable and not impossible to reach. But other factors are relevant too. People who are high in *n Ach* will accept tougher goals than will those who are low in this trait. People are more likely to accept a goal if they have reached it in the past (or even come moderately close to reaching it), if they trust the person who set the goal, and if they compare themselves with others who have reached it.

Feedback. As we have seen earlier, feedback often contributes to satisfaction. Yet the research suggests that feedback is motivating only if there is a goal involved. Although the control logging crews kept production records, they had no impact. The truckers had always had access to their load weights, but they paid little attention to this information until goals were set. Once a goal is set, some knowledge of results is required so that workers can determine where they stand at any given time.

Participative goal setting. One way to ensure that goals are accepted is to allow those involved to set them themselves, either individually or in a group. Particularly when goals are set by one's fellow workers, one feels under

---

[26] The research has been conducted both in experimental laboratories (often with psychology students as subjects) and in industry. See, for example, Gary Latham and Gary Yukl, "A Review of Research on the Application of Goal Setting in Industry," *Academy of Management Journal*, Vol. 18 (December 1975), 824–45.

considerable social pressure not to be a shirker. However, the experiments that have contrasted *own* and *imposed* goals suggest that own (participative) goals are not necessarily more motivating than imposed goals, particularly if the latter are set by competitors or trusted supervisors.

Money. Monetary rewards are not essential for successful goal setting (as the truck-loading case illustrates). But earning more money is often a goal in itself, and in our society considerations of equity suggest that people should earn more if they work harder on paid jobs (in sports, of course, it is a different matter). An unfair goal, one not sufficiently rewarded, is not likely to be accepted.

Commitment. Goals are more likely to be motivating if people commit themselves to goals voluntarily, publicly, and then recommit themselves.[27] Goals set by others are less likely to be accepted truly voluntarily than are goals one sets for oneself.

All this suggests that job redesign and goal setting are complementary rather than competitive approaches to improving organizational effectiveness. Without natural work units it may be difficult to set goals at all. Workers assigned to enriched jobs or self-managing work teams are more likely to set tough goals for themselves than are those who work on traditional, routine tasks.

Goals provide more than generalized motivation. As we discuss in Chapter 11, goals give subordinates a clearer picture of what they are supposed to accomplish. Furthermore, goals set standards against which higher management can evaluate subordinate performance. Indeed, when there are clear goals and feedback is provided, the subordinate can tell for himself whether he is performing adequately. Thus, the need for detailed supervision is reduced, and employee satisfaction is enhanced.

Goals may take many forms. Budgets and sales quotas are examples (see Chap. 11). Management-by-objectives is a process by which both financial and nonfinancial goals are set on a systematic basis.

Use of goals

On jobs that provide little satisfaction, leisure may be a strong reward. Some organizations allow employees who have finished their day's work to go home and still collect eight hours' pay. In England this practice is known as "job and finish." In North America, electric-meter readers, letter carriers, garbage collectors often work on this basis.[28] In these occupations close supervision is impossible. (Of course, if an employee finishes much too soon, the supervisor has an indication that the work has been assigned inequitably. Still management must be careful not to kill incentive by using a few free minutes as an excuse to give to raise an employee's workload.)

---

[27] Gerald Salancik, "Commitment and Control," in Barry Staw and Gerald Salancik, eds., *New Directions in Organizational Behavior* (Chicago: St. Clair Press, 1977).

[28] "Cities using this incentive for garbage collection crews have found overall productivity increasing substantially." E. S. Savas, "An Empirical Study of Competition in Municipal Service Delivery," *Public Administration Review* (November 1977), 723.

Some problems. Goals are not without drawbacks. They work best when they are specific and easily measurable, but not every important goal (for example, employee development) can be made highly specific. Emphasis on any specific goal may result in other goals being ignored that are almost equally important. Individual goals discourage teamwork; group goals discourage individual responsibility. Goals must be frequently reemphasized, or they begin to be ignored; on the other hand, overemphasis on goals which employees have not accepted truly voluntarily may lead to frustration and revolt. Indeed, as we discuss in Chapter 4, goal-setting is one of the most critical of leadership activities.

New work schedules

The basic assumption behind job redesign is that changes in work content will result in increased satisfaction and productivity. By contrast, many organizations are acting as if they believed that employees' primary demands were not for improvements in the nature of work but for greater freedom to leave it. The last few years have seen the growing acceptance of new approaches to work scheduling: the ten-hour-day-four-day week, flextime, and job sharing, as well as the expansion of an older arrangement, part-time work.

What these plans have in common is that they are designed to provide greater opportunities for employees to enjoy their life *off*, as opposed to *on*, the job. The 4-day week provides longer weekends. Flextime permits workers to choose a work schedule that fits into their off-the-job activities. Work sharing and part-time work permit employees to spend fewer hours on the job. For some workers these new work schedules represent a changing life style, which downgrades work as a source of satisfaction. But for many women it represents just the opposite: an opportunity to combine work with family life. Indeed work schedules have become a major issue for some women's groups.

The 4-day week

The 10-hour day, 4-day week (sometimes called concentrated workweek or the 4–40 plan) was the first of the recent innovative approaches to work scheduling which have been tried widely in this country. The advantages of the plan are clear. By concentrating the work week into four days, the plan provides an extra day to run errands, to take trips to the country, to engage in recreation at home, and (for some) even to hold a second job. Further commuting time is reduced. This is an attractive package and, according to polls, a high percentage of workers now on conventional work schedules would prefer to shift to the new plan.

In practice experience with the 4–40 plan has been mixed. Some organizations report decreased absenteeism, reduced turnover, and higher productivity. In some tight labor markets, the plan provides the organization a valuable competitive edge in recruiting new employees. Unmarried and childless younger workers find the new schedule particularly attractive, especially if they participate actively in weekend recreation (in fact, it seems as if attitude towards recreation determines attitude toward the plan).

On the other hand, many companies have participated in 4–40 and then dropped it. The workers were enthusiastic at first but then found that the gain of the three-day weekend was more than offset by the fatigue of the 10-hour day and the loss of free evening time. Working mothers in particular find it difficult to raise children under these conditions. Organizations that must operate five days a week find it hard to schedule the fifth day (half crews on Monday and Friday are a common but rarely satisfactory solution). Further, unless supervisors put in a 50-hour week, they must leave part of the workforce unsupervised. Finally, under many union and government contract rules, work in excess of 8 hours per day must be paid on an overtime basis.

Not untypical was the experience of the Chyrsler Corporation Tappan, New York, parts depot. Started in early summer, the program was terminated in October. "The biggest complaint was caused by the need to rotate jobs Monday and Friday." a union spokesman said. "We found that workers wanted to stay on their own jobs." Enthusiasm for 3-day weekends was seasonal, waning when employees' children returned to school. Further, the 10-hour day gave them little time at home.

In some situations, concentrated workweeks make greater sense. It is greeted with enthusiasm by salesmen and work crews who travel a great deal and can return home only over weekends. Workers in out of the way posts have even more unusual schedules.

A uranium mine in northern Canada flies its personnel up to 500 miles to their work at the beginning of the week. They work 11 hours a day for 7 days and then are flown home for a full week layover. Meanwhile a second crew takes over.

Similar schedules are common for oil rigs, while firemen in some communities work a 24-hour day followed by two or more days off. But these are special situations. Under more normal conditions, 4–40 has created more problems than it solves. Most unions oppose the 10-hour day unless overtime premiums are paid for the last 2 hours.

Flextime

Unlike the 4–40 plan, the main virtue of flextime is lack of rigidity. First introduced into Europe, this new work scheduling procedure is now widely enjoyed (for example by some 40 percent of Swiss workers) as an alternative to the age-old and until now presumed inviolate tradition of fixed working hours. The plan spread to the U.S. in the early 1970s, and by 1978 covered an estimated 3.5 million workers.

The principle behind flextime is that each employee should have some freedom to choose his or her work schedule. Flextime presumes a required *core* period in which all employees are expected to be at work. Typically, the core might be from 9 to 11 A.M. and from 2 to 4 P.M. In addition to this 4-hour core there is a *band* of other hours in which employees can work, perhaps 7 to 9 A.M. and 4 to 6 P.M. plus part of the lunch period. Some organizations allow employees to work less than 8 hours on some days in exchange for more than 8 hours on other days, as long as their weekly or monthly total equals a "normal" number of hours. Often workers keep track of their own hours, or a mechanical device may be activated by each workers' special key. Thus, aside from the core period, employees—depending on their personal elections—will have different work schedules. Now, what are the advantages of flextime?

- Flextime is especially advantageous to working parents, since it permits them to adjust their hours to their childrens' school schedules. Beyond this, employees can adjust their work schedules to allow time to visit dentists, to run errands, or to avoid traffic jams.[29] Since employees set their own hours of work, they are less likely to be late or absent. There is less reason to take a full day off just because of an unavoidable midday appointment.
- In turn, flextime can have an impact on supervisory-employee relations. Supervisors have less need to act as policemen. Further, the plan greatly reduces demeaning requests for "personal time off" and irritating investigations over whether tardiness or absence is legitimate.
- Individuals differ in their physiological rhythms. Flextime permits them to adjust working hours to when they are likely to perform best and to enjoy leisure when they want it most.
- Even more critically, through flextime management says to employees: "You're adults, you're responsible. We're substituting your self-control for externally imposed supervisory control." Since individuals know their needs and values better than any outsider, they are in a better position to undertake tradeoffs (is it better to take off two hours today and work longer tomorrow?). The resulting boost in morale should be reflected in better feelings about the organization and also improved performance.
- Finally, flextime reduces the double standard that exists when managers are permitted to schedule their own work hours and employees are not.

Many organizations report substantial benefits from flextime: increased productivity, greater satisfaction, reduced tardiness, absenteeism, and turnover, and less time spent on coffee breaks (people who set their own schedules are less likely to be fatigued than are people who work schedules set by others). By contrast with the 4–40 plan, few organizations that have embraced flextime have abandoned it.

Nevertheless introducing flextime is never easy; further there are a variety of situations for which it is not suited. In the first place, flextime creates many problems where teamwork is required, such as on an assembly line, or in activities such as nursing or police work, where one person cannot leave his post until relieved by another.[30]

Complex scheduling arrangements are often required, especially when minimum-size work crews are needed at all times. From management's point of view, it is far easier to let employees work out these scheduling details by themselves. Once employees become accustomed to taking responsibility on a group basis for scheduling, they may also take responsibility for other

---

[29] On the other hand, flextime may disrupt carpools.

[30] Individuals can trade their assignments so that the requisite number of people are always present, but arranging these trades may be difficult. Sometimes even assembly-line work may be modified to permit flextime. The early bird who works on one end of the line may produce a bank which the next person on the line, who reports to work later, may handle later on. Adjustments of this sort, however, are always complex.

aspects of work, thus facilitating the kind of participative atmosphere in which self-managing work teams may develop. Running an operation with some people absent may require those on duty to learn unfamiliar jobs. All in all, flextime is consistent with job redesign.

Another problem relates to supervision. If 12 hours elapse between the time the first employee reports for work and the last one leaves the office—but the supervisor is on duty for only 8 hours—then the office will be unsupervised for 4 hours. Possibly this is actually an advantage. The supervisor will be forced to delegate authority during this 4-hour period and to engage in planning rather than detailed supervision, something that may be good for both worker and supervisor.

In practice, flextime is most common in professional and clerical work. This kind of work usually requires less teamwork than does manufacturing. Further, clerical activities tend to be heavily female, and at this stage in society's development working mothers feel the greatest need for the flexibile hours.

Flextime plans differ in the degree of flexibility they allow. Some plans require workers to pick a schedule and then stick to it; others allow schedule shifts on a daily basis, sometimes even without advance notice. Some permit workers to pick the length of their lunch hour and to take breaks of various lengths during the day; others allow flexibility only with regard to the starting and quitting time. Although some jobs permit greater flexibility than do others, employers frequently feel they need uniform policies to prevent cries of favoritism.

Some organizations permit employees to vary the number of hours they work per day or even per week, usually with the provision that time lost in one period be made up later on. In the Swiss countryside, for example, the 1800 hour work year is the norm. Workers put in long hours in the winter and then spend much of the summer on vacation or tending their farms. In the U.S., flexibility of this sort would create financial complications. The Fair Labor Standards Act requires overtime premiums for work in excess of 40 hours per week. Government contracts and many unionized firms are required to pay similar premiums for those working in excess of eight hours per day.

Almost the ultimate form of flexibility allows the worker to decide on a day-to-day basis whether he wants to work or not. West Coast longshoremen, for example, report to the union hiring hall when they feel like it, and senior (class A) longshoremen are pretty well guaranteed work (or at least show up pay). As one man put it: "A real San Francisco longshoreman is an independent cuss. He's not a slave to the calendar. He figures out what he needs and he works to meet his needs, but when the day is nice, and the steelhead are running, why work?"

Perhaps some day a large proportion of our society will enjoy such freedom. So far, the number is small.

Part-time work represents another form of flexibility. Demand for part-time work is increasing rapidly, particularly among mothers, students, and older workers. By the late 1970s, over one-third of female employees and

Part-time work

one-eighth of male employees worked on a part-time basis, and demand for part-time jobs is even greater than its supply. Part-time work was once also temporary work, but a growing number of employees now have permanent part-time positions.

It is understandable why part-time work is attractive for many workers. Organizations are also learning that many qualified employees are available only on a part-time basis. Very often part-time workers have better productivity records and lower absenteeism and turnover than full-time workers. Professionals may produce almost as much work in a six-hour day as they would in eight hours. Further, there are many jobs that don't require full-time coverage.

Nevertheless, many of the disadvantages of flextime also apply to part-time work. Scheduling and supervision are often difficult. Usually it is just as expensive to train a part-time employee as a full-time one. The social security tax structure acts to make part-time employees more expensive than full-time ones. On the other hand, many employers provide part-time employees relatively fewer fringe benefits, even though the trend is rapidly changing toward treating both groups equally.

Part-time work is concentrated in sales and service activities, such as fast foods. However, Control Data runs a factory in St. Paul, Minnesota, that is staffed completely by part-timers. So far, there are few part-time managers, but part-time work is attractive to talented professionals who might otherwise be unavailable:

> I am an assistant vice-president and economist at the Federal Bank of Boston. I am the head of the National Business Conditions Section at the Bank, and for two years I have been a part-time worker. How can a supervisor work part-time? The Director of Research certainly entertained some doubts when I told him that after my daughter was born, I wanted to work only 20 hours a week. In large part, it has worked because while I am the official head of the section, I share my supervisory work with the other economist in it. Like team teaching, we have team management, with one member of the team being slightly more equal. I also have bright, well-motivated workers in my section who are happy to take responsibility for their work. I do about the same job I used to do, but for less pay. I also work harder while at the bank. And of course, I take a lot of work home, which I also did when I worked full-time.[31]

Job sharing. This is a form of part-time work that has attracted considerable attention. Here a single job is divided between two people, each of whom works part time (say 20 hours a week or 6 months a year). In some cases a husband and wife may share a single professional position (with complications if their marriage falls apart). Although there are some philosophical attractions to this form of work schedule, particularly for those who view it as a step towards eliminating the differences in sex roles, the main advantage is that the job in question is staffed on a full-time basis. Nevertheless, job sharing has the disadvantage that it will work only if two individuals can be found, each of whom is willing to work an unusual schedule that directly complements his partner's. When one partner quits or becomes unhappy with the arrange-

---

[31] Francine Gordon and Myra Strober, *Bringing Women into Management* (New York: McGraw-Hill, 1975), p. 88.

ment, a replacement may be difficult to find. Other forms of part-time work are more flexible and therefore more popular.

Union attitudes

The bulk of the experiments with unconventional work schedules have occurred with non-union white-collar workers. Unions are rather suspicious of these new developments, and this is almost as true in Europe as it is in the U.S. One reason for this suspicion is that management sometimes introduces new schedules in union plants without consulting the union; the union insists this is a matter for joint negotiation. From the union point of view, the solution to work schedule problems is shorter hours without lower pay. Eight hours a day is the most anyone should ever work, many unionists say, and every effort should be made to reduce this figure. Part-time work is opposed unless part-time workers receive fringe benefits equal to those of full-time workers. Flextime is feared because it may blur job jurisdictional lines. Further, since flextime supposedly leads to higher productivity, management should pay higher wages for workers who partake of it. Some unions look upon flextime chiefly as a means for management to reduce its overtime payment.

Recently, however, as their members have shown greater interest in flextime and part-time work, white-collar unions in particular have begun to drop their opposition.

Conclusion

Job redesign and new work schedules are designed to counteract the growing work discontent that many (but not all) observers have noted in recent years. Beyond this it is hoped that they (as well as goal setting) will contribute to higher productivity.

According to its advocates, job redesign harnesses workers' unused abilities and fosters teamwork. Through enlarging workers' discretion, job redesign also makes work more challenging and as a consequence raises both productivity and satisfaction. In terms of expectancy theory, job redesign and goal setting techniques both make it easier for workers to convert effort into performance. Further, they make performance itself more rewarding, particularly if performance permits workers to demonstrate valued skills and to attain fair, accepted goals. Finally, job redesign smooths work flow and reduces the need for close supervision.

However, job redesign is not as universally appropriate as some of its advocates make it sound. Challenge is motivating particularly for those with high *n Ach;* for those low in *n Ach,* greater challenge may be oppressive. For many workers, the best part of job redesign is that it permits them greater opportunity to socialize on the job.

Furthermore, the opportunities to redesign work are relatively limited. Conceivably, automobiles could be made on a completely craft basis and the assembly line eliminated. But to do so would be prohibitively expensive. In many situations, the range of feasible changes may not be broad enough to make a major difference. Workers are not likely to find self-actualization on an assembly line or even in a reorganized dog food factory. Job enrichment may give rise to unrealistic expectations that workers will be given ever-increasing freedom to make essential work decisions. Few managements are prepared to permit this.

Efforts to introduce job redesign are not always successful. Job redesign may require changes in pay rates, promotional policies, and supervisory methods. All this may engender resistance from unions, middle and lower management, and even from other workers who may be jealous of the seemingly special privileges being given to the workers whose jobs are being changed.

On the other hand, job redesign's novelty should not be exaggerated. Craftsmen, for example, enjoyed enriched jobs long before the term *job enrichment* was invented. Indeed, some observers believe that as the more routine jobs are taken over by machines, the average level of challenge will increase in the jobs that remain—without an explicit job redesign effort.

Despite these cautions, most people would like a little more control over their work lives, and job redesign may help provide this. Further, job redesign permits more efficient use of manpower in many cases (apart and beyond any questions of satisfaction or motivation).

A number of organizations have concentrated, however, not on changing the nature of the job but the hours one works. New work schedules are often thought of as alternatives to job redesign. The demand for new work schedules has been largely associated with the growing number of women in the work force. Flextime permits greater flexibility in planning leisure activities and in coordinating work and family relations. It gives workers considerably more control over their work lives.

Despite other differences, workplace reforms share the common denominator of allowing workers greater freedom: to decide *how* to do the job, in the case of job redesign; to decide *when* to do it, in the case of flextime. Furthermore, new work schedules are difficult to introduce without changes in the way work is organized. Flextime may require job rotation, job enlargement, or group decisions as to how tasks are to be handled when some workers and even the supervisor are absent.

Neither job redesign nor new work schedules exhaust the possibilities of workplace reforms. Many workers are more concerned with hygienes than motivators; for them higher wages, better job security, and the various amenities enjoyed by management (for example, a more comfortable workplace environment) may be more important than either a slight increase in job discretion or greater freedom to choose when to do one's essentially boring work. Other workers want opportunities to get ahead, particularly greater opportunity to participate in key decisions affecting their own careers. These issues will be discussed in later chapters.

Worker satisfaction and motivation are closely related to supervisory style, as we shall see in the next chapter.

supervisory behavior: balancing structure and support

The supervisor plays a key organizational role. But what does the supervisor *do?* In particular, how does a supervisor mobilize subordinates' energies to work towards organizational goals?

The thesis of this chapter is that among the most important things the supervisor does is to provide subordinates what we call Structure and Support—terms to be defined later on—and that the nature of this Structure and Support should vary, depending on the circumstances. Our analysis will provide another opportunity to apply the principles discussed in Chapters 1 and 2, especially Expectancy Theory.

Before proceeding, let us note three important cautions.

1. Supervisors do much more than merely supervise subordinates. They make technical decisions; they represent their departments in dealings with other departments, higher management, and outside organizations; they are involved in endless paper work; they engage in long-range planning, and so forth. These other activities often are more vital to effective organizational functioning than are the direct boss-subordinate relationships that we discuss in this chapter.

2. Even with regard to their subordinates, supervisors do much more than merely provide Structure and Support. For example, they provide supplies, information, and technical assistance; and in many instances they help

administer the compensation system, which may (but unfortunately often does not) provide rewards for effective performance.

3. Finally, just as supervisors do more than supervise subordinates, so subordinates' satisfaction and performance are affected by many aspects of organizational life other than the supervisor's behavior. Subordinate satisfaction is heavily influenced by factors such as their personalities, the nature of their tasks or organizational-wide practices regarding compensation, promotional opportunities, job security, and fringe benefits. Few of these may be under the individual supervisor's direct control. Subordinates' productivity may similarly be influenced by their previous education and training, whether they work on up-to-date equipment, and even the state of the business cycle. These factors also are outside the supervisors' direct control, although frequently they can take steps to moderate their effects.

With these cautions in mind, let us examine the supervisor's dealings with *individual* subordinates. (The supervisor's related role, as *group* leader, is treated in Chapter 6.) We begin with a historical introduction describing the blind alleys down which research darted before our present concepts evolved. We then examine in general terms what may be called a Contingency Theory of Leadership, a theory in which Structure and Support play key roles. Next we explain the theory (especially Structure and Support) in practical, job-related terms. Finally, we summarize the conditions under which Structure and Support should be used, reexamine the relationships between the two concepts, and place the supervisory role in broad context.

Blind alleys

Supervision may be the most researched and least understood of all management concepts. Over the years much effort has been invested in studying boss-subordinate relationship, yet until recently the various investigations seemed to be running down dead-end alleys. Frequently researchers' findings were widely publicized through a management community anxious for quick cures for supervisory problems. Again and again, however, management would apply these findings and then abandon them because of their limited application. Meanwhile further research would prove these managers' instincts right.

Why were these efforts so pointless? Largely because researchers, abetted by practicing managers, were seeking a *one best way*, a simple how-to-do-it formula which would resolve all boss-subordinate problems and simultaneously maximize both productivity and satisfaction in all management situations, from managing an assembly line to leading a jazz band. Progress began only as researchers realized that effective supervision depended on the circumstances (and under some circumstances, supervision made little difference). A quick tour of major blind alleys may put our later discussion in perspective.

Traits

Early research was based on the psychology of individual differences. It was directed toward finding a single trait or series of traits that would distinguish between leaders and nonleaders. Armed with psychological tests, researchers compared "bishops and clergymen, salesmanagers and salesmen, and railway presidents and station agents"[1] as well as presumably effective and ineffective leaders at the same organizational level.

The results of this research were disappointing. Traits that seem related to leadership in one situation appear not to be related in others. Only a few generally valid generalizations were developed, and these are not very useful.[2] There has been some success in developing tests to predict who will make a good supervisor in a specific situation.[3] (However, a test—if one existed—for selecting symphony orchestra conductors might be of little use in selecting factory foremen, college presidents, or football coaches.) Further, the research provided little insight into what effective supervisors *do* or how to make them better.

Human relations

By the 1950s, the emphasis had shifted from identifying effective leaders (personality) to describing *what* effective leaders did (behavior). But the hope was still high that a single style of leadership behavior would emerge, one that would be best under all circumstances.

Consistent with the emphasis on human relations during this period, researchers generally believed that the key element in effective supervision was concern for subordinate welfare. Among the first studies was that of the home office of the Prudential Insurance Company. Twenty-four work groups were examined; half were high and half low in productivity as determined by prior work records. Among the critical findings was that supervisors of high-productivity groups were more likely to be *employee-centered* than *production-centered* and to exercise *general* rather than *close* supervision.[4] Note the differences in attitude expressed by two supervisors in this study.

Production oriented: "I handle the amount of work given each clerk, watch the dates and time the work so that everything gets out on schedule. If a letter comes in late, we have to speed up handling it—give it special attention. . . . I have to watch this to make up for time lost in other departments."

Employee oriented: "If you keep your employees from being hounded, they are more likely to put out the necessary effort to get the work done on time. . . . I tell them 'if you feel the job is getting you down, get away from it for a few minutes.'"

---

[1] Victor Vroom, "Leadership," in Marvin Dunnette, ed., *Handbook of Industrial and Organizational Psychology* (Chicago: Rand McNally, 1976), p. 1529. Perhaps the best single summary of psychological research on leadership traits and leadership general is Ralph M. Stogdill, *Handbook of Leadership* (New York: Free Press, 1974).

[2] For example, leaders as a whole appear to have a bit more self-confidence than do nonleaders, but the relationship is not strong, and many leaders are less self-confident than the average nonleader.

[3] Mention should be made of a highly controversial theory relating supervisory effectiveness to a personality trait called LPC (attitudes toward Least Preferred Co-workers). LPC appears to measure the psychological closeness supervisors feel to their subordinates. According to this theory, supervisors high in LPC are most effective in situations that are moderately "favorable" to the leader. In situations that are highly favorable or highly unfavorable, low LPC supervisors (presumably more autocratic) are more effective. Fred Fiedler, "The Leadership Game: Matching the Man to the Situation," *Organizational Dynamics* (Winter 1976), 6–16.

[4] Daniel Katz, Nathan Maccoby, and Nancy Morse, *Productivity, Supervision, and Morale in an Office Situation* (Ann Arbor: University of Michigan, Institute for Social Research, 1950).

Low-production supervisors spent more time explaining changes in work methods to subordinates and were more likely to call meetings to explain procedural details. High-production supervisors were less likely to be punitive when subordinates made mistakes. Other studies suggested that members of high-production groups tended to show more pride in their work group and that their supervisors themselves were less closely supervised by their bosses. High-production supervisors spent more time listening to employees' problems and showed more concern for their employees' welfare.

Based on this and similar studies, it was widely concluded that the secret of supervisory success was to emphasize people over production. Gradually, however, some serious questions arose concerning the universal validity of this conclusion.

1. The initial findings were not replicated everywhere. A study of railway track maintenance gangs showed no significant relationship between productivity and closeness of supervision. The difference perhaps was that work in an insurance office was so highly routinized that employees knew their jobs thoroughly and almost any amount of close supervision was resented as an unnecessary form of nagging. Work on the railway was less standardized; unexpected problems often required the supervisor's attention.

2. It was widely believed that close supervision caused low productivity, but this may have confused cause and effect. Close supervision might be an understandable reaction when a supervisor's subordinates are performing ineffectively. By contrast, a supervisor who is assigned to a highly productive group has no need to supervise closely. The evidence today suggests that supervisors vary their behavior, depending on the needs of the situation. Thus, they are less likely to supervise closely if subordinates are competent and well motivated.

3. Early studies concluded that employee-oriented supervisors were able to maintain high productivity because of their concern for employee satisfaction. In other words, supervisor's concern for employees caused employee satisfaction and this, in turn, caused higher productivity. Later studies indicated that productivity and satisfaction were often independent and that supervisory behavior which appeared to raise satisfaction might have a negative effect on productivity, and vice versa.

People and production

By the 1960s some scholars were arguing that the successful supervisor should be concerned both with employee welfare (people) and high productivity. Aside from some research that tends to refute this hypothesis, the question arose whether this formulation might be so broad that it is almost meaningless and certainly not useful. Granted that stressing production is a good thing, the real problem is *how* one obtains high production: through detailed supervision, for example, or through granting subordinates broad discretion.

Structure and support

In part to answer questions such as these, a different stream of research began to develop measures of supervisory behavior somewhat more precise than the ones just mentioned. Perhaps the most important research was done at Ohio State. Here, utilizing sophisticated psychometric techniques, a group studied leadership in a wide variety of circumstances (from air crew leaders to school administrators). Eventually they isolated two dimensions, which have been refined and revised over the years. We will call them Structure and Support.[5]

- Structure relates to supervisory activities that define the nature of subordinates' jobs. Examples include assigning goals, training, and coordinating subordinate activities.
- Support reflects the extent to which the supervisor is friendly to subordinates, is approachable, trusting, and demonstrates consideration for their needs and feelings.

A variety of psychological instruments (chiefly questionnaires) have been developed to measure each dimension. Supervisors have been asked to evaluate their own behavior, subordinates have evaluated that of their bosses, and evaluation questionnaires have been filled out by bosses and peers of the people being evaluated. Literally hundreds of studies have been made.

What does all this research tell us about the relationship between these two dimensions and such other variables as subordinate productivity and satisfaction? Do supervisors displaying high Support have more productive subordinates than those who display low Support (as human relations advocates would argue)? Is Structure positively related to production? (In other words, are traditional supervisors right when they insist that close, detailed supervision is the best way to get subordinates to do their jobs?)

Actually, there was but one consistent relationship at first: subordinate satisfaction was positively correlated with supervisor Support. Otherwise, the relationships were confused. There were positive relationships in some cases, negative relationships in others, and in some instances the relationship was not significantly different from zero.

Contingency theory

In the early 1970s a series of research breakthroughs occurred which gave students of supervisory behavior new hope but forced many of them to abandon the expectation of ever finding one best way to supervise. This new research provides the basis for what has been called Contingency Theory (since appropriate supervisory behavior is *contingent* on a variety of factors to be discussed below). The heart of Contingency Theory consists of the following insights.

1. The key relationship between Structure and both satisfaction and productivity may be curvilinear.[6] As the next chart suggests, if subordinates receive too little Structure, that is, if they are provided too little information

---

[5] The original two terms, still widely used, were Initiating Structure and Consideration. For a review of the research, see Edward A. Fleishman, "Twenty Years of Consideration and Structure," in E. A. Fleishman and J. G. Hunt, eds., *Current Developments in the Study of Leadership* (Carbondale: Southern Illinois Press, 1973) and Stephen Kerr and others, "Toward a Contingency Theory of Leadership Based on the Consideration and Initiating Structure Leadership," *Organizational Behavior and Human Performance*, 12, No. 1 (August 1974), 62–82. The Ohio State group was not alone in deriving these two dimensions. A variety of other studies, utilizing other methodologies, have converged on dimensions roughly equivalent to those used here.

[6] Empirical evidence for the concept of curvilinearity is weaker than for the rest of theory, and curvilinearity should be considered an untested hypothesis.

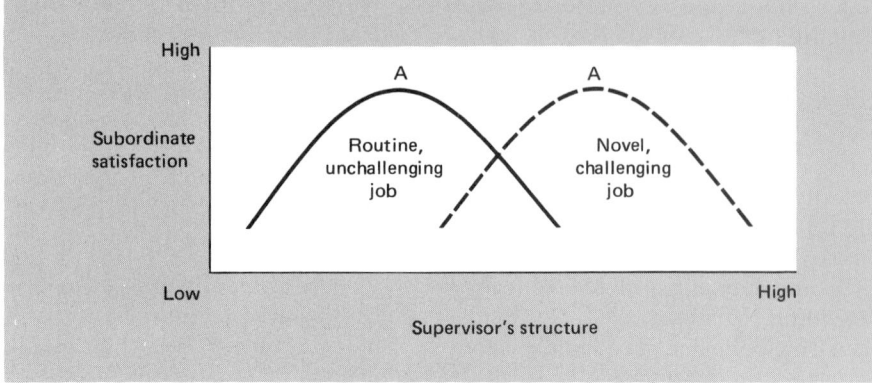

as to what they are supposed to do or how they are supposed to do it, they become anxious. Increase their Structure, provide them more guidance, and their satisfaction will also increase. But increase Structure too much—beyond point A on the chart above—and helpful guidance turns into oversupervision. When this occurs, employees become frustrated and satisfaction begins to drop.

2. The ideal amount of Structure (point A) varies from one situation to another. Thus, workers on a routine job will want much less Structure than those on new, complex tasks. The latter will welcome much more guidance from the boss. (But even on nonroutine tasks there may be a point beyond which still more Structure becomes annoying.)

3. The relationships between Support and either production or satisfaction are more complex. By and large, the more Support the better, but in some instances an increase in Support will make a big difference (for example, for a highly dependent worker); in other instances, extra Support may have little impact.

4. Appropriate supervisory behavior changes almost from minute to minute.

At 7:55 A.M. the boss emphasizes Support as she greets her subordinates coming to work. At 8:00 she switches to high Structure, as she hands out regular assignments. Later, presiding over a meeting of experienced subordinates who share in solving a difficult work problem, she exerts relatively low Structure.[7] At 11:00 she provides some help (high Structure) to a new employee who is having trouble learning the job. At 11:30 she gives the employee a word of encouragement (Support) without providing further direction. She has lunch with several subordinates; they talk about fishing (Support). So it continues through the day as the supervisor constantly switches supervisory techniques depending on the needs of the moment.

On balance, we may say that one supervisor exerts more Structure than another, but this "average" style of supervision masks the fact that one of

---

[7] Alternatively, we may say that she is sharing Structure, since the group provides the Structure as much as the boss.

the keys to supervisory effectiveness is the ability to react flexibly to constantly changing interpersonal contacts.

5. The final insight derives from Expectancy Theory. It suggests that the supervisor's main job is to strengthen the arrows in the expectancy theory diagram. Specifically, the supervisor ① makes it easier for the subordinate to convert effort into productivity, ② increases the likelihood that higher productivity will be rewarded, ③ ensures that rewards are distributed more equitably, ④ possibly even changes the value (in terms of satisfaction) of these rewards to employees, and ⑤ helps improve feedback. Together these activities should increase the subordinates' work efficiency, the rewards they receive from effort, and their general job satisfaction. In short, subordinates should expect higher effort to lead to valued rewards.

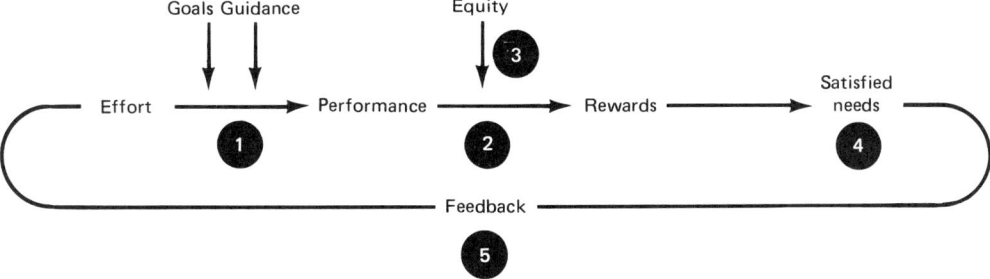

APPLICATION OF EXPECTANCY THEORY TO SUPERVISORY BEHAVIOR

HOW THE SUPERVISOR CAN STRENGTHEN THE EXPECTANCY RELATIONSHIP

1. To strengthen the likelihood that increased effort will lead to higher performance:
   - provide clear goals; that is, indicate the nature of the performance desired (this is one element in Structure)
   - indicate how these goals are to be reached; for example, through rules or training (another element in Structure)
   - make the work environment more pleasant (especially through providing Support) so that work becomes easier
   - provide the tools, supplies, and information needed to do the job
   - encourage the development of cohesive work teams and, through participation, obtain efficiency-improving suggestions from subordinates (see Chap. 6)

2. To increase the perceived likelihood that greater performance will lead to rewards:
   - work with higher management to recast the reward and promotion (career) system, so that rewards and promotions more clearly reflect performance
   - provide rewards of their own; for example, praise for higher productivity
   - redesign jobs so that completed work becomes a reward in itself (see Chap. 3)

3. To increase the feeling that the relationship between reward and performance is equitable, monitor the rewards, ensuring that:
   - rewards are commensurate with performance
   - rewards are distributed fairly
   - employees have opportunities to participate in deciding how rewards are to be distributed
   - employees have their grievances heard when apparent inequities occur

4. To increase the value of rewards in terms of satisfaction:
   - encourage participation and initiative, thus facilitating the satisfaction of egoistic needs on the job (in other words, change employee orientation from instrumental to expressive)
5. Develop (or influence higher management to develop) adequate methods of feedback, so that employees can more accurately perceive the effort-reward relationship.

The remainder of this chapter explains how Structure and Support help smooth the *path* between effort and the *goal* of effective performance.[8]

Structure

It is easy to see how Structure is related to productivity. After all, if employees don't know what to do, how can they do their jobs? More surprising, however, is the fact that lack of sufficient Structure is a major cause of employee dissatisfaction. According to a major nationwide study, the two characteristics of workers' jobs most closely related to overall job satisfaction are (1) having a "nurturant" boss (i.e., Support) and (2) receiving adequate help, assistance and guidance (i.e., Structure).[9] A similar national study of employed males found that 35 percent lacked clarity about the scope and responsibility of their jobs and 38 percent lacked enough information to do their jobs effectively.[10] Both factors (scope-responsibility and information) are provided through Structure.

Even workers who highly value the freedom to make decisions for themselves need information to make such decisions. When given an order, they want some explanation of what is to be done, why it is to be done, and what limits will be placed on their freedom—as well as relevant background information necessary to help them do a better job or to satisfy their natural curiosity. They prefer their boss to be easily available to answer questions or to provide assistance when needed.

We shall consider two elements of Structure—setting goals and providing guidance in meeting these goals—as well as a third factor closely related to Structure: providing the key tools and information to do the job.

Setting goals

The supervisor has the responsibility for seeing that subordinates do not flounder around and that their efforts are not wasted but instead are efficiently directed toward higher performance. Concrete goals direct effort and reduce uncertainty. Under most circumstances, clear standards also contribute to satisfaction.

---

[8] Contingency Theory is often called the Path-Goal Theory of Leadership. For a review, see Robert J. House and Terrance R. Mitchell, "Path-Goal Theory of Leadership," *Journal of Contemporary Business* (Autumn 1974), 81–97.

[9] Robert Quinn and others, *Survey of Working Conditions* (Washington: Government Printing Office, 1971). The six next most important factors, in declining order of importance, were: (3) "labor standards problems," such as safety hazards or poor transportation; (4) promotional policies; (5) closeness of supervision; (6) a technically competent supervisor; (7) autonomy in matters affecting work, and (8) a job with "enriching" demands.

[10] George Graen, "Role-Making Processes Within Complex Organizations," in Marvin Dunnette, *Handbook of Industrial and Organizational Psychology*, p. 1206.

Explicit goals. Some jobs are so routine, of course, that no one has any problem knowing what to do. Under such circumstances, supervisors who emphasize goals sound overbearing. Nevertheless, there are times when assignments are clear to the boss who makes them but totally unclear to the subordinates who receive them. It is far from uncommon for a subordinate to spend time on one thing when the boss puts higher priority on something else. Hardnosed as managers are supposed to be, many find it difficult to operationalize their goals or to be really specific as to what they want their subordinates or the work group as a whole to accomplish. As the above surveys suggest, employees quite frequently say, "I'm not really sure what the boss wants me to do," or "when I was hired nobody told me what my exact responsibilities were."

Supervisors, imbued with the human relations point of view, too often avoid the unpleasantness of being explicit about their expectations (although they may crack down later without warning on the unsuspecting subordinate who does not meet these unspoken expectations). Although setting and insisting on high standards sometimes leads to hostility, failure to be forthright about expectations may lead to greater difficulty still. Goals are accepted under most circumstances, provided they are reasonable in terms of employees expectations (see Chap. 6), and provided the supervisor's insistance on meeting goals is combined with a measure of Support (especially understanding).

Setting difficult goals. Tough goals, as long as they are felt to be fair and reasonable, contribute both to productivity and satisfaction. Reaching a difficult goal provides a real sense of achievement. Among the great secrets of charismatic leaders—from Joan of Arc to Vince Lombardi, the football coach—is their ability to persuade their followers to accept and work for seemingly impossible goals. Usually a two-step process is involved. First, these leaders inspire belief in the goal, to dream the impossible dream. Second, they develop their subordinates' confidence that they really do have the ability to reach this goal, to make the impossible dream come true.

Employees want to know not only *what* to accomplish but also *how* to accomplish it. If employees lack appropriate training and instruction, their efforts are wasted, and both productivity and satisfaction suffer. Supervisors can provide guidance to their subordinates in a number of ways:

Guiding employee efforts

- By supervising them closely on a minute-by-minute basis, telling them exactly what to do.
- By providing detailed advance instructions (rules) covering most contingencies.
- By providing broad forms of training that impart general skills.
- By making themselves available for questions, but otherwise letting subordinates work things out by themselves.

Typically, supervisors use a combination of these techniques. The particular mixture used in any situation depends on the nature of the job, on the subordinates' previous training and skills, and to some extent on the subordinates' personalities and orientation toward work. Although insufficient guidance can be frustrating and can lead to misdirected effort, forcing people to solve problems by themselves often provides a useful learning experience. Guidance that is too close can be felt as restrictive (thus indicating lack of Support) and sometimes leads to reduced productivity and heightened resistance to change.

Effective supervisors generally explain the *why* of their instructions; they give their subordinates the theory, the overall framework within which particular instruction fits. Provided with this framework, subordinates can cope with unusual problems without having to run to their boss for continual instructions. Patient explanation and demonstration by the supervisor is frequently an essential first step. But in many areas it is more effective to give trainees a chance to think things out by themselves. If subordinates cannot arrive at a satisfactory solution on their own, the supervisor should then offer suggestions.

Providing technical assistance

Even the most motivated workers find it hard to get their work done without adequate means of doing it. Therefore, the provision of tools, supplies, and above all essential information is among the most important parts of the supervisor's job. The importance of this function was underscored by a nationwide study. Outranking all other items on a long list, the statement, "I receive enough help and equipment to get the job done" was "very important" to 69 percent of employees studied.

The supervisor is, for the most part, dependent on higher management and other departments to obtain the needed supplies and information. For this reason (as we discuss in Chap. 11), the supervisor's external relations are a key to internal success.

Support

One of the presumed lessons of the early human relations movement was that supervisors should be supportive, treat their subordinates as human beings, look out for their welfare, be fair, listen to their problems, and so on. Today we are less convinced than we were thirty years ago that this is *all* that is required to make a successful supervisor; but clearly, support is an important element in determining employee satisfaction and willingness to cooperate in meeting management's objectives. Regardless of what else it might be, Support is a stress reducer. As a form of hygienic management, Support helps reduce the feelings of dissatisfaction and oppression that many workers feel when they are confronted by the pressures, rigidities, and sterilities of their jobs. By reducing frustration, Support helps create conditions under which people will accept Structure with minimal resentment and, one hopes, some enthusiasm. A further valuable by-product of Support is the strength it gives employees' beliefs that work effort will lead to satisfying rewards.

"Treating people as human beings," "being fair," "showing interest in them as individuals"—all these sound rather trite, and being nice is not enough. Supervisors must adjust to the special needs and expectations of their subordinates as a group and as individuals. As we shall see in Chapter 6, Support is related to legitimacy: the supportive leader is one who behaves in a way that subordinates feel is appropriate for a supervisor.

Three of the critical elements in Support are: (1) creating a feeling of approval, (2) developing personal relations, and (3) providing fair treatment.

Creating a feeling of approval

The personal, one-to-one relationships between supervisors and their subordinates have a lot to do with the way subordinates view their jobs. Because subordinates are dependent on their boss, it is important for them to feel that the supervisor approves of their work and of them as individuals and is concerned with their personal development.

Supervisors can communicate their feelings of approval of subordinates in many ways: taking an active interest in them as people, listening to their problems, giving praise when justified, showing tolerance when mistakes are made, and so forth. However, the subordinate's psychological perception, the *feeling* of approval, is what is significant. The overall quality of the boss's attitudes toward subordinates—particularly confidence in their ability—may be more important than any act or even combination of acts.[11] If the boss trusts the subordinate, this will show through, and the subordinate will trust the boss. In fact, the existence of such feeling of mutual approval determines how individual acts are interpreted. If such a feeling exists, employees may excuse their boss's mistakes; if it does not exist, they may exaggerate these mistakes out of proportion. Similarly, in the absence of approval or trust, supervisors' attempts to show interest in employees may be seen as meddling.

The meaning of courtesy also depends on subordinate attitudes. Saying "please" or "do you mind" is appreciated, but employees soon see through superficial gestures if they conflict with the rest of the boss's behavior. In some situations cusswords are better evidence than icy courtesy that the boss likes you. Or take praise. Although most human beings like praise, they become suspicious when it is applied too heavily. Further, praise for good work is not enough. People have bad days as well as good; a real feeling of approval assures the individual that the boss will show tolerance for an occasional mistake. In short, the existence of a feeling of approval means that the supervisor has demonstrated a personal loyalty to subordinates. Until that happens, loyalty will not flow the other way.

Note, though, that approval means different things to different people. We once interviewed two lacquer-mixers who worked pretty much by themselves at opposite ends of a long factory floor. They did the same job and were under the same foreman (who said both did a good job). The first mixer said: "I've got a good boss. He knows I know the job, so he leaves me alone, he never bothers me." The second mixer said: "My foreman doesn't care whether I'm dead or alive. He's a bum foreman who doesn't show any interest in his men or how they are doing."

Obviously, the two workers looked upon supervision very differently. The first saw supervision as restrictive, to be avoided if possible. The second expected help and reassurance from the boss. Both workers were anxious to

---

[11] Raymond Miles and J. B. Ritchie, "Participative Management: Quality vs. Quantity," *California Management Review*, Vol. 13 (Summer 1971), 48–56.

win approval and acceptance, but what came through clearly as acceptance to one worker seemed outright rejection to the other.

Development. Closely related to feeling for approval is concern for the subordinate's development. Training is technically a form of Structure, but beyond this the supportive supervisor is interested in helping subordinates prepare themselves for promotion.

Developing personal relations

A feeling of approval is more likely to result if the boss shows personal interest in subordinates. Consequently, effective managers make time to get to know their subordinates and to help them with their problems both on and (to a limited extent) off the job.

Need for personal relations. People like being treated as individuals. Yet as far as the typical organization is concerned, the average employee is nothing more than a personnel number or a job specification. The organization is impersonal; only the immediate boss can make it personal. Particularly to a new employee, the supervisor *is* the organization, and what the boss does helps mold the individual's conception of the organization as a whole. An insensitive supervisor can easily undo all the organization's efforts to create a good impression through public relations and fringe benefits.

Home problems affect efficiency on the job, so good managers listen to employees' problems and offer assistance in some areas. Ordinarily, all they can do is listen, but even this provides relief for someone in distress. In any case, the more the managers learn about the people who work for them, the better they can understand employees' behavior and how to deal with it. (Of course, managers should not seem to pry or meddle.)

Even more important, good informal relations on matters not directly related to the job set the stage for better communications on problems related to work. Any social barrier will create a communications barrier.[12] Employees rarely feel completely free and easy when talking to the boss about their work, for they are quite aware that it is the boss who hands out rewards and punishments. But when they talk about the employee's fishing trip, the employee is the expert at the moment, even if there is no true equality between them. Some of the air of permissiveness and informality created by discussing baseball and the weather might carry over to on-the-job affairs. Once the boss and the subordinate know each other as individuals, both will feel freer to bring up mutual problems.

To put it another way: good managers try to reduce the number of orders they give by encouraging people to ask them questions, rather than by telling these people what to do. For this approach to work, however, subordinates must feel confident and secure enough to go to their boss when difficulties arise. In an atmosphere of approval and mutual understanding, subordinates will feel more comfortable in asking questions, and the boss's advice or even criticism will be less likely to be resented.

[12] As we note in Chapter 6, there are substantial differences among cultures in what people think is the appropriate social distance between boss and subordinate.

Setting the tone. Obviously, it is the superior who sets the tone of the relationship, not the subordinate. First, the manager must be available to all comers. The boss who is barricaded behind a wall of formality or is always "busy, busy, busy" is not likely to develop satisfactory informal relationships. Nor is it enough to be a good fellow a few times a year. In most companies the permissive atmosphere of the annual Christmas party stands out in sharp contrast to the distant relationship that is normal for the rest of the year.

The manager must take the initiative by maintaining regular and frequent contacts with subordinates. Some managers make periodic "howdy rounds," talking to each employee in turn. Even if these encounters consist only of idle chatter, still they provide an opportunity for employees to bring up problems that are bothering them. In other words, the manager opens up the contact and lets the subordinate decide what topics should be covered.

Providing fair treatment

Since subordinates are directly dependent on their bosses, they are understandably anxious to receive fair treatment from them. The boss can demonstrate a sense of fair play by letting each employee know exactly what is required and by exercising consistent discipline. Decisions must be based on grounds that are accepted as legitimate by subordinates. An appeals procedure (see Chap. 11) can be provided. Above all, there should be an all-out effort to treat everyone equally, so that rewards seem proportional to contributions.

Treating people equally is not as simple as it sounds. The conscientious manager is torn between two conflicting, though universally accepted, platitudes: "Avoid favoritism" and "Treat people as individuals, in accordance with their special needs." Those special needs can lead to apparently inconsistent treatment and can create endless bad feeling within the group.

With all the good will in the world, the manager may begin to play favorites unconsciously and to follow the normal tendency of either favoring the passive, dependent, "good" employee or paying the most attention to the aggressive individual, to "oil the wheel that squeaks the loudest." The manager must avoid both extremes.

Making exceptions. What about making exceptions in special situations? Obviously, treating people fairly does not mean treating everyone in exactly the same way. It does mean that when an exception is made, it must be accepted as legitimate by all members of the group. There is a general rule, for example, that vacations must be taken during the summer months. Ann Lawrence's husband is sick, so the boss lets her have February off to take him to Florida. Is this favoritism? Only if Ann's fellow employees think so. An exception of this sort will be accepted as fair if the group (1) knows why it was made, (2) accepts it as justified, and (3) is confident that another employee in the same situation would receive the same treatment.

Granting special favors when the circumstances permit not only lessens a subordinate's feeling that the organization is arbitrary and "heartless," but it may also lead to an "exchange of good turns." In a sense it is a form of implicit bargaining. As a worker in an assembly plant described it:

"My boss is great. She came in one bitterly cold morning when the shop was still half-frozen. She went out to the cafeteria and brought back a big can of hot coffee, which she handed all around. While we can't be bought, the thought was there, and we appreciated it. As a result, everybody worked a lot more, despite the cold."

The assumption behind this approach is that if the manager does more for subordinates than is absolutely required, they will respond in kind. It means, for example, that if Jane comes to work with a strained ankle, the foreman will find her some work that she can do sitting down; if a waiter is suddenly deluged with customers, the hostess will relieve some of the pressure by setting up tables and pouring water. The hope is that when an emergency arises, subordinates will reciprocate by working overtime or by producing more than their usual stint. Thus, an atmosphere is created in which both supervisor and subordinate exhibit a flexible attitude toward their mutual obligations.

Structure and support: when to use them   Having discussed the nature of Structure, Support, and associated activities, it may be useful to summarize the conditions under which these two significant supervisory activities are especially appropriate. The following paragraphs try to make sense out of the sometimes conflicting research. In reading them, please remember that we considerably oversimplify the picture in that we assume that there is but one kind of Structure and one kind of Support, when in fact there are many forms of each.

When structure is needed

A key point about Structure is that when there is too little of it, workers become frustrated and confused. Increased Structure, when there is too little, improves job satisfaction, but excess Structure is viewed as harrassment and depresses satisfaction. However, the optimum degree of Structure with respect

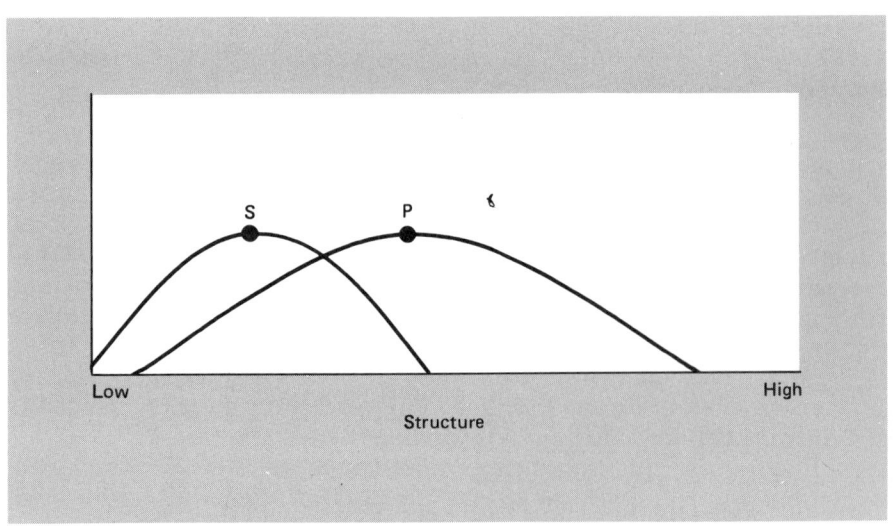

to satisfaction (point *S* in the chart) may well be lower than the optimum degree with respect to productivity. Put another way, the pressure represented by increasing Structure past point *S* may raise output, but at the cost of making workers less satisfied. If Structure is increased too far, workers begin to rebel: grievances, absenteeism, and turnover may increase; there may even be sabotage. Eventually (at point P) the cumulative impact of excess structure may begin to reduce productivity. How soon point *P* is reached may depend on a number of factors. Where production rates can easily be checked and supervisors can easily discipline workers who perform inadequately (for example, in nonunion companies) and where alternative jobs are scarce, the supervisor may be able to get away with a considerable degree of increased Structure before worker frustration becomes great enough to decrease production.

With this general observation, let us look at the various conditions that may influence the relationship between Structure and production and satisfaction.

Job characteristics. Not much Structure is required on routine jobs. In effect, the jobs themselves are already structured. The supervisor may have to assign individual tasks, to train new workers, and to help solve unexpected emergencies. Beyond this, structure becomes redundant and resented. Under these circumstances, perhaps the supervisors' chief functions are to provide Support, to monitor supplies and maintenance, and handle "foreign affairs" with other departments.

On jobs that are complex, uncertain, and ambiguous, subordinates appreciate a more directive role by the supervisor. Under these circumstances, Structure is viewed as help (but even then, too much Structure becomes annoying).

Need for decisive leadership. The technology of many jobs requires decisive leadership, tight coordination, and high structure. The conductor of a symphony orchestra must exercise strong leadership, and there is little room for individual discretion (a rock group, on the other hand, may practice considerable participation). Military aircraft crews prefer low Structure under routine flight conditions but react positively to it in simulated combat. Decisive direction of subordinates is also often required by surgeons and ship captains. In each of these cases, subordinates must get their satisfaction from the excellence of their performance as a team rather than from their ability to exercise individual discretion.

Decisive decision making may be important even when teamwork is not necessary. A study of a parcel delivery service indicated that drivers, who see their bosses only a few minutes each day, are likely to prefer bosses with strong authoritarian attitudes, whereas positioners, who handle parcels on the dock and work in close contact with their bosses all day long, prefer those who are not authoritarian. Since drivers spend only a short time with their boss, apparently they prefer someone who is decisive and inclined toward high Structure.

Training. Untrained, inexperienced workers require more Structure than those who already are trained.[13] Once employees are trained, they have internalized Structure, so they need less from their supervisor.

Availability of information. Greater Structure is necessary when only the boss has access to the information needed to make critical decisions; the reverse is true when the subordinate has this information.

Subordinate desire for discretion. There are substantial differences in the amount of responsibility people are willing to accept on the job. One person may flourish under highly Structured supervision that another might find extremely restrictive. One of the authors learned this lesson the hard way when he was working in a government agency some years ago. Imbued with the principles of good human relations, he explained in detail the background of every letter he dictated to the secretary assigned to him. He asked for comments on style and even suggested that if she wished, she could draft some of the letters herself. At last she burst out, "I'm not paid to do that kind of work. That's your job. You just tell me what to do."

High Structure can be particularly frustrating for employees who have strong ego needs and who are expressively oriented toward their jobs. They want a fair amount of freedom to develop their own approaches to work problems, and anything perceived as close control may be particularly threatening to their egos. On the other hand, instrumentally-oriented employees and those with weak ego needs may be somewhat more tolerant of bosses who supervise them closely, particularly if these bosses adhere to the civilities of Support. In fact, for some highly dependent employees, close supervision may provide security and a sign that their boss is interested in them as individuals. In addition, there are some employees who have become so accustomed to the authoritarian approach in their culture, family, and previous work experience that they regard low Structure as no supervision at all. They abuse the privileges it bestows upon them and refuse to accept the responsibilities it demands.

Consider the case of two hospital floors supervised by two very different head nurses.[14] The first head nurse (Miss Smith), though extremely courteous, was strict and uncompromising with nurses who violated regulations. She insisted that conversations be kept to a minimum and handed out detailed, unambiguous work assignments to her nurses.

The second head nurse (Miss Rogers) had a much more informal, almost kidding relationship with her subordinates and patients. She consulted with her nurses about problems and changes and succeeded in developing a strong feeling of comaraderie on the floor.

Now you might suppose that all the nurses would have preferred Miss

---

[13] According to one study, autonomy (low Structure) is negatively correlated with satisfaction for new, untrained employees; for more experienced employees, the reverse is true. Ralph Katz, "Job Longevity as a Situational Factor in Job Satisfaction," *Administrative Science Quarterly*, 23, No. 1 (June 1978), 204–23.

[14] This case is based on the research of Edith Hamilton.

Rogers' floor to Miss Smith's—but they didn't. The hospital let nurses choose which floor they wanted to work on; both floors were quite popular, but with different groups of nurses. In general, the older women liked the security of Miss Smith's floor, where everything went according to predetermined routine. As one older nurse put it:

> "I honestly feel I need a responsible person nearby to supervise me. I need guidance, and therefore I prefer to work where there is fairly close supervision. . . . I like to do things in an orderly way. . . . [on Miss Rogers' floor] things are done too sloppily."

Most of the younger nurses preferred the independence allowed them by Miss Rogers.

Why these differences? For one thing, nurses' training has become less strict than it once was, and the younger nurses have never experienced close supervision. More important, these differences may reflect an attitude toward authority that the younger nurses developed in their formative years at home and at school, an attitude influenced by the wide range of freedom permitted to modern children. Indeed, subordinates' feelings toward their boss are often colored by the relations they had with their parents and the emotional maturity and security they developed as children.

Substitutes for supervisor's Structure. There is less need for the supervisor to provide Structure if subordinates can obtain the equivalent of Structure from other sources. When the job itself is routine and highly programmed, additional Structure becomes superfluous. When employees are well trained, they have learned the equivalent of Structure. Employees can obtain needed information and supplies from staff departments, thus reducing the need to obtain them from the boss. In bureaucratic organization, rules, rather than the boss, often provide Structure.

Structure can also come from one's peers. Self-managing work groups decide how they are to perform their work; at times they set goals. Work groups often train new members. Workers often pass on to each other the information necessary to do the job. Social controls, especially professional standards, help guide employee behavior. At times, workers police one anothers' quality. All this reduces the need for supervisory Structure.

When Support is needed

By contrast with Structure, there is relatively little danger that the boss will provide too much Support.[15] But since Support comes in many forms, the trick is to provide the particular form required to meet the needs of the individual subordinate. Virtually all subordinates welcome Support, but in some circumstances this supervisory activity becomes critically important; in other circumstances it is of no great significance. When is Support particularly important?

---

[15] Of course, if the boss showers the subordinate with endless attention, this attention becomes viewed as lack of Support.

1. For the dependent worker or the worker brought up in an authoritarian culture, the supportive supervisor may be a substitute parent, someone whom the subordinate can lean on in time of trouble.

2. For workers with high social needs who are assigned to routine jobs, the activities of the supervisor may facilitate or hinder the development of a friendly, cohesive work group. For example, supervisors can cooperate with or disrupt activities such as pay-check-number pools, birthday parties, after-work parties, and the like. Good social relations are especially important, also, when the job is anxiety arousing, or intensive teamwork is required.

3. Supervisory Support acts as a stress reliever that counters the frustrating nature of some jobs. When the job is substantially *more* or substantially *less* challenging than employees want, supervisors can make themselves available to listen to gripes. Where the job is less challenging, they can also seek to divert workers' attention to social activities; where it is too challenging, they can provide encouragement. In such circumstances, the extrinsic satisfaction provided through Support makes up for lack of intrinsic satisfaction inherent in the work. By contrast, where the job is already satisfying (and offers neither too much nor too little challenge), supervisory Support is much less necessary.

4. Support is particularly important where the technology or layout of the job requires the supervisor to have constant interaction with subordinates. The personality or style of the rarely seen boss matters little to subordinates. But if the job requires close teamwork, dealing with the boss on a minute-by-minute basis, then Support becomes crucial.

5. Where Support is provided by other people in the organization, particularly by one's colleagues, then receiving Support from the boss becomes less critical. Similarly, Support becomes less important if the organization enjoys benevolent personnel policies. If your rights are set out in the union contract or the company personnel rulebook, then the boss's opportunities to tyrannize are greatly reduced.

The relationship between structure and support

Support and Structure are closely interrelated, particularly in the eyes of the subordinates who receive them. When less Structure or more Structure is provided than the subordinate wants, then this inappropriate level of Structure is felt as lack of Support. Too little Structure means that the boss doesn't care. Too much Structure constitutes nagging. Put another way, whether Structure is viewed as Support depends on how much Structure the subordinate wants.

On the other hand, Support can counteract the oppressive impact of Structure. Support makes the exercise of power more palatable.[16] The same supervisor behavior may appear intimidating or benign, depending on whether

---

[16] Research suggests that for supervisors low in Support, high Structure leads to high levels of grievances and turnover. However, for supportive supervisors, extent of Structure is almost unrelated to either grievances or turnover. For the classic study, see E. A. Fleishman and E. Harris, "Patterns of Leadership Behavior Related to Employee Grievances and Turnover," *Personnel Psychology*, 15, No. 1 (Spring 1962), 43–56.

the supervisor is viewed as Supportive. When the supervisor is considered to have the welfare of subordinates at heart and is accepted as a member of the team, then close attention (high Structure) is welcomed. Under these conditions, subordinates may be delighted to have the supervisor provide them help and show interest in what they are doing. By contrast, when the supervisor is seen as a hostile outsider, this same help and interest is perceived as excessively close supervision and resented.

Conclusion

Supervisors have a great impact on organizational life through their everyday contacts and their influence on motivational systems. We have stressed Support, as a contributor to a satisfactory work environment, and Structure, as a means of strengthening the expectancy relationship between effort and satisfaction. Both are important, although to differing degrees under various circumstances. Further, they are related to each other: excess Structure is felt in insufficient Support; on the other hand, Support makes up for inappropriate Structure.

One thing emerges from all the research: there is no single best way to supervise. Consider a few examples. Foremen on the automobile assembly line can allow subordinates only a limited amount of discretion; here the good foreman is the person who shows concern for the inevitable frustrations induced by the work process (Support). He should be able to obtain adequate supplies for the workers, but otherwise not engage in Structure himself—the assembly line provides plenty of this already. By contrast, the symphony conductor must be a close supervisor (high Structure); there is little opportunity for independent decision making in a symphony orchestra. Technical competence and an ability to coordinate activities is what counts here. Concern for subordinates' feelings is a desirable plus, but essentially secondary, given musicians' identification with making good music. As a consequence, some of the best conductors have been unfeeling autocrats.

Supervisors play an important role, but it would not be wise to exaggerate their significance. Supervisors' freedom to vary their styles of supervision is heavily constrained by factors such as technology, company policy, and union contracts. About the only reward directly under their control is praise; and praise, unaccompanied by other rewards, soon loses its value. Support may be the only element most supervisors are reasonably free to vary. Furthermore, the supervisor is rarely able to deal with subordinates just as individuals. Subordinate behavior is almost always affected by the groups within which they belong, as the next chapter discusses.

Some managers mistakenly assume that providing Structure is invariably resented by employees. Employees, not unlike citizens in a democracy, recognize the contribution of leadership in providing direction, facilitation, and the resolving of intra-group problems. A supervisor who can't or won't "make things happen" is resented as too passive. The supervisor/leader has an important function to perform in aiding people to get their work done, in obtaining needed resources and support from outside, unambiguously specifying assignments, and setting the "rules of the game." Living in anarchy or in an excessively ambiguous, ill-defined work setting is discomforting, to say the least.

Only in such supervisory structured environments is it possible for the employee to believe that there will be some correspondence between effort and accomplishment and reward.

group behavior: organization consequences

We have seen that social needs are among the most powerful and compelling on-the-job motivations. People who make up organizations behave as members of groups, and that membership influences their attitudes and behavior toward the job and the organization. Groups may exercise far stronger control over their members than management does, and management must work through these groups to achieve its ends. But before considering problems of the leadership of groups, we must first understand why groups develop and how they function.

Why groups are formed

Companionship

The need for relationships with others is one of the strongest and most constant of human drives. As we have discovered, many jobs call forth only a small fraction of a person's total abilities. To management, someone may be just another unit of labor or a number; to friends on the job, that person is an individual. To colleagues, employees can be themselves and express their true feelings.

Research indicates that employees who have no opportunity for close social contact find their work unsatisfying, and this lack of satisfaction often reflects itself in low production and high turnover and absenteeism. Many years ago, Elton Mayo observed that employees in a textile plant who worked at isolated jobs were highly dissatisfied and consistently failed to meet production standards. Staggered rest periods helped a little. But when the company permitted these workers to take rest periods *as a group,* production and satisfaction both increased.[1] Similarly, researchers in hospitals have discovered that maids feel uncomfortable when they work only in the company of high-status personnel (doctors, nurses, etc.) with whom they cannot associate with ease. Several hospitals have found that when three or four maids are grouped together as a team, turnover falls and a much better job is done.

Identification

The difference may be subtle, but people want more than just to have friends: they want to *belong.* Feeling part of a large organization is often a vague, nebulous attachment; but sharing experiences with immediate colleagues is among the most meaningful and potent sources of job satisfaction.

Extensive studies during World War II indicated that soldiers' willingness to show bravery and make sacrifices was correlated not with loyalty to country or understanding of the war issues, but with loyalty to the immediate group. In other words, men committed acts of heroism that were motivated largely by the desire not to let their buddies down.

Having learned this lesson, the army abandoned its system of bringing individual replacements into combat units and instead began rotating units as a whole.

Other studies indicate that smaller groups tend to enjoy higher satisfaction than do large ones. In large departments where everybody does the same job, people find it hard to form stable social groupings and often have low morale. Many companies with large secretarial pools are putting up waist-high barriers on the office floor to encourage the development of social groups and team spirit. In part, the extraordinary success of Japanese companies is due to the sense of belonging they engender in their employees.

Understanding from friends

The daily work routine is rich in opportunities for frustrations and tension. Whether we are harassed by an overbearing customer, an obstreperous typewriter, or a picayune inspector, we all seek a sympathetic ear, preferably from someone who has had similar experiences and can thus understand our troubles. Organizations that lack this outlet sometimes rely on the clumsy and expensive system of employee counseling, in which outsiders hear out employees' troubles.

Guide to acceptable behavior

Whenever we are thrown into a new social situation, we are not sure how we are expected to behave. Our work days are filled with ambiguous situations. How much time should I take for a coffee break? Must all copy be shown to the advertising manager? Even where there are established rules, one question remains: Is everybody expected to live by the letter of the law?

---

[1] Elton Mayo, *The Human Problems of an Industrial Civilization* (Boston: Graduate School of Business Administration, Harvard University, 1946), pp. 42–52. It should be noted that other factors were introduced that contributed to the improved morale and productivity. The work was broken up into self-contained tasks, and the rest periods themselves helped combat fatigue and monotony.

Most employees do not want to violate the generally accepted "rules of the game"; at the same time they do not want to conform to restrictive rules ignored by everyone else. They want to know the "right" thing to do. The group plays an important role by providing all its members with a kind of guide to correct behavior—correct not in terms of any written policies, but in terms of what is actually acceptable.

Help in solving work problems

A new sales clerk may not be sure how to handle a complicated problem of returning some merchandise. Lab technicians may be hesitant about asking the boss to repeat instructions, yet they are afraid of ruining the experiment without additional information. In each case the employees turn to fellow workers for assistance, often preferring this source of help.

The group's solution to a problem may differ from what management expects, and it may even be more efficient. Red tape is eliminated; shortcuts evolve; informal channels of communication are established to cut across department boundaries. By the same token, work groups may also engage in featherbedding and work restriction.

Many jobs that appear superficially dull and routine are made more interesting by the individual ingenuity and spontaneity encouraged and protected by the group. Although it may appear to the casual observer that management has defined a rigid series of job requirements, work groups provide a setting that spurs the individual to modify the job situation to make it more satisfactory: for example, extra work breaks can be obtained because employees spell one another; unpleasant tasks assigned to one person can be rotated or shared by group agreement. The key point here is that all of these new activities take initiative and energy. Thus, on jobs that appear to require little of either, an outlet can be found in the informal modifications of the environment that are sanctioned by the group.

Certain jobs can be done by isolated workers, but working as a group often results in higher individual motivation and a faster work pace. Even schools are experimenting successfully with teaming students together, rather than allowing them to work alone or wait their turns to recite. Team members provide mutual help, which increases the rate of learning.

Protection for the membership

Groups help to protect their members from outside pressures and authority. As we shall discuss later, groups often resist management's demands for additional output. Most dynamic organizations change work methods and routines faster than the individual can adjust to them. A determined work group can materially alter the pace at which these changes are introduced.

Without a sense of group allegiance, an individual worker's behavior could injure fellow workers. The work group often disciplines members who try to earn the supervisor's favor by squealing on fellow employees, by turning out too much work, or by failing to help their fellow workers on the job. Group members often agree on the level of output each will put forth, so that no one member will outperform the others.

At one time, a market analysis office was required to prepare reports for top management. As time passed, the analysts made these reports increasingly elaborate, using colored graphs, photographic reproductions, and more detailed data. Some of this window dressing had real value, but most of it was designed to catch the boss's attention. After realizing that they were spending tremendous amounts of uncompensated overtime on their efforts to outdo one another, the analysts agreed on standards to limit their competitive efforts.

The most common target of group power is the immediate manager. Most managers quickly recognize that although they have authority, it would be foolhardy to make certain decisions (see Chapter 6). The members of the group can express their displeasure by cutting down their work pace, sabotaging the work (discretely, of course, so that blame will be hard to place), working strictly according to rules, or making their boss look inept to superiors.

Multiple group memberships

Rarely do participants in an organization belong to just one group. Take Adam Kopka, a mechanical engineer, who is friendly with other workers in his project group: two electrical engineers, a technician, and a chemist. In addition, Kopka is identified with members of two other project groups who report to Ann Fisher, the manager of the Special Projects Department. Kopka also associates with other mechanical engineers scattered through the laboratory. His lunch group and afterhours bowling associates may include still other people. Now each of these groups has a different membership, although there may be a great deal of overlapping. For some purposes, one group is the most important to Adam; for others, another. The mere fact that he belongs to several groups, however, may subject him to considerable stress when there is a conflict between group interests.

Suppose that the mechanical engineers feel that they are losing influence in the laboratory, so they adopt more sophisticated mechanical engineering standards in their design work. As long as Adam is in the company of his fellow mechanical engineers, he feels this is a fine decision. Back in his project group, however, he is under pressure to emphasize other project goals. Now he feels under cross pressures; he cannot be loyal to both groups. His fellow engineers want him to insist on a design that will require substantial mechanical engineering time and effort. The project group wants a simplified design that upper management will quickly approve and fund.

How work groups are formed

When engineers design the plans and technology for a new factory, and when architects design the office layout, they are also designing the social relations that will prevail within the organization. Management determines where people will work and what opportunities they will have to contact each other during the day. It also determines rates of pay, conditions of work, and the various factors that are associated with each job. From these basic elements, long before the first employee enters the building, a sophisticated observer can predict the social relations that will exist within the organization.[2] In most cases, those who work in close proximity with each other will begin

---

[2] For two such studies, see A. Zaleznik, C. R. Christensen, and F. J. Roethlisberger, *The Motivation, Productivity and Satisfaction of Workers: A Prediction Study* (Boston: Graduate School of Business Administration, Harvard University, 1958); and Leonard Sayles, *Behavior of Industrial Work Groups* (New York: Arno, 1977).

interacting; friendship and solidarity will follow. Depending on the number of status elements provided by management, certain groups will "lord it over" those perceived as having less prestige.

But management decision making also omits many factors that become part of the group dynamic. Most jobs are poorly defined by management, and little consideration is given to differences in personality. At the outset, when new employees are thrown together by layout and work location, it will be difficult to achieve a harmonious intermeshing of people and jobs. Bill chatters constantly while working next to Alice, but Alice prefers solitude. Henry sends over undecipherable hand-written documents to Joyce and expects her to make a final check of serial numbers. Joyce and Bill argue about turning the thermostat up or down.

In a few weeks, the rough edges and minor interpersonal frictions will wear away. Alice will change work locations with Joyce. Between them, Bill and Joyce will convince Henry to write more carefully and to do his own checking. Bill and Joyce will work out a way to share the leadership role so that they do not come into direct conflict.

Grouping employees is almost like pushing and pulling on the poles and strings that control a big, amorphous tent so that the tent eventually covers everyone comfortably, both big and small, tall and short. Thus, the crystallization of groups is also a process of filling in the blank spots, making consistent the inconsistent and incompatible elements originally provided by the organization.

The group becomes an organization

Once these groups have been established, there is a dynamic, self-generating process, a spiral that moves faster when issues arise that are of common interest to the members.

> Employees learned that Ellen Phipps, the newly hired analyst, had been openly criticized by a supervisor other than her own at a divisional meeting. This incident, considered to be unfair and a reflection of interdepartmental jealousy, caused the group to pull together. Each group member voiced the same sentiments: "How awful! Shows what we're up against here!" As employees began to complain to each other, it became evident that they shared the same sentiments toward the company. The increased discussion of "poor Ellen" strengthened the sense of grievance as well as the group's cohesiveness.

Thus, we can expect:

New issue ⟶ increased group interaction
Increased interaction ⟶ stronger in-group feelings

Then the group begins to develop an identity as something more than a mere collection of people. A customary way of doing things evolves, a set of stable characteristics that are hard to change. The group becomes an *organization* in itself.

The impact of the group

What happens when the group becomes an organization within the organization? In effect, it contains in miniature the characteristics of the larger institution: it has goals, leadership, rules, and so on.

The group serves to differentiate many activities that the formal organization ignored or assumed to be inconsequential. A value is placed on everything:

- The lunch period beginning at 12 noon is preferable to the one beginning at 12:30.
- Analysts hold more important jobs than coordinators (although their pay is the same).
- The front of the office has higher status than the back.
- Employees hired before the merger deserve greater deference than those who came after.

Every group requires an internal structure. *Structure* here means a set of unique characteristics that determine the members' relationships to one another and to supervision, the standards of conduct that are approved and enforced by the group, its system of rewards and punishments, and its system of communication.

The group differentiates these functions in order to establish a mechanism for regularizing its activities. Placing a value on each activity increases the likelihood that allocations and decisions will be made harmoniously. The right person can now have the appropriate work location and equitable priority in taking vacations. The group becomes a tight little island of certainty in a wider sea of uncertainty.

These aspects of group life are in equilibrium because (1) they are all interrelated, (2) a change in any one of them has an immediate effect on all the others, and (3) the members strongly resist changes in any part of this interrelated system.

Group standards of behavior

Groups are able to eliminate interpersonal frictions and uncertainty in their daily activities by evolving mutually agreed-upon standards of behavior. These routines, SOP's (also called *programs* or *repertoires*), ensure that everyone will respond consistently to given cues. Some responses make work more pleasurable. Members of the accounts receivable department always go to lunch together; those who do not go do not *belong*. Other customs make the job easier or heighten the quality of workmanship. Waiters agree among themselves to share all tips equally and to help one another serve and clear tables during rush hours. If college professors must miss classes, their colleagues will try to stand in for them. All these customs reflect the expectations of group members with respect to one another's behavior.

Probably the most important group standards protect the members of the group against real or imagined outside dangers, particularly from upper management. Production workers may agree on a level of output and exert pressure on those who deviate from it—especially on those who produce more than the accepted bogey (standard). In much the same way, students often resent overachievers in the classroom.

Group standards of good workmanship and high quality often make management's task easier, for the group will deal with the troublemakers and reduce the need for management to impose discipline. If a standard allows workers to be five minutes late, the group will prevent its members from abusing this privilege.

A group of white-collar employees was frequently given the afternoon off when the ball team played a home game. Without any prompting from management, the employees agreed among themselves to come in an hour early to compensate for the short days. Employees who were unenthusiastic about this informal change in the schedule were pressured into conforming, and management gained the extra work time.

Larger groups, particularly in the professions, often maintain ethical standards designed to further the goals of the overall membership. Many professionals—attorneys, accountants, or scientists, are tempted to take short cuts that would save them time and money, and they may be absolutely certain that these short cuts would go undetected. Yet the standards that they have internalized during years of training and association with a professional group hold them to certain fixed patterns of behavior.

These standards may make it harder for management. They may handicap an administrator who finds it difficult to dissuade engineers from goldplating their work (setting higher quality standards than are necessary). Many times, groups urge their members to underproduce, to reject new assignments because they do not approve of the work, and even to coalesce in opposition to the appointment of a new supervisor. Groups may resist almost any directive of management that will require them to change their established practices. A famous study of our government shows how even the President of the United States becomes frustrated when he seeks to impose his priorities on well-established informal department norms.

As Franklin Roosevelt remarked . . . "To change anything in the Navy is like punching a feather bed. You punch it with your right hand and you punch it with your left until you are finally exhausted, and then you find the damm bed just as it was before you started punching. . . ." [3]

Group attitudes and values

In addition to group standards of behavior, there are also group standards of attitude or values. People who work together closely adopt similar attitudes toward the company. Everyone is expected to share opinions such as "Most people don't realize how difficult our job really is"; "Inspection is trying to make our job rough"; and "You've got to have an MBA to be a supervisor."

In many cases, these standards are without factual basis. They are myths that have risen from the group's fears or wishes. Yet the group's acceptance of them is a fact—a fact that management must take into account.

As we have said, the individual becomes wedded to the group as a result of constant association and socializing. Members begin to think and act alike,

---

[3] As quoted in Graham Allison, *Essence of Decision* (Boston, Mass.: Little, Brown, 1971), p. 86. Allison provides a fascinating account of how differences in group standards among segments of the government and armed forces shaped U.S. and Russian activities during the Cuban missile crisis. John Kennedy's experience seems to have been similar to Roosevelt's.

not only in order to enjoy the fruits of group membership, but also because the process of living together reinforces certain feelings and attitudes in the mind of each member. These attitudes may have existed only weakly before, if at all. Before going to work in XYZ Company, a recently graduated chemical engineer considered himself only moderately well-trained and useful. After working in a research group composed entirely of chemical engineers, however, he decided that chemical engineers are the most skilled and valuable group in the laboratory. Through constant interaction with a group, certain predispositions are reinforced, or even distorted, in the minds of the members.

Pressures to conform

Why are most people so anxious to conform to group standards? In the first place, as members of the group, they look at things from the group point of view; they tend to identify with the group; and since it helps them meet their needs, they accept its goals. Even those who have misgivings about the validity of the standards go along anyway, because they want to be highly regarded by their peers. Finally, the group has effective means of punishing those who insist on doing things their own way.

Ostracism is one of the most effective forms of group punishment for deviant behavior. A member who overproduces, fails to share important information, or is officious may become isolated from fellow workers. In extreme cases, no one will talk to the offending workers or even acknowledge their presence. In less extreme cases, deviants may be excluded from ordinary on-the-job social activities. When they have trouble, no one will come to their aid. Sometimes the group resorts to more direct techniques. Someone may "accidentally" let management know about some of the deviants' mistakes. Their equipment or desks may be "adjusted" while they are away.

The punishments devised to enforce group standards are sometimes highly ingenious.

In one office, supervision was lenient in permitting employees to arrive late for work. When one person began to abuse this privilege by arriving very late every day, the group was afraid that management would start to crack down on tardiness. Whenever this employee came in late, fellow workers warmly applauded. This gesture served to emphasize their displeasure and, it was hoped, would encourage management to deal individually with the tardy member.

It would be a mistake to assume that all group members conform. Not only do groups differ in their cohesiveness, but individuals differ in their response to group pressures. Interesting experiments have been designed to assess the susceptibility of individuals to group pressure. At one extreme are those who will deny what their own sense organs tell them to be consistent with group opinions. At the other end of the spectrum are those who are unshakable in their own beliefs, even in highly ambiguous situations when the group provides useful information that should cause them to modify their attitudes.

Group orientation

Groups also differ in their overall orientation. Some groups are used to working with problems that can be quickly solved and for which there is quick feedback; others expect to work months, even years without knowing how successful they have been. This sort of difference exists between manufacturing and research. Some groups are comfortable with uncertainty and risk-taking; others demand clear proof and no ambiguity. Some groups are more aggressive and demand improvements for personal comfort; other groups are more passive and less likely to challenge upper management's decisions.

These differences can lead to problems of cooperation when groups must work together, as in the company described below, which is anxious to launch new products.

> The finance department wants a quick pay-back of any new investment, because it keeps an eye on capital costs and knows the stock market's sensitivity to quarterly profit improvements.
>
> The development department knows that any important breakthrough is going to take several years.
>
> The marketing department is impatient with any constraint. For years the company was dominated by Finance; but now power is shifting to Marketing, and it is eager to show what they can accomplish in expanding the company's product line.

At any meeting, people's statements will be shaped by their group loyalty. If the company forms a new product team, however, and the team continues to meet together regularly, some members may develop loyalty to the team that rivals their loyalty to their department. This can produce conflicts similar to those faced by engineer Kopka (see "Multiple group memberships" at the beginning of the chapter).

Group commitment creates problems

As group members convince themselves that *their* norms, values and perspectives are the correct ones, they inevitably come into conflict with outsiders and often with the larger organization.

Resistance to outsider requests

Although groups seek to regularize their internal relationships, they do not wish to have routine external relations. Most of them learn to be unpredictable to outsiders. That is the group's source of power and status: it can resist demands and challenges. Groups that are predictable (e.g., they can be held to tight workload standards) are easily manipulated, and their internal routines are constantly subject to disruption.

Also, groups tend to exaggerate the differences between themselves and nongroup members—the outsiders—to the point of caricature. They stereotype the outsider.

> From the point of view of manufacturing, researchers are long-haired, sandal-wearing, blue-sky thinkers. From research's point of view, production people are short-sighted, antiintellectual bores.

This caricaturing has several effects. It is a source of cohesion. Interaction is facilitated by conversation about such common symbols as "the stupidities of the outsider." In addition to its role as a rallying cry, these strong cleavages between the group and the outsiders encourage *self-confirming prophecies*.

> Henry had never dealt with accountants until his department was burdened with an "excessive" charge for overhead. By the time he got an appointment with one of the cost accountants he was angry, convinced they were narrow-minded number crunchers. Understandably, his first words were, "Now look, I know you don't care what happens to operating departments, but your stupidities are hurting my. . . ." Before he could finish the tirade, the accountant countered with a few words of her own about managers who tried to "pass the buck for their inefficiencies." As the argument continued, Henry became more convinced that his original prediction—that it would be impossible to reason with accountants—had been correct; they were indeed impossible people.

Obviously, had Henry predicted more reasonably, he might have received a more courteous, responsive reception. Such confrontations provoke the basic competitiveness and hostility among groups.

Each group is seeking to dominate the other; groups refuse to yield to the outsider. (This is the same quest for status that may take place within a group during its formative period.) If the accounting group senses that it is making concessions as a result of complaints from operating units, it assumes that a greater number of accounting decisions and practices soon will be questioned. Its prestige will suffer, and work will be more cumbersome and less satisfying. It is not fun to be at the bottom of the status ladder, to take orders or blame from everyone. It is, however, very satisfying to be deferred to at the top.

Over time, groups in every organization evolve a relatively fixed hierarchy. Although the formal organization chart may show accounting, manufacturing, purchasing, and inspection at the same level, the confrontations we have described result in a consensus, making it clear who outranks whom. Again, group action modifies the formal organization.

Competition and conflict are understandable, since groups are characterized by different orientations and experiences. Sales actually sees customers and understands their problems; Manufacturing never deals directly with the public. Since these departments evolve differing goals (suboptimization), values, and even language, the stage is set for converting a single organization into a set of warring factions.[4]

Suboptimization: group goals

Groups tend to *suboptimize* rather than to commit themselves to the goals of the larger institution. They evolve their own goals, reflecting their own special interests. Engineers demand a new high-temperature test facility; marketers want to hire a social psychologist; machinists need a more generous incentive scheme. These objectives evolve out of the process of working to-

---

[4] A good case study of the differing perspectives of functional groups is provided in Andrew Pettigrew, *The Politics of Organizational Decision Making* (London: Tavistock, 1973).

gether and socializing. Group members convince one another that they need to achieve these goals to help the larger organization accomplish its objectives or to improve their own working conditions. Group members grow righteous about the fairness of their demands.

> The installation of a new computer in the Y Corporation was delayed two years by interdepartmental struggles. The Finance group claimed that new equipment should be under their jurisdiction, but Production and Sales supported the establishment of a new information processing department. Finance feared that the creation of a new department would mean a loss of prestige; Production and Sales believed that the new computer would not be helpful to them if it were placed in an existing department. Thus, costly equipment was wasted for two years because of these special interest groups.

For most groups, goals such as maintaining or increasing their share of the total organization's budget, increasing the quality of their facilities and perquisites, and gaining increased recognition are more important than improving the effectiveness of the total organization. Each group rationalizes any conflict between its particular interests and the concerns of the larger institution by insisting that its goals are consistent with those of the total system. "What's good for us is good for them, too!" Thus, group loyalty can be expensive in terms of overall organizational needs.

Status systems

As soon as a loose aggregation of individuals develops into a genuine group, subtle status differences arise. A rough definition of *status* is "the measure of a person's prestige within the group." It is an index of how important a person is in the pecking order, and the degree of acceptance as a leader.

Status is generated by group interaction. It provides a sense of security. The person whose status is underestimated may become insecure. Consider the senior who is mistaken for a sophomore or the professor who is introduced as a student. Moreover, status helps to guide the interrelationships among group members. A person with high status expects and receives greater deference than one with lower status. Status systems facilitate the operation of any organization.

> A progressive mental hospital endeavored to eliminate all outward distinctions in the dress of patients and staff. The result was chaos. Important identifications could not be made, particularly when bizarre behavior was exhibited. In violation of the formal rules of the hospital, the staff began carrying their keys in easy-to-observe places on their persons, so that they could distinguish patients from fellow staff members.

How is status determined? What criteria do groups use when assigning higher standing to Ms. A than to Mr. B? Some status decisions are based on the attitudes and behavior of management; others are entirely the product of the informal organization of the group.

Determining group status

Status often depends on job title. Obviously, a superintendent is more important than a general foreman, and a general foreman outranks a foreman. Engineers outrank technicians; secretaries are above stenographers.

Pay is an important consideration when determining job status. Higher pay means higher status, and even a difference of a few cents per hour may have a significant effect on a job's status. The new manager may find this bewildering and unreasonable.

> Consider the checkers and the loaders in one newly unionized plant. The checkers received $5.70 an hour; the loaders, $5.60. The checkers insisted that since record-keeping involved greater responsibility and required a high-school education, they should receive a pay increase of at least 30 cents. The loaders felt that since their job required considerable skill and physical effort, they should be paid as much as the checkers. The union succeeded in raising the checkers' salaries by 20 cents and the loaders' salaries by 30 cents—and the checkers were more unhappy than ever.

The frequency of paychecks also helps to determine an employee's status. Some organizations have monthly, semimonthly, and weekly payrolls. Receiving a paycheck on a monthly basis may be less convenient, but it carries much more prestige than receiving a weekly wage, which may be computed on an hourly rather than an annual basis. Sometimes unskilled, casual workers receive their pay every day.

Work schedules are also a useful index. The hourly employees come in at 7:30 A.M., the office clerks at 8:30, and the executives dribble in from 9:00 on—but the executives often work late at night. The freedom to choose one's hours without punching the time clock is a mark of distinction. (Henry Ford once made all his executives punch the time clock, thus lowering even further what was already rock-bottom morale.)

Which employees are allowed to eat in any of the company lunchrooms? Are tables reserved for them? Can they leave the building for morning coffee? Do they receive a daily copy of *The Wall Street Journal?* The allocation of these special privileges follows status lines.

Where does the employee work—in the field or in the home office, in the new building where the important operations occur or over in the "boneyard"? Working near the end of the production line carries more status than working near the beginning, for the finished product is more valuable, and the job is more responsible. In some offices, those who work closest to the boss enjoy the most status. To be able to say "I work on the fourteenth floor" may be the pinnacle of prestige.

Among the job factors that affect status are: clean vs. dirty jobs, freedom from supervision, amount of training and skill required, and opportunity for promotion. A study of the restaurant industry revealed substantial differences in the status enjoyed by employees who worked with various vegetables.

At the top were luxury or decorative items such as parsley, chives, and celery. At the top of the regular vegetables were green beans. Next came spinach and carrots. Next to the bottom were sweet and white potatoes, and onions were considered the most undesirable of all. . . .

Comments of the workers showed that they valued highly vegetables with lack of odor, with crispness, and cleanness in handling, whereas the vegetable that had an odor and that stained the hands or was sloppy to handle was held in low esteem. The low standing of potato peeling is too well known to require comment, but here at least the workers said they preferred potatoes to onions because they did not smell or stain the hands. . . .[5]

Most jobs carry with them certain *symbols* that indicate varying degrees of status. In the army, shoulder insignia denotes officer rank. Paratroop boots, berets, or wings indicate that enlisted men belong to elite outfits (and for this reason, during World War II, many men wore this apparel without authorization).

In industry, too, there are countless widely recognized symbols. Clothing is often an indicator. Executives (and often, office people) wear coats. Foremen wear white shirts. Hourly-paid workers wear work clothes. The chef's hat and the machinist's apron are more specialized symbols of prestige.

Among executives, the type of office helps to determine status. Is it a private office? How large is it? What type of desk does it have? Is a private secretary in evidence?

Status depends on *who one is* as well as what one does—That is, on the attributes or characteristics that the employee brings from community and home. Among the qualities that confer status are education, age, seniority, sex, and ethnic background. A great deal of unrest in contemporary organizations results from the growing resentment against traditional status assignments nurtured by work groups. Covert discrimination against women, blacks, Mexicans, Jews, Catholics—the list could be a long one—fortunately is diminishing, but the problems will not simply disappear.

In many organizations, as management moves to correct past discriminatory practices—for example, in promotion of women or blacks—the company often meets resistance from other employees who are unwilling to give up their status advantage. Individual behavior also influences status. People with pleasant personalities, specialized skills, or leadership traits ordinarily enjoy high status positions, as do those who conform closely to the behavioral standards of the group. The person who does not know how to behave is likely to lose status—in the exclusive club as well as on the factory floor.

Thus, there are several indicators of status, including title, pay, type of work performed, and symbols. In a sense, each is a thermometer that measures a different aspect of status. If all status thermometers give approximately the same reading, status is not likely to cause trouble in the organization. But when thermometers read differently, when the various indicators of status give inconsistent or ambiguous measures, there is often unrest and dissatisfaction.

Status inconsistency and ambiguities

[5] William F. Whyte, *Human Relations in the Restaurant Industry* (New York: McGraw-Hill, 1948), p.36.

More prestigious group members expect to occupy the more prestigious positions. The longer service, better educated employee in a restaurant kitchen would resent being assigned to onion peeling, particularly if junior employees were chopping greens and celery. The violation of a group standard would produce a disturbing status inconsistency. The same problem prevails when an employee is promoted to a department manager's job but is not given the type of office usually assigned to employees of that rank.

Often a supervisor is unaware that the group has drawn subtle distinctions between various jobs, work locations, and types of equipment. Seemingly innocent changes in job assignment or work location may precipitate ill feeling and resentment.

> The metal-drawing department had four kinds of machines. Although all workers in the department received the same wages, there were noticeable differences in ease of the machinery's operation. From the group's point of view, it was a promotion to move to a Z machine, but a demotion to move to an X machine. This attitude made it much harder for management to transfer employees as production needs dictated. It led to many grievances, particularly when management tried to move informal leaders to "lower-ranking" jobs.

Thus, the group's conception of what is right and fair is integral to understanding employee reactions to the work situation. Status anxiety may be expected where there is status inconsistency. An employee with a prestigious family and educational background, working on a low-status job would be uncomfortable and likely to demonstrate aggression. Someone without a college degree working with colleagues who have degrees would be insecure and might overreact to a critical comment by the supervisor. Thus, *status anxiety* can mean "hypersensitivity," a condition that explains many communications and morale problems within organizations.

Trouble can develop when the status of an individual or group has not been clearly established. In a sense, group relations are characterized by a culture lag: status relationships do not keep up with technological and organizational changes. Newly created groups suffer status anxieties, that become evident as the group reaches out for recognition and symbols of prestige, such as office space.

> The bookkeeping-clerical operations of a large bank always occupied a status position beneath that of the front-office groups that dealt with the public. With the addition of expensive computers, the back-room operations took on added importance. In fact, some of the key computer and systems specialists were paid higher salaries than were the loan officers and other front-office personnel. Understandably, there was much resentment when these computer people began to request the special perquisites—such as executive dining room privileges—that had been enjoyed in the past only by the high-status officers. It took several years for top computer management to attain high status.

In such cases, management is confronted with a dilemma. Management argues that each group should be treated equally; yet, this policy is bound to generate trouble if status distinctions are ignored. The manager's problem is complicated by the fact that low-status departments may be struggling to get ahead and raise their relative position in the organizational community.*

Excessive status consciousness may cause as much trouble for management as total disregard of status distinctions. Status systems can be outmoded by dynamic organizations and thus cannot or should not always be observed. Employees ranked as low in status by the group may be equipped to handle more responsible jobs.

Emergence of functional roles and informal leadership

In addition to a ranking system, the group also provides itself with additional specialized roles. One or more members will serve as "gatekeepers," connecting the group to other parts of the organization. In R&D labs, researchers with contacts in production or marketing perform a critical function by transferring information; [6] other group members represent their colleagues in negotiations with management for improvements in amenities and perquisites. Another activist group member helps to reconcile squabbling employees, thus facilitating the internal regularity of relationships. Still others may be an excellent source of technical information related to work problems.

All of these group-appointed specialists gain status from recognition by their colleagues. These specialists are fulfilling leadership roles parallel to the leadership role handled by a formal supervisor. Understandably, they are often called *informal leaders.* Management attempts to make use of these influential employees to gain information or to help evolve a consensus on some subject in dispute. The easiest way for management to identify who is playing these roles is through observation. Informal leaders will be those whom

1. others contact more frequently than they do nonleaders.
2. the group is most likely to follow. When an informal leader expresses an idea or suggests an action, most of the group will concur.

Managers need to be aware of another characteristic of these informal leaders: they engage in *uncertainty absorption.* When asked for advice, informal leaders may filter information to transform ambiguous and complex issues into a simple, direct conclusion.[7] At times, such simplifications and conclusions can be wrong or misleading.

* Competition for improvements in working conditions and benefits appear to be most common among groups that are more than halfway up the ladder. Their position is somewhat ambiguous, since they are almost the best, but not quite. They seem to have a grudge against the company, and they seize on real or imagined slights. If they are unionized, these groups utilize the grievance procedure to put pressure on both union and management.

[6] Cf. Michael Tushman, "Special Boundary Roles in the Innovation Process," *Administrative Science Quarterly,* Vol. 22 (December 1977), 587–606.

[7] This concept was introduced by Herbert Simon and James March, *Organizations* (New York: Wiley, 1958), p.165.

> The marketing group was eager to know when the corporate lab would come up with a substitute for the newly banned phosphates. When they asked the best-known project leader, Sue Cohen, her answer was that the substitute should be ready for final testing "in a few weeks." There were still a number of unresolved technical questions—this type of research always has uncertainties—but Sue did not think it would be useful to communicate all the details to Marketing; after all, Marketing wouldn't understand anyway.

Thus, every group produces informal leaders—individuals with high status who are followed by other members of the group. Someone must take the initiative to solve the group's problem. The leader circulates through the group, urging a united front for dealing with problems or devising punishment for an uncooperative fellow member. When developing consensus on what needs to be done, a successful leader is careful to sound out the members and to smooth over internal differences of opinion by persuasion and suggested compromises. At times the leader represents the group in dealing with the supervisor, the union, or other work groups.

In summary, the group's ability to survive is aided by the leader who

1. initiates action
2. facilitates a consensus
3. provides a link or liaison between the group and the outside world: managers, other work groups, the union

Group cohesiveness

There are significant differences among groups as well as among the members within each group. One of the most important differences is the degree of internal unity or cohesion. All the elements of group behavior that we have mentioned are influenced by this factor. If the group is united, it is probable that all members will conform strictly to group standards, partially as a result of heightened pressures to conform. It is also likely that a small leadership core will represent without challenge the feelings of all members. By definition, cohesive groups are internally consistent in their measures of status; they are more likely to act in unison when their expectations are violated by management, one of their own members, or even another group.

New employees may find it difficult to gain acceptance by highly cohesive groups, and this can create problems when management must fill a vacancy. There may be a trial period—like a fraternity initiation—during which newcomers must prove themselves. The new members must show that they are willing to live up to the norms of the group, that their personalities are acceptable, and that they accept their status within the group. Exclusiveness can come as an unpleasant shock to the unprepared employee.

For management, it is not enough simply to recognize that such differences exist among groups. Management must also predict the conditions that will produce either united or disunited groups. From our own research and that of others, the following factors emerge as some of the determinants of group cohesion:

- High-status jobs
- Relatively small size
- All work very similar in job content
- Clear physical boundaries setting off the group from others
- Ease of communication among members
- Absence of internal competition for promotion and recognition

Changes in accustomed ways of doing things and sudden cancellations of prerogatives will also draw employees together. Management opposition to solidarity may serve only to strengthen the group.

Further, a group is likely to be stronger and more cohesive if it has engaged successfully in cooperative action in the past. This is the familiar circular pattern: cohesive groups are more successful, and successful groups are more cohesive. Success also depends on whether the group occupies a strategic position in the flow of work and on many other factors.

In contrast, when members find that their group does not protect them or win benefits for them, they are unlikely to abide by group standards. In fact, members may begin to seek other affiliations that offer more security and status. This defection further weakens the group, which then becomes less and less successful.

The agony and the ecstasy

Clearly, individuals require group support. They try to develop group structures where these structures do not exist. In the process, relationships become easier and more regular, and commitments and identification become more intense. All of this can help—but also hinder—the larger organization.

Highly cohesive groups can be intolerant of change and unmindful of the needs of "outsiders." The standards that helped to eliminate interpersonal frictions can also inhibit acceptance of new procedures, equipment, and people. An organization can become frozen if there is strict adherence to the group status system and work standards. Intergroup cooperation can come to a standstill.

If the organization faces a dynamic environment where change is imperative, management may consider methods of reducing the culture lag introduced by rigid groups. The increasing use of task forces, special projects and teams, and interdepartmental committees reflect an effort to unfreeze group-based attitudes by mixing a variety of employees in temporary systems.

. . . the creation of changes in persons involves, essentially, a changing of the cultures in which the person finds himself. Isolation from the ordinary environment tends to shear away the person's or group's preoccupation with, and allegiance to, "things as they are." [8]

---

[8] Matthew Miles, ed., "On Temporary Systems," in *Innovation in Education* (New York: Bureau of Publications, Teachers College, Columbia University, 1964), p. 454.

Commitment to group goals and values can also produce a strong momentum that will overcome efforts to change the direction or reduce the size or status of a particular program. Long after technology or markets have changed, members of an established group can insist that their work is as useful and productive as ever. While in the early stages of any new development, group loyalties and enthusiasms might have been most useful; later they could become a handicap.

Conclusion

In this chapter we have attempted to analyze one important component of the organization: aggregations of employees, or groups. Although the boundary lines that determine group membership are affected by management's job assignments and supervisory practices, each group develops a momentum of its own. As a result, there is an informal organizational structure that does not appear on any organization chart.

People join groups for a wide variety of reasons. Ultimately, it seems that group members are searching for satisfactions not provided directly by the job or by the supervisor—satisfactions such as companionship and protection.

Informal groups have a life of their own. Members of each group develop their own methods and perspectives; they have their own leaders and a minutely defined status hierarchy. These are the stable, enduring components of group life, informal organization that management dare not ignore.

Management sometimes tries to evade this reality by emphasizing the organization as a whole, even to the point of trying to disperse destructive cliques. Yet, loyalty to the group, to one's fellow workers, is much stronger than loyalty to the larger organization. Indeed, the only way management can develop overall loyalty is to encourage teamwork and informal relations. The group may exercise far stronger control over its members than does management itself.

Other managements seek to bypass the group by telling supervisors to deal with each employee as an individual. It is certainly true that supervisors must spend much time dealing with the personal needs and idiosyncrasies of subordinates, yet it is unrealistic to consider the group merely as the sum of the individuals concerned.

We like to think of organizations as being unified in seeking to achieve their goals. More realistic is the view that organizations are heterogeneous; each major group has its own goals and seeks to win benefits to further its narrow interests. These group actions grow out of an increased differentiation of elements within the groups' jurisdiction. Jobs, the physical environment, and individual members take on new values as the groups reassess the status of people and their work. As a result, new constraints—behavior standards, values, and goals—develop within the larger organization. In addition, the group seeks to differentiate itself from outsiders, often resulting in increased friction with anyone who does not belong.

the supervisor as group leader

Ignoring the group, Chapter 4 looked at the role of the supervisor. Chapter 5 dealt with informal leaders, but not with the formally appointed leader called the supervisor. Here we combine the two and look at the complex role of the supervisor as a group leader.

The previous chapter suggests that an effective informal leader follows the social norms of the group, takes various actions to strengthen the group internally, and represents the group to the outside world. As we see in this chapter, successful supervisors seek to perform these same functions. Indeed in many situations successful supervisors are accepted by their subordinates as informal leaders.

In analyzing the role of the supervisor as a group leader, this chapter makes the following interrelated points:

1. Much of the supervisor's authority comes from the group, which would resent and resist authority unless it accepted the supervisor as *legitimate*.

2. On the other hand, the supervisor can do much to strengthen or weaken the group.

3. Through various forms of formal and informal participation, the supervisor enlists the commitment of group members to organizational objectives.

Legitimacy

From a formal point of view, managers receive their authority from above, from their superiors who define the managers' powers and responsibilities and who sometimes write these down in an organizational handbook. Another view is that managers receive their *real* authority from below, from their subordinates, and that the statement of authority from above is merely a hunting license; for in spite of statements of formal powers, if their subordinates are unwilling to obey them, then they have no real authority.

How can managers induce subordinates to obey them? Of course, they can use bluster and force and can threaten to discharge those who resist. If enough pressure is applied, then subordinates may comply. But as we saw in Chapter 2, their compliance may be grudging and resentful.

Alternatively, subordinates may wish to comply because the organization is doing what they want to do themselves. Individuals lost in the wilderness gladly take directions from a leader who seems to be taking them back to civilization. Symphony orchestra members exercise little autonomy, but they follow their conductor willingly because they want to create good music. Similarly, a junior research scientist will obey the boss with enthusiasm if he or she sees the boss's directions as helping solve his or her research problems. Note that in all these case the subordinates would have followed their boss's instructions even if he didn't have the formal title. They obey because their ends are identical with those of their leader.

Relatively few cases involve sheer coercion or the boss telling subordinates to do what they really wanted to do in the first place. Most situations occupy a middle ground (sometimes called a *zone of indifference*): Subordinates obey the boss because they accept the *legitimacy* of his order, that is, because according to their norms and values it is expected and proper for the boss to give a particular order and for them to obey it.

Thus, supervisors support their legitimacy by establishing a series of relationships with subordinates. But they must also recognize that the process of legitimization occurs in a group and cultural setting; and in that setting, the view of one person is greatly influenced by the views of associates. The group makes it easier for the boss, though, for it often informally disciplines those who violate group expectations by not obeying legitimate orders.

As we mentioned in Chapter 5, every group has customs, proprieties, and expectations that its members believe are proper. A manager who violates these standards acts in an "illegimate" fashion and does so at his or her peril. Subordinates can retaliate in numerous ways, ranging from refusal to do more than their normal share in time of emergency to wildcat strikes and sabotage. In contrast, the manager who respects the group's standards often wins its cooperation and, at times, finds that the group will modify its standards in management's favor. To take an example of the impact of such standards:

Train crews in a marshaling yard were handling 150 trains a day. Through short cuts (often violating safety rules) they were able to finish their work in six hours. The rest of the time they could sleep or read.

We can identify several standards in this condition: (1) 150 trains a day represent a proper work load; (2) the remaining time can be spent as the crews wish; and (3) certain rules will not be enforced.

CHAPTER 6
the supervisor as group leader

Then management decided that since the crews had so much free time they could handle 200 trains. Immediately the crews began to follow all the rules. They would never move a train even a few feet without having someone to go to the rear and wave a red flag. As a result, the crews put in a full day's work, but productivity fell to 50 trains a day. Soon management gave up its demands for 200.

Here management violated group standards, broke the implicit contract, and acted in what the group felt was an illegitimate fashion. The crews retaliated in a way that left management helpless.

In the remainder of this chapter we shall consider what the group views as the legitimate use of authority. First, however, a word of warning: though we shall use the word *group* rather freely here, you should remember that social groups tend to overlap and that any given employee may belong to several groups with varying expectations (see Chapter 5).

How can a manager exercise power legitimately? The answer seems to depend on at least three factors: (1) his job legitimacy, that is, on his right to hold his power in the first place; (2) the way he behaves on the job; and (3) the demands he makes on subordinates. These three factors are obviously interrelated; for example, the manager can ask more from subordinates if his right to hold his job is legitimate, and if he makes his demands in a legitimate fashion.

To some extent people obey leaders just because they are invested with the symbols or titles of authority. Soldiers are trained to obey those who wear officers' insignia, regardless of the individual merits of the wearer. Royal coronations and presidential inaugurations transfer a certain "magic" to kings and presidents.

Job legitimacy

Nevertheless, every group has definite expectations about what qualifications their leader should possess. A leader who fails to live up to these expectations is considered unfit for the job—and this holds true for a foreman or a President of the United States. The important thing is that the leader be respected.[1]

Background. Certainly there are expectations about the leader's background: her ethnic group, his college or degree (a Dean without a Ph.D. or a hospital director without an M.D. can find it harder to win support from subordinates).

The nature of the qualifications subordinates expect in their leaders will, of course, vary substantially from job to job. Thus, in many American companies the fair-haired boy or girl who is promoted solely on the basis of family connec-

---

[1] Respect need not mean liking. As Machiavelli advised his Prince, it is often better to be feared than to be loved.

tions may find it hard to win cooperation. On the other hand, family connections are almost essential if one is to be considered a legitimate king (and, in some European firms, a legitimate company president). In some organizations a manager is expected to have worked up through the ranks, and an outsider who is brought in over the head of someone subordinates feel deserves the job will have to face strong resentment (though "proper" behavior may ultimately win him respect). In other cases, it is traditional for leaders to be brought in through special channels; thus, for a long time in the army, officers won greater respect if they started their careers in West Point, rather than as privates. But traditions can change: In recent years the army has made it easier for enlisted personnel to become officers; on the other hand, many large companies have increasingly reserved management ranks for college graduates.

Technical ability. It is important for supervisors to be technically skilled in their work, even if they rarely practice their skill on the job.[2] Indeed, subordinates often subject a new supervisor to a period of testing and initiation to determine whether he measures up to their standards. If subordinates feel their supervisor is master of skills they themselves regard as important, then in a way he has beaten them in a fair race—he has earned his job and is respected for doing so. To put it another way, managers will find their authority more easily accepted if they are authorities *on*, as well as authorities *over*.

The feeling that the boss should show technical skill is particularly strong among people who take pride in their work and closely identify with their occupation (for example, building tradesmen, professors, or research scientists). With such subordinates, Structure is rejected unless one is technically proficient. Technical skills are also very important where close coordination is required between members of a work team—as in flying a plane, conducting an orchestra, or operating on a patient.

Managerial behavior

Subordinates normally have well-defined expectations about how a "good" manager should behave, both on and off the job, though these may vary greatly from one situation to another.

In giving orders, for example, authority may be emphasized or underplayed. North Americans tend to resent the outward display of authority, and often feel it proper that their bosses go through the forms of consulting with them. Engineers, scientists, and professors seem to hold this expectation particularly strongly. But there are many other cultures in which a boss is expected to be firm.

Of course, all supervisors are expected to be fair and to treat people in a "nice way." But the nice way in the university would be very out of place in the army. An officer, for example, is expected to have a "military bearing"; a professor should display a "scholarly attitude." Some groups expect their supervisors to "act like a boss," and subordinates take advantage of them if

---

[2] The leader's technical skill need not duplicate that of his followers. A pilot can't overhaul an engine; perhaps a conductor can't play all the instruments in an orchestra; yet both derive status from their technical ability.

they don't rule with an iron hand; in other groups it is a great compliment to say that the supervisor "doesn't act like a boss."

This much is clear: a manager should become familiar with subordinates' expectations as soon as possible. The manager may eventually wish to change these expectations, but he must recognize the likelihood of resistance if he tries (see Chap. 9).

Social distance. Perhaps the most subtle of these expectations about managerial behavior concerns the social distance (or status differentiation) the boss should keep from subordinates. In most situations, a boss is expected to be "friendly" (and this is particularly true where the American tradition of equality prevails), but the meaning of friendliness varies greatly from one situation to another. Usually there are well-defined expectations about how close the relationship should be. Military officers should be aloof from enlisted personnel, for example; deans should invite all new faculty to dinner (but not visit their classes); plant managers are expected to make "howdy rounds" in the plant and to be good fellows at the company picnic (but perhaps only there); supervisors should show interest in their subordinates' vacation stories and (in some plants but not others) go out drinking with them on payday.

A wide variety of factors is relevant here. At sea, there is a traditional social gap between officers and seamen. This distance is reinforced by means of separate uniforms and separate eating and sleeping arrangements. Yet this gap is rapidly breaking down under the impact of automation, and on smaller ships the traditional formality tends to dissolve. Further, there is more of it in the navy than in the merchant marine, and on European ships (where officers and sailors may have very different backgrounds) than on American ships.

The question of expected social relationships is closely tied with technology. In a scientific laboratory, a premium is placed on widespread communication of information and widespread participation. Here status differences are expected to be played down, and social relations are close. But where instant obedience is expected (as in the armed services), social distance (and frequent rotation of supervisors) reinforces legitimacy. Indeed, it is feared that if enlisted personnel become socially close to their officers and learn their personal inadequacies, they may begin to question the officers' orders.[3]

Appropriate social distance varies even more among countries. Australians insist on greater affability than do some stiffly correct, status-conscious Europeans; North Americans may fall in between.

Finally, the youth rebellion of the last two decades has considerably changed expectations about social distance. Respect for authority has declined, and supervisors are expected to be less aloof than they once were. This process will be accelerated by job redesign and other changes that give workers greater

---

[3] Technological change, however, has largely outmoded the brave infantrymen of Tennyson's day, whose job was "not to reason why," and put in their place technicians who are expected to make decisions on their own. Along with this, the social aloofness of officers has tended to decline. (Morris Janowitz, *Sociology and the Military Establishment,* 3rd ed. Beverly Hills: Sage, 1974.)

freedom or require that supervisors and subordinates interact with each other more frequently. Social distance facilitates obedience, but inhibits communications, and the pendulum has swung toward closer boss-subordinate relations.

Work customs. Managers should also be sensitive to the indirect effect of their actions on work customs or norms. Take status, for example. Assigning younger salesclerks to advantageous store locations may enable them to earn higher commissions than their seniors, thereby splitting the work force into two hostile groups. Even innocent decisions about parking lots or the arrangement of tables in the cafeteria may upset delicate social relationships and lead to turmoil and antagonism.

Time-honored social relationships sometimes conflict with management's formal rules. Since many offices permit employees almost unlimited free local phone calls, a new manager almost precipitated a strike when she tried to stop this practice in her office.

Work demands

On most jobs, an implicit contract between boss and subordinates governs what work the boss may legitimately demand. Legitimate demands are obeyed almost automatically; excessive ones meet resistance. Implicit bargaining plays a very important role here.

Most employees realize that they assume certain obligations when they accept a job, and they acknowledge that the boss has a right to insist on a "fair day's work." In effect, they feel, "Since I work here, I must obey orders and try to do a job. I realize that it is the boss's job to get work out and the company's job to make money. So I'll do my *fair* share."

But employees have definite expectations of what constitutes their "fair share." They resent what they regard as "being taken advantage of." As we saw in the train marshaling case, they resist producing more than their usual amount, and those who do so are subject to punishment by their peers.

Employees generally question working outside the limits of their customary job description (whether written or not). Regardless of the union contract, for example, a group may consider it unacceptable for maintenance personnel to be asked to do production work—or vice versa.

A manager's instructions are more likely to be accepted if they seem to be concerned with getting the job done, rather than with the arbitrary exercise of authority for authority's sake. Employees object to being given busy work after their "fair day's work" is done.

On the other hand, technical instructions concerned with the job are considered legitimate—unless the individual making them is felt to be incompetent. Similarly, subordinates accept orders that are obviously required by the situation. They resent rules that are imposed for no apparent reason. Thus, no-smoking rules are hard to enforce unless employees are convinced there is a real fire hazard. The manager must be able to justify rules as essential to getting the job done, maintaining plant safety, and so forth.

Conversely, subordinates often feel that the boss who fails to enforce legitimate regulations is remiss. Mine workers in one situation placed the blame for accidents on a foreman, since it was his job to see that rules were followed.

Employees often expect the boss to show *leniency,* to ignore minor or technical violations of rules as long as the job is getting done. As we have seen, they also expect that under unusual conditions (say, when they have bad days) the boss will give them a break and not insist even on the fair day's work. This expectation also involves a form of implicit bargaining, for in exchange for this "good turn" the employee may feel some obligation to work harder in genuine emergencies.

To conclude, we have seen that legitimacy is largely determined by subordinate expectations, and that these expectations in turn are established and enforced *in part* by the various forms of implicit bargaining. At first, the bargain may be little more than an armed truce; but over time, expectations will be that the bargain *should* be observed by both parties. Gradually, expectations "harden" and acquire what anthropologists have called the "crust of custom."

A system in equilibrium

Thus, the manager-subordinate relationship can be conceived of as a system in equilibrium. Strong forces operate against all parties to restore them to equilibrium, should they ever stray away. The manager is confined and restricted by subordinates' expectations. Accepting those expectations makes the managerial job rather easy; ignoring or flouting them is risky, though sometimes—if the organization is to deal successfully with external challenges—the risk must be taken. Before doing so, however, the manager should pause and consider the move and perhaps devise an approach that will achieve his objectives without a frontal attack on what subordinates feel to be right and proper.

It should be emphasized that expectations arise through means other than implicit bargaining. Some expectations are established by the culture generally, and efforts to change them solely through the group are doomed to failure. The manager's task is made even more difficult because subordinates may belong to a number of different groups, each with its own set of expectations. Indeed, there are times when expectations are quite difficult to determine.

Although supervisors misconstrue their function if they try to win popularity contests, they should also recognize that whatever they do, they do in a group context. Their effectiveness depends to a large extent on the willingness of group members to accord them legitimacy.

Building a work team

Not long ago a nationally known concern distributed to its supervisors a pamphlet entitled "Deal with Individuals, not Groups." Its message was simple: individuals, if properly handled, will work for management's objectives; groups will inevitably oppose management. Cater to the employee's competitive spirit, reward individual efforts, break up attachment to the group, the argument ran, and you will be surprised how much the employee puts out.

Fostering competition is not management's only means of breaking up group cohesion. As we saw in Chapter 5, groups can be made so large and heterogeneous that team spirit becomes difficult to develop. Similar effects can be obtained by modifying technology and work arrangements. In restaurants even the height of the counter separating waitresses from kitchen personnel affects their ability to work together.

Advantages and disadvantages of cohesion. Of course, certain dangers arise when the work group becomes too tightly knit. Such a group may be reluctant to accept new employees as members, particularly when they belong to minority groups. Further, though there may be more cooperation within the group, cooperation with outsiders may suffer. Thus competition and ill feeling may develop among rival groups.

On the other hand, members of cohesive groups gain satisfaction from working together. Turnover and absenteeism are frequently lower. Further, it may be easier to supervise a closely knit group, since its members provide Structure and Support for each other. The supervisor need not repeat information and orders to every member; the informal leader will act as an effective channel of communications to and from the supervisor. A quarreling, disorganized group finds it hard to work together and may direct its aggression against management in the form of poor workmanship, sabotage, grievances, and wildcat strikes.

But does cohesion increase productivity? Research suggest that cohesive groups produce either substantially more than the average or somewhat less. Particularly where the job requires close cooperation among the members of a work team, the mere existence of cohesion makes work more efficient. In general, however, cohesion results in higher productivity only if the group accepts management's demands for higher production as legitimate. If the group is unified for the purpose of protecting itself against management, then greater cohesion will mean less production. All cohesion means is that the members will adhere more closely to the group standards, whatever they are.

Where management cannot develop groups with goals compatible to organizational objectives, it may become necessary to resort to measures that will weaken or eliminate informal groups. Continuous movements of personnel, particularly those showing leadership potential, and supervisory patterns that stress dealing with the individual are two possible ways of keeping strong groups from developing.[4] In most instances, however, given a sound overall program of human relations, it is in management's interest to promote teamwork.

Developing teamwork. What can supervisors do to develop teamwork? Most important, they can develop sensitivity to the facts of group life discussed in the previous chapter. They can familiarize themselves with the social geography of the groups they supervise and learn to identify the patterns of leadership, status and friendship that exist within them. Understanding these patterns can help in a host of ways. Also supervisors can:

- Put friends together. True, this arrangement may lead to more talking on the job, but a number of studies suggest that production is higher when employees

[4] These were among the techniques used by the communists during the Korean War to break down the morale and cohesion of American prisoners.

are permitted to pick their work mates, and this is particularly true where the work requires cooperation.
- Provide special help to isolates, the lonely employees who have no friends. Informal leaders may assist in the isolates' integration.
- Make sure that new employees are carefully introduced to the group. Many companies have a "big brother" or "big sister" system in which an older employee familiarizes every new employee with the formal and informal requirements on the job.
- Assign personnel in a way that will avoid the growth of conflicting subgroups.
- Cut down on transfers *between* departments, within the limits of union seniority rules.
- Rotate jobs *within* the group, in order to strengthen each employee's identification with the team as a whole, rather than with the individual job.
- Locate coffee machines and schedule workbreaks so as to facilitate off-the-job contacts.
- Provide financial incentives. Group incentives may do more to encourage cooperation than individual bonus plans do.
- For employees who are constantly moved from department to department (such as maintenance personnel or internal auditors) provide some opportunities to work together as a common group and to feel they have a home base.
- Establish self-managing work teams and organize group meetings to discuss key problems. Both forms of participation contribute to group cohesion.
- Be aware of antagonism and conflicts among group members and seek to mediate and resolve these. If conflict is serious, Organization Development techniques may be necessary.

Developing group participation

Beyond representing the subordinates with higher management, many supervisors have discovered that they can obtain better results by giving their subordinates an opportunity to participate in decision making, either through consulting with the group or by allowing subordinates to make and implement decisions by themselves.

Industrial engineering in a metal-plating department has been trying for a long time to figure out an equitable way of dividing up work. The operation was unusually complex and erratic, and every time the engineers made a suggestion the workers were quick to prove that it was unfair to someone. The engineers were about to give up in disgust when the workers asked, "Why not let us decide?" In a short while they had worked out job allocations that even the engineers agreed were superior to theirs.

Participation of this sort leads to gains all around. Management gains, in that better decisions are often made by people close to the job. When subordinates are given the necessary freedom (as in self-managing work groups), they often do an impressive job of working out their own methods of scheduling, quality control, and so forth. They develop easier and better ways to do the job; they exchange ideas on how to improve productivity; and they question their boss's ideas and provide him with additional information he can use in making decisions. (In expectancy theory terms, group decision making can increase the likelihood that effort will lead to production.

> The Superintendent of machine operations was convinced by the Safety Department that long-sleeved shirts were a hazard, even when rolled up. So she posted a notice that beginning next Monday wearing long sleeves on the job would be prohibited.
>
> Monday morning, four workers showed up with long sleeves. Given the choice of working without shirts or cutting their sleeves off, they refused to do either and were sent home. The union filed a sharp grievance, asking for back pay for time lost.
>
> Then the Personnel Department stepped in. The rule was suspended for a week, and a special meeting was called with the union grievance committee. The safety director explained that if a worker's sleeve got caught in a machine his or her whole arm might be ripped off. The union agreed to the rule provided it was extended to management (who originally had been exempt on the grounds that they didn't get close enough to the machines). The next Monday, the rule was reinstated. A few workers, forgetfully, arrived in long sleeves. The others handed them a pair of scissors and insisted that the offending sleeves be eliminated on the spot. Later, a union vice-president and a company time-study expert were treated in the same way. The rule was in full effect.

Furthermore, employees who have had the experience of regulating themselves are far more capable of making sound decisions when emergencies arise. Since they make the decisions by themselves, there is less need to refer every problem to the manager. As a consequence, the manager can concentrate on long-term planning and handling relations with other departments.

Employees gain the satisfaction of exercising greater control over their work environment, as well as the feeling of success from having accomplished something by themselves. (As expectancy theory puts it, their effort is rewarded by a feeling of achievement.) Just the experience of working together develops cohesion and enhanced morale, especially for employees high on n Affiliation.

Participation is often a means of generating commitment. People are willing to work harder for objectives they set by themselves. (For example, one of the best ways to raise money for a charity is to have rich potential donors on the fund-raising committee.)[5] Once a group makes a decision, group pressure forces everyone to go along. Beyond this, participation reduces the need for the supervisor to utilize Structure. The mere fact that the group is given the power to enforce and implement rules increases the likelihood that they will accept the rules, even rules to which they might otherwise object. In other words, whether or not a group accepts management's objectives depends not only on *what* is demanded but also on *how* it is demanded.

How can supervisors stimulate participation of this sort? To some extent, they can permit it to develop naturally, merely by refraining from close supervision. If they simply say, however, "Take over," fumbling and confusion are bound to result. In the following section we see how supervisors can encourage participation through meeting with subordinates to consider mutual problems.

---

[5] Explicit, public commitment is an especially effective form of motivation, particularly when the commitment is voluntary. Gerald Salancik, "Commitment and Control," in Barry M. Staw and Gerald Salancik, eds., *New Directions in Organizational Behavior* (Chicago: St. Clair Press, 1977).

Later on, we consider how the informal organization of the group can also be used to encourage participation.

Holding meetings

Effective managers frequently call their subordinates together when they have problems of common interest. Of course, individual problems can be discussed and worked out together in private conversations, but *group* problems require *group* discussion. Such meetings need not be formal. Indeed, meetings range all the way from a regular session of the board of directors to an informal discussion between a supervisor and two mechanics at a machine that has been causing trouble.

In some companies, most major decisions have long been made by committees, particularly at the higher levels of management. At lower levels it is now accepted practice for supervisors to hold regular meetings at which subordinates can raise questions, discuss common problems, and consider new developments. Increasingly, such meetings are being held even on the hourly-paid level, though they are still probably more common in organizations such as restaurants, hospitals, stores, schools, and libraries than in manufacturing plants.

Meetings of this sort may be used for three different purposes:

Information-giving. This meeting is simply a substitute for posting a notice or speaking to subordinates one by one. Obviously, taking the whole work force away from their job is an expensive procedure, but it ensures that everyone will be notified of new directives or information that is important to the whole group. Furthermore, such meetings give subordinates a chance to ask questions, raise objections, and discuss the implications of the announcement.

Consultation. Just as managers can ask individuals for suggestions on how to solve a problem, so they can call a meeting for the same purpose. Though the manager will make the final decision on whether or not the suggestions are accepted, people derive great satisfaction from knowing that their ideas are being considered, and even more if they are used. A group exchanging opinions and experiences often comes up with better suggestions than any one person working alone. A suggestion that has evolved from the contributions of many members of the group is more likely to be implemented with enthusiasm by the entire group than is a suggestion that is the brain child of one person, whether manager or subordinate.

Group decision. Just as supervisors can delegate authority to individual subordinates to handle problems that involve them alone, so they may call a meeting and delegate authority to a group to handle problems that involve the group as a whole. Of course, there is little difference between a meeting called to solicit suggestions and a meeting called to enable the group to make decisions on its own. But by waiving its veto power, management thrusts upon the group the responsibility for choosing between alternatives.

Group decison making: subject for controversy

Most business meetings are called for the first two purposes mentioned above—for information-giving or for consultation. Yet the greatest amount of interest and conflict about group meetings centers on the third purpose: group decision making. Some observers feel that group decision making is a cure for every business ill. Others concede that group decision making may have *some* value at the top management level, but ask, "Are lower-level managers and rank-and-file workers capable of making group decisions? Can they be trusted to make what is from management's point of view the right decision? Won't subordinates avoid responsibility and try to get out of work? If given the power to make decisions, won't they wander into areas that are none of their business?"

The issue is hardly this clear-cut. Participation is not an all-or-nothing matter. As the accompanying chart illustrates, there are degrees of participa-

---

THE PARTICIPATION CONTINUUM

Boss provides Structure
↓ Increasing participation
Subordinates provide Structure

1. Boss solves problem, making use of available evidence.
2. Boss obtains information from subordinates, then makes decision independently, on the basis of this information.
3. Boss shares problem with subordinates, either individually or as a group. Boss asks for ideas and suggestions, but makes the final decision.
4. Boss shares problem with subordinates, either individually or as a group. Together they work out a decision based on common input.
5. Boss delegates solution of problem, either to individual subordinates or to the group. They make the final decision.

---

tion, ranging from the situation in which the boss makes all the decisions alone, allowing the subordinates no input (*1* on chart), to the situation in which the boss delegates full power to act *(5)*.[6] Note that consultation and delegation can involve either individual subordinates or the entire group. The chart reminds us also of a point made earlier: participation is related to Structure. Low participation means the boss provides the Structure. High participation means Structure comes from either individual subordinates or the group as a whole.

When to use participation

How much participation should management allow in a given situation? A number of factors are relevant.

---

[6] The analysis that follows is influenced by Victor Vroom and Philip Yetton, *Leadership and Decision-making* (Pittsburgh: University of Pittsburgh Press, 1973) and by Frank Heller, "The Decision Process: An Analysis of Power Sharing," in Robert Dubin, ed., *Handbook of Work, Organization and Society* (Chicago: Rand McNally, 1976). See also George Strauss, "Management Practices," in J. Richard Hackman and Lloyd Suttle, eds., *Improving Life at Work* (Santa Monica: Goodyear, 1977).

Subordinates' ability to make decisions. Who has the necessary information, skills, and background to solve the problem at hand? If subordinates have critical information, it is important to involve them in the decision-making process. Especially if the information is widely distributed, participation should involve the group as a whole; but if only a few people have this information, participation should take in only these few. Participation is not meaningful (at the most it is pseudo-participation) if subordinates are unable to contribute meaningfully to it. On the other hand, one should not jump to conclusions as to who can contribute what:

In a meeting to discuss proposed changes in Britain's genetic engineering rules, one scientist complained that local safety committees (which included laboratory assistants) were being asked to comment on scientific issues they were not qualified in. One [member] replied that even washing-up women can contribute to the discussion: they may not appreciate the nuances of science, but they understand better than many scientists the importance of not putting hypodermic syringes into plastic disposal bags.[7]

Importance to the parties. How important is the issue to the various parties? Other things being equal, subordinates should be given greater opportunities to participate when subjects are important to them. When matters are of critical importance to management, subordinates may participate by providing information only (see 2 on chart).

Actually, there are many areas in which management does not care (within broad limits) what decision is made, so long as there is no excessive dissension. For example, management is largely unconcerned with how employees divide up dirty work, as long as the work is done, or how rest periods are scheduled, so long as the time alloted is not exceeded. And because no vacation schedule can satisfy everyone, managers save themselves a major headache by letting the group do scheduling. (Note, however, that supervisors still must preside over the process by which the decision is made. If they say merely "you decide," without helping to establish procedure, there may be endless bickering and confusion. It is the supervisor's responsibility to help the group resolve its internal difficulties.)

In other areas, the supervisor's objectives coincide with those of the group—in matters of accident prevention or avoiding traffic jams in the parking lot, for example. Possibly, management should reserve a veto power over decisions in such matters, although it is unlikely that the group will make decisions that are, from the supervisor's point of view, far wrong.

Conflicting interests. There are some subjects that are appropriate for only restricted forms of participation. Because of legal requirements, for example, the question of *whether* to eliminate racial desegregation in a department is not appropriate for participation; the question of *how* to do it may be. Participation in the normal sense is not feasible in areas of basic conflict be-

---

[7] *Economist*, March 17, 1979, p. 95.

tween superiors and subordinates; for example over whether the company should grant a wage increase or make layoffs.[8]

How can supervisors keep participation from encroaching on areas of basic disagreement? One way is to set clear limits to the group's area of freedom. Instead of asking subordinates "How much vacation time should you get?" the supervisor might ask "How many people can we spare at any one time during vacation and still meet customer needs?" or "Who should go when?" And supervisors should make it clear in advance that they reserve the right to reject proposed decisions if they feel that (from their point of view) these decisions fall outside the previously set limits.

Organizational commitment. Participation in a broad range of issues (not just vacation schedules and parking lots) is particularly appropriate where subordinates and management are committed to the same organizational objectives. Participation works well with academicians, professionals, and members of higher management, since these people are likely to have roughly the same objectives as do their bosses. Among workers who lack intrinsic interest in their work, participation may be effective only within a narrow range. Participation is also unlikely to be successful where there has been a history of labor-management strife.

Winning subordinate acceptance. Participation, of course, is a means of winning acceptance for organizational objectives. The supervisor is interested in getting not only a sound decision but one that will be accepted by the group. An *adequate* decision that is enthusiastically implemented may be better than one that management prefers but subordinates resist. Thus the participative process is particularly appropriate when the decision is difficult to implement.

Subordinate desires and expectations. As we mentioned in discussing Structure, individuals vary considerably in their desires to make decisions on their own. In part, this reflects personality differences; for example, need for independence or n Achievement. Education and upbringing make a difference. College graduates and younger workers generally expect more opportunity to participate than do older, noncollege trained workers.

Cultural factors are also important. There are substantial differences among cultures in terms of the value given to participation or the willingness of subordinates to accept the responsibility for making suggestions. The North American concept of participation is completely foreign to many parts of Latin America. In Japan, by contrast, management from the bottom up and widespread consulation are much more prevalent than they are here.

There are also differences among occupational groups. Professionals value participation more than nonprofessionals. In collegial organizations, such as universities, few major decisions are taken without widespread consultation.[9]

---

[8] Both topics are standard fare in collective bargaining, which itself is a form of participation.

[9] Indeed, despite expectations of high participation, some professionals suffer from "decisional saturation," being asked to participate in more decisions than they want. Joseph Alutto and James Belasco, "A Typology for Participation in Organizational Decision Making," *Administrative Science Quarterly*, 17, No. 1 (March 1972), 117–25.

Supervisory belief in participation. Participation will not work—at least not for long—if the supervisor does not have faith in it. For participation to be successful, supervisors should believe that the process will lead to useful suggestions being made. Where supervisors have confidence in their subordinates' abilities, satisfaction tends to be high.[10] Where such confidence is lacking (for example, where the supervisor views participation as merely a morale builder), employees eventually see through the deception; consequently, the desired payoff in terms of morale does not result, and productivity is less likely to improve than without such "counterfeit participation."

Some organizations require regular meetings as a standard practice at all levels. Unfortunately, supervisors may call these compulsory meetings merely because they are told to do so. They go through the motions but never become involved in the spirit of consultation. An office worker once described her experience to us:

"We have meetings once a month. The office manager asks us if we have any questions or suggestions. Sure, we have lots of complaints, but no one has the courage to bring them up. Once in a while someone who is looking to make a good impression asks some silly question, although she already knows the answer."

A belief in participation does not require the boss to hold endless meetings, to consult at length prior to taking action, during emergencies, or to discuss trivia. Indeed, subordinates will generally mistrust participatory gestures if they are inconsistent with the boss's overall leadership style, and they may well perceive such gestures as manipulation rather than genuine power sharing. Actually, the mere act of holding formal meetings is less important than the manager's willingness to consult with subordinates informally when problems arise. When consultation takes place around the drawing board, over the machine that has broken down, or in the cafeteria, status differences create less of a barrier to communication than they do at a formally called meeting.

Group vs. individual decision-making. Is group decision-making more effective than individual decision-making? The answer seems to depend on the nature of the group, the problem being considered, and what is meant by "effective." Groups sometimes turn out higher-quality solutions than do individuals, although this isn't always the case. In solving problems that have one definite solution, a group is more likely to be accurate than is an individual. Furthermore, group problem-solving has the advantage of enlisting a variety of backgrounds and experiences; thus, the range of solutions is usually greater, and the group solution is more likely to represent a balanced point of view. Meetings are particularly useful when the participants represent various departments whose coordination is required to implement the final decision, for the discussion tends to force the departmental representatives to look at the problem from an organizational rather than a departmental point of view.

The give and take of unstructured brainstorming often generates innovative new ideas that individuals might never think of by themselves. When

---

[10] J. B. Ritchie, "Supervision," in George Strauss and others, eds., *Organizational Behavior: Research and Issues* (Belmont, California: Wadsworth, 1976).

groups represent different interests, they may reach a compromise which all are committed to implement. By contrast, when united on a single goal group members tend to make bolder decisions than would individuals acting alone. Since the decision is made by the group no one individual can be held responsible if it turns out to be a mistake.

On the other hand, individuals are more capable than groups of handling subtle relations—whether in threading a needle or in developing a complex theoretical formula. Thus, groups may be more efficient than individuals in solving crossword puzzles, but individuals are better at devising them. Great works of art are almost without exception the products of single individuals.

In addition, meetings are time-consuming. Decisions reached in them take longer than do those of individuals, particularly if time is computed in terms of total man-hours expended. Sometimes, of course, the higher quality and easier acceptance of decisions reached through meetings makes them worth the extra time involved. On the other hand, managers on occasion pass the buck to meetings when they are psychologically unprepared to make decisions themselves. Meetings under these circumstances accomplish little.

A crisis that demands immediate decisions does not permit a formal meeting. But a meeting may be useful, if held before the crisis, to develop procedures in anticipation of a future emergency. Furthermore, a participative atmosphere and experience in working together to develop plans will often result in greater teamwork when a crisis actually occurs and when decisions are made with little or no participation.

There is the risk that presenting a problem to a group to discuss may lead to greater conflict than existed before, and skillful leadership is required to prevent this. The danger of conflict is particularly great when vested interests are involved (for example, when a group is deciding whether "soft jobs" should be rotated or assigned on the basis of seniority). The less cohesive the group, the greater the difficulty in reaching agreement, though experience in making decisions of this sort may help cohesion develop. Organization development techniques may also reduce internal tensions.

The relative advantages of group, over individual, decision making were effectively summarized long ago by well-known executives from two companies with vastly different attitudes toward committees:

"If you can name for me one great discovery or decision that was made by a committee, I will find you the one man in that committee who had the lonely insight—while he was shaving, on his way to work, or perhaps while the rest of the committee was chattering away—the lonely insight that solved the problem and was the basis for the decision."

"It stands to reason that if you get five men together and one man is wrong, the mistake will be picked up. Or if one man has a good idea, the others will contribute to it and develop it. And if they have good ideas, what comes out may be better than the separate ideas added together." [11]

Participation: a summing up

A strong case can be made for participative management, in which the manager meets with subordinates to discuss a wide variety of work-related

[11] Ralph Cordiner, former Chairman of General Electric, and Frank Abrams, former Chairman of Standard Oil of New Jersey, as cited in Justin Longenecker, *Principles of Management and Organizational Behavior* (Columbus, Ohio: Merrill, 1958), p. 27.

problems. Ideally, participation leads to greater cohesion and a greater acceptance of management's objectives. An atmosphere of cooperation can provide essential need satisfactions for subordinates: the social satisfaction of working together, a feeling of identification with the group and the overall organization, and a pride in accomplishment. For management, such cooperation, if achieved, makes life a lot easier, since subordinates provide their own Structure. Participation is particularly useful during periods of change.

The advantages of participation can be oversold, however. There are many areas in which the interests of subordinates and management conflict. Subordinate acceptance of the legitimacy of management's demands and behavior does not necessarily mean that these subordinates will "internalize" and work enthusiastically toward management's objectives. It may mean only that they will put in a "fair day's work." That "fair day's work" is largely determined through implicit bargaining and may be fairly low. To the extent that subordinates expect to be consulted, participative techniques may act as hygienes rather than motivators, that is they will reduce dissatisfaction without increasing productivity.

In a sense, strengthening group cohesion through participation may make management's task harder, for the group will now develop expectations that its acquiesence is required for everything management does. Meetings are time consuming. If subordinates are given genuine freedom to make important decisions, there is no guarantee that these decisions will be those managment wants (and the very process of discussion may lead to friction among group members).

Group decision (*4* and *5* on the chart) may be appropriate when management is really indifferent about the decision (as with scheduling coffee breaks) or management is sure the group has the same objectives as management (as in time of war or in some professional organizations). Many of the advantages of participation, however, can be obtained through forms of consultation in which the boss obtains the necessary information from subordinates (*2* on the chart) and possibly allows them to make suggestions *(3)*, while retaining the final decision for himself. Consultation may provide a lower degree of commitment to the final decision than having subordinates make decisions themselves, however the quality of the decision may be just as high and subordinate input into the decision process will in some degree increase its acceptance.

Working through the informal organization

It would be impractical for a supervisor to call a meeting every time there is a minor problem. Often supervisors can work out acceptable solutions by themselves, taking into account the group's standards and expectations. But at other times, supervisors make use of the informal organization of the group.

As we mentioned in the preceding chapter, groups evolve their own leadership. Informal leaders play key roles in every organization, and without their cooperation management must face an uphill battle against sabotage and apathy.

Informal leaders

Note this classic story of how two boys' club recreational directors handled the same problem in different ways. The problem was this:

> The younger boys were to use the play center till 9 o'clock, then they were to leave and make room for the older boys. But, instead of going home, the younger boys would hang around the door, bang on the windows, and generally create a nuisance.
> Again and again the first recreational director asked the boys as a group to go away—but with no results. Faced with the same situation, the second director turned to one member of the group and merely said: "Listen, Joe, the time's up. Be a good fellow and take your gang out of here." Joe, who was the informal leader, complied immediately and the group left.[12]

Why was the second director so successful? He recognized the informal leader's special status and gave him an opportunity to gain still more status through proving his power to the director. Under the first director's approach, the informal leader could exhibit his power only by opposing the director's will; had the group obeyed the director, the informal leader would have lost status.

The situation is very much the same in business and industry. A manager can either fight the informal organization and its leaders or work with them. If the informal leaders fail to win recognition by working *with* management, they will get it by working *against* management.

Management is often heard to complain, "All our trouble is caused by a few ringleaders. If we could only get rid of them, our trouble would disappear, morale would rise, and our employees would be loyal once again." Unfortunately, these "ringleaders" are often informal leaders; the trouble they cause reflects the desires of the group. In dealing with them, a certain amount of bargaining is often required. Eliminate the informal leaders, though, and the group may become still more antagonistic to management, morale may fall even lower, and new ringleaders will step to the fore. In a nonunionized situation it may be possible to eliminate ringleaders one by one till finally nothing is left but a cowed, disorganized mass of individuals who docilely obey orders. However, such individuals may never show a gleam of initiative or teamwork.

What is the alternative to firing ringleaders? Working with them. There are numerous ways in which a manager can build up good relations with the informal leaders. Among other things he can pass information along to them first, ask their advice on technical or human-relations problems, and assign them to train others.

There are, however, several dangers that the manager must guard against:

1. The informal leader is often hard to identify. The outstanding employee who does the best work and cooperates most readily with management may *seem* to be the informal leader, whereas these characteristics may actually make him a social isolate. On the other hand, the "loud-mouth" may serve as the group's *spokesman* rather than its actual *leader*. The group may even

---

[12] William F. Whyte and Burleigh B. Gardner, "The Man in the Middle: Position and Problems of the Foreman," *Applied Anthropology*, 4, No. 2 (Spring 1945).

have different leaders for different purposes. Sometimes the members of the group will follow one individual when they act in cooperation with management and another when they are antagonistic. Finally, there may be no identifiable informal leader at all.

2. The informal leader who works closely with management may lose status with the group by doing so and become known as a "company stooge." This danger is particularly acute when there is antagonism between management and the work group generally and the informal leader is asked to do things that the group does not accept as legitimate.

3. Carried too far, cooperation becomes favoritism. It is one thing for the manager to give the informal leader information and to ask for his advice. It is quite another to give him easier work or special favors. Nothing could be more effectively calculated to drive him from his leadership position.

Working supervisors

The working supervisor is a group member to whom management may show special attention without giving rise to charges of favoritism. Working supervisors are common in process plants (such as oil refineries), in many offices and laboratories, in self-managing work teams, and also in some of the older, more traditional industries in which craft skills still prevail. They also exist in some professional groups.

Since working supervisors often gain status because of their seniority and technical proficiency, subordinates may be more willing to accept orders from them than from the formal supervisor. This is particularly true where the supervisor has not come up from the ranks, where coordination of the work force requires a high degree of technical skill that can be acquired only through long years on the job, or where constant attention and order-giving are required, as with a steel mill crew.

We have observed situations in which management has impaired output and demoralized the work group by deliberately or inadvertently taking away the working supervisor's power and prestige.

Union steward

The union steward is ordinarily an informal leader who commands respect outside union matters: Provided the over-all union-management relationship is friendly, the manager may wish to pass on information to the steward first, use him as a sounding board for proposed changes, and even ask his advice. Again if relations are good, this consultation can be handled outside the context of formal collective bargaining and in a way that will not lead to the loss of the manager's power or the establishment of precedents that management may later regret. Such consultation has the great advantage of permitting the steward to participate in solving technical and human-relations problems in a constructive, positive fashion; otherwise, in order to display his status, the steward has to resort to the essentially negative activity of processing grievances. In a strongly unionized situation, the supervisor will never be able to develop cooperative relations with his subordinates if he bypasses or ignores the union.

communications: the information transmission process

Much of what is said about management and personnel relations simply assumes that human beings will understand what they say to one another as they interact at work. In fact, we have given most of our emphasis to *what* should be said—correct tactics and strategies to improve personnel relationships—and rather little attention to *how* it should be said. But people are constantly misunderstanding one another in their day-to-day organizational relations.

"I thought you wanted me to start that new job *after* I finished what I was doing."

"How did I know he was *serious* about quitting?"

"I *discount* almost everything I hear from those jokers in Corporate Communications!"

"But I was sure you meant London, *Ontario.*"

In this chapter, we shall explore the source of these misunderstandings and the methods to improve interpersonal communications.[1]

---

[1] This chapter seeks to provide a somewhat simplified overview of the subject of communication theory, which has received substantial attention from social psychologists. For good summaries of the research literature see Richard Farace, Peter Monge, and Hamish Russell, *Communicating and Organizing* (Reading, Mass.: Addison Wesley, 1977); Nan Lin, *The Study of Human Communication* (Indianapolis, Ind.: Bobbs Merrill, 1971).

On the surface, face-to-face communications appear simple. Have you ever listened to two old friends talking together? Rarely do they use complete sentences; often a single word, a grunt or a groan or a raised eyebrow communicates as much meaning as lengthy speeches would convey between casual acquaintances. A few syllables go a long way.

But successful communication does not necessarily take place automatically whenever two people get together. Let's examine a situation more typical of business life. The shop-clerk tells his boss with pride, "This is the heaviest day we've ever had." But the boss thinks the clerk is lazy and looking for an excuse not to unload new stock. So he answers angrily, and the subordinate concludes that the boss is overbearing and ungrateful.

CHAPTER 7
communications: the information transmission process

The communication process; the sender's world

Most of us have a simple, straightforward view of communication:

Sender's thought or idea → Converted to words and speech → Receiver's hearing → Receiver's understanding

Were the process that straightforward, life would be much simpler. Let's look at reality, then: first, the sender's world.

Intention. The sender, whether colleague or boss or subordinate, has something to communicate to the other person: information, instructions, a point of view, some data.

What is transmitted

Impression management. The presumably logical, objective content of communication is complicated by other motives. Often, the sender "stage manages" the communication to convey an overall impression of personal prestige, helpfulness, or power.[2] We are all familiar with acquaintances who use each contact to communicate a total image of themselves. Listen to this manager, instructing a subordinate:

"I could tell—when the VP called me into her office to give me this assignment—that she really relied on my extensive knowledge of food chains. Then I asked for you to work with me, because this is going to be so big and important that I hoped you could get a part of the glory. Now here is what I want you to do first on this supermarket project of mine."

It's pretty obvious what's being communicated: self-importance and "I want you to think of me as your powerful protector."

Emotional state. The sender unintentionally is also saying things about his or her own emotional state. Some of this reflects the immediately preceding circumstances. Pushed? Panicky? Under stress? Relaxed? The sense of agitation or calm will be transmitted along with the actual words the sender is using.

[2] Much of the work on impression management is the product of Erving Goffman. See *Relations in Public* (New York: Basic Books), 1971.

Covert feelings. The sender also has hidden feelings (some may be even unconscious) toward himself (or herself) and toward the recipient of the communication. Imagine the difference in the tone of the interchange if the sender is feeling guilty and inadequate, rather than self-confident.

The receiver may be distrusted or disliked or, contrariwise, a close and dear friend who can always be relied upon to do the right thing. These inner, private feelings surface in a variety of ways in actual communication. And added to these are the emotions generated by the apparent attitude of the intended receiver. Does he or she appear interested in, and receptive to, what is being said, or resistant, even hostile? This feedback, in turn, shapes the message that goes out.

Modes of communication

Intended and unintended meanings are transmitted to the other person by more than simple words; there are many dimensions to the mode of communication.

Argot and jargon. Occupational and professional groups evolve their own specialized language that sociologists call argot. Some argot reflects the need to invent precise but simple ways of saying things that have to be used repeatedly. Generations of managers learn to scrawl ASAP on notes, to indicate that something is important, wanted as soon as possible. It is easy to forget that a newcomer may not be familiar with all these specialized terms, although at times they may be used simply to symbolize group solidarity or to exclude outsiders.

Differences in how groups use everyday terms can cause trouble. This example is from NASA's bio-satellite program:

> The investigators (bioscientists) thought they were being specific when they asked for a sterile system [one free of all bacteria] to conduct monkey urine. But the engineers (designing the satellite) didn't understand the meaning of "sterile.". . . The engineers took *sterile* simply to mean "clean—void of all obvious dirt and contamination." As a result, invisible bacteria could live in the system, which would infect and kill the orbiting monkeys.[3]

We have become sensitive to the complex language forms, the long cumbersome sentences and erudite language associated with government documents and social science monographs. Their authors believe that this jargon is important to signify the importance of what they are saying.

Symbols. Many words have strong emotional meanings that go far beyond their dictionary definitions. When a manager says she isn't sure the union shop is "desirable" (presumably because it forces workers to join a union), she is communicating to the union that she doesn't like, trust, or accept unions and probably hopes to weaken them. In much the same vein, when a new employee is told he can't have a parking place in the lot near the executive offices, he hears this as meaning: "You haven't arrived yet; you're really not one of the important bosses."

[3] Leonard Sayles and Margaret Chandler, *Managing Large Systems* (New York: Harper, 1971), pp. 233–34.

Of course, semantically speaking, all words are symbols; they serve to represent reality, but they are not reality. There is thus ample room for misunderstanding, as the quotations at the beginning of the chapter suggest. Each of us uses words slightly differently, with different intended meanings and connotations. When a prospective employee is called "aggressive," is that term communicating virtue: energy, initiative, and perseverance? Or does it mean irritatingly pushy, even belligerent? Speech gives great leeway for nuance, connotation, and hidden meanings.

There are nonverbal symbols, too. An Afro haircut, a flag in one's lapel, a white coat (in the lab or hospital)—all are saying things about the status and beliefs of the wearer, and they can trigger rather strong reactions in the other person.

Interaction styles. One communicates by the patterning of one's interaction as well as by words. Some people speak in long monologues; others use short bursts followed by long silences. Some are good at synchronizing their talking and silence periods with the interaction patterns of other people; they are flexible. Still others are rigid and cannot adjust.[4] Speaker and listener like each other and listen better when they have a comfortable interaction pattern, when their speaking and silent periods are synchronized.

Nonverbal cues. Almost everyone has now heard of body language and how much is communicated by posture and facial expression. A scowling speaker's words sound threatening; many people are suspicious of those who don't look them squarely in the eyes. The position of one's hands can suggest fear or openness, and there are countless other cues given by bodily actions and positions.[5]

Even the distance between the speaker and the listener connotes something about how friendly they are and their relationship.[6]

Spatial relations. Communication is also affected by the surrounding physical environment, the ease or difficulty with which people can converse. As generations of students and teachers have discovered, chairs arranged in a circle, where people face one another, stimulate easy give-and-take more than the typical, rowed lecture hall does. Even height differences have their impact: the listener who is lower than the speaker often feels repressed or demeaned. Open offices are designed to encourage spontaneous exchanges

---

[4] For a more complete description of how interaction patterns affect communication, see Eliot Chapple, *Culture and Biological Man* (New York: Holt, 1970), pp. 245–67.

[5] A summary of the best work in this field is presented in Ray L. Birdwhistell, *Kinesics and Context* (New York: Ballantine, 1972).

[6] Edward Hall has developed what he calls the science of "proxemics," and he believes that there are cross-cultural differences in terms of what one considers an appropriate and comfortable distance separating two people engaged in discourse. In the U.S., we become oppressed and discomforted when the speaker comes too close; but in Latin America, getting close to your listener is viewed as friendship. Hall's work and that of others are summarized in John Short, E. Williams and B. Christie, *The Social Psychology of Telecommunications* (London: Wiley, 1976), pp. 46–49.

of information; closed-in offices can intimidate people and reduce communication.⁷ Too much grandeur can be overwhelming.

"I found it hard to really listen to what he was saying. He was behind that huge mahogany desk and sitting in an oversized executive chair, while I was perched on a small armless one. It wasn't until he came around from behind that barrier and said, 'Let's sit around the coffee table' that I could begin to feel easy enough to hear the subtleties of what he wanted me to do on this new job."

Of course, there can be too much of a good thing. People also need privacy, some sense of personal space that is violated only at their request. Many open-office plans are discomforting for that reason; they also inhibit frank interpersonal discussions.

Tone. Communication also has an overall quality or tone that influences the hearer. If the speaker appears to be supportive, the message that comes through is very different from the message of a speaker who appears to be antagonistic. In recent years, much emphasis has been placed on "transaction analysis," which, in part, emphasizes these differences in tone. TA asserts that all communication represents one of these three levels:

      Parent   Child   Adult

With the *parent* tone, the sender is emphasizing that the receiver is somewhat childlike, and words like *should* and *ought* are dominant. The speaker is evaluating and judging the other person.

A supervisor dispairingly whines at a subordinate, "Haven't you learned to keep this work area neat yet and those files orderly? It's about time you started acting responsibly."
Such a parental judgmental tone typically evokes a childlike response: "Aw, can't you see I'm busy; I do the best I can." And, of course, that seemingly irresponsible reply will stimulate an even more critical rejoinder.

To avoid this spiral of parental criticism and childlike, irresponsible reply, the tone should be more *adult*—less judging, complaining, or self-justifying. Each party deals with issues as problems they will explore together.⁸

The world of the receiver

But receivers of communication are not passive receptacles, either. They also seek to make certain impressions. They have emotional states that may impede understanding, and they have feelings about the senders.

When we are insecure, worried, or fearful, what we hear and see seems more threatening than when we are secure and at peace with the world. Rumors of all sorts spring up when management makes a change of any kind

---

⁷ A growing field, sometimes called environmental or ecological psychology, deals with the impact of physical arrangements on human interaction. See Robert Sommer, *Personal Space: The Behavioral Basis of Design* (Englewood Cliffs, N.J.: Prentice-Hall, 1969).
⁸ For a good overview of transaction analysis, see Thomas Harris, *I'm OK—You're OK* (New York: Avon Books, 1973).

without adequate explanation, even a change as simple as moving desks around the office. This is particularly true during an economic recession. Then, statements and actions that under less trying circumstances would have passed unnoticed become grounds for fear. "Yes, Joe might be right. They are going to double the workload." "I saw the foreman looking at the seniority list. I guess the rumors are right; a lot of men will be laid off because of the new equipment." By the same token, when we are angry or depressed, we tend to reject out of hand what might otherwise seem like reasonable requests or good ideas.

The receiver's expectations

Listeners usually hear what they expect to hear, rather than what is actually being said. On ceremonious occasions such as the opening of a new building, in a context emphasizing good will and good cheer, no one will interpret the speaker's remarks as bad news. But if a summons to the head office is associated with criticism, it is difficult not to interpret the big boss's comments as censure, regardless of what is said there.

If the sender is perceived as trustworthy or even friendly and supportive, what is said is likely to be accepted and believed. Conversely, a disliked or distrusted person will find it difficult to communicate anything but the most banal facts. This is an aspect of stereotyping. We tend to hear good and true things from those we like; those we dislike speak untruths.

In labor management relations, where there has been overt conflict, it is difficult for management to have credibility in statements to the leaders or members of the union. Everything is suspect. "They're just saying that to frighten or deceive us."

Stereotyping. People expect to hear comments reflecting the speaker's associations, as we noted in Chapter 5. Outsiders are often perceived as threatening or upsetting to the group norms and routines; therefore, almost any request made by the outsider may be interpreted as inappropriate or pressureful. The same request for service from an insider would be heard as appropriate.

Many years ago, an experimenter clipped an item from a well-known union publication titled, *The Four Goals of Labor*. He then pasted it up with a caption: "from the National Association of Manufacturers." Not surprisingly, when the material was shown to union members they were overwhelmingly critical of it as an unfair, biased representation of labor's goals.

Influence of reference group

Clearly, the group with which we identify ourselves—the reference group, as psychologists call it—creates some of this bias. Advertisers discovered long ago that as individuals, we rarely change our minds by ourselves. Our attitudes toward politics, music, recreation, work pace, and all other activities and interests are largely colored by the group with which we identify.

As noted in Chapter 6, the manager may be wasting time trying to convince an individual employee to work harder when there is a strong group standard to the contrary. The employee would be risking ostracism in going along with the manager's request. Similarly, management often uses slogans and posters to indoctrinate workers with the importance of promoting safety, cutting scrap losses, making suggestions, or engaging in good housekeeping. They even send personal letters to employees' homes. The trouble with these efforts is that they are directed to the *individual*, whereas the basic attitudes and convictions are determined by the *group*. Thus, if fellow workers see the supervisor as harsh and unfair, chances are that the employee will feel the same way.

In a large organization, the difficulties of perception are compounded. An announcement may go to dozens of groups with different occupational and status interests. What each group "hears" depends on its own interests. An announcement that the company has purchased the patent for a product that will be manufactured in a new plant on the West Coast may be heard in these different ways.

Design engineer: "This may be an indication that the company prefers to go outside the organization for new ideas, and that is bound to hurt our status."
Production engineer: "This new product will mean more work for us. Some of us may have a chance to move out West."
Worker: "The new products aren't going to be manufactured in the home plant. That means if business should get slack, we're likely to be laid off. A bad trend."

Ignoring information that conflicts with what we already "know"

Most of us resist change. We tend to reject new ideas, particularly if they conflict with what we already believe. In some ways our communications receiving apparatus (sense organs and brain) works like an efficient filter. When we read a newspaper or listen to a political speech, we tend to note only those things that confirm our present beliefs. On the other hand, we tend to ignore anything that conflicts with our beliefs. Sometimes our filters work so efficiently that we do not hear new information at all. Even when we do hear it, we either reject it as a fallacious notion or find some way of twisting and shaping its meaning to fit our preconceptions. Because we hear and see what we *expect* to hear and see, we are rarely disappointed.

Communications sometimes fail to have the desired effect because they run counter to other information that the receiver possesses. Statements that hard work leads to promotion are ignored in a company where promotions often are made on the basis of seniority or favoritism. A guarantee that "the company never cuts an incentive rate because employees are earning too much" is disregarded if rates have, in fact, been cut as a result of minor engineering changes.

Cognitive dissonance. In recent years, a great deal of psychological research has been conducted on the mechanisms by which human beings cope with what they perceive to be irreconcilable communication inputs, or *cognitive dissonance*.[9] This research suggests that one can predict very strong differences between the reaction to information that is consistent with what the receiver already believes, and the reaction to new information that is inconsistent with those beliefs. These differences are summarized below.

---

[9] For a fuller discussion, see Elliot Aronson, *The Social Animal* (San Francisco: Freeman, 1976), pp. 85–139.

Communication is consistent with existing beliefs	Communication is inconsistent with existing beliefs
Seeks additional exposure, more information	Avoids exposure
Accepts information as valid	Rejects validity
Remembers what is heard	Easily forgets
Memory is accurate	Memory distorts information

This sort of bias is one of the reasons why company newspapers (so-called house organs) find it difficult to gain worker acceptance. Once employees become convinced that the paper is just a management mouthpiece, many will believe nothing it prints, no matter how objective or verifiable. So, too, with pamphlets and other give-aways. If these are tagged as propaganda, all the information they contain becomes suspect, even useful information about health and household safety.

> During February, 1971, the National Emergency Warning Center (an arm of the U.S. Office of Civil Defense) transmitted a coded message to all civilian radio stations, warning of an impending nuclear attack. Although the message was sent in error, its form and content were precisely correct, and nearly all civilian stations were supposed to go off the air after announcing that "the President has directed an emergency action notification." Even though every station knew the correct procedure, and each had been drilled in its response, all but a small number ignored the message. Apparently most station managers found the coded alert inconsistent with what they believed to be reality.

It is difficult for a manager to shed a reputation for being hardboiled or unfair. He may go through a training program and emerge with every intention of turning over a new leaf, but subordinates will be suspicious of his motives and assume that his new approach is just a trick. They will distort and misconstrue every move he makes. He is now unpredictable.

Defensive avoidance. By a somewhat similar mental process, we ignore or distort much that is threatening, unnerving, or requiring upsetting changes in our routines, beliefs, and actions.

Social psychologists reassessing why Pearl Harbor was unprepared for a Japanese attack even though a number of warnings were issued from Washington believed that the warnings were never "heard." Our military high command deceived themselves into thinking that each announcement simply confirmed their pre-existing belief that the Japanese either were not going to war or were likely to move toward other targets.[10]

Noise. Related to these concepts is the one of noise. The sender's communication often must compete with a number of irrelevant stimuli: not only

[10] Irving Janis and Leon Mann, *Decision-Making* (New York: Free Press, 1977), pp. 120–29.

literal noise, which muffles and distorts sound, but other people speaking, visual and aural sensations emanating from a wide variety of sources. Air traffic controllers, trying to hear the pilot of an incoming plane, can be deluged with a variety of other sights and sounds, so a critical word is lost or confused with another term. In one mid-air collision, the controller thought the pilot knew where the other plane was because he missed hearing the pilot use the word. *think*. The controller heard the pilot say only, "It has passed us," so the controller stopped worrying about how close the two planes were to each other.

Living in a world of words and being deluged by sounds all the time, we learn to tune out many things. While a mother usually hears her child crying, the father often sleeps through, although he would hear his wife call. Many things a manager says are ignored, actually never heard, because they sound so much alike: "Work efficiently. . . . This order is very important. . . . Save materials. . . . The company is depending on you." To themselves, they say, "So what else is new?" Thus, before we can hear a message, we must learn to discriminate between background noise (timeworn clichés) and significant, relevant, new information, worthy of attention.

Unfortunately, in critical situations—safety emergencies, work crises—it is likely that general confusion will cause critical words to be missed or misinterpreted.

Thus it is not only easy, it is almost inevitable for substantial error to creep into communication because of this thicket of distorting obstacles:

SENDER'S INTENTION
↓
Impression management
↓
Emotional state
↓
Covert feelings
↓
Multiple modes of communication
↓
Tone
↓
RECEIVER'S WORLD
↓
Emotional state
↓
Stereotyping
↓
Reference group beliefs
↓
Cognitive dissonance
↓
Defensive avoidance
↓
Noise
↓
RECEIVER'S UNDERSTANDING

Improving communication

Among other things, good communication requires solving simultaneously two quite different problems. Managers must learn to improve *transmission*—what words, ideas and feelings are actually sent to the other person. At the same time they must cope with their own *reception*—what they perceive the other persons' reactions and statements to be. We shall devote the rest of this chapter to a discussion of several methods by which a manager can maximize success in communicating. At first glance, these techniques may appear mechanical substitutes for mutual trust and understanding. However, a wide variety of research confirms the efficacy of considering communications as both a psychological and technical problem.

CHAPTER 7 communications: the information transmission process

In communicating, the temptation is to adjust to *yourself*. You have the need to say something and to say it in a particular way. In fact, often you communicate when your emotional needs to speak are strongest and the odds of being understood the lowest.

Adjusting to the world of the receiver

"I was just boiling with rage. He had done it wrong again, so I explained why we needed to keep this particular customer: how much they had purchased in the past, who else would be impressed with their being a steady customer, their tie-in with the consolidated buying syndicate, and all the rest. But I could tell the production scheduler wasn't understanding!"

Of course he wasn't! The manager was gaining satisfaction by venting his feelings; he was not trying to get through to the other person.

How does the speaker adjust to the *receiver?* Several passive techniques are available, as well as more dynamic ones. The passive techniques involve thinking ahead and endeavoring to be aware of the listener's needs, possible symbolic interpretations, and the right time to communicate. Dynamic techniques revolve around *feedback* and reinforcement, to be discussed later.

It is extremely difficult to get through to a listener whose expectations and predilections are contradicted by what you are trying to communicate. If your typist has been in the habit of preparing only a single carbon, you must *stress* a request for two carbons. If being sent to the front office is regarded by employees as a sign of impending discipline, you must take pains to communicate that this is not the reason if, in fact, it is not.

The receiver's expectations

In short, you must be sensitive to the private world of the receiver, try to predict the impact of what you say and do on the other person's feelings and attitudes, and tailor your messages to fit your receiver's vocabulary, interests, and values. Managers who work with a variety of groups in the organization must learn techniques of "simultaneous translation" to avoid misunderstandings. The greater the gap between your background and experience and that of the receiver, the greater the effort you must make to find some common ground of understanding.

As we have seen, symbols play a vital role in the private world of the listener. Here is a case in which effective communication was blocked until symbolic meanings were taken into account.

Awareness of symbolic meaning

139

> To help in the preparation of market analyses, the district sales manager asked the salespeople to compute correlation coefficients from their records. These coefficients could be calculated quite simply and painlessly by use of a simple formula. But the sales representatives refused to do what they were asked. One excuse followed another: the computations were too complicated, it was clerk's work and not part of their job description, the coefficients were really useless, and so on. There seemed to be no way to convince them to perform this simple task.
>
> Why was this modest request greeted with such stubborn resistance? The very degree of the salespeople's reaction was the key to the problem. Investigation revealed that coefficient correlations had been tried three years earlier, when the department was headed by an inept supervisor who was universally disliked. Among other things, he had tried to revamp all the departmental procedures and in the process had introduced this statistical technique. Ever since, the sales representatives had associated the term "coefficient correlation" with autocratic supervision. To them, it had become a symbol of oppressive management. Once the company had plumbed this seemingly irrational attitude, it was a simple matter to develop a different terminology for the operation, to conduct training in how the computations should be carried out, and to gain ready acceptance for the whole activity.

The moral of this story is clear: if there is extraordinary, unexpected resistance to a proposal, try to find out whether some symbolic meaning is associated with it.

Often, those who wish to communicate must prepare the way for effective listening by taking the time to prove that they share certain symbolic values that they presume to be of importance to the others.

A supervisor describing some new work procedures to her department: Here is the way we are going to handle Eastern Division Receivables. The procedure grows out of that hassle we had with the comptroller's office and the computer people. We're always the forgotten ones in these new procedures, and the computer people get their way. This time we took "first place" in the final agreement on procedures, and we aren't going to have to handle those silly blue forms anymore either, the ones that took us all so much time. Now, here is how we'll have to handle the. . . .

The speaker is showing solidarity with the group and with some previous issues that have riled people: the status of the computer, the blue forms, the position of the comptroller's office. These have nothing directly to do with the new procedure she wants to communicate, but if her listeners feel that she shares their values and needs, they are more likely to listen with alertness and sympathetic understanding and accept her as a credible source of new information.

Where these common symbols do not exist, the sender may have to build up systematically some shared experiences and, thus, shared symbols, before communicating more difficult, more controversial subjects.

Critical timing

Messages can come too early and too late; theoretically, there is an ideal time when the odds are greater that the message will get through.

Communications come too early when they presume to deal with problems or subjects that the listener has not experienced: "I didn't understand a word they were saying about human relations problems because I had never worked and certainly had never been a supervisor." On the other hand, an employee who is frustrated by a problem may be highly receptive to new ideas.

Similarly, when people are away from their regular work environment or work group (and not frightened), they may be more receptive to materials that conflict with their prejudices, predispositions, and "conventional wisdom." An engineer described his experiences as part of a company task force:

> I've never learned so much so quickly. Part of it was being thrown in with finance and marketing people from other parts of the corporation and working as a team overseas. Everything was new to me; I had never done this sort of work before, and there was nobody there to tell me what I expected to hear.[11]

Thus, it may be useful to wait until there is time available to get people to another location (e.g., taking executives to a resort "retreat" to rethink corporate policy) or away from their normal associations.

A manager can also make the mistake of asking a subordinate to communicate results or findings prematurely. At least, when the manager wants the subordinate to continue to be open-minded and alert to new possibilities (say in R & D) too-early communications may rigidify expectations. Don't get people to take a stand too early, in other words, until you are sure they have as much information and data as they need to draw sensible conclusions.

Communications come too late when opinions have already hardened or the subject has become a battleground between groups or individuals. One way of limiting the amount of noise or distortion is to communicate your message before those other beliefs or attitudes come into play. Then the communication will meet less resistance and your chances of getting it accepted will be greatly increased.

Management announced that Foreman Green would retire in a few months and would be replaced by a man named Williams from another department. One of the men felt that Williams had done him an injustice years ago and spread the word among his fellow employees that Williams was a tyrant who played favorites.

Long before Williams set foot in the new department, a petition was sent to top management requesting that a different foreman be assigned. And once Williams showed up, everything he said and did was fitted into the picture the employees had already established. Every job assignment he made was scrutinized for favoritism. Even harmless statements were often interpreted as threats.

---

[11] A harsh, devious form of this principle is involved in brainwashing, which involves separating the individual from all familiar supports (friends, home, etc.) so he will be more receptive to the constant haranguing of his captors. Less devious is the value of foreign travel in stimulating learning.

A situation like this is an ideal breeding-ground for misunderstanding and unrest. Yet management could have minimized the problem by taking positive action before the picture of the new supervisor was established, perhaps by having the employees meet him as soon as the announcement was made.

It is a waste of time to try to communicate during an argument or bitter debate, when the person has to defend his preconceptions. During such acrimonious discussion, to concede (or even to "hear" accurately) would mean admitting that you are less worthy than the other person.

When issues have become polarized in an organization, informal groups pressure their members to hold only orthodox views and not to concede anything to outsiders.

"There was no use talking with the Shipping people about anything after that battle over losing the Krystar business. Anything you said to them about procedures, they interpreted as being just a continuation of the arguments. And no one from Shipping would dare agree with anything we said in Production or even listen to us—he would be massacred by his colleagues for heresy."

Feedback

Perhaps the single most important method of improving communications is *feedback*. This term, adopted from electrical engineering, refers to the ability of certain complex machines (technically, systems) to check on their own performance and to correct it if necessary—often called cybernetics.

We all use this principle of feedback in our human communications—perhaps without realizing it. Even in casual conversations we are constantly on the alert for cues to whether we are being understood (such as attentive nods from the other person). A good teacher is always interested in audience reaction among students. If they seem confused or drowsy, the lecture isn't getting across. Good managers are equally conscious of the need to determine subordinates' reactions to what they are trying to communicate.

An interesting study illustrates the importance of feedback.

Two students were placed in different rooms, and one was asked to communicate to the other the position of an interconnected series of dominoes placed on a grid. Both had identical grids in front of them. The sender was permitted to explain to the receiver, in any way, the relative positions of the dominoes. Yet it was impossible to complete the task successfully when the receiver was forbidden to respond—that is, when communications were entirely one-way. No matter how painstakingly the sender explained the pattern, the receiver never understood all of it.

Apparently, some opportunity to ask for further information, at least to answer "yes" or "no" to the questions of the sender (e.g., "Did you understand what I said?") is essential if complex information is to be communicated. Without feedback, false perceptions creep in, and even a small error that goes uncorrected may become magnified into a major distortion.

This experiment also revealed that communications gain in speed and efficiency as more and more feedback is permitted. Limiting receivers to "yes" or "no" responses is less effective than allowing them to expand their comments to whatever they deem appropriate.[12]

Face-to-face communications are superior, under most circumstances, to written orders, printed announcements, or business letters. The sender must experience direct feedback from the receiver to know what the receiver is hearing or failing to hear. How else can the sender become aware of the hidden meaning—the symbolic significance—the receiver is ascribing to the words? What better way to bring out into the open contradictory information already in the receiver's mind that may cause the communication to be rejected or ignored?

Another reason for the greater effectiveness of personal confrontation is that most of us communicate more easily, completely, and frequently by voice. Probably the greatest advantage of such communications is that they provide immediate feedback. Merely by looking at the audience, skillful speakers can judge how it is reacting to what they are saying. If necessary, they can modify their approach or vary the intensity of voice. (The human voice can provide a wider variety of emphasis and pace than any printed page, regardless of the number of type fonts used.)

Even better feedback is possible if the recipients of the message are allowed to comment or ask questions. This gives supervisors an opportunity to explain their meaning or to consider unexpected problems. (Printed material can provide explanations, but few writers can anticipate all the questions that might be asked.)

It is almost impossible to criticize someone's performance in writing without giving serious offense. The cold type or words always sound more harsh and condemnatory than they may have been intended, and such written criticisms often provoke strong emotional counterreactions. The result is that the recipient tends to reject the entire message as having come from a hostile source. The same criticism discussed in a face-to-face exchange can be made much more acceptable and thus will be heard.

Furthermore, we usually ascribe more credibility to what we hear spoken than to words attributed to someone in print. Employees conditioned to the "slick" releases of public relations offices tend to discount many of the printed announcements they read. Actually hearing the boss say that the company is in serious trouble, however, may carry a great deal more weight than would a statement in the house organ, particularly if employees have an opportunity to ask the boss direct questions.

U.S. Secretaries of State like Kissinger and Vance have had to travel a great deal to develop mutual understandings and to convey subtle elements of our country's foreign policy. No memoranda or letters can substitute for face-to-face discussion. With direct contact each can check what the other is hearing and thinking:

"Tell me now, in your words, what you think this assignment is all about."

---

[12] For a fuller description of this experiment by the original researcher, see Harold Leavitt, *Managerial Psychology*, 4th ed. (Chicago: Univ. of Chicago Press, 1978), pp. 119–20.

"I think I hear you telling me that the first part is clear, but the second half of that assignment seems ambiguous. Is that correct?"

Written communications

Written communications still have an important place; they may be indispensable in some circumstances. Lengthy, detailed procedures should be put in writing, so that the person to whom they are addressed can have a chance to study them at leisure. The spoken word exists only for an instant, then vanishes. The written message provides a permanent record to which receivers can refer to make sure they understand what has been said, and to which senders can refer as evidence that they have in fact said it. Frequently, too, the relative formality of written communications gives the message greater weight than it would have if it were delivered orally.

For very important messages, both the spoken and written word may be used in combination. If a new procedure is to be introduced, the supervisor might call a meeting of subordinates to give them a rough outline of the change and to: (1) explain why the change is necessary, (2) answer their questions, and (3) perhaps make adjustments to meet objections. Once general agreement has been reached, the new procedure can be reduced to writing for future reference.

Assessing nonverbal cues

How do we know if the person to whom we are communicating understands, agrees, or sympathizes with us, or is indifferent, unconvinced, or confused? In a face-to-face situation, we can observe other people and judge their responses by their total behavioral set. We can watch for nonverbal cues—the expressions of puzzlement, anger, or comprehension that flicker across the face of the listener, or the subtle body motions that reveal impatience, animosity, or agreement. These cues give eloquent expression to attitudes that the receiver may be reluctant or unable to express in words.

Indeed, by their posture and facial expression, the set of their lips, the movement of an eyebrow, people often tell us more than they do in hours of talk or scores of written memoranda. A subordinate is seldom eager to challenge the orders of a superior. But in the course of informal, face-to-face discussion, an alert supervisor can detect the subordinate's lack of enthusiasm by tone of voice and general physical behavior.

Few of us appreciate just how much valuable information these nonverbal cues transmit. As many have observed, when communication is at peak efficiency, words are often superfluous. Good examples of this are the hospital operating room, the jazz band, and some small interdependent work teams in industry. The close coordination necessary for these groups to achieve their goal is attained largely through small bodily movements and expression changes.

Reinforcing words with action

Words by themselves are suspect. Employees are more likely to accept new propositions when they observe an actual change in behavior or participate themselves in the process of change. Supervisors in one company were told that they would have the final say in granting individual pay increases, a radical departure from past practice. Most supervisors were skeptical about whether management really meant what it said. But this feeling disappeared when they began filling out recommendation forms themselves and sending them to the personnel department (a minor clerical job that in the past had been done in the superintendent's office). The consistent reinforcement of verbal announcements by action increases the likelihood that the communication will be accepted.

Employees learn that their supervisors, not the personnel department, control pay increases when they see them taking this action and hear directly from them that they are to receive the increase. Where Personnel does the notifying, employees perceive otherwise.

Management must be careful not to allow supersalesmanship techniques to dominate its thinking in communicating to employees. One cannot advertise one type of personnel program and deliver another. In the same vein, low-pressure statements are probably more effective than high-pressure pronouncements. Instead of telling workers how generous their pension benefits are, it may be more effective to give them comparative data on pension plans for the industry or community and let them draw their own conclusion.

Once management has acquired a reputation for accuracy and credibility, it can do a more effective job of communicating information on new problems.

Early in World War II, when the radio stations of most countries were widely suspected of distorting the war news, the British broadcasting system adopted a policy of frankly reporting Allied setbacks. This gave the British an advantage in morale and tactics over their enemies when the tide turned in favor of the Allies, for Europeans of all nationalities were ready to believe the news of the German rout—simply because it came from a source that had proved itself trustworthy.

Using direct simple language

Written communications should be as readable as possible. Every manager must ensure that statements are couched in simple, direct language. Government agencies have been the favorite butt of jokes about gobbledegook, but many private organizations also are guilty of torturing simple statements into complicated puzzles and using specialized and complex jargon. Low readability is undoubtedly a factor in the breakdown of communications. (And since most people talk more simply than they write, that is another reason for using face-to-face communications whenever possible.) High readability, however, is not an answer in itself to the fundamental barriers to communication that we have discussed.

Emotionally charged rhetoric should be left to debating teams. Strong adjectives and expletives, innuendoes and exaggerations cause most listeners to turn off, not on, and raise questions concerning the credibility and balance of the speaker. Crowds, particularly in political gatherings, can be aroused by demagoguery, but most reasonably intelligent listeners, alone or in small groups, reject the inflated statements of the silver-tongued politician.

Introducing a helpful amount of redundancy

Communications engineers have developed techniques for measuring the amount of redundancy in a message—roughly the amount of repetition it contains. The supervisor who wants to give a direct order or transmit technical information should make sure that the message includes substantial redundancy. Then, if any word or phrase is misunderstood, there are other elements in the communication that will carry the point. To give a very simple example:

> A firm manufacturing several thousand varieties of chemical compounds used a numerical coding system to refer to each of the products. Increasingly, management found that mistakes were creeping into the ordering system. When a supervisor requested a shipment of compound #28394, a clerical error would occasionally result in a wasted shipment of #23894. Each digit was crucial, and the slightest mistake was costly. Eventually, the firm adopted individual names for each compound, and these words had a great deal of built-in redundancy, as do nearly all words. If a clerk ordered "calitin" instead of "calithin," the shipping department knew what he meant.

If each word is crucially important, it pays to say the same thing in several ways. In giving complicated directions, it is wise to repeat them several times, perhaps in different ways, to guarantee successful transmission.

At times, however, a manager may want to avoid redundancy and concentrate instead on introducing novelty or originality into communications. We tend to ignore many of the messages we receive, simply because they sound so familiar. Most of us repeat our favorite clichés so often that people no longer listen to what we say; it is all so predictable. ("I know what the boss is going to say the minute he starts on that line about us all being one big happy team.")

There is some need for surprise, in modest doses to be sure, if we are to gain the attention of those with whom we wish to communicate. This is particularly true when our message contains something that contradicts expectations. To repeat our previous example: if your typist has been in the habit of preparing only one carbon, you must stress your request for two.

communications: the problem-solving process

"My boss doesn't give a hoot about me. As far as he is concerned I am another piece of machinery."

"I'll say this about my boss: no matter what your problem, she'll hear you through."

Effective communication requires effort both by the sender of the message and the receiver. The previous chapter was concerned with the sending of the message. In this chapter we shall deal with the specifics of the receiving or listening process. Listening is one of the most important of all management tools. Yet, though people learn to listen before they learn to talk, relatively few listen well.

Listening is sometimes viewed as interviewing, and in this chapter we use the two terms, listening and interviewing, interchangeably. This may cause some confusion, since most people think of interviewing in the sense of formal interviews connected with getting a job. By *interviewing* we mean much more than this: we mean deliberate, active listening whose purpose is to draw other people out, to discover what they really want to say, to give them a chance to express themselves fully, and to assist in the solution of mutual problems.

The following interchange illustrates dangers that arise when managers fail to listen.

Jane: Bill, I think the time has come for us to investigate new office copying equipment.

Bill: No, our budget won't stand it. We invested too much when we decided to buy rather than rent Brand X equipment three years ago.

Jane: But we can rent this time, and we'll have equipment available when we need it. The cost won't be much more than our present repair bills, and we'll save on clerical time. Furthermore. . . .

Bill (interrupting): No, this isn't the year. We don't have the budget. You'll have to do a better job with what you've got.

Jane: If you only knew how badly off we are now. . . .

Bill: No.

Of course, Bill may be right, but he hasn't listened to Jane. He has cut her down, injured her self-esteem, and cast doubt as to her ability to handle her job. The next stage may be escalation:

Jane: You're just being pig-headed because it wasn't your idea.

Whether Jane says this or not, she feels it. What could have been an objective discussion leading to cost-benefit analysis has degenerated into a personal flareup. Note how differently the scenario might have been:

Jane: Bill, I think the time has come for us to investigate new office copying equipment.

Bill: Tell me more what you have in mind Jane.

Bill doesn't have to agree with Jane after the discussion is over, but her feelings about him and the job will be very different if he hears her out.

Historical background

Management first became aware of the value of listening in industrial relations during the 1930s as a consequence of studies conducted at the Hawthorne plant of the Western Electric Company. These studies were primarily concerned with the determinants of morale and productivity. Attempting to uncover basic feelings, however, the researchers found that questioning subjects about specific aspects of their jobs resulted in superficial, lifeless answers. Even worse—or so it seemed at the time—instead of giving straightforward responses, interviewees tended to talk about what interested them most at the moment.

Following this clue, the interviewers tried a radically new experiment, they sat back and let the interviewees direct the interviews. Now they discovered that people began to express their *feelings.* Employees launched into long tirades (to which the interviewers patiently listened) revealing attitudes that might otherwise have been kept carefully guarded. In fact, some employees expressed attitudes that they had not been consciously aware of themselves. As a consequence, the interviewers discovered surprising relationships about which they would never have learned by asking direct questions.

More important: the employees benefited greatly. Just by talking freely in the presence of a sympathetic listener, they got their problems off their chests and felt better. They experienced what psychologists call *catharsis* (from the Greek: to make pure). In addition, merely by talking things over, the employees began to gain insights into the nature of their own problems. Once they had relieved their feelings by speaking openly in a receptive environment, they were able to look at their problems more objectively. And their clearer understandings, supplemented by further discussion, often enabled them to work out solutions (at least to those problems that they were in a position to solve themselves).

Impressed by the value of the Hawthorne experience, Western Electric instituted a program of formal counseling. Specially chosen counselors were trained in the use of *nondirective* interviews. (By *nondirective interviews* we mean—as we shall explain later—a type of interview in which the interviewer encourages the interviewee to express his own thoughts with considerable freedom—as contrasted to directive interviewing, in which the interviewer asks direct questions and tries to keep the discussion within predetermined limits.)

These "free-floating" counselors were given no regular supervisory duties. Their function was merely to listen to employees' problems without giving advice. Other companies rapidly followed Western Electric's example. Particularly during World War II counseling was very popular, especially to help women workers.

The counselors faced a tough ethical problem of what to do with the information they received. If they repeated to management what they had been told, the workers would no longer trust them. On the other hand, if they could use their information in a discreet manner, they might be able to eliminate the causes of trouble. Often the counselors compromised by giving management general reports without revealing details that might identify individuals.

In recent years the use of such counselors as a personnel tool has declined. It was discovered that this technique has many drawbacks, including the following:

- Although counseling might help an individual make a better adjustment to a poor environment (say to an inept supervisor), it did not improve the environment itself. Employees often began to feel that they were wasting their time talking to a counselor who could do little for them, and they ended up almost as frustrated as before.
- Counseling is directed almost entirely toward changing *individual* attitudes and behavior, in spite of evidence that group attitudes are often more important than individual attitudes.
- The counseling system gave subordinates a chance to bypass and tattle on their supervisors. Naturally, the supervisors objected.
- The counselors discovered that they were spending most of their time with a few disturbed individuals who really needed deep psychotherapy rather than counseling.

The basic trouble with "free-floating" counseling was its separation from line management. Line management emphasized downward communication; counseling provided upward communication. But the two forms of communication went along different channels.

Management began to learn that effective communications must go both ways. Upward communication and downward communication, listening and order-giving, are both more effective if done by the *same* person. Furthermore, if they are merged into the same process, something new and better emerges. Thus, there has come the realization that interviewing or active listening is not a special technique for use by personnel experts only, but a vital aspect of good management generally.

Listening as a management tool

To enumerate the uses of listening would be almost to itemize the functions of management itself. Listening is useful for bosses dealing with subordinates, for subordinates dealing with their bosses, for staff people dealing with line people (and vice versa) and for colleagues at the same level dealing with one another. Listening is obviously well suited to formal interviews, such as those used for hiring, exit, and requests for transfer. But it is also appropriate in less formal situations, such as the following:

Low morale: finding out the cause of employee dissatisfaction, turnover, or absenteeism.
Discipline: discovering why employees are performing unsatisfactorily and helping them to evolve means of correcting themselves.
Order-giving: getting reaction to and acceptance of orders, to see that the person who receives the order really understands it.
Resistance to change: gaining acceptance of new techniques, tools, procedures.
Merit rating and evaluation: helping an employee correct his weaknesses.
Grievance-handling: finding out the real causes of a union grievance and getting the union officers to agree to a constructive solution.
Settling disputes: finding out the causes of the disputes between employees and getting them to agree to settlement.

The listening approach is not something to be applied only when dealing with specific problems. It is a general attitude which the manager can apply day in and day out in dealings with fellow supervisors, subordinates, and the boss. In a nutshell, it is a matter of always being ready to listen to the other person's point of view and trying to take it into account before taking action oneself.

Establishing confidence

Managers must take the initiative in encouraging subordinates to come to them with their problems. They must show that they are willing to hear them out. Otherwise minor irritations may grow to tremendous proportions, even before the manager has become aware of the danger.

If the initial discussion is a pleasant experience, the subordinate will come back more freely and more regularly when new problems arise. If it has been an unpleasant experience and if he feels he has been "put on the spot," he will be reluctant to reveal what is on his mind in the future.

The manager should be aware that some of the people who report to him will be easier to get to know than others. Some will talk quite freely and easily. Others will hold back because of fear or natural timidity. Managers must be careful not to spend all their time with those to whom it is easy to talk.

To avoid the charge of favoritism, and to insure that he is able to deal with the problems of all his employees, the manager must go out of his way to make contact with employees who are reluctant to come to him. The manager must recognize that there is an invisible barrier which separates him from his subordinates. For some, this status difference is of little importance, but for many it makes effective upward communication much harder.

Finally, listening takes time. The manager should make time available for his subordinates to talk to him. But if he doesn't have time at the moment, it is far better to postpone the discussion to some specific hour than to rush through a discussion in an abrupt, distracted manner.

Initiating action

Nondirective listening is useful not just when someone initiates action for you (as Jane tried to do with Bill in the case that begins this chapter), but also when you try to initiate action yourself, that is, when you try to get your boss, your subordinate, or someone at your own level to accept your ideas.

Suppose you are the division manager, and you want to introduce a new system of quality control. Although you have not yet consulted the production supervisor, you have heard through the grapevine that she has strong objections to the new system. Yet her cooperation is essential if the system is to succeed.

You feel fairly certain that your plan is good and that the production supervisor's objections are not well grounded. You are the boss, of course, and you could give her a direct order to put the plan into effect. (Question: How would the supervisor react to this order? How loyally would she carry it out?)

Instead, you decide to listen to her point of view. In spite of the grapevine, you can't be sure you know what her objections are until she has spoken to you, personally. (Question: What would happen if you had already made up your mind and just went through the formalities of listening?)

So you call her into your office, explain to her that you would like her reactions to the proposed plan, and briefly explain what is involved (assuming she is not aware of this already). You emphasize that you still have an open mind as to whether to adopt the plan at all and that within limits (which you are careful to explain) the details of the plan are subject to modification.

You then ask for her comments. You listen carefully and encourage her to express herself more fully. As she speaks, she relaxes and explains her point of view with more restraint than she would if she felt she were on the defensive. Instead of trying to answer her arguments, you encourage her to tell you everything she thinks and feels about the change. When she finishes, you briefly summarize what she has said, to make sure you understand—and also to indicate to her that *you* understand.

After speaking her piece, she feels free to listen to your point of view, which may have changed since you heard her comments. You fill in some of the areas where you feel she was misinformed and indicate the points on which you have changed your own thinking. You agree that many of the problems she raises are real ones and ask for her suggestions in dealing with them. You make concessions yourself. Eventually, you work out a detailed program which includes as much of her input as seems feasible (subject, of course, to similar consultation with other affected managers).

At the end, even if the supervisor is not fully convinced of the wisdom of the modified plan, she agrees to carry it out and probably feels pleased that you consulted her.

The above example illustrates the flexibility of the listening technique as a means of initiating action (though we must emphasize that the results are frequently not as good as we have pictured). Note the steps you went through in the above example.

1. Stating the nature of your proposal, indicating that it was tentative.
2. Listening carefully to the supervisor's reactions.
3. Summarizing these to indicate that you understood them.
4. Seeking her cooperation in working out a solution, careully indicating the framework within which the solution must be made.
5. Modifying your original proposal in the light of her suggestions.
6. Making a joint commitment to carry out the agreed upon action.

Off-the-job problems

Managers sometimes use listening techniques to help employees solve personal off-the-job problems. Normally stable individuals have unexpected trouble and try to use their boss as a wailing wall. However, the bosses should be careful not to run their subordinates' personal lives.

The manager should be particularly cautious when sensitive areas are reached in the course of a discussion. What most people want is a sympathetic, understanding listener rather than an adviser. They may ask for advice, but actually they want only a chance to talk. Even when advice-giving is successful, there is the danger that the employee may become over-dependent on his boss and run to him whenever he has a minor problem.

The manager should be still more careful when deepseated personality problems are involved. In such a case it is wise to refer the person to a professionally trained specialist rather than to play amateur psychologist. The average manager is not equipped to do counseling, nor is this part of his job. The patient-psychiatrist or client-counselor relationship is just not consistent with that of subordinate and boss. And the nondirective technique may trick subordinates into blurting out confidences they will later regret.

The use of the nondirective approach

In understanding how the nondirective approach should be used, it is helpful to think of the interview as running through three stages: feelings, facts, solutions.

1. Feelings. The interviewee is encouraged to release his feelings; the interviewer is concerned with helping the interviewee express himself. This stage is the most purely nondirective, for the interviewer still has little idea where the discussion will go.

2. Facts. Having blown off steam, the interviewee is now ready to look at the facts rationally. In this stage the interviewer can be more directive and may even use "probes" (to be discussed later) to bring out information that the interviewee has not already volunteered. In fact, the interviewer may contribute additional information on his own.

3. Solutions. Once the facts have been assembled, the interviewee is in a position to weigh alternate solutions and pick the best one. As we have mentioned frequently, it is preferable to help the interviewee work out his own solution; however, the supervisor may have to be rather strongly directive to make sure that the solution is consistent with the needs of the organization.

These, then, are the three major stages of the listening process, although it may switch back and forth from one stage to another as different problems are considered. Still on a given problem the interviewer should stick to the order indicated: feelings, facts, solutions. Certainly one should avoid the common human tendency to jump to a solution before getting all the facts.

Equally important, he should not waste his time trying to isolate the facts before the interviewee has had a chance to express his feelings, to blow off steam. Why? Because feelings color facts, and as long as someone is emotionally excited he is unlikely to approach problems rationally. Furthermore—and the point is subtle—the feelings of the people concerned in the situation are themselves facts that must be considered. For instance, the office manager has been having trouble getting Bill to do a full day's work. The most important fact in this solution may be the manager's intense dislike of Bill as a person. Until the manager's feeling is recognized as a complicating element, "facts" he presents will be distorted by his antagonism toward Bill.

Does this mean that the interviewer should never express himself—that he should never try to correct the other person if he is wrong nor try to change his opinion? Of course not. It may be enough for the psychiatrist or the professional counselor merely to listen. The manager must also take action. But in most cases, before he takes action he should wait until he has heard the employee's whole story.

The nondirective approach is not a magic solution to all human-relations problems, of course. There are times when a supervisor may have to be quite firm and directive in the solution stage of the discussion to make sure that the solution is consistent with the needs of the organization. For instance, the supervisor may listen patiently to the subordinate's objections to a new system; the subordinate may persist in his resistance; and the supervisor may still have to overrule him, explaining why, and insist that the system be used. However, the subordinate will have had the satisfaction of being consulted, of knowing that he had his day in court to present his side of the story.

Listening techniques   Skillful listening is an art, and like all arts it requires training and experience. It can be learned better by practice than by reading a book, especially when the practice is supervised by an experienced instructor. Fortunately, one can gain unsupervised practice every day of the year.

Each manager must develop a system that is comfortable for him and that fits his personality, but he should avoid using the same technique with all people and for all purposes. An interview held for disciplinary reasons will naturally be different from an interview held for the purpose of order-giving.

Regardless of the form of the interview, here are a few hints that may prove useful.

Encouraging the other person to talk

Your primary objective is to get the other person to talk freely, *not to talk yourself.* The best way to find out what the other person wants to say is to listen, and the best interview is usually the one in which the interviewer talks least.

But listening is not easy, for our natural impulse is to talk. This is particularly true when we feel threatened by what is being said to us—for instance, when we are being criticized. Under these circumstances our normal impulse is to defend ourselves rather than to listen.

Listening is more than just not talking, however. It requires an active effort to convey that you understand and are interested in what the other person is saying—almost that you are helping him say it. A friendly facial expression and an attentive but relaxed attitude are important. A good listener also makes use of door-opening comments such as "uh-huh," "I understand," "That explains it," "Could you tell me more?" or "I'd be interested in your point of view."

Even silence can be used to keep a person talking. When he pauses in his discourse, he is either being polite and giving you a chance to talk, or else he wants you to comment, to evaluate what he is saying. Merely by not taking his challenge, perhaps by a nod, by waiting through his pause, you indicate that you have nothing to say at the moment, that you want him to continue talking.

Reflective summary

One of the most effective ways to encourage the other person to talk is the *reflective summary,* in which you try to sum up the feelings the other person has expressed, disregarding the factual details and incidents. For example: "The reason I want to quit is that the so-and-so boss keeps pestering me. He won't give me a chance!" Then he (or she) stops, wondering whether he has gotten himself into trouble by saying too much. Your response, "He won't give you a chance?" encourages him to tell the rest of his story, but it does not commit you in any sense. Such a summary serves a number of purposes:

1. It shows the other person that you are giving his ideas careful consideration and that you understand him—in other words, that you are being fair.
2. It gives him a chance to restate and elaborate his attitudes if he feels that you haven't quite grasped his point.
3. It serves to highlight what he has really been saying. Often people are surprised to learn what their words have meant to someone else, and are rewarded with deeper insight into their own attitudes.

The reflective summary is particularly effective if you reflect not only what the other person has actually said, but can somehow put into words what he has tried, unsuccessfully, to express. Be careful, however, not to hear more in his words than he intends to put into them. For if he finds you reading things into his words that he did not mean to be there, he will be doubly careful to watch what he says.

Your summary should indicate neither approval nor disapproval of what the interviewee is saying. It should simply indicate that you are listening attentively. For instance, he says, "It's got to the point where I may lose my temper and take a poke at the boss." If you were to say, "Well, that's quite understandable," you would almost be inviting him to carry out his threat! A more satisfactory response would be "You are sore at him because. . . ."

There are limits, however, to the extent to which reflective summaries are appropriate. It sounds patronizing and manipulative to parrot the interviewee's phrases without any indication that you are responding to their meaning. For example:

Employee: "So I want to find out exactly what I'm expected to do. How many units am I expected to do a day? It seems I'm getting a run around."

Boss: "You want to know exactly what you're expected to do. You want to know how many units a day you're supposed to do? You feel you are getting a run around."

The boss has heard the employee's words but has failed either to hear the fact-related question or to respond to the employee's feelings. Possibly the boss might have responded as follows:

Boss: "Perhaps we can do something to make your work assignment clearer, but I'm concerned about your feeling that you've been getting a run around."

Active listening requires that you put yourself in the other person's shoes. Only if you can understand the message sender's own frame of reference and his world of reality, can you really grasp the real meaning of his or her message.[1] Though few of us can qualify as psychiatrists, we can learn to listen with a "third ear" by asking ourselves such questions as: "What did Joe really mean when he told me he was 'fed up'? Was it his assignment? His family? His chances for promotion? Me, as his boss? Why did he remain silent when I asked him for details?"

Listening empathetically

There is a hidden content in many communications that can only be inferred by the listener. (This underlying element is frequently referred to as the *latent* content as distinct from the *manifest* content.) Although the listener should keep his imagination in check, he should try to go beyond the logical verbal meaning where there is some evidence that emotional feeling is involved. Most communications are, in fact, a combination of fact and feeling.

A good example of this hidden content is provided by the word *communications* itself. An office manager complains to the personnel director that all

---

[1] Empathetic listening does not necessarily mean that you *agree* with the other person's message, only that you are trying to *understand* it. Some authorities argue that the interviewer should *accept* the interviewee's feelings. We disagree. Perhaps acceptance is required for psychotherapy. But if an employee says, "I think Race X is inferior, and I'll be damned if I work with one of them," the boss may perhaps try to understand this feeling but has no obligation to accept it.

her human-relations problems stem from "poor communications." If the personnel director wants to be of assistance, he will try to get behind the manager's use of the word *communications*. The manager might mean that there are divisive cliques that tend to distort her orders or that she, the boss, never hears the "real truth" about what is going on in the office. She might be using the word *communications* to mean that cooperative teamwork is lacking, or to mean many other things. The point is that the words used by a speaker may not be very informative until we have an opportunity to question him on what he really means in terms of actual observable behavior. The listener must try to get back to the *referents* of the speaker and to avoid the easy assumption that both people are attaching the same meaning to abstract terms like *poor communication*.

Empathetic interviewing means also that you respond to the other person's comments as a person, yourself, not as a machine. To the best of your ability, you show sincere concern (insincere concern is easily discerned and is worse than nothing). There is nothing wrong in demonstrating emotion yourself; on the other hand, there is no need to match the other person's display, emotion by emotion. But it helps to be spontaneous, *yourself,* which means that none of the suggestions made in this chapter should be made mechanically. Unless you are straightforward and honest, you are unlikely to receive honesty in return.[2]

Probes

The "free-floating" counselor is interested primarily in getting at underlying feelings. And as a manager you, too, are interested in the feelings of your subordinates. But if you know that you must *act* on the basis of what you learn in the discussion, you will also want to get all the facts, the whole story.[3] This means that after the feeling stage has passed, you should to some extent direct the interview. Tactfully and calmly, you should steer the conversation, but without forcing the interviewee into an area he does not want to enter, and with no hint that you have already made up your mind.

One way to direct the interview is to build on what the interviewee has already said. By repeating certain words selected from what he has said, you can indicate that you would like him to talk more about this particular area. This device is called a "probe." For example, in explaining how a fight started between himself and another employee, Bill says, "Joe was always riding me. When he picked up my lunch bucket, that was the last straw." Now if the supervisor wants to find out more about what Joe has done to arouse Bill, he has a good chance to insert a probe: "You say Joe was always riding you?" Then he stops and waits for Bill to go on. Notice that the interviewer does not say: "What did Joe do to make you so sore?" Rather, he simply repeats the employee's own words.

Weighing alternatives

Sometimes it is enough if the interview helps you find out how the other person feels about the situation and what the essential facts are as *he or she*

---

[2] For a good discussion, see Jack Gibb, "Defensive Communication," in Harold Leavitt and Louis Pondy, *Readings in Management Psychology,* 2nd ed. (Chicago: Univ. of Chicago Press, 1973).
[3] In other words, your interviewing is "organization centered," not "client centered."

sees them. In other instances, however, you may wish to help him devise a solution. How can you do this without seeming to impose your own ideas on him? The following approach may be useful.

Let us assume one of your managers wishes to discipline severely an employee who has been a troublemaker. The manager's first suggestion may be to fire the troublemaker immediately. If you keep aking for additional suggestions, she may suggest lesser penalties. Finally, she may even come around to suggesting certain changes in her own behavior.

Now, after the manager has offered all these suggestions, you would attempt to get her to examine each one:

What would its probable effect be?

How would the other employees react?

How would it help her solve her problem?

By helping the interviewee think through her problem, you may succeed in having her come to a conclusion that is hers, not yours. And if it is hers, she will be much more likely to act on it with enthusiasm.

Things to avoid

Too much warm-up

Many people feel that before getting down to the subject of an interview, particularly if it is an unpleasant one, they should try to place the interviewee at ease by discussing some irrelevant topic—baseball, traffic jams, the weather. This approach may relieve the supervisor's anxiety, but it intensifies that of the worker, particularly if he has some idea of why he has been called in. While he is on the "hot seat," he may be thinking, "Why doesn't this character get down to business? Why does he have to play cat-and-mouse? What's this building up to?" Such "warming-up" is useful at times; however, the interviewer should be careful to use it only when it actually reduces anxiety.

Premature judgment

The listener should avoid giving any indication of pleasure or displeasure at what the subordinate says. Judgment must be suspended until all the facts are in. This restraint is extremely important, because subordinates look for verbal or facial cues that will tip them off to what the superior wants or does not want to hear. (Of course, unconsciously, we are always forming impressions, even on the most meager facts. However, supervisors should be aware of their predispositions and try to keep them from warping their judgment or communication.)

Criticizing or moralizing puts the other person on the defensive. Even if he does not argue back, he will begin to edit what he says in order to win the interviewer's approval. He will concentrate on proving that he is right rather than on giving an honest explanation. Certainly, putting some one on the defensive makes it harder to find out what that person really thinks.

Even praise or sympathy should be avoided until the end of the discussion, for it makes the interviewee think his present approach is correct and encourages him to avoid the hard work of thinking the problem through.

Direct questions

One of the most frequent errors made by inexperienced interviewers is transforming the interview into a game of "twenty questions." Bill has fallen into the habit of coming to work late and his supervisor is anxious to straighten him out before discipline becomes necessary. Having had some training in human relations, the manager suspects that a home problem is involved. His end of the conversation may run something like this:

"Do you have trouble starting your car?"
"Is there any trouble at home?"
"Does your alarm clock go off on time?"
"Did you have a drink too many last night?"

To each question Bill replies, "No, it isn't that." And to himself he says, "That's none of his business." And then another question is shot at him.

Here the manager, not Bill, is directing the interview. Note that every one of these questions is phrased in such a manner as to put Bill immediately on the defensive and make him overcautious in what he says. Some of the questions, such as, "Did you have a drink too many last night?" are downright insulting.

The listener rarely knows the right questions to ask; if he did, he would probably know the answers as well. The other person's problem is usually more complex than it seems at first glance, and direct questions tend to narrow it down too quickly.

To complicate matters, most subordinates try to say what they think will please their supervisor. Direct questions often imply the kind of answer the supervisor wants, or at least give the subordinate an "out." For instance, the question "Did you have trouble starting your car?" provides a ready excuse for a tardy worker.

If the supervisor wants to find out what the subordinate really has on his mind, he should leave the situation as free as possible to permit the subordinate to emphasize the things that are important to *him*.

If possible, the interviewer should avoid questions that can be answered with a simple yes or no. "Well, do you like your job?" "Do you think the tools are in bad shape?" Questions of this sort shut off discussion because they can be answered by a relatively meaningless "Oh, I guess so," "I suppose you might say that."

Arguing

Little is gained from argument, particularly in the early stage of the interview. Yet everyone has a strong human tendency to correct the other person when he says something that is obviously wrong. Especially, if the interviewer himself is attacked personally, he must exercise tremendous restraint not to answer back.

For example, an employee says he is having trouble doing the work because the stock has been changed. "The company must be buying cheaper material these days." Now if you know that there has been no change whatsoever in the materials, you will be strongly tempted to "set the employee straight" on this point, although his complaint may be a symptom of something much more basic. If you give way to this temptation, you may simply transform the interview into a fruitless argument.

Hard as it may be, you should avoid being defensive, even when criticized. This is difficult, because often even your unconscious feelings are revealed through facial expressions.

Advice-giving

When you finally get the complete picture as the employee sees it, you may be able to provide advice or information that has not previously been available. But again it is often better to help him work through his own problems. In any event, you should hold off giving advice until *after* the interviewee has told his entire story—until you have all the facts.

Active listening at the wrong time

Nondirective listening is not the solution to every problem. When someone is legitimately asking for information, for a helping hand, or for some resource you can provide him, he may have no need to talk things out. Sometimes managers abuse the nondirective technique by shifting the discussion from the technical aspects of the question at hand to the subordinate's motives in dealing with it. Such abuse occurs most commonly when the manager has a psychology or social work background. For example, a subordinate may have a sound practical objection to something the boss may want to do. Instead of listening to the objections themselves, the excessively psychologically oriented boss may look upon the subordinate's attitude as an example of hostility and may seek its emotional basis. Such an approach often adds to the hostility it is designed to alleviate.

Masterminding

Many people go through the motions of the nondirective interview but violate its spirit. They hope, by asking shrewd questions, to manipulate the interviewee into believing that he is thinking through his problem by himself, though the way questions are worded inevitably forces the interviewee to arrive at the interviewer's own predetermined conclusion.

Masterminding is used with various degrees of sophistication. One of the less subtle forms makes constant use of the leading question, the "don't you feel. . .?" approach: "Don't you feel it would be better for the company and your own future if you came to work on time?" Questions like this usually permit only one answer. They are thinly veiled forms of advice, judgment, or just plain bawling out.

The basic purpose of nondirective listening is to enable the listener to find out how the individual sees the problem or situation at issue, and then to help him think and, above all, *feel* his way through to a solution. The goal of this whole philosophy is for the supervisor to be perceived as a source of help—as a person who can assist the subordinate to develop and do a better job.

introducing change: the managerial issues

We live in a world of change. We Americans, in particular, have learned to expect change as part of our everyday life. We pride ourselves on being modern and up-to-date in our habits and behavior. Still, we may be more traditional than we think. To be sure, we accept and even welcome changes in terms of material things, such as household gadgets or cars. But we tend to resist changes in our interpersonal and job relations, because these changes threaten the security of the orderly and familiar ways we have known in the past, and often our status, as well.

One of the most important measures of an organization's strength is its ability to change. In fact, it *must* anticipate environmental changes by altering its own policies and structure in time to meet new conditions as they arise. In this chapter we shall discuss why there is resistance to change and what can be done to deal with it.[1]

Types of resistance to change

Of all the types of resistance to change, perhaps the one most commonly recognized is the resistance of many

---
[1] For a good discussion of the problems involved in introducing change, see Gerald Zaltman, Robert Duncan, and Jonny Holbek, *Innovations and Organizations* (New York: Wiley, 1973) and Everett Rogers with Floyd Shoemaker, *Communications of Innovations: A Cross-Cultural Approach* (New York: Free Press, 1971).

employees to technological change—to automation, for example. Such resistance is readily understandable. In some instances, technological change means that employees must agree to work on faster machines with increased workloads. In others, it requires the acquisition of new skills and even a new approach to work; for example, the worker must learn to watch and adjust equipment rather than to operate it manually. In still others, as in the case of locomotive firemen and flight engineers, it may mean the loss of work altogether.

But other forms of change are also resisted: changes in organizational structure, methods of compensation, and so forth. Take the case of a clothing store, once famous for its high-quality merchandise, which is located in an area from which high-income customers have moved. A new owner resolves to introduce a lower-priced line and to induce the sales force clerks to engage in high-pressure salesmanship. The salesclerks are likely to react violently to changing well-established patterns.

Resistance to change is sometimes as deep-rooted at the managerial level as it is at lower levels. In many companies one hears constant complaints about "old fogies" who are hampering progress. As we explore elsewhere, there are problems involved in reeducating managers to improve their supervisory practices, to give higher priority to accident prevention, and so forth. Indeed, managers tend to resist the introduction of almost any new personnel practice. They may regard a new system of job evaluation as a threat to existing status relationships, or the introduction of affirmative action hiring rules as a threat to their traditional prerogative to hire whomever they wish. Similarly, managers may object to the new patterns of relations that may be imposed by the introduction of the computer.

Resistance to change may show itself in unexpected ways, for instance in aggression, regression, and in all the negative reactions discussed in Chapter 2. It may appear as absenteeism, resignations, requests for transfer, and lowered productivity. One clear sign of resistance is a series of apparently "emotional" or "irrational" objections to minor changes. These often indicate that more deep-seated problems are involved.

It should be emphasized that not all change is resisted. Some forms of change are welcomed (such as new typewriters). Aerospace companies engage in constant technological and organizational change with relatively little resistance. It is not change itself which causes the resistance, but the meaning of the change for the people involved. Thus, one should expect greater resistance to change in a company which is contracting or stationary in size than one would in a company which is expanding, even though the expanding company has a larger number of changes—the reason being that in the expanding company the changes are less likely to threaten employees' social or economic status.

What causes resistance to change?

An obvious reason for resistance is economic. Workers resist automation when they fear they will lose their jobs; they are unimpressed by arguments that in the long run there will be more jobs in other parts of the country.

Economic factors

What concerns them most is their economic welfare.[2] Craftsmen may fear that new developments will reduce the economic value of their skills; managers oppose a change that helps the company as a whole but hurts their individual promotional opportunities.

Sometimes the economic factors underlying resistance to change are obscure or not immediately apparent. In one plant, employees began to damage parts they were sending to a new plant overseas. Formerly, the parts had been shipped to a domestic plant. Was this blind resistance to change? Not at all. Investigation revealed that the employees were afraid the company was shifting more and more of its operations to the overseas plant and feared that eventually they would lose their jobs.

We must, however, guard against the common misconception that workers generally—and particularly their unions— blindly resist all forms of technological progress. The Clothing Workers Union developed special programs designed to encourage management to introduce such changes. They recognize that only through rising productivity can their wages be raised. Similarly, the United Mine Workers cooperated with coal-mine owners in an extensive mechanization program, which resulted in substantially fewer jobs in the coal fields but higher earnings for those who remained. Foreign visitors to this country express surprise at the extent to which American workers have learned that technological change benefits them. There is, however, a significant gap between intellectually recognizing this relationship and accepting change in a particular case.

Inconvenience

Equally understandable is the resistance to a change that threatens to make life more difficult. A worker fights the assignment of extra duties; he has learned his old job so well that it requires no attention any more, whereas the new job requires surface attention. Similarly, executives dislike the inconvenience of being reassigned from one location to another. Even if the company pays their expenses, there is the bother of buying and selling houses, packing, and readjusting to new work and a new environment.

All of us develop a vested interest in our usual way of doing things. Our everyday habits provide us with a certain security in our life. Some of these habits are quite trivial: We drive to work by a fixed route every day, even though other routes are equally good; when our usual route is temporarily blocked, we are annoyed by the inconvenience of having to change our pattern.

Learning new ways requires the expenditure of energy, and human beings are generally lazy. For even the simplest job there are "tricks to the trade" that take time to learn. When a person is thrown into a new situation, old tricks no longer apply and the security of the familiar is lost.

Commitment

Commitment makes change more difficult. Even if the old way isn't working, we have much invested in it. To admit we were wrong is humiliating, to do so publicly is doubly so. Thus we defend and persist in our errors; and

---

[2] For similar reasons, workers may object to bigger workloads, even when there is no demand for greater physical effort. They reason that they may work either themselves or their friends out of a job or that management is getting "something for nothing."

the longer we persist, the greater our commitment. When the Edsel seemed to be in trouble, Ford sank millions of dollars more to keep the ill-fated project going. Similarly, the United States' commitment in Viet Nam continued long after its disastrous results were clear. As Under Secretary George Ball put it as early as 1965, "Once we suffer large casualties . . . our involvement will be so great that we cannot—without national humiliation—stop short of achieving our complete objectives."

Uncertainty

The new way is always strange, threatening, and laden with uncertainties—even if it is an improvement over the old. We have a chance for a new job at higher pay. Should we take it? Maybe not. How hard will it be? How long will it take to learn? Will we be able to meet the challenge? Who will our friends be? The opportunity may be very good indeed, yet there is a strong tendency to let well enough alone.

One reason for this fear is the lack of factual information. We know our present circumstances; we don't know what the new ones will be. Some people are gamblers by nature, but the average person hesitates to venture into uncharted waters. The uncertain is always threatening.

New equipment is introduced into the plant. What will it mean to our job, our status, our security? A new boss is assigned to the department. What will the new policies be? How will they affect us? Often the rumor mill exaggerates the potential threat of a change. Until management clarifies the impact of the change, such rumors can panic a group of employees.

Uncertainty caused by lack of information may be corrected simply by providing answers to questions—assuming that management is aware of what questions are being asked. But there is another kind of uncertainty that cannot be dissipated by information: the anxiety that springs from the individual's fears about how *he himself* will react to the new situation. Every soldier is assailed with doubts the night before his or her induction. What will army life be for me? Every veteran is delighted to provide information, but no one can predict how *I* will react. For this sort of uncertainty there can be no quick remedy.

Symbols

Symbols raise special problems. Remember that a symbol is something that stands for something else. The flag symbolizes one's country; the Bastille, prerevolutionary oppression in France; the top brass's parking lot, their special status; the restaurant's white table cloth, its general excellence. A symbol cannot be eliminated without threatening in people's minds the things for which it stands. There was widespread emotional reaction to the change in the Canadian flag. Consider the following case from industry:

The new manager of the Integrity Insurance Company had little difficulty with her "modernization" program until she decided it was a waste of money to print policies on high-quality parchment paper. Her proposal to substitute a cheaper but still durable paper led to a storm of protest from the company's insurance agents: the new paper wouldn't look or wear well, it didn't look right, the customers would think it cheap. Investigation revealed that to the agents the parchment paper was a symbol of Integrity's reputation as a leader in the industry. They began to fear that these changes would mean that Integrity would be just like any other insurance company.

Small changes may symbolize big ones, particularly when employees are uncertain about how extensive a program of change will be. When a situation begins to shift, subordinates search for indications of what lies ahead. A symbol represents a whole framework of treasured relationships and values; subordinates unite to protect it against attack just as if everything it represented were actually in danger.

Threats to interpersonal relationships

As we mentioned in Chapter 5, anything that disrupts the customary social relationships and standards of the group will meet with strong resistance. In particular, employees oppose changes that threaten their status or their painfully acquired, socially valued skills.

Vests and coats in one clothing center were made by separate groups of tailors, though to an outsider their skills seemed readily interchangeable. Over the years the demand for vests had fallen off while an acute shortage of skilled coatmakers developed. Yet in spite of the combined urging of union and management, the vestmakers refuse to transfer to coatmaking. As a result the vestmakers lost over $60 a week. Why did they persist in this apparently illogical attitude?

The vestmakers were a small, tightly knit clique of friends who were proud of their skill. They had a long-established union local of their own. They feared that if they were transferred to coatmaking their clique would be broken up, and they would become the least-skilled coatmakers rather than highly skilled vestmakers. Thus, the change threatened their prestige and their social arrangements.

Even when no change in physical location is involved, most changes tend to upset interpersonal relations. Take the situation in a small firm that had just hired a new purchasing agent.

Previously, department heads had ordered their own supplies. Now the department head merely filled out a purchase order; the purchasing agent decided on the supplier and negotiated the price. Though this policy saved the department heads from being pestered by salespeople and saved the company money, the department heads were highly antagonistic. They missed the feeling of importance that came from dealing directly with sales representatives; the purchasing agent was far less obsequious to them than the salespeople had been, and he threatened their authority by suggesting at times that they might use cheaper, lower-quality material. This fact may help explain why they began complaining about red tape and about how the purchasing agent made their jobs harder, not easier.

Every manager develops patterns of informal relations with subordinates. And every new supervisor requires a long period of initiation before being accepted by subordinates as their legitimate leader, in part because they fear that the new manager may not follow previous patterns of informal relations. In fact, *all* new members of a group have a hard time until they develop satisfactory relations with their colleagues—and one of the reasons why people resist being transferred to new jobs is that they dislike the disruption of old relations and the work of establishing new ones.

Other changes may threaten an employee's opportunity to provide leadership. Before automation, a crew chief on a press directed the team that worked with him; after automation there was less need for teamwork and less opportunity to issue orders. Under the old scheme the plumber scheduled his own work; under the new scheme he must wait until someone calls him, thus reducing his discretion and status and substantially changing his social relationships with others.

Individuals adjust their pattern of social relations to fit their own special personality needs, just as they adjust other elements of their life in the formation of habits. Over a period of time, assuming an employee is not anxious to quit his present job, he has probably developed a good fit between his personality needs and the requirements of the job. The individual who wants to boss others around, even if he is not officially a supervisor, has probably found a position in the work group that permits him to initiate activity; the worker who wants to avoid social pressures has probably found a job where no one can push him, not even the person who works next to him. Changing work procedures and systems, and introducing new equipment, upsets these convenient, pleasant job patterns. The sequence of work may be so drastically changed that the employee who was formerly isolated must now work with a high-pressure colleague, and the leader is left with no one to lead.

Resentment toward new orders and increased control

Whenever management institutes change, it must substantially increase the number of orders it gives to subordinates. This results in a change in interpersonal relations, and this second change, in turn, may well lead to resistance.

Some people resent taking any orders at all. Others have become accustomed to a certain level of control from higher management but resist any attempt to increase this control. On routine jobs or on jobs where employees are used to being their own boss, direct orders from management are relatively rare. When change occurs, they become subject to all sorts of unusual pressures from supervisors, staff people, and the big boss. Suddenly they find that someone is checking up on them and barraging them with far more orders than usual. This sharp increase in control reduces their feeling of autonomy and self-reliance. It emphasizes their dependence on higher management.

Similarly, members of management often resist change when it is initiated by staff people who normally have little control over (or even contact with) the line people who must carry out the change. Staff people have a strong incentive to promote change because it increases their prestige and influence; for almost these very reasons, however, line people have a tendency to resist change.

Resistance of this sort occurs also in the relations between staff groups. Engineers often resist suggestions by purchasing agents to use new materials which have come to the purchasing agents' attention through salesmen. Engineers feel that they should have exclusive authority to specify material, and that they should tell the purchasing agent what sorts of material should be used—not vice versa. So when purchasing agents try to influence the engineers, they are reversing the usual channel of communication.

Some experts argue that one of the main problems in introducing change is that it is introduced in an intermittent fashion. The organizations that have greatest difficulty are often those that make changes only once in a while. The trick, these experts claim, is to make change almost continuously, to make change for the sake of change even if there is no compelling reason for change at the moment. Perhaps this suggestion is too extreme. Still, it does emphasize the point that living with change is very different from leading the same placid existence day after day.

Rather than distribute the disruptive impacts of change throughout the organization, some companies have established separate departments that specialize in change and uncertainty. In this way they protect the routine efficiency of regular departments from being disturbed.

Union attitudes

Unions are also likely to resist change unless management consults with them, either formally or informally. It is not enough to inform individuals. Every union has certain institutional needs that must be met if it is to retain its members' loyalty. If management makes a point of working with the union, the union may cooperate in introducing the change. If management ignores the union, the only way the union can preserve its status is by opposing management.

What happens when management decides to introduce new equipment that will require workers to learn new jobs and assume new responsibilities? The typical approach in some companies is for the industrial engineer to make all the necessary plans, perhaps in consultation with the supervisor. When the equipment arrives, the supervisor assigns people to the new jobs and the personnel department computes the new pay rates. Almost inevitably, the union will find something wrong with the change and file a grievance—and perhaps even sponsor a slowdown or wildcat strike. Why? Were the union to accept management's action passively, it would be abandoning what it regards as its proper role. The only way to save face is to fight the proposed changes.

In other companies, management customarily informs the union of proposed changes long before they are made, asks for suggestions on how the seniority clause should operate when workers are transferred, and bargains over wage rates for the new job. The union's status is preserved, and it assumes responsibility for resolving what might be a bitter dispute over who will be assigned to the new jobs. Of course, in bargaining over wages the company may have to make concessions; but over all, it may cost less than trying to force the change over the union's objection, for workers are in an ideal position to ensure that unwelcome change will prove unsuccessful or costly.

The computer: an example of resistance

Workers are not the only group to resist change. Some of the most clearcut examples of stubborn resistance to change have been managers' reactions to the computer revolution. Though computers have been widely installed, many managers have strongly opposed the management science techniques that the computer makes possible. No doubt these techniques have been oversold, but there is little question that managers have failed to realize the techniques' potential.

Why has there been such resistance? In the first place, management science techniques often require that records be kept more accurately than ever before, thus making the line manager's life more difficult. More important, many managers believe that computer systems reduce their discretion. Information they need is "locked up" in the computer where they can't get at it; further, they believe that computer-processed reports are often inaccurate.

Computer language frequently baffles line managers, which makes them dependent on computer experts. In some cases computers actually make decisions that line managers once made themselves (for example, regarding line balancing and inventory control). Many managers fear that the computer will reduce their status or even cost them their jobs. Although this fear arises because the managers don't understand what the computer does, it is nevertheless very real. In a sense, knowledge is power, and the computer shifts the location of knowledge. (No wonder in many organizations there is power struggle over who "owns" the computer.)

The introduction of computer-oriented techniques is often hindered by poor personal relations between computer specialists and line managers. The typical computer expert (who is often young) is convinced that he or she has mathematical proof that a proposed change will result in greater efficiency. The specialist is prepared to explain the method of analysis to line people, but if they cannot understand it, they should accept the word of an expert:

I've developed a program that should save the company thousands of dollars in terms of reduced inventory, will eliminate stock-outs, and will greatly speed up customer delivery. Though I've simulated the organization and know my program will work, I just can't get them to accept it. They tried a bobtailed version of my plan on an "experimental" basis, but they didn't use it right. They said my plan wasn't practical. I know it would have worked had they given it a chance. Instead they sabotaged it.

Line managers, on the other hand, tend to be antagonized by this cocksure attitude. To them management is more art than science: "Computer specialists haven't any experience doing what we do," they say. "And they don't take the human equation into account." Given this attitude it is understandable that line managers often consciously or unconsciously sabotage efforts to introduce computer-oriented changes into management practices.

The hostility line managers show to management science techniques is only an extreme example of the resistance they frequently show to proposals initiated by staff departments.

So far we have dealt with change as if it involved only two groups: one seeking change, another resisting it. Obviously, this is not so. Apparently simple changes may involve a host of people who may not seem concerned at first. A change may appear to affect only Mr. *A*, but it affects his relationship with Ms. *B*, who becomes upset, thus hurting her relationship with Mr. *C.* Mr. *C* in turn deals with Mr. *A* in a less friendly fashion than usual, which further upsets Mr. *A*. Eventually, a comparatively minor change touches off a major crisis.

Change must be seen in organizational terms. Rarely are managers and

CHAPTER 9
introducing change: the managerial issues

Change and the overall organization

their immediate subordinates the only ones involved. Very often the need for change develops first: profits decline, competition adopts new products, equipment begins to wear out and get out of date. Management may cling to its traditional ways at first, even though to an outsider the need for adjustment may be obvious. Eventually, one group within management (usually a staff department) may become aware of the problem and propose a solution. Now it must sell its solution to other groups. Line personnel may resist because they have the difficult task of implementing the change. Other staff people may resist also: the controller, for instance, because the change is too expensive, or the personnel director because it would disrupt a tricky union relationship.

While the plan is under consideration, rumors fly, restlessness increases, and sometimes exaggerated fears arise. When the plan is finally tentatively adopted at higher levels, management must try to win the acceptance and cooperation of those at lower levels, and sometimes from the union. Often the change may have widespread and unexpected ramifications, and it may disrupt precariously balanced relationships.

The process should not be considered entirely a one-way street running, for example, from staff to line to subordinate employees. Line management will seek additional information from staff, raise objections, and suggest modifications in the proposed plans. Staff people may now be the ones who are resisting the changes proposed by line. Subordinates will react in the same way—openly if they are permitted to speak out, under cover if they are not. (For example, they may "modify" management's plans through outright sabotage.) Often subordinates propose change that higher management will "resist."

In organizations where human relations are sound, change is usually taken in stride. But in organizations where tensions and dissatisfactions are high, changes will be more difficult to accomplish. For example:

The high degree of [social] integration, the relative lack of conflict, and the level of job security in the chemical industry provide an atmosphere in which technological change is more accepted by workers and management than in the automobile industry, where, because of its history of labor-management strife and its irregular employment patterns, workers are naturally suspicious of the motives and effects of technological innovation.[3]

In some situations, stresses that are not obvious in ordinary circumstances become evident when change is introduced, almost as if the change is the straw that breaks the camel's back. Consider the following ingenious study conducted at General Electric:

The experiment was concerned with two sets of groups of workers, all doing repetitive, no-attention work. First these employees went through a "manipulative period" of several weeks. One set of employees, the "Favored Groups," received praise and friendly help from their bosses and were protected from disruption. The other set, the "Disfavored Groups," were nagged and pestered by management in a number of annoying ways. As might be expected, the Favored Groups developed positive attitudes toward their treatment while the Disfavored Groups expressed feelings of considerable aggravation.

[3] Robert Blauner, *Alienation and Freedom* (Chicago: University of Chicago Press, 1964), p. 153.

Nevertheless, neither treatment seemed to have a significant effect on the various groups' output rates.

At the end of the manipulation period, all special treatment stopped, except that shortly thereafter slight changes were made in each group's production methods. In both sets of groups both quantity and quality of output went down but the effect was very significantly greater in the formerly Disfavored Groups than it was in the Favored Groups.[4]

The lesson for management is that although morale may have little impact on productivity under normal conditions, it may well make change more difficult. The impact of change on an existing organization is always difficult to predict.

Violation of expectations

One concept may help summarize much of what we have said about resistance to change. In previous chapters we suggested that in most well-established groups there are generally accepted (legitimate) norms about the rights and responsibilities of both managers and subordinates—and that the nature of these rights and responsibilities is established by implicit bargaining. Change violates the implicit bargain. Unless the manager is careful in introducing change, the action is likely to be regarded as illegitimate, and subordinates will seek to restore the previous equilibrium by resisting the change.

Reducing resistance to change

Let us examine the problem of introducing change in still another framework. Take a situation in which workers are producing at 70 percent of the efficiency that might be expected on the basis of purely technical considerations. Obviously, certain forces are operating to hold the rate down. For instance:

1. Dislike of work.
2. Fear of working oneself out of a job.
3. An informally set "bogey."
4. Dislike of the supervisor.

Yet another set of forces must be operating to keep the rate *as high as* 70 percent. These may be:

1. Fear of losing one's job—or at least fear of losing special privileges.
2. Pressure exerted by the supervisor.
3. Financial incentives (if there is piece work).
4. Fear of being caught idle.

Presumably, at the 70 percent rate of production, the two sets of forces have reached a balance (this has been called a quasi-stable equilibrium). That

---

[4] Stanley Schacter and others, "Emotional Disruption and Industrial Productivity," *Journal of Applied Psychology* 45, No. 4 (August 1961), 201–13. The description of the experiment is somewhat oversimplified, but it gives the essential picture of what was done.

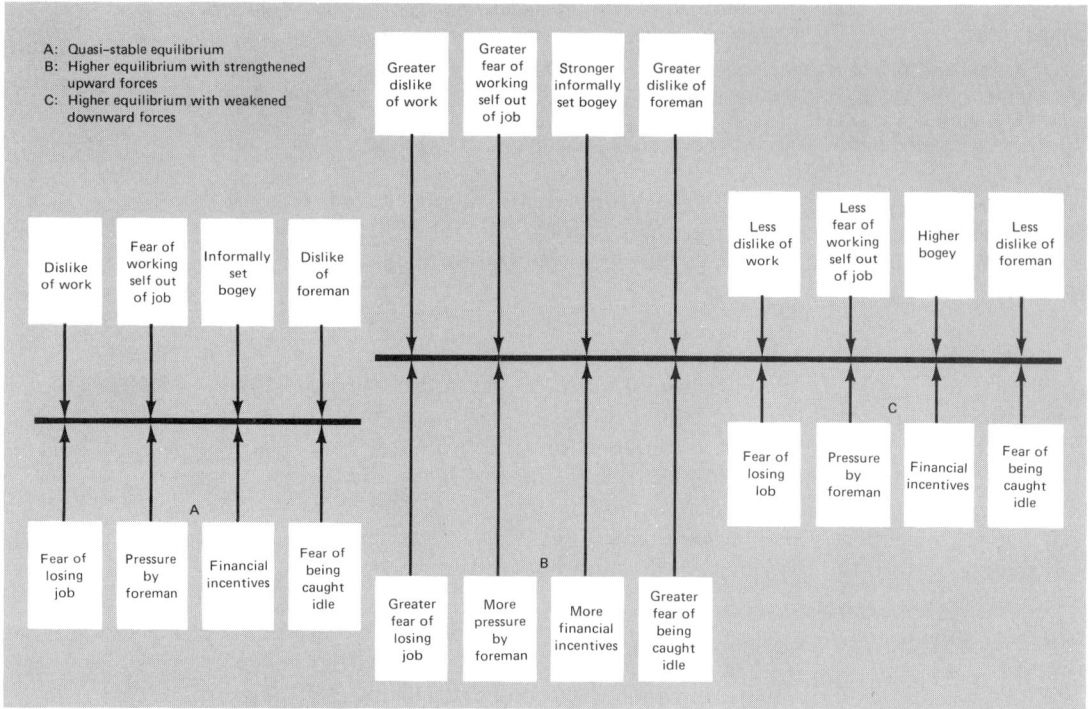

is, a system has been established in which one set of needs is balanced off against the other. (See *A* in the diagram.)

Now, if management wants to increase production, the typical approach is to strengthen the upward forces (*B* in the diagram), perhaps by having the supervision apply even more pressure or by installing piece work. This method of introducing change we shall call *overcoming resistance*. Of course, the higher production climbs, the more employees' resistance is raised, until finally a new equilibrium is reached where the two sets of pressures are once more in balance. However—and this is a crucial point—at the new equilibrium, stronger forces are operating on each side, and tension is at a higher level. Frustration is greater, and employees are more likely to devise techniques to insulate themselves from the pressures acting on them. From management's point of view this is an inefficient way of doing things. It is like trying to stop a car by using the brakes without taking one's foot off the gas.

Fortunately, there are more efficient ways of accomplishing the same objective. Instead of strengthening the upward forces, management can weaken the downward forces (*C* in the diagram), perhaps by making the work less disagreeable or by inducing workers to change their bogey or by reducing their dislike of the supervisor. This method we shall call *reducing resistance*. Here, too, a new equilibrium will be reached at a higher level of production, but it will be at a lower level of tension. It is like stopping a car by taking one's foot off the gas but by not using the brake. Though frequently method

2 (reducing resistance) cannot be used without some of method 1 (overcoming resistance), method 2 strains human relations less.

In overcoming resistance, management seeks to apply enough pressure on employees to induce them to do what is expected. The most obvious way to overcome resistance to change is simply to threaten to fire employees if they don't adjust or to promise to pay them more if they do. This, of course, is the traditional approach, which we discussed in Chapter 2, and it leads to the problems we described at the time. Employees may respond to threats either by quitting altogether, by sabotaging the change once it has been introduced, or by implementing it in a half-hearted manner. What about trying to deal with resistance by promising employees economic rewards if they will accept the change? If the reason for resistance in this case is largely economic—and in many cases it is—obviously an economic reward is a good answer, for it helps reduce the cause of resistance and thus helps get the change accepted with less tension.

On the other hand, economic rewards are less successful if the reason for resistance is noneconomic. An executive may be offered a salary increase to move to a new location. Let us assume that the executive's immediate reactions to this offer are that the new location is very unpleasant and that he has misgivings about the type of work he will be doing and the colleagues he will be associating with.

Confronted with such a choice, the executive will probably experience painful indecision. Indecision is always frustrating, even between attractive alternatives. He may even try to get the salary increase without leaving town, perhaps by going to work for another company. And regardless of what he decides, for years to come he may resent having been forced into the decision. If he stays, he may deplore his economic sacrifice every time he pays a bill. If he goes, his attitude may make it difficult for him to adjust to the new situation.

A large chemical company used a new approach in staffing a new laboratory in a remote section of the country. Their approach emphasized reducing causes of resistance. First, the company publicized the importance and challenge of the new laboratory's work and hinted broadly that assignment there would offer great opportunities for promotion. Then it invited a small core of experienced engineers to accept positions in the new lab and told them that they could invite less-experienced employees to join them. However, management made it clear that those who were invited were free to reject the invitation. The potential candidates and their families were brought together from all over the country at the site of the new lab and were given a chance to get to know one another and to investigate housing possibilities. As a consequence, the firm had little trouble recruiting able engineers to work in the new location.

In the discussion that follows, we shall emphasize methods of reducing, rather than overcoming, resistance.

As we mentioned earlier, much of the resistance to change has an economic motivation. People either fear that the change will result in an immediate loss of job or earnings, or else they fear that it will affect their long-run job security of chances for promotion. The easiest solution in such a case is

Through economic incentives

simple but expensive: guarantee that these fears are groundless. If a sales representative refuses to handle a new line of goods merely because he or she fears a loss of commission earnings, management might guarantee that earnings will be no lower with the new goods. It is quite common in union contracts today for management to guarantee that no one will be displaced by technological change. Certainly, too, if new equipment is to be introduced that will displace people, the change should be made in a period of expanding employment when the displaced employee can be offered another job that offers equally good security and pay.

Such guarantees are extremely useful in smoothing over change. The difficulty is their expense. The very reason for change may be the desire to cut costs because of economic necessity. Even in such a case, management may reduce resistance if it can truthfully show that the change will be an improvement in the individual's own (not just the company's or the other workers') economic prospects in the long run.

Though the bulk of this chapter is concerned with noneconomic means of handling resistance, you should not draw the wrong impression from our allocation of space. *Economic motivation is very important in our society.* When the cause of resistance is economic, all the noneconomic techniques that we are about to discuss will be meaningless.

Through two-way communication

Resistance to change that springs from fear of the unknown can be reduced simply by providing appropriate information. This information should explain not only *what* is to happen but also *why.* And it should be sent to the whole organization, to those both directly and indirectly involved.

This question of communications raises all the problems that we discussed in Chapter 7. Is the information really understood? Does it answer the questions actually being asked? Here, as in most areas of human relations, only *two-way* communication will serve the purpose. When major change is contemplated, superiors and subordinates should sit down and discuss the proposed plan in a way that will bring doubts and questions out into the open. After all, even though management's ideas may work in theory, employees may have the know-how to make them work in practice. Indeed, what management diagnoses as *employee* resistance to change is sometimes really management resistance to listening to employee suggestions.

Through group decision making and commitment

Most people have a strong desire to participate in decisions that affect them directly. Group decision making actively involves subordinates in the process of introducing change and enhances their sense of control over the environment. Often group approaches to change involve three somewhat distinct stages: (1) unfreezing old attitudes, (2) tentative change, and (3) commitment or refreezing attitudes.

Unfreezing attitudes. People often resist change because they hold certain fixed attitudes, to which they adhere in spite of all evidence to the contrary. Group decision making helps them *unfreeze* these attitudes so that they can reexamine them.

A classic example occurred in a pajama plant.[5] During World War II the company's staff psychologist tried to persuade management, in view of the general manpower shortage, to abandon its policy of not hiring women over thirty. The top-management group immediately opposed this suggestion, insisting that older women took too long to train, had a higher absenteeism rate, and never worked at top speed. When the staff psychologist mentioned the good performance of older women currently employed, management dismissed them as exceptional cases.

Shifting to another approach, the psychologist tried to involve management in a minor research project to find out how much money the company was losing through employing older women. Management itself determined the criteria to be used (production rates, turnover, absenteeism, and learning speed) and also decided how the data were to be gathered. In short, management became actively involved in the project. To management's surprise, the data showed that older women were better on all counts. Highly excited by these findings, management changed its policy and even spread the word of its shift to other companies.

Notice that the psychologist failed when he tried to attack management's stereotypes head-on. But he succeeded when he induced management to unfreeze its old attitudes by engaging in the research study. By doing this, management opened its mind to objective evidence. In a sense the approach used was like double-clutching. Instead of shifting directly from one attitude to another, the group went into "neutral" before taking up its final position.

Change: establishing new group standards. In Chapter 5 we mentioned that groups develop certain standards of proper conduct and that individuals who fail to live up to these standards are subjected to pressure to conform. When an individual member of a group decides to accept a change imposed from above, he fears that his fellow workers will criticize him for playing along. But when the entire group is involved in the decision leading to the change, just the opposite occurs: the individual who *refuses* to accept the change is pressured into accepting the group decision. In effect, group decision making may lead to the establishment of new group standards that are rigidly enforced.

Commitment and refreezing attitudes. Group decision making commits each member of the group to carry out the decision that is agreed on. It refreezes the group. Even if a member has reservations or second thoughts, he is under strong pressure to implement the decision. Providing employees with information and arguments may influence them one way or another, but they themselves must decide whether to accept or resist a proposed change if they are to feel committed to the ultimate decision. Beyond this, commitment is greater when:

1. commitment is made public,
2. there is commitment to a *specific* course of action rather than some vague set of values,
3. those involved feel they have made the commitment voluntarily, without coercion,

[5] A. J. Marrow and John R. P. French, "Overcoming a Stereotype," *Journal of Social Issues*, Vol. 1, No. 3 (1945), pp. 33–37.

4. group members believe the commitment is irrevocable, and
5. those involved are reminded of their commitment at some later date.[6]

But commitment is a two-edged sword. As we have seen, it causes people to persist too long in such disastrous actions as the Edsel folly and the Viet Nam war. Unfreezing commitment is often extremely difficult.

Furthermore, although group decision making may be a useful tool in reducing resistance to change, it is by no means a cure-all for management's problems. It works effectively when management is relatively indifferent to what the group decides (for instance, management may not care how the work is divided up so long as the job is done). Group decision making may also prove effective when management and employees have overlapping but not conflicting interests. But when there is no community of interest or when participation is foreign to a group's experiences, group decision making is of little use in reducing resistance to change.

Through bargaining

How does bargaining differ from group decision making? In group decision making, management gives the group freedom to make its own decisions (within limits). Bargaining implies a willingness to talk things over and to make compromises in an effort to get the group's approval of proposed changes. However, management does not agree in advance to accept any decision made by the group. Normally, it accepts only some of the group's proposals and only as a *quid pro quo* in exchange for the group's accepting the rest of what management wants.

Sometimes bargaining is implicit (as we mentioned in Chapter 2)—that is, unspoken understandings are reached on how much management will demand in the way of change, and subordinates in effect agree to accept a limited amount of change as long as management is "reasonable" in its demands.

Often, explicit and open bargaining is more useful, particularly in a unionized situation. As we have seen, unions insist on being consulted on every matter that affects the welfare of their members. Some changes, such as pay cuts, may clearly require union approval. In other instances, although management has the power to make a change on its own, it may be caught up in a swarm of grievances if the union does not approve of what it does. When workers are transferred from one job to another, for example, the union may charge that the seniority clause of the contract has been violated.

Many managements insist on their "prerogative" to make all decisions by themselves. When the union attacks their actions, they try to limit the discussion to the strictly legal question of whether the contract was in fact violated. They feel that once the union is given a say, it will be difficult or impossible to operate efficiently or to make any decisions at all.

There are times when management probably should stand on principle, particularly to show that unrelieved obstinacy on the part of the union can provoke equal obstinacy on the part of management. But management should

---

[6] See Gerald Salancik, "Commitment and Control of Organizational Behavior and Belief," in Barry Staw and Gerald Salancik, eds., *New Directions in Organizational Behavior* (Chicago: St. Clair Press, 1977).

set an example of reasonableness—at least to the extent of listening to the union's point of view. This may not be enough, however. A union is seldom satisfied just to be informed or to be given an opportunity to air its objections, especially if these objections always prove fruitless. If management wants to win the union's support in introducing change, it must give careful, open-minded attention to union grievances. Perhaps it should even let the union participate in the decision-making process itself.

Regardless of whether management lets the union participate in decision making, management must be prepared to make concessions and to accept union suggestions that it may not completely agree with. A reasonably adequate solution enthusiastically supported by the union is better than a perfect solution strongly opposed by the union.

Many of these same principles apply to dealing with nonunion groups. The interests of management and subordinates often conflict. Regardless of how assiduously management uses the techniques of consultation and group decision making, there will be occasions when subordinates are unwilling to accept everything management wants. Under these circumstances it is simply common sense for management to make some concessions to the subordinates' strongest objections, if only as a means of winning more complete acceptance of other aspects of the proposed change.

Collective bargaining is difficult with nonunion groups, for there is no established mechanism to rely on. With small nonunion groups, however, at least it is possible to discuss problems with the group as a whole. With larger nonunion groups, management can deal with informal leaders or specially selected committees.

Management is under no obligation to bargain over every change it wants to initiate. On occasion it must push proposals through without regard to subordinates' objections. But whenever management acts this way, it should be fully aware that it may be preparing the way for costly resistance later on.

Handling symbols

How can management minimize resistance when it has to change or eliminate some feature that has acquired symbolic meaning? First, management should indicate clearly that changing the symbol is not the same as attacking the values the symbol stands for. Thus in switching from parchment paper for insurance policies (see p. 163), the sales manager might emphasize that the change will help create the modern, up-to-date atmosphere that customers of the Integrity Company expect.

Sometimes it is possible to replace one symbol with another: when a new state is added to the Union, the old flag is discarded, but a new one takes its place. Similarly, if it becomes necessary to move top management's cars from the front to the rear parking lot, special areas marked with special signs might be reserved for them.

Making changes tentative

When the individuals concerned participate in making the final decision on whether or not to accept a change, it is sometimes useful to ask the group to go along with the change on a tentative, trial basis at first. This approach has two advantages:

> Members of the resident medical staff often had guests in the hospital cafeteria for Sunday dinner, but crowded conditions frequently made it impossible to find a whole table for themselves. They had the cafeteria director place a sign on a group of tables: "Reserved for Medical Staff." Immediately, several other high-status groups asked for similar consideration. To avoid the inflexibility and embarrassment that would arise if a majority of tables were specially reserved, the director changed the notices to read: "Medical Staff Are Requested to Use These Tables." This request could be justified on the grounds that it would make doctors easier to reach in case of emergency calls, and it also minimized the feeling that this was an additional symbol of the doctors' higher status.

1. It enables employees to test their own reactions to the new situation and provides them with more facts on which to base their decision.
2. It helps to "unfreeze" employees' attitudes and encourages them to think objectively about the proposed change. A change introduced on a trial basis is less threatening and generates less resistance than a permanent change.

However, when the individuals concerned do not participate in making the final decision, tentative changes may be unwise. They prolong the period of uncertainty and tension and the length of time in which the group is supervised closely. And there is always the chance that employees will in effect "participate" in the final decision—by resisting it or sabotaging it.

Slow change or quick?

Should change be introduced slowly or quickly? The answer is not clear. Many people believe in "making haste slowly," on the grounds that slow changes are less disruptive than fast changes and provide greater opportunity for adjustment. Given time, the new will blend with the old.

Fast changes, if forced on people, may lead to violent resistance, and the resulting shock may disrupt the entire organization. There may be some resistance to slow change, but it will be less intense at any given time. Indeed, if the change is introduced slowly enough, it may not even be perceived—or else the organization may become accustomed to constant, gradual change as a natural process, as the fashion industry has.

Slow change entails certain dangers of its own, however. It is bound to be less effective if it is just patched onto an existing set of practices than it might be if it were fitted into a new framework. In theory, management should evaluate the likely long-term ramifications of every proposed change before introducing it. Unfortunately, however, when management introduces slow change, total reevaluation is rare (often because management wants to avoid "trouble"), and practices are continued that become increasingly inappropriate to the changed situation.

The story is told of how during World War II the British army ordered a time study of their standard procedure for firing artillery. Most of the operation seemed efficient enough, except that just before the gun went off two men came to attention. When the time-study man asked why, he was told, "We've always done that." Only after considerable research did he discover that the original purpose was to keep the horses from jumping (though horses had not been used for years).

When change is so gradual that people do not recognize that it has occurred, they may well continue to behave in ways that were appropriate only in the old situation. If change is to be made slowly, management would be wise to give everyone concerned an over-all picture of what is eventually intended. Otherwise employees will begin to wonder, "Something is happening, but we don't know what," and exaggerated fears will arise about where the change is leading.

Actually, if employees fully understand and accept the change, there is little reason not to make the change rapidly. Adjustment is required only once, and there is small likelihood of anachronistic holdovers from a former period. Fast change eliminates the need for the constant series of adjustments that are required by slow change and leave the organization in that continual turmoil.

Other techniques

One of the most common and most difficult problems in introducing change is that of bringing in a new manager. Ordinarily, if the old manager has been well liked, the new one will have two strikes against him, for none of the employees will believe that he can be as good as his predecessor. At the outset, everyone wonders what changes the new manager will make. His most inconsequential acts are carefully examined for clues to his future policy and may be exaggerated into foreboding of future disasters. His subordinates may resent him as an outsider and prepare themselves to reject everything he does.

Let us examine this problem and how it was handled in a specific situation; our example will illustrate several techniques that may be helpful in introducing change in a wide variety of situations. The following case describes how a new supervisor was introduced into a large restaurant:

Since the old supervisor had developed warm relations with her subordinates, the restaurant manager was afraid that her departure might have a bad effect on the morale of the whole organization. Consequently he prepared the way for her successor with great care. First, he discussed the problem of a replacement with both the old supervisor and the chef, her chief assistant. The chef proposed a candidate for the job; though this candidate had to be rejected, the reasons for the rejection were fully explained to the chef.

When the new supervisor was finally selected, she was introduced to her subordinates at a general meeting. The manager announced that the old supervisor was leaving and went on to say how much she meant to the restaurant. The old supervisor spoke with great emotion about how sorry she would be to leave her associates. Then she introduced the new supervisor, extolled her virtues, and asked her employees to show the new woman the same cooperation they had given to herself. Finally, the new supervisor promised to do her best to follow in her predecessor's footsteps.

For the next few days the new supervisor followed the old one around, getting to know people and trying to learn the supervisor's routine and methods of dealing with people. On the old supervisor's last day, the whole kitchen staff gave her a farewell party.

Although the new supervisor decided that she would eventually make certain changes in the operation, she spent her first few weeks trying to follow the human-relations pattern established by her predecessor. Only after she was fully accepted by the group did she begin making changes.[7]

What techniques were used here to win acceptance for the new supervisor? How might these techniques be used in other situations?

Consultation. The manager respected the key position of the chef in the informal organization and requested his opinion on the change. When he felt the chef's opinions had to be rejected, he was careful to explain why.

Other organizations may use similar techniques to involve key subordinates in the selection process and thus substantially increase their acceptance of the final decision. Universities, for instance, typically appoint faculty members to the committees that choose presidents or deans.

Induction. The old supervisor was careful to introduce the new supervisor to all key personnel and to explain the customs of the organization. Doubtless this did much to save the new supervisor from making a social faux pas, to help integrate her into the social pattern of the organization, and to minimize the amount of disruption caused by the change in command.

Ceremony. The meeting at which the new supervisor was introduced and the farewell party for the old supervisor both served a ceremonial or symbolic function. They formalized the fact of change and helped the old supervisor pass on some of her prestige to the new.

There is a tendency in our cynical society to play down the importance of ceremony. Yet it is no coincidence that throughout history every strong, stable institution—be it church, state, university, or company—has been noted for the ceremonies by which it helped focus individual loyalty on the organization as a whole.

Ceremonies are particularly important in time of change. Take, for example, the traditional ceremonies observed at the crucial moments of our life: birth, graduation, marriage, and death. The presence of relatives and friends and the giving of gifts and flowers help symbolize friendship and the unity of families. By involving ourselves in the formalized rites of the ceremony, we somehow protect ourselves from some of the fears and pains of moving from one stage of life to another. The heightened emotional atmosphere helps prepare individuals for major changes in their relationships with others. Indeed, we have learned to expect really important changes to occur in this way.

Probably more important, the use of ceremony is a public proclamation that in spite of apparent change the basic values remain the same; the new pays obeisance to the old. The English cry, "The King is dead; long live the King." The French say, "Plus ça change, plus c'est la même chose." In primitive

---

[7] Adapted from William F. Whyte, *Human Relations in the Restaurant Industry* (New York: McGraw-Hill, 1948), pp. 319–31.

countries, oil companies may hire medicine men to sprinkle holy incense on new oil wells, thus showing their willingness to come to terms with the older culture.

Avoiding change until acceptance is assured. The new supervisor avoided making changes until she had developed informal, social relations with her subordinates. This is in conflict with the old adage that a new broom should sweep clean—or that new managers should make all their changes at once. True, as we suggested earlier, it is sometimes (but certainly not always) desirable to complete change quickly rather than to let it drag on. Even so, it is usually wise for new managers to wait before taking action until they know more about the organization and the people with whom they are dealing.

In earlier chapters we distinguished between the manager's formal and informal authority, pointing out that the first arises from one's official position, the second from the respect accorded one's technical and leadership skills. Managers who have both informal and formal authority can win acceptance of their ideas more easily. But new managers have only formal authority and in effect must force their ideas on their subordinates. After a few months they begin to accumulate informal authority; as they become trusted as individuals, their ideas meet with less resistance.

Building on the past. In the restaurant case, the new supervisor made it clear that she had no intention of throwing out past practices wholesale. As anthropologists and missionaries long ago discovered, it pays to learn the customs of the people with whom one works, particularly their ceremonies, symbols, and expected ways of doing things. Changes can be introduced more easily if an adjustment is made to the past. There are times, of course, when one may wish to cast out all the old patterns of behavior and start completely from scratch. However, in doing so one also casts out the good with the bad, the baby with the bath.

using discipline for effective performance

We have purposely avoided the topic of discipline, so that we could discuss other problems first. Discipline is required only when other measures have failed. Suppose you have clearly instructed an employee in his or her duties, have listened to his problems, have tried to help him do better, and have tactfully criticized his performance, yet he still fails to meet the organization's standards. Then what? Then reluctantly, you are forced to resort to discipline.

But can discipline be made consistent with what we have said about general supervision? We think it can.

In the first place, the best discipline is self-discipline, the normal human tendency to do one's share and to live up to the rules of the game. Once people understand what is required of them, they can *usually* be counted on to do their jobs effectively and with good cheer. Yet some people (perhaps most of us) find that the possibility of discipline lurking in the background helps our better selves win out over our lazier selves. As one worker put it:

"If you can get away with one thing you always try to get away with something bigger. It's human nature. If you can sneak out of the plant with nails one day, the next day it may be a hammer, and the day after a buzz saw. But if you know they are going to check your lunch box, then you don't get into the habit of taking things in the first place."

Ordinarily, if employees feel that the rules by which they are governed are reasonable, they will observe them without question. That is to say, they will respect the rules not because they fear punishment, but because they believe in doing things the *right* way. Coming to work on time; following the supervisor's instructions; avoiding fighting, drinking, and stealing at work; punching the time clock—all these are accepted by a majority of employees as reasonable rules, as necessary conditions of work.

Standards accepted by the group are frequently enforced by the group. (See p. 120, our story of how machinists enforced the rule against long-sleeved shirts.) Still, it is useful for management to back up the group when it is seeking the same objectives as management. The following quotation from a worker on an automobile assembly line illustrates a common feeling:

"Who needs a guy who doesn't do his share? Or someone who is late and makes the rest of us work harder to keep up? We ignore guys who are too lazy to do a good day's work; the foreman should give them hell! But if he's just trying to irritate a pain-in-the-neck foreman, more power to him!"

Most employees are tolerant when a co-worker has an occasional off day, provided he does his part the rest of the time. But they resent seeing someone else "get away with murder" while they are doing a full day's work. In fact, unless the culprit is disciplined the rest of the group may adjust to his low level of performance.

Thus, consistent proof that all rules are being enforced serves to strengthen the informal group's efforts at correction. Clearly, good managerial practices will vastly reduce the need for discipline. But if employees realize that infractions of rules will be disciplined, good management will become even better.

Avoiding discipline

Of course, discipline is to be avoided if possible. Too often management views it as the first, rather than the last, step. How can the need for discipline be minimized?

1. Management should avoid introducing too many rules, especially rules that seem unrelated to the job at hand.

2. Management should make every effort to convince employees that the rules it introduces are reasonable. The United States' disastrous experience with Prohibition shows the futility of trying to enforce a law that seems unreasonable to the majority.

3. In many instances, failure on the job is due to poor assignment. The employee's skills and interests do not match the job. If that is the problem, it may be corrected by better training or a transfer.

4. At times, too, the problem arises from the failure of management to explain what the job requires or to be sufficiently alert to employee progress. Here, of course, better communications are required. Many apparent discipline problems are merely misunderstandings that can easily be settled in face-to-face conversation.

Steps such as this may help establish "positive discipline," an atmosphere in which subordinates willingly abide by rules that they consider fair. In such an atmosphere, unnecessary causes for discipline are removed, and the group may exert social pressures on wrongdoers.

Types of discipline

Assuming discipline is required, we must determine the severity of the penalty. Many companies now provide what is called progressive or corrective discipline, which calls for increasingly severe penalties each time a person is disciplined. Except for very serious wrongdoings, an employee is rarely discharged for a first offense. This is particularly true if the firm is unionized, since arbitrators insist that the offender be given a second chance unless the offense is particularly bad. Frequently they will insist that the employee receive a warning about the nature of the punishment for future violations. Before sustaining discharge, some arbitrators insist that evidence be provided to show that the supervisor made an effort to rehabilitate the rule violator. Progressive discipline implies that some effort be made at rehabilitation.

Ordinarily, the sequence of penalties under progressive discipline is as follows: (1) oral warnings; (2) written warnings; (3) disciplinary layoffs; (4) discharges.

Oral warnings represent an informal form of correction. When an individual fails to maintain standards, or breaks a rule, a clear oral warning that repetition may eventually call for discipline is in order. The supervisor should, of course, concentrate on helping the subordinate figure out ways to prevent these troubles from recurring.

Written warnings are the first formal stage of progressive discipline. Psychologically, perhaps, they are not different from oral warnings, but they are made part of the employee's record—and they can be presented as evidence if more serious penalties follow or if the case is taken to arbitration.

Disciplinary layoffs (to be distinguished from layoffs due to lack of work) are next in severity. Usually they are for several days or weeks; layoffs in excess of a month are uncommon. Some companies skip this stage of discipline altogether, particularly when it is hard to find a trained replacement, on the grounds that it is too cumbersome to replace an employee for just a few weeks. Moreover, the disciplined employee may return from his layoff in an even nastier mood than when he left. On the other hand, there are some employees who pay little attention to oral warnings but to whom actual punishment, such as loss of income, is convincing proof that the company means business. A layoff may shock them back to their sense of responsibility.

Discharge remains the ultimate penalty, but one that is being used less commonly. The expense of training a new employee makes the loss of an experienced one very costly to the company, and the hardships that face an individual who has been discharged make arbitrators and unions reluctant to permit its use. Many arbitrators, indeed, refer to discharge as "industrial capital punishment"—and for good reason.

Consider the impact of a discharge on a man of say 55, with 30 years' seniority. In the first place, he may lose pension rights which would eventually be worth $60,000 or more, plus substantial vacation benefits. Few high-paying employers would be willing to hire a man of his age, especially after they check his references and discover his discharge. Certainly he can expect less pay than he was getting from the job to which his 30 years' service had carried him. Further, as a low-seniority man, he is now fully susceptible to all the winds of economic misfortune. Assuming he loses $6.00 an hour for the rest of his life, his financial loss may be as high as $150,000.

No wonder one arbitrator told us: "I am very reluctant to let someone be fired unless I feel the company's grounds are justified, both morally and legally. I think the employee should have every chance to mend his ways." Faced with this attitude among arbitrators, companies are forced to place greater emphasis on their selection and training programs. Workers who are discharged today are often individuals who simply don't care for their jobs, younger employees with no family responsibilities, or persons with severe behavior problems, such as alcoholics or psychotics.

Demotion is seldom used as a disciplinary measure; it is ordinarily reserved for situations in which an employee has been mistakenly promoted or is no longer able to perform his job. As a disciplinary measure, demotion has a number of disadvantages. Losing pay over a period of time is a long, slow form of constant humiliation, as compared with the sharp slap of a layoff. Also, if a company is going to retain a trained employee in any capacity, it makes more sense to use his highest skill.

Managers whose performance is substandard are rarely laid off or formally demoted. Instead, they are often quietly transferred without cut in pay from responsible jobs with substantial promotional opportunities to dead-end jobs with little or no opportunity for salary increase or promotion. Or, in some companies, they are requested to "resign."

Most firms find that it is best not to treat either managerial or hourly paid employees so harshly that they give up hope or lose motivation.

The red-hot-stove rule Inflicting discipline puts the manager in a dilemma. How can he or she expect his subordinates to continue to regard him as a source of help, when discipline is by nature painful? Can he impose discipline without generating resentment? We think so—through what Douglas McGregor called the "red-hot-stove rule." This rule draws an analogy between touching a hot stove and undergoing discipline. When you touch a red-hot stove, your discipline is *immediate*, with *warning*, *consistent*, and *impersonal*.

Apply these four characteristics to discipline. When you burn your hand, you are angry with yourself. Sometimes you are angry with the stove too, but not for long. You learn your lesson quickly, because:

1. The burn is *immediate*. There is no question of cause and effect.
2. You had *warning*. Since the stove was red-hot, you knew what would happen if you touched it.
3. The discipline is *consistent*. Everyone who touches the stove is burned.
4. The discipline is *impersonal*. A person is burned for touching the stove not because of who he or she is.

In short, the act and the discipline seem almost one. You are disciplined not because you are bad, but because you have committed a particular act. The discipline is directed against the act, not against the person. There will still be resentment against the source of the discipline, but as the discipline becomes automatic, the resentment is reduced. As one worker put it: "I really had it coming to me. I was looking for trouble. I can't blame the forelady. Her job was to enforce the rules. That's what she is paid for."

Let us see how the red-hot-stove rule works out in practice.

Immediate discipline

The manager should begin the disciplinary process as soon as possible after he notices a violation of the rules. (Of course, if he has lost his temper he should wait until he has cooled down.) Note what happens if he delays action:

Jane Jones has a bad tardiness record. She comes in a half-hour late, but thinks the manager hasn't noticed it. By noon, Jane decides she has nothing to worry about.

The manager *has* noticed it, but she is busy with another problem and she figures it might be a good idea to let Jane stew awhile. Late in the afternoon, just before closing time, she calls Jane into the office to give her a two-day layoff.

Naturally, Jane feels she has been treated unfairly and resents both the discipline and the manager. She assumes the manager has been harboring a grudge instead of being honest and open. In the future, she will never feel secure with the manager and will always wonder, "What's she going to pull on me next? Why does she have to play this cat-and-mouse game with me?"

If the discipline quickly follows the offense, it is more likely that the offending person will associate the discipline with the offense rather than with the person imposing the discipline—that is, the discipline will seem more automatic.

Of course, immediate discipline does not mean that an individual should be judged without full investigation. But it does mean that the manager should take notice of the offense as soon as possible and push the investigation with all due speed.

For instance, a man comes in to work after two days' absence. According to your records, he never called in to report sick: therefore, he is subject to discipline. "Immediate discipline" requires that you call him into your office for an explanation as soon as he gets to work. If he claims he was unconscious under a doctor's care during this period, you obviously are not going to discipline him until you have a chance to investigate. Even here you should push your investigation as rapidly as possible.

When the facts of a case are not clear, and yet immediate action is necessary, many companies provide for suspension. The employee is told that he is "suspended" without pay and that he will be informed later about what discipline will be imposed. This technique may be used when tempers are so high that calm appraisal is impossible, or when the guilt is obvious but the amount of penalty can be determined only after further investigation. Suspension also makes possible a consultation among various levels of management before the final penalty is determined. Since suspension is a form of layoff, however, it should not be used unless the offense calls for at least a layoff. If the suspension is longer than is justified by the offense—or if no suspension was justified at all—arbitrators will usually order back-pay.[1]

Advance warning

If discipline is to be accepted without resentment, both the individual who is being disciplined and his fellow workers must regard it as fair. And *unexpected* discipline is almost universally considered unfair. This means that (1) there must be clear warning that a given offense will lead to discipline, and (2) there must be clear warning of the amount of discipline that will be imposed for a given offense.

Assume that a rule has been posted for several months but that the manager has never disciplined anyone who violated it. Clearly, no one expects the rule to be enforced in the future either. Now the manager grabs one employee and makes an example of him. The victim might well cry, "Why me?" Discipline without warning violates the workers' expectations of fair supervision. Further, if the case were taken to arbitration, the company could lose.

Does this mean that once an order is laxly enforced, the company can never again enforce it? Perhaps, in a unionized situation, for an arbitrator could rule that a *precedent* of no enforcement has been established. If, however, there has been at least some enforcement of the rule (that is, if the company has not given clear evidence of its acquiescence to nonenforcement), the company can begin strict enforcement once it has issued clear warning of the change in policy.

We have already discussed the need for effective communications. Once more, let us emphasize management's responsibility to make sure that employees really know what the rules are and how they are to be enforced. Failure to communicate such information deprives employees of clear warning. Among other things, a communications program might include the following:

- The immediate supervisor, perhaps with the help of the personnel department, explains the rules to all new employees just after they are hired
- Bulletin-board notices are posted and handbooks are distributed to employees
- In some cases, lists of penalties are included in the union contract
- When rules are changed, the immediate supervisor calls a group meeting or notifies individuals informally
- When a rule is about to be violated or actually is violated (provided it is a minor, first offense) the supervisor issues an informal warning

[1] Traditionally, when a worker is discharged, he is expected to leave the plant immediately, even if he has an appeal in process. Several unions have proposed that, except for the most serious and obvious rule violations, the individual be allowed to continue to work until his or her case is finally resolved. This is the practice in a number of government agencies as well as in portions of Swedish industry. It is also the position of the American Association of University Professors with regard to the discipline of faculty members. This is increasingly the case in the government sector since courts have ruled that in some cases government employees have the right to have a formal hearing before they are discharged and to receive full pay—whether they work or not—until a final decision emerges from the hearing.

Many arbitrators interpreting the legal meaning of the contract might say that posting a notice on a bulletin board constitutes clear warning. But in terms of human relations, this is not enough. Written communications should be supplemented by oral communications. The better job management does of explaining a new rule and why it is necessary, the easier it will be to enforce it—simply because workers will be more likely to accept it as reasonable. Regardless of the legal requirements of arbitration, management is clearly to blame if employees unwittingly violate rules because they don't know what is expected of them. Good communications pay off by significantly reducing the amount of discipline that must be imposed.

Consistency

If two individuals commit the same offense and one is more severely disciplined than the other, naturally there will be cries of favoritism. One of the quickest ways for a manager to lose the respect of his subordinates and to lower the morale of the work group is to impose discipline in a whimsical, inconsistent way.

Consistent discipline helps to set limits (that is, to inform employees what they can and cannot do); inconsistent discipline inevitably leads to confusion and uncertainty. When some rules are permitted to go unenforced, employees may either (1) decide to ignore all rules, or (2) become confused about what is really required of them.

For instance, one day the boss lets Mary, his secretary, get by with handing in a report that is full of erasures. The next day he bawls her out for a sloppy report that is actually less sloppy than the previous day's. Under the circumstances, it is hard for Mary to know what standards are expected of her. She may well decide that the discipline has nothing to do with her act and "learn" only that the boss has a personal grudge against her. Not only won't she learn the rules, but she will be resentful as well.

Everybody wants to know the limits of permissible behavior. One way to establish these limits clearly and dramatically is to punish those who exceed them. We all tend to be unhappy and insecure in a situation where we are not sure what is expected of us. Child psychologists, for instance, have learned that children are not necessarily happier when they are given absolute freedom. One reason they get into so much mischief is that they are trying to find out how much they can get away with, at what point Daddy will spank.

The rules of fair warning and consistency require discipline to be neither greater nor less than expected. If the degree of discipline comes as a surprise, the organization may have failed to give adequate warning; if the punishment is less than expected, it will be difficult for the employees to accept a more serious penalty in the future. When there is uncertainty and misunderstanding as to whether the offense is to be punished and the degree of punishment, then the policy is inconsistent. If the rule-breaker sees the supervisor making arbitrary decisions, then he or she might blame the supervisor rather than the improper action for the discipline.

Consistency is hard to maintain. Some people we like; others we do not. Sometimes we see a rule violation as a personal insult, a direct challenge to our authority. Other times, prompted by our natural instinct to be understanding and kindhearted, we are tempted to give the rule-breaker another chance.

One source of inconsistency is management's tendency to be stricter in slack times and to ignore rule violations when manpower is short.

Crawford had a terrible absenteeism record. He missed work for two days without a legitimate excuse. Normally, given his record, his offense would justify an immediate two-week layoff. However, Crawford's services were badly needed on a rush job. No one else could take his place. So the supervisor added the incident to Crawford's personnel record and warned him that a further violation would lead to discharge.

Keeping Crawford on solved the immediate problem of maintaining production. But the long-term effects might have been more serious. What did Crawford and the other workers learn from this incident? One of several things: (1) The absentee rule was not to be enforced strictly, (2) the supervisor was playing favorites, or (3) strict discipline in time of slack work was merely a dodge to get around the seniority provisions of the union contract. In any case, the employees' respect for their supervisor probably took a nose dive.

Often a supervisor finds it easier to transfer a problem employee to another department than to face the hard task of disciplining him. In one case an employee who had consistently failed to live up to company rules had been transferred 11 times without any record of disciplinary action appearing in his personnel folder. This employee could hardly be blamed for not knowing what standards of behavior were expected of him. No one had taken the trouble either to help salvage him or to rid the company of a constant expense.

Consistency in enforcing discipline may be expensive in terms of lost production, but inconsistency may be even more so. Although the evidence is incomplete, it appears that the automobile plants that are most hesitant about enforcing rules against wildcat strikes (work stoppages not officially authorized by the union) have had the worst record of such strikes. Yet if a whole department goes on strike, it may be very costly to discipline everyone. Not only will the company lose the production of that department, but workers in other departments may walk out in sympathy.

Wildcat strikes are set off by a variety of causes (frustration with the work or slow handling of grievances, for instance). Obviously it is better to eliminate the causes than to punish the symptoms.[2] Still, if no discipline is imposed, workers "learn" that they can engage in such strikes with impunity. Companies that have been willing to sustain the short-run costs have found that wildcat strikes have decreased. Further, when management takes a firm stand, the union finds it easier to discourage its members from taking matters into their own hands. Many union leaders have told us candidly that they find it hard to observe the no-strike provisions of their contracts when management doesn't take the initiative in disciplining violators. "We can't be more against strikes than management."

Consider another problem involving consistency of discipline. We have heard foremen say, "I can only catch a small proportion of the rule violators,

---

[2] Indeed, if workers are prevented from wildcatting, they may release their aggressions in other ways—through slowdowns and absenteeism, for example.

but those I catch I punish severely." Is this fair? Many workers consider it a form of Russian roulette. Adventurous souls may try to see how much they can get away with, making a game of this procedure. Furthermore, scattered instances of discipline hardly constitute a clear warning.

If the rule is on the books, the manager should make an effort to enforce it, and enforce it uniformly. If that is impossible, the rule may have to be revised or dropped altogether. Sloppy enforcement of one rule encourages employees to disregard other rules.[3]

In some cases, 100 percent consistency is impossible. For instance, unless every employee is searched before leaving the workplace, it may be impossible to eliminate stealing. Unfortunately, since searches are expensive and deeply resented, the company must often rely on stern punishment of anyone who is accidentally caught stealing. Since workers generally accept antistealing rules as reasonable, there is usually little resentment of this policy, inconsistent though it seems.

Does consistency require that the penalty be determined by the offense, regardless of the personal history and background of the person who committed it? Of course not. We have already said it is common industrial practice to be more lenient on first offenses. Arbitrators are reluctant to let "industrial capital punishment" be imposed on an employee unless a reasonable effort has been made to rehabilitate him or her. Certainly each case should be considered on its own merits. Among the factors commonly considered are length of service, records of past performance and discipline, organizational practice in similar cases, and the extent to which the employee should have known the practice in question was prohibited.

Three employees are caught gambling, for example. One has been disciplined for the same offense before; the other two have not. The first employee is discharged; the other two are given written warnings. This, we would argue is a more consistent punishment than it may first appear to be. Although each case should be considered on its own merits, the overall disciplinary program must be kept consistent. Certainly if two individuals with the same personal histories commit the same offense, they should be treated equally.

How long should a rule violation be held against an employee? Current management practice tends toward disregarding offenses committed more than a year or two ago. Thus, an employee with a poor absenteeism record would start afresh if he maintained a good attendance record for a year.

There has been considerable discussion in industrial-relations circles about whether or not good personnel policy requires the posting of all rules and the setting of standard penalties for violations. For example: "Rough-house: First offense, warning. Second offense, one-day layoff. Third offense, one-week layoff. Fourth offense, discharge."

Those who favor such lists argue that they provide effective warning and greater consistency. Those who oppose them feel that they make it harder

---

[3] Often it is more effective to reward the good than to punish the bad. This is a good way to deal with rules that are difficult to enforce. Rather than penalize absenteeism, the employer may provide attractive prizes or extra holidays for employees with perfect attendance records. One problem here is that denying an employee a prize may itself be viewed as discipline.

for management to distinguish between various degrees of guilt. Mandatory discharge for stealing would mean that the employee who is seen taking a box of safety clips would receive the same penalty as one who was caught robbing the safe. One company with a rigid series of penalties was obliged to impose only a one-week layoff on an employee who had altered his output records—this was the standard penalty for inaccurately reporting production figures. Actually, the employee had been doctoring his records for years and had received hundreds of dollars in unearned incentive payments as a result. Had the company not set up a specific penalty in the rule book, it could have imposed a far more severe penalty.

Impersonality

We have said that a good supervisor encourages subordinates to express themselves freely and tries to play down differences in status. He tries to build the feeling that he and the worker are on the same team. Doesn't the imposition of discipline seriously endanger this relationship? It may. In fact, the disciplined worker might easily murmur, "That so-and-so. I thought she was my friend. I'd rather have a boss who wasn't such a hypocrite and then I'd know where I stood."

It is not easy to impose discipline without causing the person disciplined to feel resentful and aggressive. But the manager can minimize the danger to the relationship by imposing discipline as impersonally as possible. Discipline has the least negative effect if the individual feels that his behavior at the particular moment is the only thing being criticized, not his total personality.

In its opening stages, the disciplinary interview is not much different from most other forms of interview. First, state the problem as you see it; then ask for the subordinate's point of view, and listen. Ask *how* it happened, not *why*. Offer every chance for explanation. Try to avoid this sort of exchange:

Supervisor: Late again, I see. Didn't I tell you yesterday, if you were late once more this month, I'd give you a layoff. . . .
Employee: But . . .
Supervisor: (ignoring him) Well, you've had your last chance. You better go home.
Employee: But I did get here on time—only the superintendent called me in to her office to discuss the Savings Bond drive.

Instead, do your best to draw the employee out and try to discover the real story. Don't ask for his excuse, but concentrate on the *basic* reasons for the rule violation. Has he been poorly instructed on the job? Has he lost his motivation? Is he having trouble at home? Why? (Of course, you should have asked yourself some of these questions long before the employee's misconduct led to discipline.)

Sometimes your interview will give you all the facts you need. In other cases you may need to investigate further, perhaps by checking with other members of management. Avoid making a decision until you have the whole story, but reach your decision as soon as possible.

Once you have decided what discipline is appropriate, impose it quietly and impersonally. Suppose in a lateness case that the employee shows general irresponsibility, and that his only excuse for his latest tardiness was that he forgot to set his alarm clock.

Supervisor: Well, I can see how it happened. But from the company's point of view, not setting your alarm clock is not an adequate excuse, particularly since this has happened three times this month.
(Pause—to listen to objections.)
You have already received two written warnings this month, and the rules now require that you receive a day's layoff.
(Pause—again for objections.)
Jim, you've got to figure out a way to get here on time. You do a fine job when you are here, but the rule (and I think it is a fair one) is that if this occurs again within 30 days you will receive a week's layoff; and if it occurs again you will lose your job. I don't want this to happen. Now what can be done about it?
(Then discuss positive means of avoiding trouble in the future. Try to get him to suggest a workable plan—or suggest one yourself. Even if this doesn't work, end with):
Jim, will you try harder to get here on time in the future?
(The answer is likely to be "yes" and you have, for what it is worth, a positive end to the interview and a positive commitment to do something.)

Note that the discipline here has been imposed impersonally and the employee has been given every chance to express his objections. After imposing discipline the supervisor reverts to his role of *helping*. The interview ends on a positive note.

After disciplining a subordinate, you may understandably tend to avoid him or alter your attitude toward him in subtle, hardly noticeable ways. But these shifts in attitude are particularly dangerous, for they generate corresponding alterations in the subordinate's attitude. Eventually, the whole relationship may be destroyed. By contrast, if you treat the employee as you always have, you indicate that by-gones are by-gones, that it was the act that was punished, not the person.

Simple as this advice may seem, it is hard to carry out in practice. Both parties are upset by what has happened. It is easy to understand why the person who has been disciplined is resentful, but the act of imposing discipline is also emotionally distasteful to the person who imposes it. Most of us feel guilty when we hurt other people—even when such a feeling is not justified. To protect ourselves from guilt feelings, we have to build up a feeling of anger. But, since we fear the anger of the person we have disciplined, we become unapproachable and cold after we have imposed the penalty. As a result, we seem to be disciplining the other person *as a person,* rather than as the violator of a specific rule. Naturally his response is, "The boss is out to get me."

It requires a great deal of maturity to approach discipline without a sense of guilt or hostility, particularly if you feel that a subordinate's disregard of the rules is a reflection on your own managerial abilities.

Supervisors too frequently have the tendency to avoid taking corrective measures until drastic action is needed. Confronting people with their inadequacies is often personally painful. In any case, it is too easy to assume that the other person is aware of his limitations. Besides, keeping records is time-consuming. Evaluations are frequently subjective and often difficult to defend. Criticism leads to counter-criticism. And so to keep good relations on the job, the supervisor often keeps his opinions of his subordinates to himself until the situation becomes intolerable, at which time the supervisor imposes a disciplinary action without warning—thus turning suddenly, in the eyes of the subordinate, from a permissive, namby-pamby boss to an unfair, autocratic ogre.

Consider the case of Alton Scotia, who filed a grievance after being hired in January, as technical writer for a research project, and then was fired in December for "failure to learn his job." As Ruth Van Duzen, his former boss, describes it:

Our project is working under heavy pressure, and we have no room for people who can't pull their weight and certainly no room for people who still must be trained. Al's record looked good, and so we hired him as a full-fledged professional. That was our mistake and it didn't work out. I gave him several different kinds of assignments and each time his reports were so poor that I had to have someone else do them over. I don't think he understood what we were doing here; he even said so himself. I gave him the simplest work I could find and here he made mistakes.

I sat down with him twice to go over his work in detail. He doesn't take criticism well and we got into a nonproductive fight over his writing style, which frankly I think is simply awful (I've kept copies of his work to prove it). I could have kept a complete log of everything he did wrong, but this would have been too time-consuming; and, in any case, he didn't learn from the little I told him. It was clear he wasn't going to straighten out. Certainly my two meetings with him should have made it clear that he was in trouble. I hoped that he'd have sense enough to recognize the situation and quit by himself; but when he didn't, I had to let him go. Why should he hang around on a job where he doesn't fit?

Naturally, Al saw the situation somewhat differently.

The trouble is all Ruth's. She's a lousy supervisor. She would never explain what she wanted (I told her I didn't understand her assignments), but I did the best I could. She kept switching me around from job to job, so I could never learn. But she had criticisms of my work only twice—and these were very petty. She and I have different ideas as to style. Since she never said anything again, either good or bad, I assumed I was doing OK. I never had any idea my job was in jeopardy. According to laboratory regulations I'm supposed to get a written evaluation every six months and a formal warning before discharge. I received none of these. Not only am I out of a job, but my professional reputation has been besmirched. I am really going to fight this injustice!

The role of the union

As yet we have said little about the role of the union in matters of discipline. Unions rarely object strongly to discipline provided it is applied consistently and the rules are clearly publicized and generally considered reasonable. Of course, union officers may go through the motions of filing a grievance at the request of a disciplined member, much as a lawyer defends a guilty client, but they often feel as this union officer did:

"I've got to go to this grievance meeting and fight for that so-and-so. He had it coming to him and got what he deserved. How can he think he is so much better than anyone else that he doesn't have to follow the rules?"

Management should not expect the union to discipline members who violate the contract.[4] When the union does impose discipline, it is abandoning its traditional role as the worker's defender, and management is failing to assume its responsibilities.

Management must also be realistic about the union leader's political position. Often union leaders feel obliged to defend members whom they themselves think are guilty; to do otherwise would be to risk defeat at the next election. Once management recognizes that union leaders must often perform what is for them an unpleasant job, life becomes a good bit easier for both management and the union.

Management may be able to reduce the number of grievances prompted by disciplinary action by bringing the union into the earlier stages of the disciplinary procedure.

Bill Jones has been absent frequently. According to accepted plant practice, after five no-excuse absences, he can be laid off for a month. Jones' foreman informs the department steward that he intends to enforce the rule against absenteeism and that the steward might try to "straighten Jones out" before he gets into real trouble. Where the foreman-steward relationship is a good one, the steward will often warn the employee informally that continued violations may lead to a penalty that the union will find difficult to reduce.

In this way the union is given an opportunity to play a constructive role without being burdened with the responsibility for applying discipline.

Quasi-legal procedures

The presence of a union need not impair management's efforts to maintain a satisfactory disciplinary policy. But it may force management to adopt what might be called a "quasi-legal" procedure.

Most union contracts require (1) that the company may discipline employees only for "just cause," and (2) that any employee who feels unjustly disciplined may appeal to higher management through the grievance procedure and, if management's answer is unsatisfactory, to arbitration. The arbitrator makes the final decision on whether the discipline was for just cause. He may sustain the company's action completely, or reduce the penalty, or decide the penalty was entirely unwarranted and eliminate it altogether.

The grievance procedure provides a valuable protection to the individual worker, awkward though it may be for management. Management has the right—one might even say the *duty*—to establish the rules under which the organization shall operate. But a channel of appeal must be kept open from management decisions on whether or not these rules have been violated. Thus, the grievance procedure operates as a means of enforcing consistency.

In our Anglo-Saxon tradition, the accused is assumed innocent until proved guilty, and in establishing guilt the burden of proof is almost entirely on management. For instance, to prove that a worker has been loafing on the job, more than the supervisor's unsubstantiated word is required. Management must be able to produce objective, factual data which show that other

---

[4] There are a few exceptions in the building and clothing trades, where powerful unions may discipline members who violate the contract.

employees on comparable jobs consistently produce more than the alleged offender. And it must show that the worker's low production was not due to poor material or faulty equipment. Similarly, the union may challenge any rule that has not been clearly communicated to the employees or consistently enforced.

As a consequence, disciplinary matters must sometimes be handled in a legalistic, courtroom manner, particularly when they reach the arbitration stage. Unfortunately, both union and management may find themselves devoting more energy to legal intricacies than to dealing with the human problems involved. Each side tries to build up an air-tight case and to poke loopholes in the case of the opposition. The billowing clouds of legal technicalities often serve as a smoke screen that obscures the underlying human problems. Fortunately, the company that maintains a generally fair disciplinary policy as part of its standard procedure is less likely to become involved in the legalisms of arbitration.

The existence of the grievance procedure means that the supervisor's disciplinary penalty may be reduced or eliminated, either by higher management or by an arbitrator. It is even possible that an employee who the supervisor is sure has flagrantly violated the rules may be totally exonerated. Under these circumstances the supervisor naturally may feel frustrated when his or her decision is not backed up. However, such possible miscarriages of justice are the price that must be paid for development of a judicial system that permits every accused employee to have his "day in court." A basic tenet of our society is that it is better for the guilty to go free than for the innocent to be convicted.

The reason why "guilty" employees are acquitted at higher stages of the grievance procedure is usually that the supervisor has failed to gather evidence, to be consistent in his application of discipline, or to communicate the requirements of the job to employees. Hence it is important for higher management to train and advise supervisors on the requirements of a sound disciplinary policy. Even with training, managers find discipline difficult. They must prove incompetence before discharging an allegedly incompetent employee, and this requires them to keep "a little black book" listing the employee's inadequacies—hardly the way to develop trust or to build a cooperative relationship. If a discharged employee successfully appeals his or her case through the grievance procedure, the manager must resign himself to work with this employee, despite the fact that their relationship may be permanently poisoned. No wonder many managers will put up with incompetence—hoping perhaps that some day the employee will quit or retire—rather than spend the time, energy, and emotion required to begin a disciplinary process which may have an uncertain chance for success.

Government imposed standards

Until recently only unionized firms had to worry about discipline procedures being challenged. The nonunion employer was legally free to discipline or discharge employees for any reason at all. Recent legal developments, the full implications of which have not been fully worked out, tend to restrict the previously unfettered rights of nonunion employers in this area. Three trends are involved.

Protection against discrimination. Various legislation protects employees against discrimination on the basis of race, ethnic background, sex, or age (if between 40 and 70). Women, members of ethnic and racial minorities, and older workers all have recourse to a variety of government agencies if they feel their discipline is really a form of discrimination. The easiest way for the employer to protect itself against such charges is to show that discipline occurred for "just cause." But, as in arbitration, the employer is required to demonstrate that the employee received adequate note ("advance warning") as to company rules and the requirements of the job, that the discipline was imposed in a consistent manner, and that the extent of discipline was not disproportionate to the nature of the offense committed. When older workers are discharged, not because of wrong doing, but because they can no longer do the job, it becomes particularly important to prove that discharge was due to the workers' demonstrated inability to meet the minimum requirements of the job, not because of advanced age. Often, this is difficult to prove.

Government employees. There are even stricter standards regarding government employees. Apart from protections under various civil service laws and regulations, the Supreme Court has ruled that long-term government employees may acquire a "property interest" in their jobs. In turn, this can entitle them to a hearing and other procedural protections against discharge or layoff.

Free speech and free private lives. Other court decisions have given employees at least some rights to free speech, even when they call attention to their employers' misdeeds. In contrast to the earlier legal principle that employees owe absolute loyalty to their employer, the new doctrine suggests that employees have the right to "blow the whistle" against their employers when, for example, the employers try to hide the fact that they have been polluting the environment.[5] A California engineer won legal damages from an employer that had discharged him for "disloyalty" (he had reported that the company's new computer console violated the state safety code). Five states have laws forbidding employers from infringing on their employees' political freedom. Some courts have extended free speech to include life styles and have held that employers may not impose "unreasonable" restrictions on clothing, hair style, and so forth. The predominant view, however, is that an organization may require its employees to adhere to common standards of dress and grooming, providing these standards tend to enhance the organization's public image. The Supreme Court, for example, has held that policemen may be required to keep their hair reasonably short.

There are other decisions which restrict employers' rights to interfere

---

[5] For a discussion of the circumstances under which courts seem likely to intervene in cases of whistle blowing, see Kenneth Walters, "Employee Freedom of Speech," *Industrial Relations,* Vol. 15, No. 1 (February 1976), pp. 26–43.

with their employees' private lives (such as their extramarital affairs) unless it can be proven that this off-the-job behavior has a direct impact on the company's welfare.

Taken as a whole, these trends suggest that arbitrary disciplinary procedures will be increasingly subject to governmental regulations. An indication of the future: The Oregon Supreme Court has held it illegal to use "a socially undesirable motive" to discharge an employee; for example, an employee may not be discharged just for agreeing to serve on a jury.

Conclusion

Basically, discipline is a form of training. When discipline problems arise, it may be as much management's fault as the workers'. Many disciplinary problems grow out of management's failure to inform employees of what is expected of them.

On the other hand, effective discipline depends on more than one-way communication in which the supervisor tells employees what to do and punishes them if they don't. Employees may be aware of a rule, yet refuse to accept it. For instance, if many employees take extended lunch hours or use sick leave as a vacation, the remedy is not to punish the guilty but to win group acceptance of a new standard. Once this has been accomplished, discipline will be needed for only the small minority of recalcitrants.

For discipline to be accepted, the rules must be effectively communicated, and the penalties inflicted must be consistent. Discipline helps employees learn the requirements of their job; and if discipline is applied impersonally, without personal animus, it may increase subordinates' respect for their superior.

On the other hand, although fear of punishment may motivate many people to obey the rules, actual punishment almost always breeds resentment and reduced motivation in the person disciplined.[6] Thus the most effective disciplinary system is one in which rules (and their punishments) are so well accepted that discipline is almost never used.

---

[6] Hoyt Wheeler, "Punishment Theory and Industrial Discipline," *Industrial Relations*, Vol. 15, No. 2 (May 1976), pp. 235–43.

decision making and organization levels

So far our discussion has concentrated on a two-level organization: an employee and a supervisor in direct face-to-face contact. It should be apparent, however, that as the size of an organization increases, there will be more than two levels. No longer can a single manager supervise everyone through face-to-face contact. With the addition of a number of managers comes the need for supervising and coordinating the work of the managers themselves: managing the managers. More and more levels will be introduced as the organization grows in size.

In this chapter we shall first look at the nature of hierarchies, why they exist and how they affect the role of the manager. Then we shall examine in detail two managerial decisions that affect the functioning of the hierarchy: the amount of responsibility delegated to subordinates, and the manager's span of control.

The nature of hierarchies

The term hierarchy refers to a multileveled, vertical structure. A hierarchy tells us who outranks whom within the organization, who must defer to whom; in other words, the formally prescribed status differences, often called the scalar system.

Hierarchies facilitate central control of a relatively large group; that is, large numbers of people can respond

CHAPTER 11
decision making
and organization
levels

LOGIC OF THE HIERARCHY

B's unit can function somewhat autonomously, without C's. Within B's unit, E's can operate without involving D and F. Just as important is the fact that when A wants to move information to G, the data must pass through B and E, only. Information does not have to move through a lengthy chain of contacts that would include many managers.

to the goals of a single organization. Hierarchies do this in a pyramid of semi-autonomous parts linked together by managers.

The pyramidal organization chart does not mean that there are always more people of low rank in an organization, however. In the modern organization, there may be relatively few unskilled personnel at the bottom and a bulge of skilled technicians and specialists in the middle ranges. The modern army has more captains than second lieutenants! So, in terms of manpower, the organization will look more like a diamond than a pyramid.

Hierarchies are highly efficient mechanisms for coordinating large numbers of people. They permit simultaneous central direction and specialization.[1]

[1] They exist almost universally in nature as well as the world of affairs. The human body and individual cells are organized hierarchically. See Herbert A. Simon, "Hierarchy and Organization," *Hierarchy Theory: The Challenge of Complex Systems*, ed. Howard Pattee (New York: Braziller, 1975), pp. 18–46.

Within hierarchies individuals would all have to be in direct contact with one another to coordinate their activities:

> The mechanisms of natural selection will produce hierarchies much more rapidly than non-hierarchic systems of comparable size, because the components of hierarchies are themselves stable systems.
>
> ... It was pointed out many years ago that as the number of members of an organization grows, the number of *pairs* of members grows with the square (and the number of possible subsets of members even more rapidly). If each member, in order to act effectively, has to know in detail what each other member is doing, the total amount of information that has to be transmitted in the organization will grow at least proportionately with the square of its size. However, if the organization is subdivided into units, it may be possible to arrange matters so that an individual needs detailed information only about the behavior of individuals in his own unit, and aggregative summary information about average behavior in other units. If this is so ... the total amount of information that has to be transmitted will grow only slightly more than proportionately with size. Hence, the amount of communication required per organization member will remain nearly constant.[2]

Modern hierarchies

Those students of management whose views have been labeled *scientific management* or *bureaucratic theory* conceived of a very regularly shaped pyramid represented by the familiar table of organization, or organization chart. Actual relationships among members of organizations were presumed to be consistent with this structure, with the result that:

1. Nearly all contacts took the form of orders going *down* and reports of results going *up* the pyramid.
2. Each subordinate had to receive instructions and orders from only one boss.
3. Important decisions were made only at the top of the pyramid.
4. Each superior had only a limited "span of control" (supervised only a limited number of individuals).
5. At any level except the top and bottom, people were in contact with only their immediate supervisor and subordinates.

Under the impact of behavioral research, this traditional view of the hierarchy is undergoing modification.

Up and down contacts

Traditional view. The only significant contacts in an organization were those between superiors and subordinates: giving orders (downward) or reporting back on results (upward) or requesting information (up and down).

Newer view. Researchers are becoming much more aware of the importance of horizontal, or lateral, contacts in activating organizational goals. For some time, organization theorists referred to these horizontal contacts as the "informal organization," implying that they were not really required or anticipated by management when it designed the "formal organization" (or the

---

[2] Herbert A. Simon, *The New Science of Management Decision* (Englewood Cliffs, N.J.: Prentice-Hall, 1977), pp. 111–12.

pyramid). To be sure, some lateral relationships are primarily social contacts that take place largely within informal groups, yet other lateral contacts are work-oriented, such as work-flow contacts among people who must collaborate to get a job done.

Increasingly, so-called staff groups and professionals, deriving their status from their expert knowledge rather than from the level of their jobs, are able to short-circuit the line. While they may appear at a relatively low level on some charts, they often have access to very high levels of the organization. Further, as we shall see in Chapter 12, they can also initiate requests that will compete with the orders coming down the hierarchical chain of command.

Traditional view. The manager was viewed as the sole source of power. Other sources (such as informal groups) were viewed as illegitimate.

One source of orders

Newer view. Since staff groups are in a position to reward friends and to make life less pleasant for enemies, they, too, exert power. Though staff's requests may be called "advice," line learns that to ignore this advice is perilous. In addition, fellow employees with roughly the same status in the organization exert pressure and even give orders. When an engineering group requests some drawings from drafting, engineering is giving what amounts to an order, even though the two departments may be of equal formal status.

Traditional view. All important decisions were made by top managers. The best informed and most competent people in the organization, they could set broad policies for the organization as a whole. As their policies passed down through successive levels of the organization, they were spelled out in increasing detail and transformed into operating instructions.

Decisions made at the top

Newer view. The traditional view may have been realistic when companies comprised a small number of trained (and educated) managers and a large number of relatively unskilled, untrained workers. Today, organizations hire many managerial, professional, and technical personnel. Since they are often better informed on technical subjects than their superiors, the latter must abdicate certain key decisions to them.

Traditional view. An effective organization was thought to require tight control. To achieve it, the supervisor (responsible for coordinating the work of subordinates) had to have a very limited span of control. The fewer subordinates, the better the management. This point of view resulted in quite steep pyramids. In large companies, it would not be unusual to find ten levels separating the hourly employees from top management.

Limited span of control

Newer view. As we have already seen, under many circumstances subordinates perform more effectively with limited supervisory order-giving and controlling. Also, coordination can often be enhanced if employees are in direct contact with one another (through lateral, not hierarchical relationships). "Flatter" organizations, involving broad spans of control, thus are often desirable.

No bypassing

Traditional view. Contacts in the organization were supposed to follow the table of organization. Relationships were restricted to one's immediate boss and immediate subordinates. As a result, every manager had full information about the activities and people he was responsible for.

Newer view. For reasons that will become clear in the latter parts of this chapter, timely communication often requires bypassing certain steps in the hierarchical chain. Also, every organization needs an appeal channel, a mechanism by which subordinates can go over their boss's head when they feel a serious injustice has been done to them.

Hierarchies create managers in the middle

Although we have been critical of the simple, traditional view of organizational hierarchies, it would be a serious error to ignore the importance of rank differences. There clearly are successively higher levels in all but the smallest organizations. However, requests for action do not flow only in a top-down direction.

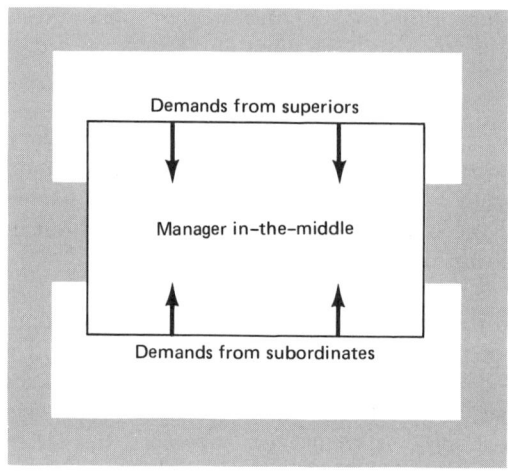

The manager is part of two groups and must satisfy the demands of both.

Managers inevitably belong to two groups: the work group they lead and the higher-management group they represent. The manager is thus a woman or a man in the middle, endlessly beset by conflicting loyalties and demands. The ineffective manager is squeezed by these conflicting pressures; the effective supervisor resists them and serves as a communications link between those above and those below.

Transmittal of supervisory styles

Supervisory styles are handed down from level to level: good supervision at the top is reflected by good supervision at the bottom. The evidence suggests that those who receive considerable autonomy are more likely to grant such autonomy themselves; those who are supervised closely will closely supervise their subordinates.

It is perfectly natural for a manager to reflect the supervisory style of the boss, for the boss is the one who hands out rewards. The actions of superiors are looked upon as clues to the behavior they expect from subordinates. A manager who is subjected to pressure from above will have a strong tendency to pass it on to those below. Transmitting pressure—and perhaps increasing it a bit in the process—is a time-honored way of relieving frustration and soothing a wounded ego. As a consequence, many managers decide:

"I can't afford to have any mistakes made in my department, or my boss will get me in trouble. If I'm going to be quizzed on everything that happens, I better check up on everything and have all the facts and explanations at my finger tips. This means I have to keep close tabs on my people."

Furthermore, managers cannot permit subordinates to exercise freedom in areas in which they, themselves, do not have freedom. Some top managements issue strict rules specifying in detail what they want subordinates at all levels to do in almost every conceivable situation. Under such circumstances, the supervisor has little discretion to delegate.

On the other hand, supervisors who are given substantial latitude feel free to let subordinates make a broader range of decisions by themselves. Knowing that they will be judged by overall results, they encourage subordinates to experiment. Nor do they penalize them for making unintentional mistakes. They recognize that as long as they produce results, the boss will back them up and refrain from meddling with petty details.

Representing subordinates. Employees are quick to recognize that their immediate supervisor has limited powers and that the levels above make many crucial decisions affecting their welfare. The effective supervisor, therefore, must speak for, protect, and represent subordinates to higher management. (You will remember that, in our discussion of informal leadership in Chapter 5, we mentioned that the informal leader functioned as an outside contact person for the group. The effective supervisor is a similar linking pin.)

Speaking out for the interests of their people when they think that management has made a wrong decision, supervisors are a voice for subordinates who have little opportunity to be heard by higher levels of authority. In a sense, they serve as shock absorbers, cushioning outside influences that jeopardize subordinates' welfare and productivity.

The existence of a hierarchy imposes an interface function on every manager except those at the very top and bottom. The manager has to move back and forth between superiors and subordinates, reconciling conflicting demands. Higher management may expect more efficiency, greater productivity, or tighter schedules than subordinates believe is realistic or equitable. Subordinates may want more facilities, firmer support, and higher compensation than those above consider appropriate.

Reconciling conflicting demands

"My boss was urging me to get that order out, regardless, by Thursday. No excuses. My staff insisted that we had to live up to our own hard-won technical standards. Every unit and component had to be completely and fully tested, even if it took all month.

They were professionals who believed in what they were doing, and they weren't going to be panicked. They said it was my job to get them the time to do high quality work."

How does a manager cope with these conflicting demands? Research suggests that it is done more expeditiously by managers who can strike a balance between initiating downward from their bosses and upward to their superiors. They prove to their bosses that they are loyal and responsible by transmitting a goodly percentage of the demands of upper management down to their subordinates. To be sure, they may make minor modifications or translations to reflect their local culture, its immediate needs, and the situation. At the same time, they prove to their constituents that they are willing and able to communicate a reasonable number of their demands up to higher levels of the hierarchy.

On occasion they are able to say "no" both to upper management and their subordinates: "What you want is excessive; I can't get it." Lack of balance is shown by the boss who simply acts as a tape recorder, repeating—even amplifying—everything from on top or, contrariwise, always siding with subordinates.

The supervisors who are able to demonstrate this balance best usually have influence. Their bosses are responsive to upward initiations. Subordinates, in turn, gain assurance that reasonable requests will be honored. When the supervisor is perpetually turned down, subordinates become disillusioned, even resentful of the pretense of participative management.

The special problem of the first-line supervisor. The lowest level supervisors probably suffer more from being middle persons than do members of any other supervisory group. Their subordinates do the actual work in the organization, but they have no one to supervise and often little chance for promotion. As a consequence, even if they are paid salary or commission, they are less likely to identify with management.

This potentiality for revolt can be ignored only at the first-line supervisors' own peril. By following supervisors' instructions too literally and failing to use common sense, subordinates can spoil work, damage equipment, waste materials, and otherwise embarrass their supervisor. By slowing down in unison they can delay schedules. Through a hundred different subterfuges they can increase costs. Thus, though first-line supervisors are subject to many pressures from above, they cannot pass these pressures down to lower levels. If they try to do so, they will only make matters worse.

The inevitable result is that the first-line supervisor must somehow come to terms with his subordinates, being particularly careful to ensure strong, continuing motivation. Often, too, he must make deals with union stewards, involving special concessions in return for an implicit agreement to keep production high.

As might be expected, expedient arrangements such as these are rarely acceptable to higher management. Consequently, supervisors sometimes become two-faced, turning one face to management and another to their subordinates. Caught inescapably in the middle, they must cope with all the problems of higher levels of management and at the same time resolve all the problems that are peculiar to their own position in the hierarchy.

CHAPTER 11
decision making
and organization
levels

Delegation

As we said at the outset, hierarchies "work" because their parts are semi-autonomous. Large numbers of people can work toward common objectives while reporting to separate bosses. Top management allows lower-level personnel to direct some of the operation; everything is not centrally controlled. But how much autonomy for subordinate managers? That becomes a critical question. How much authority to delegate, which decisions to make oneself and which subordinate managers will be allowed to make—these are important issues because the managers doing the delegating will still be responsible for the results, and their reputations will suffer if the subordinate managers fail.

In applying the broadest delegation, a manager would make relatively few decisions and would frame orders in very general terms. This would emphasize results, allowing subordinates to work out the details for themselves. Thus the manager sets goals, explains them to subordinates, fixes the limits within which they can work, and (if the subordinates are adequately trained) lets them decide how to achieve these goals. Instead of rattling off a list of orders, the manager communicates helpful information or makes suggestions, explains why things should be done, and points out how the subordinate's contribution fits into the overall plan. Subordinates have as much freedom as they can handle in complying with the aims of the organization.

Some managers seem unable to take this approach. They are inclined to give detailed instructions specifying exactly how, and in what sequence, they want things done. Compare, for example, the difference in approach used by two office managers as they handed out the same assignment.

Office Manager A: "Call Jones Office Equipment and the Wilson Supply Store. Get them to quote you prices on all their office dictation equipment. Ask them to give you a demonstration. Invite two managers to the demonstration, Ellis and Conrad, and let them try it out. Get them to put their reactions on paper. Then prepare me a report with the costs and specifications of all the equipment. Oh, yes, be sure to ask for information on repair cost . . ." (and so on).

Office Manager B: "I'd like to do something about our stenographic system. Managers who don't have secretaries of their own are complaining that it takes them too long to get someone to handle their dictation. Could you evaluate the various kinds of dictating machines and give me a recommendation on what we should do? I think we can spend $2,000. Possibly you could talk to some of the managers to get their ideas."

Office Manager A tried to think of all contingencies; and in doing so, he gave his assistant the feeling that she was little more than an errand girl. Moreover, he took so much trouble in trying to think of all the possibilities that he might as well have done the work himself.

Advantages of delegation

What are the advantages of delegation?

1. Few supervisors have the time to handle both their own job and the jobs of their subordinates. The close supervisors who try to make every decision frequently become exhausted physically and mentally. Furthermore, their decisions may not be as good as those of their subordinates, since the person who is closest to a problem usually understands it better than anyone else.[3]

Delegation is, above all, a means of internalized motivation. Delegation is really a form of job enlargement, for it gives each subordinate a sense of being more his own boss and exercising control over the work environment. In expectancy theory terms, it attempts to restructure the job so that harder work is, in fact, rewarded by greater satisfaction.

2. Subordinates can take pride in results that are directly attributable to their own judgment. People feel little involvement in their work when someone else makes all the decisions.

3. Delegation helps to develop the talents and abilities of subordinates. It is hard to train people to take the risks of decision making without putting them in a position of making decisions on their own. Employees will learn from their mistakes as well as their successes.

Pressure vs. standards. Managers who delegate more responsibility usually appear less pressured, because they are not standing over their personnel, watching their progress or constantly giving new instructions. This does not indicate an absence of standards or that subordinates are free to set their own standards. As we shall discuss shortly, delegation is rarely possible unless subordinates are given some sort of direction. High standards are essential if the organization is to be effective. They are important also for morale, since most people derive satisfaction from completing a difficult task. By setting exacting standards, the leader also implies confidence in his or her subordinates. Throughout history, effective leaders have inspired their followers to strive for seemingly impossible goals. If subordinates accept the goals of the organization as valid, they tend to feel that the pressure to do a good job originated from the goals themselves, rather than from the manager. But we shall discuss this point later.

In sharp contrast, managers who do not delegate usually appear pressured and fearful to their subordinates. In fact, they may have less self-confidence. Afraid of a mistake and of being blamed by upper management, they stay close to the work. The constant instructions they give then seem to be the product of their insecurity and distrust, not the needs of the situation.

Managerial assumptions about subordinates' abilities. The extent to which managers delegate may depend on their faith in their subordinates'

---

[3] The spread of computers has somewhat reduced this advantage of delegation. Provided information can be translated into computer language, electronic data processing makes it possible to communicate the information quickly and accurately from subordinates to the data-processing center, and the computer itself never becomes exhausted from making too many decisions.

abilities. The manager who considers subordinates essentially lazy and untrustworthy is likely to exercise close supervision. Following the precepts of traditional management, that manager, in effect, says, "People will shirk their task whenever they can. If I were to leave the shop, everyone would stop work." (No doubt, in this case, exactly that would happen.)

Other managers may believe that their subordinates are loyal and dependable but incapable of initiative or judgment. Such managers may engage in hygienic management and may even permit participation in fairly trivial areas; however, they are unlikely to delegate extensively. A significant amount of delegation occurs only when a manager has confidence in the subordinate's ability.

Influencing subordinate decision making

Effective delegation does not mean that subordinates are permitted to do exactly as they please. Quite the contrary. Delegation is feasible only when some measure or framework ensures that subordinates' decisions will be consistent with the organization's needs and that of the manager who is doing the delegating. In turn, these measures or techniques increase the advantages of such delegation while reducing the risks. There are 5 such facilitators of delegation, which we shall discuss:

- Policies
- Rules
- Goals
- Indoctrination
- Technology

Policies

Although the manager may not be able, or want, to tell a lower level of management what decision to make, it is often important to enunciate guidelines or limits that the subordinate will consider when actually making the decision. These are usually called *policies* or organizational *values* or *principles*. Top management policies require that hiring decisions not be discriminatory, for example, but lower levels are allowed to select their people.

To be meaningful and influential, broad guides for decision making must be enforced; that is, exceptions must be identified and disciplined. Otherwise, policies will be perceived (correctly) as so much window dressing designed to impress outsiders with the organization's high ethical image.

Rules

More specific and restrictive than policies, because they allow little leeway, rules can be controversial.

Rules like the following program lower-level decision making:

Every job opening must be posted on every company bulletin board.
No new equipment is to be installed without first obtaining permission of the Safety Officer.
No employee can receive a travel allowance for more than coach fare.

Rules are a means by which the decision-making activities of subordinates are programmed so that it is unnecessary for every decision to be referred to the supervisor. Rules thus save time for the supervisor; subordinates do not have to consult their boss on routine matters. Because rules provide explicit guides, many decisions can be made quickly by lower levels of the organization.

Rules set up standard operating procedures. They may be written or unwritten; they may be established by supervisory edict, training, implicit bargaining, or consultation. The significant points are that rules (1) restrict subordinate behavior and (2) are enforced, in one way or another, by management. Though many people disparage rules, particularly written rules, as "red tape," they are essential if an organization is to operate effectively.

Rules serve to limit the freedom of subordinates, thereby decreasing their feeling of autonomy. Unfortunately, subordinates cannot be given authority to do everything they want, but well-understood limits or rules make it possible for them to exercise freedom within these limits. Sometimes rules are implicit and need not be spelled out in detail.

Suppose you are the office manager, and the Big Boss tells you: "Go ahead, use your discretion in remodeling the office. Anything you say goes!" Beware! "Anything" doesn't mean that. There are certainly clearly understood rules within which you must work. You must abide by the city building codes and the union contract. You cannot exceed your budget. Further, you must go through the purchasing department, fill out the proper forms, and so forth.

If you are smart, you know that redecorating must play second fiddle to keeping production going; and unless you are on Madison Avenue, the office had better wind up looking "businesslike"—not too swinging.

When there is room for doubt, the supervisor should state the rules clearly, sometimes even in writing. Often, subordinates appear to be objecting to assuming responsibility, when they are really objecting to uncertainty. As the following sections discuss, rules have both advantages and disadvantages. They are advantageous because they establish consistency, reduce personal dependency, and permit routinization.

Establish consistency. Particularly in large organizations, rules serve to make the behavior of the parts consistent with the needs of the whole. They reduce the possibility that personal feelings rather than organizational objectives will predominate in decision making. For instance, in an effort to achieve uniformity, management frequently promulgates standard lists of penalties for disciplinary infractions. Thus, excessive absenteeism will result in the same penalty in every department, even though managers may not agree about the seriousness of this offense. The alternative would be to have one person handle all discipline.

Reduce personal dependency. From one point of view, rules are liberating. As we have noted, an employee often feels freer to take initiative when the impersonal ground rules are well established. This same effect has been observed in authoritarian countries where newspaper editors are censored. When the censor's rules are well understood, the editor feels freer to make decisions about what to print and what to exclude than when the matter hinges on the discretion of a potentially punishing censor. Without rules, arbitrary, capricious, highly personalized decision making can injure people. A society of rules (laws) can act to protect them. Rules enable subordinates to predict the consequences of their actions, an ability that is essential to personal security. Well-thought-out rules establish limits within which employees are free to act on their own. Persons on higher levels step in only when one of these limits is violated or a question cannot be answered by existing policy.

Permit routinization. Rules require the manager to initiate orders only once: when a rule is first made. Most people prefer to work without a steady stream of orders. Once rules are established and define how the job should be performed (and once people are adequately trained in the meaning of these rules), then the job can be reduced to a routine. And this can protect the ego of those who would otherwise be continually ordered around.

Excessively rigid. Rules may be too specific and detailed, however, and they may be applied too rigidly by subordinates who fail to use good judgment in handling specific cases. This is one symptom of what some people call "bureaucracy" (though the sociologists' definition is much more technical).

Unnecessary rules are difficult to enforce, and inadequately enforced rules may lead to a general breakdown of discipline. Even when they are enforced, if there are too many rules, employees may live up to only the minimum requirements of the rules, feeling they have done all the company can reasonably require. Particularly when the reasonableness of the rules is neither self-evident nor well explained, they tend to make employees feel restricted, to breed resentment and aggressiveness, and at times to provoke a desire to break the rules just to prove one's independence.

Excessively rigid rules also discourage individual discretion and initiative and make it difficult for an organization to adapt to changing conditions. They give the petty tyrant a shield behind which to vent vindictiveness. They provide inept supervisors with crutches to lean on and a way to avoid the conflicts and uncertainties of making decisions on their own. They subject able supervisors to endless frustration and make it impossible for them to operate with the flexibility required for peak efficiency. At the very least, inflexible rules lead to red tape and wasted effort.

Rules give the insecure supervisor a means of passing the buck for unpleasant decisions: "The office just issued a strict new policy—no more days off unless you're sick; my hands are tied." The supervisor hopes, by blaming higher managers with whom the subordinate does not have any regular contact, to maintain a good relationship with the subordinate. The result is a general weakening of the immediate supervisor's leadership position as well as damage to the employee's respect for the organization.

Rules have a tendency to become ends in themselves, particularly if those who carry them out forget the reasons for which they were promulgated in the first place. Consider this case:

In order to prevent salary increases from getting out of hand, top management decides that one per year is the limit for any employee. To prevent an exceptional employee from accepting a better offer from another company, a supervisor tries to put through a salary increase. The personnel department automatically turns down the supervisor's request, and the valuable employee quits.

We have no way of knowing, of course, whether this particular employee should have been given an extra increase. We would need additional facts before deciding that, but it is clear that further investigation was called for before a decision was made.

Rebellious employees can cripple an organization by following every rule to the letter. Employees of the British Post Office and the Long Island Railroad have successfully used "work-to-rule" campaigns instead of strikes, to put pressure on management.

Can't cover all situations. A limitation of most rules is that categories or "break-points" inevitably have to be arbitrary and are thus subject to abuse. Schools and clubs have had their problems with what are really "short" shorts, just as offices have difficulty in defining what is revealing clothing. Some companies limit capital expenditures to $5,000 without upper management approval. They then discover that managers make three expenditures just under $5,000 for an improvement totaling almost $15,000.[4]

Correct use. Rules are designed to set a general direction, to ensure some measure of uniformity and consistency. The basic reason for them is not to restrict the individual but to further the general welfare of the organization and the attainment of its goals. When a particular rule prevents this organizational objective from being attained, then it must give way. An exception must be made.

In summary, intelligently devised rules grant individuals in a large organization considerable freedom to make decisions on their own. To forestall completely unfettered actions, however, the decision maker is required to conform to the goals of the total organization. This insurance is provided through setting limits; that is, through establishing rules. These rules or policies can free higher-level managers from the necessity of handling many time-consuming details. Subordinates do not have to check back with their boss each time an action or a decision is called for; they know the limits within which they can operate. The higher manager need step in only when one of the preestablished limits has been violated by a subordinate or when a case comes up that is not covered by existing policies.

Unfortunately, rules and policies also have limitations. They are most useful when similar types of decisions have to be made repeatedly under relatively constant conditions. Organizations existing in a dynamic environment may find rules becoming obsolete rather quickly. They also tend to proliferate, and few are reviewed to consider their present applicability. Rules permit or even encourage the inept or autocratic manager to avoid thinking

---

[4] A good analysis of this problem appears in Christopher Hood, *The Limits of Administration* (New York: Wiley, 1976), pp. 64–66.

through a difficult decision. It is easier to say, "The problem is covered by Rule 36; therefore, the answer is obviously no."

In many ways, rules are the organization's memory, guarding against making the same mistake twice. But in the same vein, they also may place too heavy a premium on what was desirable in the past, in contrast to the present or future.

Goal setting

By setting goals, the manager can avoid the necessity for either making specific decisions or laying down detailed rules. This approach, which is in sharp contrast to detailed, minute-by-minute supervision, is often called *management by exception.* It permits the subordinate to experiment, to adjust to novel situations. (Recall the discussion of goal setting and MBO in Chapter 3.)

General direction. When orders are pharased in terms of goals to be reached, they become a challenge. A manager can say:

"We're not shipping out new orders fast enough. If we promise good service, we should be able to assure our customers that their orders leave here within 48 hours of receipt."

The alternative (detailed, how-to-do-it orders) is demoralizing:

"To increase the speed of shipment, I want you to upgrade the mail room, hire an extra expediter, and prominently post on the announcement board every order that was shipped later than 48 hours after receipt."

For accounting purposes in many companies, each department is considered a "profit center," and the departmental manager is given the goal of making the "planned profit" or of not exceeding "planned costs." Sales quotas are, of course, frequently assigned to salespeople. (In each of these cases management must be careful not to destroy incentive by raising the goals too quickly after they have been reached.) As one manager told us:

"I wanted to move into a job where there were clear standards of performance and where I could actually see what my skill and work accomplished. In publishing, as an editor in charge of a department, both my management and I get very objective data on how well my new books sell and their profitability."

There is real satisfaction in knowing "This is my job. Here I am in charge. As long as I do it adequately, no one will interfere with me. I will be judged on how well I do."

Supervision by results. Typically, when supervision by goal setting is practiced, management interferes very little, as long as the goals are met—except perhaps to give subordinates praise, promotions, or financial rewards. Only when serious trouble develops does higher management step in. The establishment of targets has advantages from the viewpoints both of management and employees.

INCREASED EFFORT. Knowing their efforts are being measured may stir subordinates to work harder than they would under merely specific rules. Even judges, with all their autonomy, differ in motivation and diligence and can be affected by measurements. Court systems have discovered that when judges are asked to make only rudimentary reports on the number of cases heard and the backlog on their calendars, they develop standards of judicial performance that gradually spread to all judges in the system.

INDEPENDENCE. There is a feeling of being one's own boss. People understand what is expected of them and are encouraged to show initiative, to develop their potentialities. There are goals to work for and a feeling of completion when they are reached.

LESS PAINFUL CRITICISM. A clear-cut set of performance standards make it easier to criticize a subordinate. Employees are often resentful when their boss talks about their personal failings, but it is quite another matter when the criticism is couched in terms of helping them improve their records. In fact, the mere existence of such records tends to reduce the need for the supervisor to prod employees. They know automatically when they have fallen down on the job.

BUILT-IN ALARMS. Higher management can discover trouble and quickly take remedial measures. As discussed in the next chapter, this is a form of feedback or upward communication.

EVALUATION. Effectiveness of employees and their supervisors can be evaluated for promotions and pay increases.

On the other hand, supervision by results can be attacked as

- overemphasizing the individual at the expense of the group
- encouraging competition and passing the buck, rather than fostering cooperation
- substituting for the single boss the more pervasive control of a number of "auditing departments" such as accounting and quality control (see Chapter 12)
- placing excessive emphasis on immediate measurable results, as opposed to significant but immeasurable intangibles such as morale, good will, and employee development

Indoctrination

When employees fully accept the goals and values of the organization for which they work, they are said to be indoctrinated or socialized. They are willing to subordinate their personal views to the higher interests of the organization as a whole. Indoctrination, sometimes called socialization, is a means of establishing organizational loyalty and commitment. Indoctrination makes it easier to delegate authority, since highly indoctrinated individuals all think in roughly the same terms and make their decisions on the basis of the same premises. If subordinates are indoctrinated, their manager can feel sure that they will solve their problems in roughly the same way that the manager would. As a consequence, there is little need to be specific about rules or goals—everybody knows them. They also know which goals are important and which can be broken when they conflict with others of higher priority. Ideally, then, with indoctrination, an organization can permit innovative, flexible means, knowing that there will be uniform ends.

Many of the most effective organizations—such as the Marine Corps or the Catholic Church—rely heavily on indoctrination. A well-trained Marine can be relied on to "fight like a Marine" even in situations where he cannot be supervised by his superior officer. The Catholic Church operated for centuries on a decentralized worldwide basis, long before the advent of modern communications, largely because the strength of its priests' faith made it unnecessary for them to receive constant instructions from Rome. To a lesser degree, many large corporations try to train their employees so that everyone in the organization can take a consistent point of view toward their job. (Large corporations develop characteristic modes of operations and ways of thinking among their employees. Someone from General Electric will approach problems in a fashion very different from that of a person from Exxon.)

Professionals are also indoctrinated, but in terms of professional, not organizational values. As long as the two are consistent (for example, as long as the company wants the scientist to engage in pure research or the company doctor to maintain employee health), decision-making power may be delegated to professionals, who will have little need for external controls. But when professional and organizational objectives conflict (for example, when a scientist oriented to pure research is told to work on applied research), then some sort of closer control may be necessary.[5] Skilled craftsmen are indoctrinated in much the same way. Their internalized sense of pride in craft often motivates them to maintain high standards of workmanship as well as to put out a fair day's work.

Indoctrination usually requires a long period of hard training. The Catholic Church has its seminaries, the Marine Corps has boot camps, many companies have management training programs.[6] Professionals, for the most part, learn their values in universities; craftsmen, in apprenticeship. Indoctrination is usually most effective, however, in organizations with high purposes and long traditions.

Indoctrination is far from being a universal cure-all for every management problem. Indoctrination can be really effective only when individuals internalize management's objectives and make them their own. The church, the Marine Corps, and other such noneconomically oriented organizations have ideological appeals that make it possible to demand almost complete loyalty from their members; but business firms will rarely, if ever, win such perfect

---

[5] We do not subscribe to the myth that every scientist wants to do pure research. Many find considerable satisfaction working in the applied area.

[6] The function of management schools in providing managers with a common point of view has been described by former IBM president Thomas J. Watson, Jr., as follows: "These schools were not only to teach general management, but—most important—they were to give our managers a feeling for IBM's outlooks and beliefs. After a time we found that the schools tended to put too much emphasis on management, not enough on beliefs. This, we felt, was putting the cart before the horse. We felt it was vital that our managers be well grounded in our beliefs. Otherwise, we might get management views at odds with the company's outlook." *A Business and Its Beliefs* (New York: McGraw-Hill, 1963), p. 91.

dedication.[7] Religious zealots may be willing to sacrifice their personal ambitions to advance the True Faith. But the typical corporate manager prefers personal success to corporate profits; and the typical worker puts personal interest above the company's, particularly when interests conflict. Thus, indoctrination in business may be considerably different from indoctrination in nonprofit institutions.

Part of indoctrination is also learning the ropes of a new organization. Studies show that organizations provide a multitude of cues to help newcomers learn norms that will facilitate consistent decision making.[8]

By observing what departments are deferred to consistently and spoken about in respectful terms, the new manager learns that requests from such departments should be given high priority as compared to "lesser" departments. Repeated words, phrases, and jargon also cue in the newcomer. Company A is always talking about new products, new technology, and pushing the state of the art, while in B one is more likely to hear about holding on to existing markets, greater sales efforts, and squeezing costs. These differences will result in very different trade-offs for the tough decisions that a manager must take.

Technology

The nature of the work itself can facilitate delegation. Where the work provides unambiguous cues and constraints that direct the actions of subordinate managers, their bosses will feel easier about broader delegations of authority. As we shall see in the section following, managers within a department store are allowed substantial autonomy because retailing produces a great many ongoing measures of relative success or failure. These measurements direct the department managers and assure their bosses. Here are other examples of situations that encourage delegation.

Most routinized production plants have clear quality and output standards that guide department heads.

Direct-mail operations can be evaluated on the percent of positive returns from mail campaigns. For most types of merchandise there are well-established return rates that indicate good or bad performance.

In magazines, quantity of advertising and renewal rates tell the publisher how well the editor is doing.

In some technologies, the work is directed by the situation, and there is little need for the supervisor to keep close watch because subordinates are responding directly to cues and controls. In a sense the boss delegates more because of these other constraints. For example, electric utility substation operators, who often work completely by themselves, report feeling that they are completely their own bosses, when in fact they have to respond to "orders" issued by dials and meters. In the same way, factory maintenance men work only when equipment breaks down, and how they do their work is normally

---

[7] In addition, the church and the Marine Corps are able to isolate their members from conflicting pressures and values in a way not practicable for most businesses.

[8] See R. Richard Ritti and G. R. Funkhouser, *The Ropes to Skip and the Ropes to Know* (Columbus, Ohio: Grid, 1977).

determined by the nature of the emergency, not by the boss's instructions. As long as the subordinates are adequately trained and the technology remains relatively constant (two determining constraints), the boss intervenes only when there is obvious trouble. The most important problems involve lateral rather than boss-subordinate relations.

CHAPTER 11
decision making and organization levels

In sharp contrast, nonroutinized activities with ambiguous results inhibit delegation. Development work on new products can be slowed by many unforeseen problems. Is a six months' delay due to inept management or legitimate difficulty in getting some circuit to work properly? How effective is the personnel work of the branch personnel officer? Personnel management is elusive to evaluate, as we know.

When someone knows his job well, merely giving him information is a substitute for an order. Note the difference between these two statements: "Bill, bring some parts over to Machine 16," and "Bill, Machine 16 is down to six parts." The second provides Bill with the information he needs to make his own decisions—and it assumes that he will make the correct one. It enables him to serve Machine 3 first if it has fewer parts than Machine 16. In addition, providing a man with abundant information has a positive effect on morale, even if he doesn't need all the information to do a good job.

Jobs can be rearranged to reduce the number of "human orders." We once observed a factory in which there was constant friction between operators and inspectors; the main trouble was the operators' resentment of what they felt was the inspectors' constant badgering to keep up quality. Only one inspector was able to keep up good relations. The secret of his success was that he rarely *told* a man he had made a mistake; instead, he showed him the offending part with the proper dimensions marked in chalk.

Thus, some technologies produce unobtrusive measures that can substitute for direct orders. Because criticism can be produced by the work itself, it may be more acceptable than the boss's negative evaluation—and it is also more certain!

It should be emphasized that the various forms of programming just discussed are, in effect, substitutes for one another and for close supervision. As one form is strengthened, another may be weakened. In times of rapid change, there may be less delegation, since goals are no longer well defined, the requirements of technology are not clearly understood, and new rules have yet to be devised and accepted. If indoctrination breaks down, then new rules must be enforced. When work becomes routine, then there may be less need for elaborate measurement of results because bottlenecks become immediately obvious and perhaps just as immediately straightened out by those involved, without need for intervention by higher management.

Integrating the forms of programming

Span of control

Although we have argued that almost all organizations become hierarchies, some are more hierarchical than others. Organizations differ in the number of levels that separate operating work from top management. In part, this number is simply a function of size: very large organizations with thousands of employees may have a dozen or more hierarchical levels. But there is no hard and fast formula by which one can translate size into levels. Earlier, some theorists thought there was. They argued that a top manager could not supervise more than a handful of subordinates, while a first level supervisor might handle three or four times as many.

Our previous analysis suggests that the number supervised—the span of control, as it is called—depends on the ability to delegate. More delegation should lead to broader spans and thus less levels in an organization of a given size.

Sears Roebuck. In 1950, Sears Roebuck had 110,000 employees in its retail division, but only four levels of supervision between the president of the company and the salespeople in the stores.[9] This flat structure was not accidental; it was a reflection of deliberate management policy to maximize the number of subordinates (the span of control) reporting to a supervisor.

Fortunately, the Sears Roebuck Company has analyzed the effect of its organizational setup on human relations within the company. Sears operates many stores that have an almost identical number of employees doing highly similar jobs. In some of these stores, 32 department managers report directly to the store manager; in others, the department managers report to 5 or 6 division managers, who, in turn, report to the store manager. Obviously, the first is a relatively flat type of structure; the second, a tall type. What has Sears observed in the operations of these two quite different organization patterns?

Tall vs. flat hierarchies

The tall organization tended to encourage close supervision. With a relatively small number of subordinates, each supervisor—whether a store manager or a division manager—was able to give very detailed instructions to, and exercise strong control over, every one of the people in the unit. But in the flat organization, the large number of subordinates made this type of supervision physically impossible. Each supervisor was obliged to rely on general supervision and good training. There wasn't time to keep a close watch on everyone. The delegation of responsibility in these stores encouraged subordinates to work on their own initiative and learn from their own mistakes. Since the supervisor could not make a decision on every problem that arose, subordinates achieved a high degree of self-reliance. The results showed themselves in the higher profits, better morale, and greater number of promotable executives produced by the flat organization.

Another obvious advantage to the fewer-leveled organization is the saving of managerial time. Problems are handled more quickly. Equally important are the better human relations associated with fewer levels. Communication is expedited; the individual employee finds it easier to identify with the work of his part of the organization.

Not every organization, of course, can arbitrarily increase the number of subordinates reporting to each of its supervisors. The ability of Sears to

[9] James C. Worthy, *Big Business and Free Men* (New York: Harper, 1959).

make use of a relatively wide span of control is a function of the following factors:[10]

1. It was possible to develop efficiency measures (controls) for the various departments so that managers could be left to make nearly all their own decisions and account for only the final results; in other words, supervision by results.

2. Department store personnel receive a good part of their compensation in the form of commissions and bonuses based on sales performance. These incentives provide them with a high degree of motivation and decrease the need for close supervision.

3. No great amount of coordiantion among department managers was required in these stores. In effect, each department could be operated relatively independently of the others, thus reducing the amount of supervision required by the store manager.

U.S. Post Office. Prior to 1955, the U.S. Post Office was also a good example of broad spans of control. In fact, the Postmaster General was directly over some 60,000 postmasters. This extraordinary span was facilitated by a rather static technology and the existence of an enormous body of finely defined rules. Rule conformity was aided by a well-staffed Postal Inspector's branch with the power to ensure that rules were followed meticulously. The problems of the interfaces between post offices, each with a very similar technology, were handled in part by a separate organization, the Railway Mail Service, which had a much taller organization.

In addition to the factors affecting span of control identified in the Sears and Post Office study, we can suggest some others. The span of control can be broader when:

1. Subordinates are doing the same or very similar work.
2. Some of the burden of coordination is handled by staff specialists or integrators. (We describe the role of integrators in Chapter 14.)
3. The nature of the job requires little communication with the boss. (More participative management may require narrower spans of control, because shared decision making involves more contact.)
4. Supervisors can spend full-time supervising, instead of being heavily involved in technical analyses or lateral relations.
5. There is no strong subordinate pressure for more levels, to provide more promotional opportunities. (Many organizations, in fact, artificially increase the number of levels, adding titles like Chief or First or Senior, to give these advancement opportunities.)

Conclusion

An organizational pyramid on paper can be misleading. Hierarchies do not operate quite as mechanistically as they did when all work was routinized and there were few specialists or professionals. Many modern hierarchies are less stratified than their

---

[10] Though the evidence is somewhat mixed, in general it supports the position that broad spans of control are associated with routine work.

earlier counterparts and much more likely to encourage a variety of lateral as well as purely vertical relationships.

We may be too quick to think of hierarchy, of clearly spelled out rank and position, as being old-fashioned and confining. Hierarchies are efficient mechanisms to coordinate the work of large numbers. As we have seen, such structures are necessary to allow large numbers of people to work cooperatively in a single organization. Nor does the existence of a hierarchy mean oppressive control or regimentation. In fact, the hierarchical model presumes reasonable autonomy for the various parts of the system: Depatment A operates somewhat independently of Department B, and both are delegated decision-making authority by their common Division head, otherwise he would not have time to do his job. Also, hierarchies will differ in their relative formality and in the amount of status difference among levels. Some are quite steep; others, quite flat.

A major problem that every manager in a hierarchy must resolve is how much authority to give subordinates. The manager is still responsible for the results but cannot do everything himself. If he can, then there is no need for the subordinate manager.

Delegation is often inhibited by the fear that the subordinate's decision will be ineffective and different from the decision the boss would make. Since responsibility cannot be delegated, the potential risk can be great if the subordinate is foolish or disloyal. There are a number of techniques of risk avoidance for the boss: carefully contrived policies and rules, clearly defined goals, and effective indoctrination. Certain technologies also more easily lend themselves to greater delegation.

The functioning of the hierarchy depends, too, on the number of levels of management—how high it becomes. Levels, in turn, depend in part on the span of control, the number of subordinates any manager can supervise. We say "in part" because, obviously, size also affects the number of levels. Larger organizations will tend to have more levels. Factors affecting the span of control were illustrated by our description of a large merchandising company (Sears) and the Post Office.

Span of control and delegation both reflect the amount of confidence a superior has in subordinate managers, and that confidence may stem from personality and culture. In some settings, people have learned to distrust the motivation of their subordinates, and subordinates may be loath to accept much responsibility. The two reinforce each other: fear of disloyalty and fear of being identified with a decision that turns out to be wrong. In such circumstances almost every decision has to be bucked up the line to top management, and there is little opportunity for subordinates to develop the decision-making skills of an effective manager.

organization design: alternative structures

Lateral relationships

An important part of management's structure problem is designing the hierarchy. In fact, most people think of organization structure as synonymous with those ascending levels. As important, however, is the design of the *horizontal* structure. The horizontal primarily deals with working relationships—more than with authority or power relationships—the ways in which people will be brought together and must cooperate to get some task performed.

Remember, work is accomplished largely through cooperation and coordination. Although individual job performance can be important, the effort is wasted unless that performance fits into the work of other people. Most organizations find that their costliest problems are those involving jobs that fail to intermesh. A claims B didn't send the report on time; B claims that A's request was not properly written. Most managers spend a heavy proportion of their time dealing with these lateral relations; that is, seeking to smooth out the work flow among employees, departments, and divisions of the organization.

Managerial lateral relations

Managers as well as workers must learn to cooperate across job boundaries. This task may be quite difficult for managers, since they are generally more competitive than their subordinates. Note the following example:

> Marketing wants to put out a low-cost computer for under $100. Production thinks it will be hard to maintain high quality if the item is mass produced, as it must be at this price. The engineers in the development department fear that the proposed product will be shoddy and hurt their professional reputations; they claim that within a year they can develop a product that will make everyone proud. The legal department is concerned about product liability suits if the product fails to function. The controller, on the other hand, stresses the importance of increasing sales this year, to relieve the cash-flow problem. Furthermore, she is reluctant to provide continued funding for Development's seemingly endless search for perfection. Until these differences can be ironed out, the organization will never attain the kind of cooperation needed for a united effort.

Far more synchronization and integration are required in management positions than in most manual jobs (including complex assembly-line work). Managers must master a number of skills: the ability to move quickly, to interact constantly with peers and subordinates, and to cope with pressures generated by interdepartmental conflicts. The manager must keep in mind that each department has developed its own set of values, goals, and methods.

In addition to these skills, the successful department head's daily routine consists of acquiring critical information from other managers, rushing through semifinished reports and materials, knowing the answers to difficult questions, obtaining permission from other departments to abandon unworkable plans, and reporting problems to trouble-shooting groups in a suitable fashion. Finally, the manager must meet fast-breaking deadlines. All of these tasks fall into the category of lateral relations.

As modern organizations become increasingly specialized, more lateral relationships develop. Managers no longer do their own planning, evaluating, coordinating, and trouble-shooting. These responsibilities are now divided among various departments that specialize in areas such as planning, quality control, scheduling, and expediting. No department can operate effectively on its own; only through mutual cooperation and persuasion will the various specialties interweave, creating a coherent system.

The role of structure

Managers often blame interpersonal conflicts on personality differences or poor communications within the organization. Although individual differences frequently contribute to human relations problems, most students of organization now realize that the structure of the organization contributes to the creation or resolution of tensions as well.

Structure shapes interpersonal relations in a number of ways. Structure determines who will work together and share the information needed to complete various tasks. Those who work together form groups. Within each group, common standards and work routines develop to smooth the problems arising from the job. Informal communications of this sort are essential for organizational success. If employees had to turn to their superior for all the information they needed to do their jobs, the supervisor would have time for nothing else.

Students of organization are often surprised by the amount of work-oriented information communicated during social contacts. During a social break, it is not unusual to hear a conversation like the following:

Bill: What a difficult week! Everything seems to be going wrong. One guy quit, another had a tonsilectomy, and now we're off schedule on the monthly P&L's. I've had to take some people off your inventory reports. Hope that's not going to put you in a bind.
Mary: Don't leave me completely up in the air; my people will be sitting on their hands unless I can, at least, get the data for the eastern division stores by Tuesday.
Bill: O.K., if you can work with that for a while, we'll just delay the other regions.

Yet when individuals with interrelated work report to different supervisors, they will probably have more trouble making the "trade-offs" we just observed. The following might have been Mary's response:

"Now look, Bill, it's your job to get me the data on time; I have responsibilities too, and I can't meet my schedule if you don't meet yours. Your department is always delaying us for one last-minute reason or another."

Of course, Bill would have responded in the same manner. After all, they work in separate worlds with different interests, skills, and objectives. The absence of constant interaction creates barriers to effective communications and cooperation.

Limitations of organization charts. Most of us have seen organization charts. They help to describe formal reporting relationships, but their simplicity may be misleading. It is apparent from the accompanying organization chart

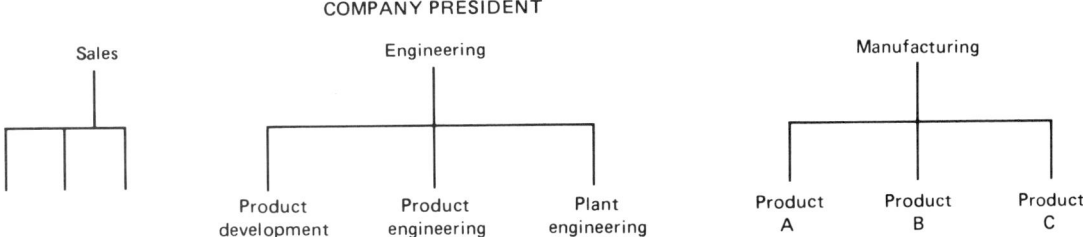

that Product Engineering reports to Engineering, but the chart does not reveal how the organization actually works. How are problems of coordination handled? Are ideas for new products generated by Sales on the basis of customer specifications or does Engineering do all the developmental work? Is the sales department involved only when the products are ready for the market? Do production engineering and plant engineering help out the various manufacturing sections when they are in trouble? Does Engineering merely set standards to which Manufacturing must conform? One must go beyond the organization chart to answer these questions. For the moment, however, we will consider the more formal relationships.

Difficulty of making choices. Galbraith poses this interesting problem. To improve the health of young people, a city wants to place physicians in local schools. Should this new physicians corps be part of the Board of Education? Should the physicians work for the Department of Health, for individual schools, or for the Youth Administration?[1] All are legitimate possibilities. Each will have different implications for the actual work of the physicians and where cooperation is likely to be easy and where difficult.

The three types of horizontal structure decisions

Teamwork does not come easily, but structure can make it more effective. What kinds of decisions must be made and how can they best be made? Basically, there are three different steps involved in the horizontal structuring of most organizations (at least, those organizations of reasonable size—over 100 people):

1. *Subdivide the organization into units.* Determine its basic divisions or major compartments. Should the organization be divided into functional compartments? Should those who share common technical and professional skills and work toward similar goals—those with the same input—be grouped together? Should the product, service, or geographic area served, the output, determine the division? Or should there be some mixture?
2. *Develop teamwork within each unit after subdivisions are created.*
3. *Coordinate the work flow between units.* Devise structural mechanisms for coordinating the major subdivisions.

The management question, of course, is how are these decisions to be made? What criteria can be found to insure a workable organization?

Designing the major subdivisions of the organization

A company can be organized in a variety of ways; but for simplicity, we shall concentrate on four basic structures: functional, product, matrix, and hybrid. The preceding chart depicts a company organized according to function. The three main functions—sales, engineering, and manufacturing—work in separate locations and are managed separately. The next chart shows the same company organized on a product basis. This

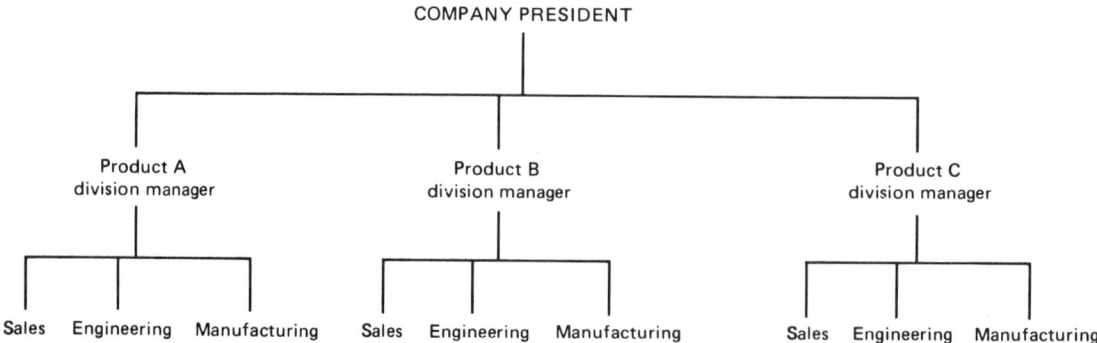

[1] Jay Galbraith, *Organization Design* (Reading, Mass.: Addison Wesley, 1978), p. 21.

method of organization produces three relatively independent minicompanies, each with its own sales, engineering, and manufacturing groups. *Functional* structures (sometimes called process structures) group people by their organizational specialities; *product* structures (also called decentralized, divisionalized, project or system structures) group people by their objectives, by product, service, client, and so forth. Some examples of this product–function distinction are indicated in the accompanying table.

Examples of product and functional organization

	Functional organization	Product organization
	A typing pool	Each typist is assigned to his own boss
	A central purchasing department	Each division has its own purchasing unit
	Separate companywide marketing, production, design, and engineering departments	Product A Design Group, including experts in marketing, design, production, and engineering
	A central-city health department	The school district and the prison each has its own health unit
	Plantwide inspection, maintenance, and supply departments	Production Team Y includes its own inspection, maintenance, and supply units
	A university statistics department teaching statistics for the entire university	Each department hires statisticians to teach its own students

As we shall see, *matrix* structure is a relatively new form of organization. It is a combination of functional and product structures. Finally, there is *hybrid* structure, an organization that is a mixture of structures and follows no common pattern.

It is important to remember:

1. Structure is a *contingency* variable. By *contingency* we mean simply that the structure chosen depends, or is contingent, on the nature of the work and the environment in which the organization must function.[2]

2. Most real-life organizations make use of more than one kind of structure. Some departments or divisions are organized one way; other parts of the organization use a different structure. Within a functional structure there may be product elements and vice versa.

[2] In recent years a vast amount of empirical literature has been written in attempt to answer the question, "What organization structure is suitable for a given technology and environment?" The following summarizes the contingency theory of organization structure: H. E. Aldrich, "Technology and Organizational Structure: A Reexamination of the Findings of the Aston Group," *Administrative Science Quarterly*, Vol. 17 (1972), 26–42; Tom Burns and G. M. Stalker, *The Management of Innovation* (London: Tavistock, 1961); F. E. Kast and J. E. Rosenzweig, *Contingency Views of Organization and Management* (Chicago, Illinois: Science Research Associates, Inc., 1973); Paul Lawrence and Jay Lorsch, *Organization and Environment: Managing Differentiation and Integration* (Homewood, Illinois: Irwin, 1967); Joan Woodward, *Industrial Organization: Theory and Practice* (London: Oxford University Press, 1965). The most comprehensive is Henry Mintzberg, *Structuring of Organizations* (Englewood Cliffs, N.J.: Prentice-Hall, 1979).

3. There is no way to eliminate interpersonal problems altogether; one type of structure eliminates some problems but creates others. There are always tradeoffs, and the task of the organizational designer is to select the structure with the least problems.

With this brief introduction we shall look in greater detail at the advantages and disadvantages of these various forms of structure.

Functional structure

Organizations are traditionally structured according to function. Functional structure is most often found in routine operations, for which technology is well established, or where the uncertainties are external rather than internal. Listed below are the advantages of functional structure.

Economies of scale. Functional structure permits the organization to take advantage of economies of scale in both equipment and manpower. When all data processing goes through the same computational facility, the organization can afford the fastest and most efficient (but sometimes most expensive) equipment. When all typing is done in a central typing pool, the company can take advantage of each secretary's special skills; slack periods in one department's demands can be balanced against rush orders in others. When all market research is centralized in a single unit, the company can afford to hire specialists in psychometrics and survey techniques. A centralized legal office permits individual lawyers to specialize in subjects such as patents, rather than to attempt (in vain) to keep abreast of rapidly changing developments in every branch of the law.

Other economies of scale are also possible. A centralized purchasing department can garner discounts for large purchases. A centralized sales department needs to send only one salesperson to a customer, and this person can sell the company's entire line. In decentralized sales organization, several salespeople (one from each division) might call on the same customer—a much more expensive procedure.

Keeping up to date and maintaining standards. Within a functional organization, employees associate with others who have the same training and interests. These groups develop a sense of occupational pride and set high standards of excellence for themselves. If a company wanted a rigid inspection policy, for example, the inspectors might be placed in separate functional units. In a separate area, they are less likely to be influenced by the departments they inspect; individual inspectors might compete with each other to see who could enforce the rules most strictly.

Functional organization simplifies communications between employees in a specialized field. When social workers are assigned to a centralized social work group, they can discuss how to handle difficult cases, and they can exchange ideas more easily than when they are separated into individual "children," "adult," and "handicapped" departments. Similarly, statisticians are more likely to discuss new developments in their profession when they work in a single department. Engineers in functional organizations are less likely to become technologically obsolescent than if they were isolated from fellow specialists in a product department. On the other hand, narrow specialization may lead to a trained incapacity to appreciate the needs of other functional groups or of the organization as a whole.

Monitoring external uncertainties. The company organized according to function is better able to keep track of external developments, particularly when it is necessary to adapt to changes in government regulations, customer demands, or scientific knowledge. Each functional group monitors developments in its own special field. Thus the health and safety department can respond quickly to changing requirements in health and safety legislation, the overseas sales department keeps abreast of the special needs of overseas customers, and the laser technology group watches the rapidly changing technology in their field.

Career development. Managers in functional organizations are likely to receive better training in their specialities and to have clearer lines of promotion than their colleagues in a "product" organization. A purchasing agent who works within a product structure may report to a plant manager; but since few purchasing agents ever become plant managers, the job may be a dead-end position or have only the most uncertain opportunities for promotion by transfer. In contrast, if the agent works in a large purchasing department, promotional opportunities will be much less ambiguous.

Flexibility in assigning people. Within the functional structure it is easier to move people from one assignment to another. Since maintenance personnel are not restricted to one product line, they can move quickly between lines to meet emergencies. Also, if the demand for Product A increases at the expense of Product B, functional structure can adjust more easily.

Despite its advantages, functional organization suffers from many drawbacks. We will discuss the nature of these drawbacks in the following case, which also illustrates the strength of product structure.

Product organization

Some years ago, one of the authors studied an electronics manufacturing company. The company was organized on a functional basis. All the electronic engineers who designed the internal logic and systems were in one department. Another department consisted of electrical engineers who converted the theoretical designs into appropriate component specifications. Mechanical engineers were grouped into a chassis department that handled the cabinetry and support hardware. The automation department designed machinery that would make printed circuits and attach any transistors or other components. The industrial engineers in manufacturing sought an overall design that would be easy to assemble.

Whenever changes occurred in any aspect of the design, interdepartmental squabbling resulted. Electrical would find inconsistencies in the electronics group's system. Automation would claim that both groups made their designs difficult to process; Industrial Engineering blamed Automation and the Electronics for poor manufacturing efficiency. Chassis, under pressure to develop more attractive and compact units, sought changes in the electronic array, to improve the appearance of the product. There was turmoil as each division blamed the other for difficulties in achieving its objectives. Problems were intensified by the natural tendency of each group to feel it had done the best job possible. No group wished to undo its completed plans just to satisfy the desires of an outsider.

ELECTRONIC EQUIPMENT DESIGN

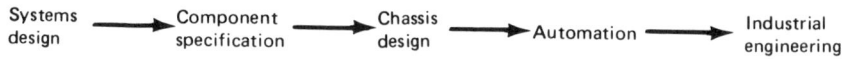

The above organization assumed (incorrectly) that each group could perform its work according to rigid, predetermined standards, and then "pass it along" to the next group. To eliminate the frictions and buck-passing (one group blaming another), top management created a series of mini-companies for each product. Thus the new organization looked like this:

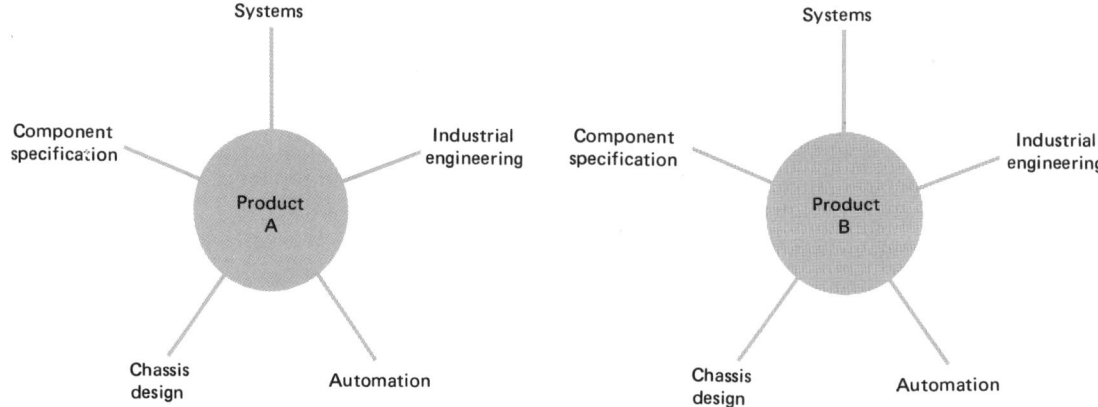

Short lines of communication. This new structure made it much easier to handle *work-flow communications*. This is a common advantage of product organization: if individuals with interfacing jobs work together, problems can be ironed out between people who know each other well; there is no need to go through a long chain of command or to coordinate activities with virtual strangers.

The advantages of short communications lines becomes especially important on new projects when members of the work group must constantly adjust to each other.

Identification with product. Functional organization leads to identification with one's function, but at the cost of less sensitivity for what happens elsewhere in the organization.

Each unit becomes jealous of its own prerogatives and finds ways to protect itself against the pressures and encroachments of others. Conflict develops on the employee as well as the supervisory level, thus forcing an extra administrative load on higher levels of management because of the need for constantly reconciling differences.[3]

By contrast, with product structure, employees obtain a clearer picture of the entire process. They become more aware of how their jobs fit into the whole scheme of things. Thus they are more likely to develop pride in the product they make. Typists, for example, are more likely to identify with their bosses' work if they are assigned to work directly with them. Statistics professors may become more concerned with how much their students learn if each department has its own statisticians. Product structure may also increase the sense of satisfaction obtained from the final product, whether the product is a complete manuscript or a student who can apply statistics to his or her field.

Pinpointing responsibility. In a product structure, each unit is technologically self-contained. This sufficiency allows the department manager to be autonomous and responsive to unexpected problems. In contrast, functional managers are more likely to say, "I can't do my job because that other department is using the wrong material [or timing or designs or isn't working hard enough or fast enough]." Within product structure there is less buck-passing, since the manager has all or nearly all the resources necessary to complete the whole task.

Thus product organization makes it easier to evaluate managers by results or output. Functional specialists, by contrast, produce inputs for other departments. This makes appraisal of their performance difficult, since no one department can be held responsible for results.

In the interest of saving time and money, the case intake department of a social work agency developed a new standardized form to be used for registering new clients. In practice, however, other departments found the form inadequate for their purposes. Yet Intake refused to modify its procedures, since for its purposes, the new form increased "productivity" (cases processed per clerk-hour), and the department manager was evaluated in terms of *his* labor costs (easy to measure) rather than in terms of his service to other departments (difficult to measure).

The absence of result measures in functional organizations may require management to supervise these departments more closely. Otherwise, each department will work in ways suited to its own needs, not the requirements of the total system.

Broad training. Functional structure leads to the development of specialized, professional skills; product structure helps to train broadly based general managers with a wide variety of skills. As suggested earlier, each product division is a bit like a minicompany, and its manager faces many of the same

---

[3] James C. Worthy, "Factors Influencing Employee Morale," *Harvard Business Review*, Vol. 28, No. 1 (January 1950), 71.

problems faced by top management: scheduling work, meeting deadlines, effecting trade-offs between operations, inducing cooperation among subordinates. Above all, these managers are judged by results. Thus, it is not surprising that a high percentage of top managers receive their initial experience in product structures.

Broad spans of control. The manager of a product organization often has a broad span of control. Since each product unit is evaluated by results (or goals) and little coordination is required among units, the manager must spend relatively little time supervising individual units.

Problems. The product organization has problems, too. The advantages of a functional structure are often lost when a company is organized according to a product structure. An increased emphasis on work flow and product reduces the emphasis on specialization. Some economies of scale may be lost, and managers will be tempted to ignore new technical developments in some of the specialities under their jurisdiction. Well-trained, motivated professionals could become anxious about their careers. Management may de-emphasize technical standards in favor of getting the product out, an attitude ironically summarized by the quip, "I don't want it good; I want it Thursday."

One final problem. How are activities grouped around the product? The nature of the product around which structure is developed is often unclear. Is it a physical good or a specific group of clients or customers? Should a container company be organized with separate divisions for cans, bottles, and so forth, or on the basis of various groups of customers; for example, beer or food companies. In a hospital, should clinics specialize according to branches of medicine (for example, orthopedic or dermatology) or according to patients (children, adults, emergency cases)? Alternatively, grouping may be determined by geography. Companies often have area managers for Latin America, Europe, and the Far East.

The "product-type" structure chosen depends on which coordinations top management finds most critical. If people who work in the same region are grouped together, they are separated by organizational boundaries from those who are working toward the same physical product. Even within the product structure there are problems concerning interdepartmental coordination. Sometimes the solution is a matrix structure.

Matrix structure

This relatively new structural form seeks to combine the advantages and eliminate the disadvantages of the product and functional structures. It provides for direct and immediate work flow supervision on a product basis as well as for specialization by function.[4] The former permits management by results, communications among employees who have the greatest need to cooperate, and a single manager responsible for the entire production process.

---

[4] For a good review of how these structures work, see Stanley Davis and Paul Lawrence, *Matrix* (Reading, Mass.: Addison Wesley, 1977).

A MATRIX ORGANIZATION IN A FOOD COMPANY

	Product dev. laboratory	Market research	Sales	Manufacturing facilities
Cereals				
Frozen foods				
Desserts				
Animal food				

(Rows labeled by Product managers; columns labeled by Functional managers)

On the other hand, professionals and specialists still have their home departments, the career satisfaction associated with working with peers, and the opportunity to work for technical excellence.

Such a neat balancing act violates one of the standard principles of scientific management, the principle of unity of command (having one boss). The distinctive feature of matrix organization is that many employees have dual reporting responsibilities; they have two bosses—one functional, one product. To see how this delicate balancing works in practice, we shall look at three versions of matrix structure: temporary project groups, contracting for services, and permanent dual reporting relationships.

Temporary project groups. The most common form of matrix structure involves the assignment of functional specialists to a short-term project group. The group is supervised by a manager or coordinator who is responsible for completing the job in a specific length of time and adhering to fixed costs and performance standards. The specialists working under this project manager must meet these demands and also perform in a manner consistent with the professional standards of their functional departments. In many cases the actual work is performed within the functional departments under the direction of the functional supervisor, with the project manager providing coordination. When the special task is completed, the members of the group return to their original assignments.

This type of matrix is associated with innovative efforts to accomplish something that has not been tried before and that cannot be made routine. It is typical of research and development work, but is also frequently found in the introduction of new consumer goods and services.

> Ellen Fisher is in charge of introducing a new soap product. She is the leader of a team of specialists—from market research, sales, and manufacturing—who have the functional skills required to launch a new product. Typically, Market Research tests consumer reactions extensively before introducing a new product. Fisher would like to bypass this step because Sales will deliver a major chain store customer (using a house brand label) if a May 1 introduction date can be met. This date is much too early, according to Manufacturing. The manufacturing team's representatives insist that production of the new soap product must be integrated with schedules for other products. "We can't produce a huge order like that overnight. It's a three months', not a three weeks' job you're asking for."
>
> Ellen's job is to negotiate with Sales and Manufacturing. She must assess the relative importance of each department's technical criteria, determine what can be modified, and decide the best overall course. The large initial order from an important customer must be weighed against possible manufacturing problems that would delay the product's introduction elsewhere. The gains from more extensive field testing must be balanced against the time and cost of these tests, especially since there are considerable data already available.
>
> Ellen is not the only one weighing these alternatives; the contenders meet frequently to debate the issues. But the final responsibility for success or failure is hers!

Matrix structure was appropriate in this situation, for several reasons.

- Management could not plan in advance the contributions of various functional specialties. Technical problems were bound to occur, but the exact nature of these was unforseeable. Further, the inevitable interdepartmental disputes were too complex and too frequent to be handled by top managers with other responsibilities.

- Expensive, highly specialized talent (such as Market Research) must be used in this project as well as in many other projects. Costly testing equipment could also be shared, permitting economies of scale.

- An overall understanding of the project's goals was required before sophisticated professional skills could be used for this project. In addition, the performance of each component part influenced the problems faced by other groups in the production of the final product. Therefore, for this project, it was essential to have one manager concerned with the project as a whole, and a number of other managers concerned with the excellence of each function.

Contracting for services. A more stable matrix structure has the product manager working through functional departments almost as if they were outside contractors. Normally, product managers have budgets and must buy the functional services; further, the managers are judged by how well they keep within their budgets (and sometimes by whether their products contribute to overall profits). In the same way, the functional managers' claim to resources depends on the payments they receive from product departments.[5]

A good example of a contracting arrangement is provided by chain department stores. For merchandise, the product manager (in this case, the store manager) must depend on functional merchandise specialists in central headquarters. Merchandising specialists are responsible for selecting the merchandise they think will have sales appeal; however, the store manager will ultimately decide which lines to carry and the percentage of the budget to be allocated to each line. If attractive merchandise is limited, each store manager will compete for the largest allocation. On the other hand, the merchandise managers find it hard to get rid of poor selling merchandise. Obviously, there is room for bargaining between the store and merchandise managers.

Permanent dual reporting relationships. Perhaps the most difficult and innovative matrix structure provides a permanent dual reporting relationship.

A state government has reorganized its Conservation Department with two equal lines of authority, one responsible for various functions and the other for geographic regions. Thus, there are statewide programs for forestry, fishery, wildlife, pure air, and water, and decentralized programs for Region 1 (comprised of several counties), Region 2, and others. The Region 1 manager will obtain staff from each of the centralized functional groupings, but these staff members will also be supervised by professional experts who see their long-term careers in terms of advancement within their functional profession. The regional manager must have the approval of those in charge of functions, since the fulfillment of regional needs must fit into the state programs.

Regional manager: "I have two kinds of problems. First, statewide offices never recognize our special, local needs. Second, members of the professional staffs, such as the wildlife staff, resent my insistence that they should broaden their skills to deal with such things as fisheries, forestry, and water pollution."

The regional managers are dependent on the functional managers, and the reverse is also true. Functional statewide programs can be implemented only through the regions, and these programs require the cooperation of regional managers.

Statewide wildlife manager: "We need to cut back on otter trapping this year if we are to preserve certain animals from extinction, but two of our regional managers with string trapper organizations in their regions are trying to sabotage this program."

The challenge of matrix organization. The matrix organization contradicts traditional managerial principles. The organization's goals are unclear, the chain of command is confused, tasks are poorly defined, and the managers' responsibility usually exceeds their authority. For many managers, this ambiguous situation is extremely threatening; others find it challenging and liberating.

---

[5] Occasionally, product managers are permitted to purchase services from outside contractors or even to seek bids from competing internal suppliers. Therefore, market prices for services may have considerable relevance for salary administration. For further details, see Raymond E. Miles and Charles Snow, *Organization Structure, Strategy, and Process* (New York: McGraw-Hill, 1978).

High-order mediating skills are required on all sides if matrix management is to work. In the Ellen Fisher example, not only must Fisher mediate among the various functional groups, but each member of her product team also acts as a linking pin. Thus the representative from manufacturing on the product team must represent both interests: manufacturing and product. In addition to arguing for manufacturing at the product team's meetings, manufacturing's representative must also fight for the product's interests when dealing with colleagues in manufacturing. Although a member of manufacturing, the representative may have a struggle. Within each of the functional groups there will be substantial esprit de corps, a unifying point of view against outsiders, even though in this case the outsider is a member of the group.

Hybrid organization

Few organizations consist of only one kind of structure—functional, product, or matrix. In real life, most organizations consist of combinations of these three basic forms. The Home Appliance Company (see chart) is a fine illustration of this. At the division level, the company is organized according to product; at the department level, it is by function; the design coordinator represents an element of matrix structure.

Whenever a new personal product (a hair dryer, for instance) is being considered, a task force is created, consisting of representatives from each of the three groups and a new product coordinator. Since these representatives

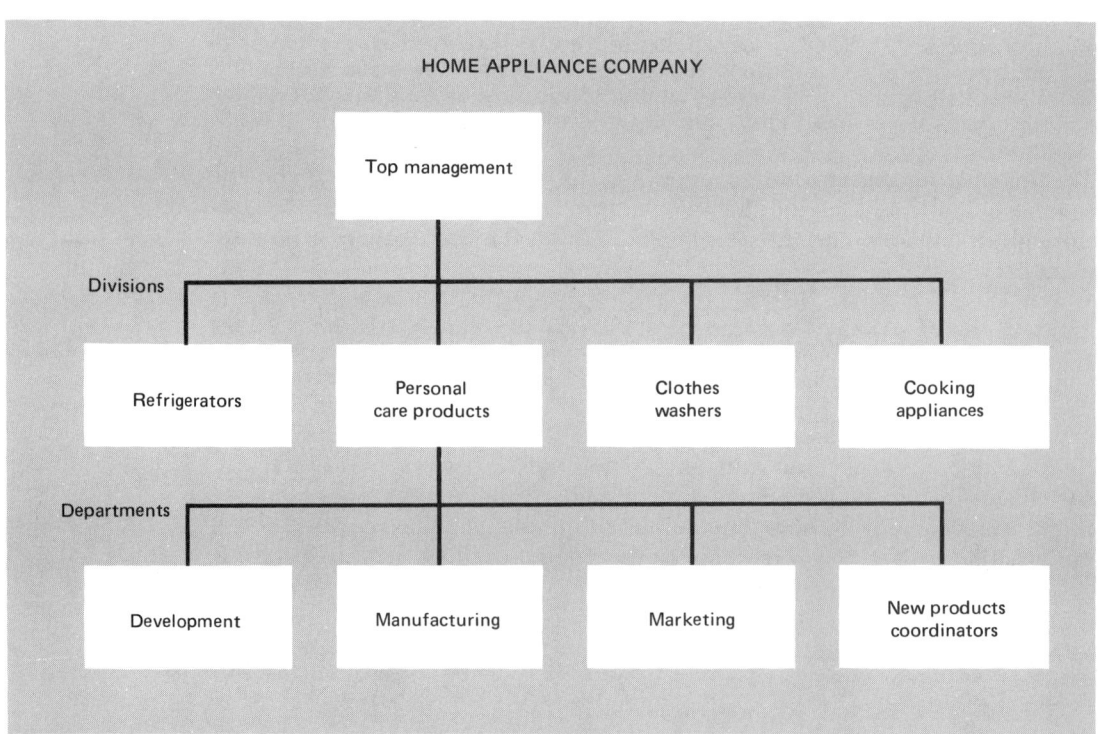

continue to report to their functional departments, a mini-matrix structure is formed; the task force works on the basic elements of the new product until it is ready to be turned over to Development.

Choosing among alternative structures

Each of these alternative structures has its advantages and disadvantages. How is the perplexed manager to decide which structure is appropriate for a particular situation? The research findings to date are not entirely consistent; however, functional structure seems to be most appropriate when there are substantial economies of scale to be gained, either in terms of equipment (such as expensive, single-purpose equipment) or manpower (for example, highly trained professionals who cannot be assigned on the basis of one professional per product group). Functional structure may also be the answer when specialized units (such as industrial relations) are required to deal with external pressures or uncertainties on an organizationwide basis.

A manager should choose the product structure when the critical problem is coordinating the workflow between units. In this situation, uncertainties arise in the relationship between units rather than between the company and the outside world. On the other hand, when coordination between units is almost automatic (perhaps because the product being made is simple and the production process is well understood and unchanging) and the emphasis is placed on rules and goals, then it might be best to use a functional organization to take advantage of economies of scale.

Finally, the matrix organization can be used in two situations: when close coordination is required for a short period and when there is a need for both close coordination *and* the economies of scale in people and equipment provided by a functional organization. Since the matrix organization is the most difficult structure to manage, it should be used to resolve only unique or particularly complex problems.

One parenthetical note must be added. Some observers believe that various structural forms have evolved in the history of American business. The earliest companies were organized functionally. These were also centralized organizations because most decision making occurred at the top of the pyramid—where the functions converged. Product or decentralized organizations came later, particularly in multiproduct companies. These enabled lower level managers (controlling a product line) to make critical decisions; few decisions, such as those concerned with capital investment, remained centralized. Now matrix organizations are increasingly common, although they are still far from predominant.

Building work-flow teams

After the major structuring of the organization has taken place, management must still make departmentation decisions. Since the typical functional or product division will have many managers, how should employees be grouped in supervisory units? There is increasing evidence that employees whose jobs are most interdependent and who must frequently coordinate with each other should be placed under a common supervisor.[6] This arrangement encourages small groups to form that will facilitate the work flow—often called socio-technical systems. As discussed in Chapter 5, members of such groups will seek to aid one another, and this can facilitate the completion of their mutual work tasks. The Ajax case will illustrate the importance of using work flow as a major criterion for structuring individual departments.

The Ajax Company case

Ajax had a functional organization. It was divided into major divisions: sales, manufacturing, finance (headed by the controller), and others.

Before

The Ajax Company manufactured small home appliances to sell to retail outlets. Every order sent in by salespeople in the field had to be processed by four different groups of employees in the home office.

   a) *Customer contact clerks* communicated with the customer if the salesperson's order was unclear, if the merchandise ordered was unavailable, or if price changes had taken place.

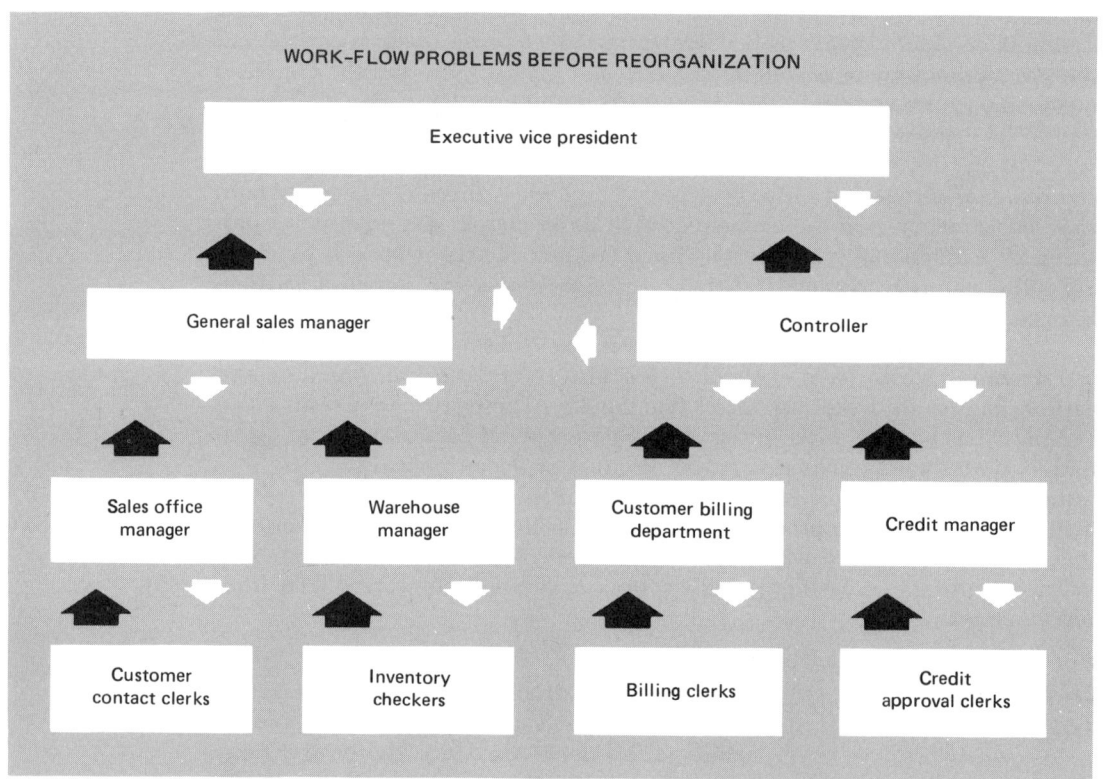

[6] This basis is often referred to as the "work flow" criterion for departmentation decisions. See Eliot Chapple and Leonard Sayles, *The Measure of Management* (New York: Macmillan, 1964). The Ajax case is adapted from this work.

b) *Billing clerks* checked the arithmetic on the order and entered correct charges and credits on the customer's account.
c) *Inventory checkers* checked to make sure that goods ordered were available for shipment.
d) *Credit approval clerks* examined the customer's credit status in order to authorize shipping.

The Ajax Company placed each technical specialty under separate supervisors, as in the diagram on p. 232. Thus, each order passed through four distinct departments and two divisions. Each specialist belonged to the organizational unit to which his function was *logically* related.

You can probably predict what happened. The design of the organization made no provision for the cooperation and communication required to complete the *total job* of order processing. There was constant conflict among employees. Inventory checkers complained that they had to track down merchandise that might later be dropped from the order as a result of the discovery of a salesperson's clerical error or a customer's inadequate credit. Responsibility for delays in processing orders were passed from one group to another. The billing clerks complained that the inventory checkers were always late with their information, and the inventory checkers retorted that their delays were the result of faulty information from customer contact clerks.

Higher management was always being called in to settle disputes. When conflict arose between an inventory checker and a customer contact clerk, for example, each would go to a superior, who, in turn, would take the battle up to the general sales manager. When the billing clerk complained that he couldn't get up-to-the-minute information from the customer contact clerks (and thus made embarrassing errors in customers' accounts), the problem might have to go to the executive vice-president. Even the sales manager and the controller were constantly blaming each other for difficulties in their departments.

After

In a reorganization of these functions, all employees processing orders were placed under a single general office supervisor who, in turn, had first-line supervisors for the various geographic areas served by the company. The new organization is diagrammed in the following chart.

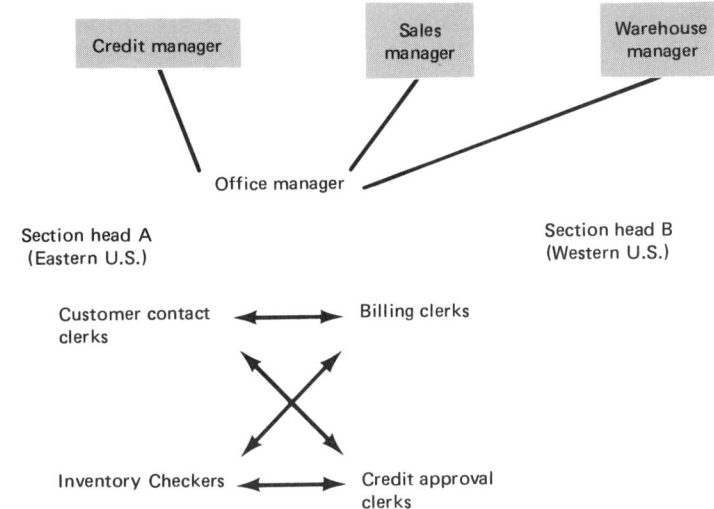

Under each of these supervisors, the specialists continue to do much the same job they had done before. Now, however, any dispute can be settled face-to-face within the immediate work group or, in exceptional instances, by the first-line supervisor. No longer is it necessary to channel complaints up the line through two or three levels of management. The new scheme saves a great deal of executive time and makes it possible to settle most problems by horizontal work-flow contacts among the employees themselves. The arrangement increases output enormously by eliminating many petty frictions.

The sales, warehouse, and credit managers now have a lateral, not a supervisory relation to the office supervisor. Each was made responsible for establishing standards of performance for the clerical employees whose work involves their respective special interests, and for auditing to be sure that these standards of performance, that is, controls, are being observed.

Work flow, an important and often neglected principle of work organization, can be applied to vastly different types of work settings: a hospital emergency room, a coal mine, and a textile weaving mill.[7]

Reorganizing a hospital emergency room

The pressure of caring for more and more patients in Midtown Hospital's Emergency Room was exerted strongly on the nurses, who made their complaints known to the head nurse. Young doctors assigned to E.R. duty were also unhappy, because they preferred diagnostic work in other areas of the hospital, and they found the E.R. nurses more difficult to work with than those in other sections.

The administrator wanted the hospital to meet its objective of providing high-quality medical care for all patients—the rich on the VIP floors as the well as the mixture of patients in the Emergency Room. The administrator was also aware that disharmony among E.R. staff was affecting the flow of patients through the E.R. Many were forced to wait unnecessarily long times, test results were being misplaced, and sometimes it was difficult to determine where a patient was—in x-ray, in the fracture room, or out of the hospital, having been discharged. The administrator was worried about the harm that might come to patients because of the staff's lack of coordination. Staff members were not working together for the benefit of the patients and the hospital.

The administrator hired a consultant who, after a work-flow study, did the following:

1. He matched nurses with doctors in separate teams so that an incoming patient would be cared for by a nurse-and-doctor unit. Each team could call on the services of a practical nurse and an aid who were shared by three doctor-nurse teams.

2. A senior physician and a nurse supervisor were hired for each shift to oversee operations. The physician was placed in charge of the Emergency Room, and the nurse supervisor was named as the doctor's deputy. One or the other was in the E.R. at all times. Doctors, nurses, practical nurses, and aids were told to bring their complaints to the nursing supervisor, who, in turn, discussed them with the physician in charge of the E.R. Together they resolved the problems and dealt with the complaint.

3. An additional senior nurse was hired for each shift, to triage the patients. That is, she quickly interviewed each patient to determine if there was a true emergency; if the patient was sufficiently ill to need a doctor, but the case was not an emergency; or if the patient could be seen in a clinic within 24 hours. This

---

[7] The hospital study was done by Grace Urrows, one of our students. The coal-mining case is adapted from E. L. Trist, G. W. Higgin, H. Murray, and A. B. Pollock, *Organizational Choice* (London: Tavistock Publications, 1963). The weaving case is based on A. K. Rice, "Productivity and Social Organization in an Indian Weaving Shed," *Human Relations*, Vol. 6, No. 4 (1953).

eliminated one-third of the workload, ascertained that emergency cases would be seen immediately, and decreased the amount of time a nonemergency case would have to wait before seeing a physician.

This plan divided large, hostile groups into small units in which the original intergroup hostility dissipated. Most decisions were left to these small groups of professionals, whose foresight resulted in more regular work loads for the entire staff. Adequate supervision of the proper kind was provided for professionals. The plan allowed for the smooth flow of patients through the Emergency Room and decreased the number of unnecessary admissions to the hospital. Thus, the hospital was able to meet its objective of delivering quality care to all patients.

The opposite type of reorganization may be observed in a British coal mine, when management thought it was introducing a more scientific organization. At one time, all the operations at the mine face were performed by a small team working together on a single shift. Since members of the team were in close contact with one another, it was easy to devise solutions for problems as they arose. Each member of the group felt responsible for the entire operation.

Management combined these small groups into much larger ones working over larger areas, believing that the change would increase efficiency. One crew did nothing but prepare the new face for blasting. Others handled the recovery of the coal that came down after the dynamite had been set off; another crew worked on timbering and moving rail lines. This new division of labor was carried out on a 3-shift, 24-hour cycle: each shift performed a different function. Each worker became a specialist. As a result, no single group of workers felt responsible for the total operation; as problems arose, each shift developed the habit of shrugging them off and passing the buck to the next shift. Communications, which at best are troublesome in a mine, were further complicated by the workers' isolation from those performing different functions. Previously, the small groups were almost self-supervising (motivated as they were by a group incentive plan); with the new plan, it became a complex management task to coordinate individual, unmotivated workers. Even new equipment did not compensate for production losses due to work-flow problems.

An Indian textile mill that had undergone intensive "job reengineering" did not attain satisfactory output levels. Each occupational group in the mill was assigned a work load based on a careful study of all the job components. In a room containing 240 looms, the following assignments were given to the 12 types of specialists:

1. Each weaver tended approximately 30 looms.
2. Each "battery filler" served about 50 looms.
3. Each "smash hand" was assigned some 80 looms.
4. Each of 9 different categories of maintenance men was responsible for from 120 to 240 looms.

These occupational tasks were highly interdependent, and the utmost coordination was required to maintain productivity. But the assignment of work loads militated against coordination. In effect, each weaver came into contact with five-eighths of a "battery filler," three-eighths of a "smash hand," and even smaller fractions of the other nine workers he depended on to keep the looms operating.

When the work was reorganized so that all workers performing interdependent tasks were made part of the same work group, production soared. Work groups were reconstructed so that a single group of workers was responsible for the operation of a particular bank of looms. The new interaction pattern produced regular relationships, facilitated communications among workers, and led directly to the increase in output.

Destroying work flow in a coal mine

Textile mill

Summary of cases   The conclusion to be drawn from these studies is that when designing the organization, the administrator should provide each work group with a relatively autonomous task. Only under these circumstances will competent internal leadership and group responsibility develop.

Ideally, the individual worker should be permitted to coordinate his or her own activities (that is, through job enrichment). If the same worker does both the typing and the filing, it is unlikely that problems will arise in integrating the two processes. The next best thing is to encourage coordination within the immediate work group. In the ideal situation, people are loyal and responsible to their fellow workers, willing to adjust their pacing, the quality of their work, and their overall efforts, in order to satisfy one another's needs.

Interdependence among units

So far, we have examined the basic structuring of organizations and the creation of departmental units. But after the various departments and divisions are established, management must still be concerned with their coordination. There will always be problems of interdependence, regardless of the company's organizational structure (except in very small companies where everyone reports to the owner/boss). Even product departments are not autonomous; they will have an impact on certain organizationwide regional, customer, or financial considerations.

How does management organize to cope with the remaining interdependence among organizational units? That depends on the answer to these two questions:

1. How much cooperation and integration is necessary between units; that is, how interdependent or autonomous are they?
2. How different are the perspectives, goals, and values of units that need to be coordinated? (The more similar they are, the easier it is for them to cooperate.)

Types of interdependence   Students of organization have identified the following types of interdependence, each with its own distinctive integration problems: [8]

1. Pooled
2. Sequential
3. Reciprocal
4. Service
5. Advisory

Pooled. Although the products of a company may be sold to various customers, the public impression created by each enhances or injures the company's total reputation. In the same way, the money each division spends and the quality of its employee relations contributes to the company's overall financial position and image. These are examples of *pooled interdependence.*

---

[8] The first three are associated with the seminal work of James D. Thompson, *Organizations in Action* (New York: McGraw-Hill, 1964).

Sequential. The Admitting Department in a hospital sends new patients to nursing floors. Manufacturing transmits finished products to Shipping. These departments are characterized by sequential interdependence; the work of one builds directly on the work of the other. More coordination is required with sequential than with pooled interdependence, because each step in the sequence depends on the one before or after.

Reciprocal. When developing a new product, a company may find that engineering, manufacturing, and marketing considerations are completely interdependent. The constant back and forth exchanges displayed in the following example are not unusual.

"We [Engineering] believe we can add a special feature that will extend the life of the appliance if Manufacturing can fabricate this new plastic. Marketing believes that this feature won't allow us to increase the selling price, so Manufacturing must keep the same total cost."

Of these first three types of interdependence, the reciprocal relationship represents the greatest amount of interunit interdependence; pooled, the least. As we shall see, reciprocal interdependence requires a greater integration effort, often involving almost continuous daily interrelationships. Pooled interdependence can be handled by more formal, slowly paced procedures (for example, hierarchical problem solving). Sequential interdependence is somewhere between the two.

Service. A distinctive and difficult type of interdependence develops from service or support activities. These centralized *functions* remain separate from the rest of the organization (as in a functional structure), but they are utilized by the entire organization, not just by the next department in sequence. Thus, data processing, maintenance, laboratory analysis, and recruiting are typical examples, since these activities benefit from economies of scale or must be centralized because professional expertise is scarce. (It would not be economical to buy expensive blood analyzers for every hospital department, so all testing is done in a central lab facility.)

Advisory. Services are not the only centralized units within the organization. Usually there are a number of specialized staff departments that inform or advise managers—or even their bosses—on difficult issues. Centralizing the talent allows for economies of scale. The company could easily hire one well-trained lawyer, a labor relations specialist, an economist, and so on.

An internal adviser can help solve questions such as the following. To the plant engineer: "We seem to be getting more machine breakdowns on line 24 than on any of the others; what's wrong?" To the company lawyer: "Our largest customer is threatening to shift to a competitor; is it legal for us to give him a special price advantage?" To the packaging department: "We're getting a lot of breakage in shipments; what's wrong with our packing methods?" Note that most of these questions concern recurring problems that

Differentiation among units

the normal organizational procedures have not been able to cope with successfully.

Organizations want the departments and divisions they create to have different orientations. Sales ought to be attuned to quickly changing market conditions; Personnel should be concerned with creating a loyal and responsive work force. Thus when the marketplace dictates a new product line, marketing might prefer dropping those employees associated with the now unsuccessful, older technology, while Personnel would favor retraining and stability in employment.

The difficulty of resolving these inevitably differing perspectives will depend upon how deep-seated are the differences among the various units that must collaborate. Research suggests that the most crucial differences in orientation revolve around time perspective, the relative uncertainty of the problems with which each is dealing, and the formality of their internal procedures.[9]

Units with a long-run time perspective like research will find it difficult to work with departments having shorter time horizons. Some groups work with problems that have formula answers: "If short sleeve sweaters aren't moving, we clean them out with cut prices." Others may be working with problems for which three equally well-trained specialists will each have a different solution, and there is tolerance for ambiguity and uncertainty. And finally, departments may differ in the relative formality of their internal organization. Some will be highly informal, while others will insist that every issue "go through channels," with a clear written record and constant referral to rules.

Integration mechanisms

Thus some organizations have minimal coordination problems; for others it is a constant challenge.

As we have said, the scope of the problem will depend on the level of interdependence among the various departments and divisions and how difficult it is for them to evolve agreements and consensus. To facilitate this total system coordination, management has a wide choice of structural mechanisms. The following are most frequently utilized.

Hierarchical procedures

When there are only a few integration problems, and these are predictable, hierarchical procedure can be used to resolve the difficulties. *Hierarchy* refers to top management's planning, rules, and procedures, which can program interdepartmental coordination. If Department A follows the monthly plan and lives up to established procedures, its work will integrate well with the work of Department B.

But the hierarchy does more than program. It provides a structure for appealing procedures that create problems after plans and rules have already been established.

The typical hierarchy is shown in the next diagram.

[9] Paul Lawrence and Jay Lorsch, *Organization and Environment.*

CHAPTER 12
organization design

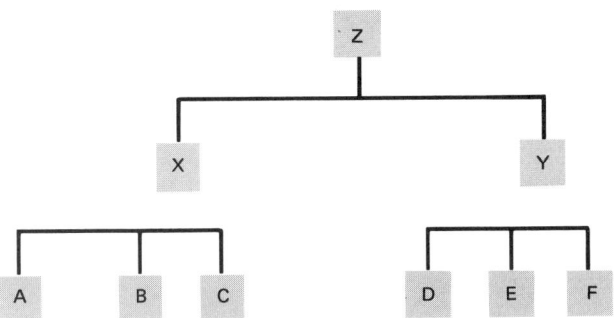

This process, almost judicial in nature, works very well as long as there are not too many complications. When there are too many complications, the dozen or more meetings necessary to resolve each one would swamp the upper-level managers. To avoid overloading the hierarchy, larger organizations add "audit" specialists to help keep the work outputs and activities of the various groups within the organization mutually compatible and consistent.

Audit specialists

According to traditional theory, a manager oversees all subordinates' actions, to be sure they are not violating the rules or standards of the organization and that they are achieving their work goals.

However, the rules, procedures, and standards of an organization may be so complicated and extensive that no single manager can administer all of them. Imagine the number of personnel, engineering, and financial procedures there are in the typical large manufacturing company. Company standards are difficult to maintain, too, because of the workers' tendency to hide or distort unfavorable information. Yet, the work of these audit specialists creates a host of human relations problems.

Standards are ambiguous

The engineers inspecting a finished piece of electronic equipment claimed that it would not operate in a room kept at a temperature of 100 degrees. The department that built the equipment argued that the humidity was too high in the room and that if the air were drier the equipment would operate at 100 degrees according to the standards set for it.

Standards conflict

The production control department told the production supervisor to ask people to work overtime because output was falling below schedule. The accounting department, however, has issued an ultimatum that all overtime work must cease, since the department has already exceeded its budgeted overtime allowance. The supervisor spends a good deal of time going back and forth between these two groups, trying to get one or the other to concede.

Auditing generates suspicions and distrust

Quality-control inspectors often say that workers hide their substandard work so that it won't be discovered and reported. This makes the job of checking quality much more difficult. Inspectors may appear overeager to find trouble, when in reality they are merely trying to do a thorough job and overcome the obstacles placed in their paths by various departments. Many operators and their managers assert, "Inspectors have to find a certain number of errors to justify their existence and their fancy budgets."

Nevertheless, periodic, after-the-fact checking helps maintain the organization as a coordinated work system.

Liaison specialists

Liaison specialists, acting as intermediaries, can aid one group to recognize how their work (or errors) impact another group. The value of a third person is that coordination is that person's sole function and he or she can appear more fair-minded to each party to an intergroup dispute. Often personnel managers, skilled at human relations, are called upon to perform this role.

Personnel manager: "In our advertising agency the creative personnel often can't understand why their work is rejected or isn't used by the business types who work with the clients. These are talented artists and writers, and they need someone who will listen to their complaints and anxieties as well as represent their needs and opinions to the fast-paced client managers. I am also able to explain to the artists some of the problems that arise from working with clients who are always changing their minds."

In addition to improving understanding between groups and proposing compromises to maintain working harmony, these intermediaries also act as *buffers.* Outside groups such as unions and community action committees want and need to communicate to the organization. A specialist who understands the source of the company's grievances and its political needs can help the organization gain a hearing and protect the basic functioning of the company's core activities. The pressures are absorbed by the liaison specialist.

Stabilization specialists or coordinators

When closer coordination is required among units, organizations employ a type of integration mechanism we have termed stabilization.[10] Unlike auditing, which is done after-the-fact, stabilization "staff" are given the authority to require line managers to obtain their permission before taking certain specified actions.

There may be such coordinators from "product" interests in a functional organization and representing "functional" interests in a product organization. Thus, in the Ajax Company case above, the comptroller's department could be in the position of requiring the order servicing organization to get the comptroller's permission before accepting an order for more than $10,000 worth of merchandise. Here are some other typical examples.

A manager would like to reduce his output tomorrow because two machines will be down for repairs. He can't make this decision himself, however, because the change in work flow will affect other departments that rely on the parts his group produces for their assembly requirements.

A manager wants to give an employee a large raise to keep another employer from bidding her away. The raise is an unmixed blessing for the manager, but it could hurt

---

[10] See Leonard Sayles, *Managerial Behavior* (New York: McGraw-Hill, 1964), pp. 103–8.

other managers who have to explain why their best employees are not getting comparable increases.

In the first case, the manager must have the production-control group check his schedule. In the second case, a salary administrator will have to approve the increase. Thus, stabilization involves making critical decisions contingent on permission from experts who keep the total organization's needs in view. As in auditing relationships, the organization's needs are often not absolute or fixed; there is room for differences of opinion. The final agreement may be the product of the representatives' negotiating skills.

A persistent problem related to auditing and stabilization procedures is that managers must contend with multiple influences, all pulling in various and often inconsistent directions. For example, the personnel department may urge managers to utilize lower-skilled employees because they are easy to hire in a tight labor market. At the same time, the engineering department may increase its demand for exacting work. The astute manager learns to sense which requirements are most dangerous to ignore, and to adjust his behavior accordingly. At times, personnel considerations predominate; sometimes engineering or perhaps financial considerations are most important.

Eventually these product or functional coordinators may get sufficiently powerful that the organization becomes, in fact, a matrix type structure.

Face-to-face contacts

If interdependence among units is great, no intermediary can comprehend all the subtleties that should be considered when working toward a compromise. When trying to come to a mutual agreement, representatives of the two groups must frequently deal with each other directly. Representatives of the concerned parties are expected to develop a common agreement. This is one of the major functions of committee meetings.

"Whenever we consider developing a new banking service, we bring together with marketing all of our operating departments, since anything new usually affects everyone sooner or later."

At times these committees are converted into special teams, task forces, or project groups to work out a new plan or program. (Once these special teams are created, the organization's pooled or sequential interdependence is converted into reciprocal interdependence.)

There are other ways to encourage greater communication between interdependent units. Purchasing, for example, can establish a field office within every operating unit. The purchasing personnel will probably develop close personal ties with the line manager of their particular office. Physical proximity (often called co-location) increases opportunities for interaction, facilitating communication between departments. Where these methods fail or are not feasible, top management may seek to improve the underlying trust and mutual understanding by sponsoring organizational development training.

Behavioral research suggests that face-to-face integration is most successful when the patterns of initiation are not one-sided. If one group constantly needs help or information from another group, or wishes to modify its initial plan but is not receptive to similar requests in return, distrust and hostility may develop between units.

In one study, the integration of sales and manufacturing was unsuccessful because Sales dominated Manufacturing. Sales constantly sought modifications in production schedules, pressured for quick adjustment to their needs, and was unresponsive to the problems faced by Manufacturing in regulating its schedules and labor costs.[11]

One of the major advantages of matrix organizations is that they force face-to-face contact between departments that must coordinate.

Slack

The opposite approach to facilitating coordination is decreasing the need for it. Departments can be made less dependent on one another by increasing *slack*. The following are examples of this.

When the purchasing department added extra buyers to its staff, it was no longer necessary to have anyone from the line departments act as a go-between to check on delivery dates and provide alternative purchase orders when delays seemed likely.

Previously, when parts were machined, they were transported directly to the assembly area. Any interruption in machining output had immediate ramifications. Now, assembly has an inventory or cushion of parts and can work for almost two days with no new supplies.

Of course, inventories and extra personnel cost money. The managerial problem is to work out the relative advantage of an additional coordination effort and compare it to the cost of more organizational slack.[12]

Sometimes organizations are referred to as being *loosely coupled* in contrast to *tightly coupled;* the loosely coupled organization has a great deal of slack.

Understanding service and advisory relationships

Even with skillful use of integration mechanisms, modern organizations find a number of coordination problems surrounding the use of service and advisory units. Special administrative skill is required to make these centralized specialists useful to the entire organization.

Service relationships

The manager of a centralized service has a tough job, as do other managers seeking to make use of the service. The support activity must be coordinated with the priorities of all the departments within the organization. Often, conflicting demands and high pressure result.

Of course, there are fewer problems if there is ample capacity—slack—in the service unit. But problems will develop the moment a modest scarcity appears. Some departments will be forced to wait or to postpone their own work because they cannot get timely service. At first, the product departments may simply pressure the service group for higher priority: "Look, we really

---

[11] John Dutton and Richard Walton, "Interdepartmental Conflict and Cooperation: Two Contrasting Studies," *Human Organization*, Vol. 25, No. 3 (Fall 1965), 207–20.

[12] For a good analysis of this concept, see Galbraith, *Organization Design*, pp. 81–85.

need that processing done fast; it's holding up eight important projects, and I know the VP would be wild if she knew we were going to have to slip our schedule."

As a result, the situation worsens. Other groups, sensing they may also have to wait, begin to pressure the service even when there is no need. They may ask for additional quantities, to be on the safe side, just in case a real shortage should develop. In effect, then, there is no such thing as a little scarcity; it quickly evolves into major shortages, as everyone rushes in "to get a fair share." The high pressure situation affects human relations within the organization.

Here is an example of a service subjected to constant pressure, as described by the supervisor in charge:

"We run a model shop that services all the engineering departments. It is our job to make parts and models for various development projects undertaken by engineers. Well, it has gotten so that nothing is routine anymore. The engineers are always engaging in rush projects—you know, someone gets a brainstorm and wants to get it under way immediately. First, they try to get you to tell them it will be done within a couple of days. By the next morning, they're calling the boss to complain you are not working on it fast enough, and by the next afternoon, they are in the office themselves, trying to get you to put their order ahead of someone else's. They can't seem to understand that it all takes time and we've got lots of other rush jobs. I don't know how much longer I can take the pressure."

Reaction to pressures. The tensions created by these pressures take their toll on departmental efficiency. The rate of personnel turnover is high. Other workers rebel against the system. They vent their frustrations by dealing aggressively with their tormentors. One observer relates a classic case of a group defending itself against excessive pressure from other groups:

Workers in the ship's store department on a large ship found that certain groups were always demanding rapid service on complicated requisitions. The ship's store workers, moving with speed and efficiency, merely announced that these offending groups would have to fill out in detail the multicopy, excessively complicated formal requisition sheets that were required by an official (but rarely observed) rule. The same pressuring groups were also denied their share of the personal items (stationery, film, etc.) distributed, in part, at the discretion of the stores department.

Unfortunately, this response may further reduce organizational efficiency and lead to additional pressure.

Low-status service personnel. If the staff of the service department has lower status than the employees pressuring for greater quantities or faster service, the service department will usually acquiesce to their superiors' demands. Often, though, conflicting feelings will accompany this action: "If we give in to Smith and rush their order, then Brown is going to be angry and report us." The solution is usually quite simple; requests for scarce departmental resources should be directed to a higher status supervisor or middle manager who can talk back to the "hoarders" and negotiate priorities. Lower-level people will be trampled without the support of higher management.

High-status service personnel. When the service group is composed of higher-status personnel than those who are demanding the service, the problem will be more serious. As we know from behavioral research, high-status employees expect to be initiators; they resent being directed by those of lower status. In this case, open conflict is likely to occur.

Actuary in an insurance company: "Some of the sales departments were trying to rush us to come up with new statistics for rate tables. We told everyone who pressured us that their work would be held back a few weeks while we rechecked all the data. If they continued to pressure us, we told them that it could be several months before the work would be finished."

Usually the product departments learn to restrain themselves, since service groups have both the power and the desire to retaliate.

Until the relative status and power of each group is established, there will be in-fighting and competition for control of the scarce resource. Eventually, these conflicts are settled—on the firing line.

Advisory relationships

In this section, we will assess the problems of integrating advisory relationships into the larger organization.

The personnel department has a typical advisory relationship (although it may have other nonadvisory functions, as well). Using this department as a case study, let us examine some of the human problems related to the advisor's role.

What is "advice"? Many theorists draw a sharp line between line and staff. The staff manager (being experienced in the field) is expected to provide technical information or advice and counsel but not to make decisions. The line manager is a decision maker. In practice, however, these theoretical distinctions are blurred.

When providing information, the personnel manager simply furnishes the facts that will help the manager make sound decisions. Personnel may:

- Interpret a disciplinary clause in the union agreement.
- Supply figures for the going rate for professional employees in the current labor market.

Or play a more active role and furnish *advice:*

"You are likely to provoke a wildcat strike if you give Bill Williams a disciplinary layoff."

"On the basis of the record, Jones looks like a better bet for the promotion, since the person on the job will have to assume a good deal of initiative without close supervision."

"If you hire Smith at that salary, you are going to have some dissatisfied older employees in your departments."

Finally, the manager can make decisions:

- Don't lay off Williams; give him a warning slip.
- Hire Green to replace the operator who left.

Sometimes there is a very narrow line between providing facts and providing advice. Thus, by selecting facts carefully, the personnel manager can actually sway the line manager's decision one way or the other. Also, what is given as advice may be interpreted by the recipient as a decision.

The temptation to exceed the advisory role. Historically, management tends to relinquish more and more functions to well-trained staff experts. When experts were first used to supplement the skills of line supervisors, the distinctions between information, advice, and decision making were rarely made. In fact, management has readily accepted expert advice without criticism. Often, since management was very anxious to avoid trouble with the unions, the industrial relations department actually *told* supervisors whom to hire, what to pay them, and how to answer their grievances, but the result was often disastrous to the prestige and status of supervisors.

In practice, it takes a strong-willed personnel manager to resist the temptation to become a decision maker. Once the manager has grown accustomed to providing advice and counsel, the next step—making the decision—may be irresistible. Even though care is taken not to usurp the line supervisor's responsibility, the personnel manager's actions may still be misinterpreted. The following case illustrates this problem.

> A grievance was filed against Gus Homes, a departmental supervisor, for failing to divide overtime equally. Homes argued that employees who failed to meet production standards on regular work should not be given overtime. The union contract said nothing about overtime, although general plant practice sanctioned equal division. The personnel director of the company, anxious to avoid any union bargaining on the overtime issue, urged Homes to change his mind. Homes refused. Some weeks later, Homes was transferred to a less desirable job. The plant grapevine reported that the manager had "given him the axe" on the recommendation of the personnel director. The truth of the matter was that the manager had believed for some time that Homes should be removed from his department. The overtime situation was just one of many reasons that seemed to justify the move.
>
> From this point on, other supervisors thought twice about refusing the personnel director's "advice." His recommendations had become cloaked with line authority; he had become another boss.

When the manager wants more than advice. Line managers may encourage staff experts to broaden their range of activities. The willingness of the personnel manager to help out on a difficult problem, for example, may provide the supervisor with welcome relief from burdensome responsibilities. In effect, the supervisor says to the personnel manager, "Good, you handle the personnel, and I'll take care of all the technical problems." Then, if a decision backfires, the line supervisor can simply point out that the advice came from Personnel. This serves as an excellent excuse.

Therefore, it is easy to understand the line supervisor's reluctance to question the expertise of the specialists top management has hired. The subordinate manager who challenges the specialist's ability runs the risk of bearing all responsibility for a bad decision. It may even be preferable to interpret advice as a decision, in order to avoid assuming responsibility and pass the buck to the expert.

Paradoxically, a manager may resent an advisory group's power and at the same time, grumble that it is failing to take responsibility for decisions. As one supervisor expressed it:

"We stay away from the industrial relations department as much as possible—they're always trying to sell you on some new program that makes more work for you. But then when you go to them with a problem, you can't get a straight answer from them; they won't tell you how to handle it. They give you a lot of pros and cons and stuff that leaves you more confused than when you went in."

Conflicting advice. We have simplified the situation by implying that at one time only one adviser (the personnel manager) is involved. In fact, in the modern organization, expertise is distributed among many specialized groups, and a problem can call for knowledge of engineering, standards, methods, personnel, and finance. The boundary lines are never clear, and each group feels that its idea is the real solution to the difficulty. Thus, a manager may be deluged with helpers who occasionally flaunt their association with higher management, as a means of gaining favor for their solution.

In some ways an advisory relationship is quite similar to pooled interdependence. Departments can be allowed substantial freedom to go their own way, but these independent decisions eventually do add up to certain commitments by the total organization.

Conclusion

In this chapter, we have discussed the design of the organization's horizontal structure: the factors that determine who will work together as a team and the mechanisms that help to coordinate various parts of the organization. A small organization is coordinated by the boss, who gets feedback and gives orders to smooth the work flow. The boss's efforts are supplemented (or sometimes frustrated) by the informal group that will seek to regulate relationships among its members. In the larger organization, subdivided and parceled out among a number of different managers, difficulties in coordination occur among managerial units and between employees who work for separate bosses. Top management has a choice from among the following major structural types:

1. Functional groupings of personnel
2. Product (or area or customer) groupings of personnel
3. Matrix organization
4. A mixture of these

Once the major subdivisions have been determined, the problem of structuring (or organizing) the personnel *within* each of these major groupings and integrating them into a smoothly functioning total system remains.

CHAPTER 12
organization
design

The internal structuring—determining who works for each supervisor—is often called the departmentation decision. We suggested that managers should be placed over *work flow units*. Employees whose jobs closely interrelate and who frequently must coordinate with one another should work together. We reviewed many examples of the conflicts that occur when difficult coordination exchanges between supervisory units must take place.

The most difficult problem of all is encouraging the managerial units to integrate their efforts for effective operation of the total organization. (What is efficient for each unit is not usually effective for the total organization. This is sometimes referred to as the suboptimization problem: departments are tempted to do things that are helpful to them but do not facilitate the work of others.)

The scope and difficulty of the integration problem depends on how much coordination is required and the different orientations of various departments.

We identified five types of interdependence, each having different coordination requirements:

1. Pooled interdependence (relatively easy to coordinate).
2. Sequential interdependence (somewhat more difficult to coordinate).
3. Reciprocal interdependence (requires a great deal of managerial attention because of the amount of coordination involved).
4. Service interdependence (a number of departments depend on a centralized support group to help them complete their work flows).
5. Advisory interdependence (specialists are available to help other managers *if* expert assistance is needed).

Finally, we looked at the problems and methods of coping with these five types of interdependence. We described a number of structural mechanisms that organizations use to bridge or link their various subdivisions:

1. Using the hierarchy (the line of authority)—making certain that formal plans, programs, and appeals travel up the line to higher management.
2. Appointing auditors to check for compliance to plans and rules.
3. Designating liaison specialists to act as go-betweens, improve communications among units.
4. Requiring managers to check with coordination specialists (we called them "stabilization roles") before doing things that could affect other departments.
5. Encouraging direct, face-to-face contact among managers working on related projects; adding committees, teams, and task forces to the organizational structure.
6. Introducing slack to decrease the need for coordination—separating the departments by making each more autonomous (adding buffer stocks of parts, making the schedules less tight, etc.).

We also explored the human relations of service and advisory relationships, discussing when they work smoothly and when friction could develop.

247

organization development and management training

Although organization development is concerned primarily with the organization as a whole, and management training deals with individual managers, the two subjects overlap, and they can conveniently be considered together. Both involve many of the problems of introducing change discussed in Chapter 9. Organization development (OD) is in a sense the broader topic and the one that has received the greatest recent attention. Nevertheless, OD grew out of management training, so it is appropriate to consider management training first.

Management training

Forms of management training. To begin with, it must be made clear that management training takes many forms and deals with many subjects. Coaching by one's boss, job rotation schemes, performance evaluation—all are, in a sense, forms of training. The manager also learns important lessons with every word of praise, every reprimand, every promotion. The subjects dealt with by management training may range from public speaking to the impact of recent tax legislation. This section, however, will focus on just one form of management training: formal programs designed to improve managerial skills, chiefly in human relations areas—how to get along with one's boss, subordinates, or peers.

Historical development. Management training became significant first in World War II, when crash programs were instituted to train new foremen. After the war, the spread of human relations and foremen's unions led companies to engage more extensively in foreman training as a means both of persuading foremen that they were indeed part of management and of reducing the petty tyrannies that earlier had contributed to the growth of blue-collar unions. At about the same time, selected groups of managers began to attend university-run executive programs, typically from two to six weeks' full time. From these humble beginnings, management training spread until it now covers all levels of the organization.

Over the years, a number of ingenious training techniques have been developed. Although useful for disseminating facts or sharpening skills, few of these techniques were effective in inducing behavioral change. During the 1960s a number of organizations experimented with a new and seemingly still more powerful technique: T-group training (to be discussed later). Powerful as this technique proved, when applied to management it, too, had shortcomings, among which was the problem of transferring abilities learned in the T-group to the job. It was largely because of the limitations of both traditional and T-group training that training specialists began turning to the broader forms of planned organizational change, which have come to be known as OD. But before considering these developments in greater detail we need to look at the requirements for effective training.

Requirements for effective training

Through trial and error, those concerned with training programs have begun to learn some of the conditions that are required for successful interpersonal training. These conditions relate both to the nature of the training program and to the organizational environment in which it occurs.

Problems as the trainees see them. The training program should start with the felt needs of the trainees themselves, and they should see it as a means of solving their *own* problems. Training in some companies is on the level of the charm school or the booster talk. Or it may be presented in theoretical, abstract terms that participants are unable to translate into practice. One way to ensure that a training program is built around problems as the trainees see them is to invite them to participate in setting up the program (or at least to survey their felt needs before launching the program). With "open" personnel systems, managers can select the courses they want to take, rather than being sent to courses whether they wish them or not.

Nature of the program

Unfreezing. The people who take part in the program must be dissatisfied with their old ways and willing to "unfreeze" their attitudes. A wise personnel director once told us that he never starts a training program until the people to be trained (as well as their superiors) are anxious for the program. If people are forced into a training program against their will, they may resent and sabotage it.

Evidence suggests that training is more valuable for managers who have just been promoted or are about to be promoted, since these are the ones most in need of an expanded viewpoint. Confronted by a new job, they are anxious to develop new skills and willing to discard old points of view. This enthusiasm for learning is especially strong among staff specialists, such as accountants or engineers, who are being promoted into line positions where they will be faced with an entirely new set of problems.

Involvement. Trainees must be encouraged to work through to their own conclusions. The only way they can understand a problem is to think it out for themselves. They suspect the fast talker who tries to trick them into accepting ready-made solutions.

A trainee can memorize what the instructor thinks is right, but this does not make it his own. Particularly in the area of emotional (as distinct from conceptual) learning, people learn primarily through experience, not through passive listening. Real learning is "gut" learning. If there is to be a carry-over from the classroom to the office or shop, it is essential that the trainee *feel* through the problem, experiencing and overcoming its difficulties while working toward a solution. We emphasize the word *feel* because many of the problems in this area are emotional, involving the ways managers see, and feel about, the people and events that affect them deeply.

Without emotional involvement, trainees are likely to develop intellectually satisfying answers that they fail to implement in practice. For example, they may do a beautiful job of analyzing a case that focuses on inability to listen to the other person's point of view—and ten minutes later totally fail to listen to another trainee's comments.

Group influence. Human-relations training is often more effective when it is conducted in groups, for most attitudes in this area are group-conditioned. For instance, a foreman will be less likely to consult with a steward if fellow foremen feel that to do so is being soft.

We have already discovered that group discussion at times provides an effective means of changing attitudes. When group norms are involved, it is easier to change members as a group than it is to change individuals. When a group of managers with common problems decides to change together, no individual has the unsettling feeling of being a pioneer, of being different. The group provides its members with emotional support, and they learn from each other.

Typically, attitudes and behaviors begin to change only when the trainees recognize that they all have problems in common which they have not been able to handle satisfactorily (for instance, handling an unreasonable steward and living under a tight budget). It helps if they can work off their resentment—let off steam—a bit before moving on to the next step. The opportunity to share one another's burdens reduces frustration and makes them more willing to consider new approaches.

Experiments with change. A training program is more effective if it makes allowances for the difficulties of giving up old ways of doing things.

Understandably, people feel more secure with old patterns of behavior that have proven reasonably satisfactory in the past. And they resent suggestions that their performance is unsatisfactory. Similarly, they object to outsiders telling them what to do; they feel that their long experience makes them more qualified than any trainer.

One approach to handling this problem is to encourage trainees to consider new practices without attacking the old ways directly; that is, to ask them to consider a range of alternatives without committing themselves to any particular one. They should be encouraged to try new ways tentatively. Only after they have tested the new procedures on an experimental basis can they be expected to change their behavior permanently. This process of experimentation with change in a "safe environment" is central both to T-groups and OD, as we shall see below.

Carry-over. For training to mean anything, it must move from the intellectual to the practical level. It must provide skills that are useful to the managers in solving problems on the job—skills that higher management will permit them to practice.

To summarize much of the above: effective training that changes attitudes should run through the three stages mentioned in Chapter 9. In the *unfreezing* stage, trainees learn to be dissatisfied with their old patterns of behavior. In the *change* stage, they experiment with new patterns in a safe environment away from everyday pressures. In the *refreezing* stage, they adopt these forms for practical use and carry them to the job.

Of the various points listed above, the last one, carry-over, may be the most critical. Training rarely results in lasting behavioral change unless there is a supportive organizational atmosphere.

Organizational climate

Training is difficult to evaluate, for reasons we shall discover. By and large, the results of training have been somewhat disappointing. Managers may report enthusiastically about a course, and their behavior may change a bit in the first few days after leaving class; but long-range improvements resulting from training—at least from conventional training—are rarely observed.

How can we explain these negative results? Except for boredom, some programs have little impact on trainees, even while they are in class. More important, what is learned in class is too often not useful on the job, especially when it conflicts with the behavior expected of the trainees by their bosses and even by their subordinates. If training is to be worthwhile, trainees must feel free to apply what they learn. When the organizational climate denies this freedom, subordinates are more likely to imitate their boss than to follow what they have learned in class.

The influence of the organization—in particular, the attitude of top management—is crucial to the success of a training program. In many companies management regards training as of only marginal importance and consequently gives it only token support. Many managers feel that training is purely a staff function for which line has no responsibility, or they institute training programs merely because it is the fashionable thing to do. Yet attitudes of this sort are quickly discerned by the trainees themselves, who may begin to feel that training is a waste of time and resent being held as a captive audience in a training class. As long as management thinks of the training process as something apart from everyday activities on the job, the chances that training will affect behavior are slim indeed.

Where higher management does not *in practice* support the objectives of training, managers feel uncertain about whether to follow the theory of the course or the example of their boss. As a result, they appear vacillating and inconsistent. Subordinates can become confused if their hard-as-nails supervisor begins to listen to them before bawling them out. Uncertain of whether their boss is going to be "tough" or practice "human relations," subordinates find this unpredictability highly frustrating. Under the circumstances, it may be a blessing that so many supervisors leave their training in the classroom and never let it interfere with their daily behavior.

In the establishment of a training course, there is often little effort to find out why managers behave as they do or to consider whether company policy or top management behavior may be the cause of whatever seems wrong; instead training is viewed as a magic cure for all ills. Managers often talk as if only their subordinates' behavior needed changing, not their own. Trainees often say, "I wish my boss would take this course. He's the one who needs it."

Too often, training programs stress dealing with only subordinates, yet the trainee's biggest problem may be dealing with the boss. Only frustration results if training teaches managers to adopt new approaches, and these managers then find that the organization won't let them do so.

Only limited results can be obtained by training lower management alone, particularly if the training is of the typical classroom variety. Possibly the best way to train foremen is to train the general foreman first; but it is difficult to train the general foreman until the superintendent has been trained, or at least induced, to behave in a manner that permits those on lower levels to try out new techniques.

Does this mean that the only way to start is with the board of directors? Perhaps. The board of directors of one of the nation's largest companies established a human relations committee, whose job, in effect, is to train top management. Top management then trained the next lower level of management and so on down the line in a carefully planned program, until finally the general foreman trained the foremen.

As we shall see, there are very definite advantages in having bosses train the people they supervise. Yet there are managers, otherwise competent, who are just poor trainers. Further, if all training is done by the boss, there is a real danger that the organization will perpetuate its past mistakes and allow little room for new ideas. Training conducted by line personnel is not the complete solution to the problem.

More important than the person who conducts the training is the organizational atmosphere in which it occurs. For training to be effective, this atmosphere must permit the manager to experiment with new patterns of behavior and to learn through making mistakes. But even changes in atmosphere must come from the top (or at least be approved by the top). Organizations are social systems, and it is difficult to change one part without changing the rest. Growing recognition of this interdependency has led many companies to establish integrated programs of organization development and to place less stress on individualized management training.

Conventional training techniques

Now let us examine some of the more common conventional training techniques. These techniques are designed for many purposes, but few, if any, completely satisfy the criteria listed above. Yet all of them have some value either as part of a comprehensive program or in organizations that are unable to mount such a comprehensive program.

Lecturing, the traditional form of teaching, gives the trainer the greatest degree of control over the training situation. Material can be presented exactly as the lecturer wishes, with little danger that anyone will talk back.

Instructors who can keep their classes constantly stimulated through the sheer force of their ideas—and who are powerful enough to effect changes in the behavior of those who listen to them—are rare indeed. A lecture is unlikely to change fixed attitudes and certainly is of little help in developing skills. It is useful chiefly in presenting background facts—for example, the meaning of a new union contract.

Lectures

The cases that we present at the ends of chapters are typical of those used in this common form of training.

The success of the case method depends directly on the ability of the instructor. Under an unskilled instructor, the trainees tend to look upon the case as a puzzle that can be solved by finding the right answer. They make value judgments about each character and try to identify the "villain." Often, too, a poorly conducted discussion will degenerate into a rambling session from which the participants derive no learning. Skillful instructors, on the other hand, emphasize useful ways of thinking about human relations rather than ways of reaching specific conclusions. They put stress on:

The case method

- Increasing the trainee's power of observation, helping that person to ask better questions and to look for a broader range of problems (for instance, not "Who is to blame?" but "Why did it happen?").
- Encouraging the group to look for more and more implications in each solution, keeping them away from pat analyses and oversimplified solutions.
- Helping students to discard vague principles, such as "Be tactful" or "Apply the golden rule," and urging them to consider not only *what* to do but *how* to do it.
- Encouraging the trainees to test their solutions against reality.

In the university classroom the case method introduces a note of realism that is absent from abstract, theoretical discussions. For management trainees in business or government, however, cases are always less realistic than the actual problems that arise on the job. Even though practicing managers may discuss cases with enthusiasm, they tend to look upon the discussion as a game in which they solve the *other* company's problems, not their own. This lack of *emotional* involvement may make it difficult to effect any basic change in the behavior and attitudes of the trainees.

Simulation

By *simulation* is meant a broad range of techniques in which trainees act out samples of real organizational behavior, to practice in making decisions or working together as a group, or both. It involves learning through doing, rather than through memorizing principles. In effect, it is a form of vestibule training. Since it is more realistic than the case method, it may lead to greater involvement.

The *management game* is one form of simulation that involves several teams, each of which is given a "firm" to operate for a number of "periods." In each period each team must decide what prices to set, how much to produce, how much to spend on advertising and on research, how much of an inventory to maintain, and so forth. Since the teams are competing with each other, each firm's decisions will affect the results of all the other firms. Typically, these decisions are fed into a computer which is programed to behave somewhat like a real market. At the end of each period the computer reports back how well each firm has done. This report provides the data needed for the next period of play. The winner, of course, is the firm that has accumulated the largest profit by the end of the game. Often the game ends in a post mortem in which the participants analyze their mistakes and attempt to generalize from their experience.

What do participants learn from such games? Primarily, how to make better decisions, to select and analyze relevant data, and to choose from among alternatives. Most management games are concerned with the external environment of business, particularly marketing, and its quantifiable aspects. Though participants gain some experience in working together, their chief concern is with making decisions, not implementing them. They provide little insight into the problems connected with organizational structure or personnel management. Only rarely is the game enlarged to afford each team an opportunity to analyze its own interpersonal problems. Management games often generate much enthusiasm among players. There is still a good deal of doubt, however, about the extent of carry-over from game to job.

The *in-basket* technique is a form of simulation that permits emphasis on internal as well as external problems. A typical in-basket exercise might be as follows:

An "executive" (the trainee) is catapulted into a new job on the sudden death of a predecessor, whose in-basket contained a number of letters, memos, and notes of phone conversations—all accumulated over the last few days. A host of urgent problems must be faced: a union grievance (as well as a poorly written proposed reply drafted by a subordinate line manager), a complaint from an important customer, and a sudden supervisory vacancy for which there are three obvious candidates.

The trainee is given a short period of time to deal with these problems, either by drafting a reply at once or getting further information. After all trainees handle their own identical in-baskets, they meet to discuss the logic behind how they handled them.

This technique provides experience both in making decisions and in implementing them. It differs from the business game in that there is no feedback on how well the decision "worked."

Role-playing is a form of simulation emphasizing human-relations problems. Parts are assigned to students to act out as they would in real life. It differs from ordinary drama in that the actors are given no lines to memorize; rather, they must improvise as they go along. Among the advantages of role-playing are these:

- It helps participants to appreciate other points of view (a foreman may play the role of a union steward).
- It helps trainees to experience a situation emotionally.
- It makes trainees more self-conscious and analytical of their behavior than they would be in real life.

Even the trainees who merely observe a role-playing session profit from observing the mistakes of others. Certainly this is a highly dramatic technique for arousing interest and stimulating class participation.

Nevertheless, role-playing has some disadvantages. It deals with problems formulated by the instructor, not with those bothering the trainee. Thus many are viewed as unrealistic. Further, the cases must of necessity be oversimplified, since they focus on the players' interactions and tend to ignore the environment in which the problem arises.

Other forms of simulation may also be utilized. Participants may be given roles—such as plant manager, sales manager, purchasing agent, and comptroller—and information about the jobs which these individuals might normally have. Then several emergencies are assumed to occur—for instance, a large rush order and a major equipment breakdown—and the trainees are required to solve the problems. Such simulation provides training in both decision making and human relations, and after each "period" the participants can profitably hold a post mortem about how they handled their problems.

The main techniques discussed share one common characteristic: the problems they consider are presented by the trainer rather than the group and are therefore looked upon as somewhat artificial or not pertinent. Thus, participants tend not to become emotionally involved or to develop insights relating to their own values or behavior. In order to obtain greater participation, a number of organizations turned to T-groups.

T-group training

T-group training (the "T" stands for training) is also known as *sensitivity training* and *laboratory training*, and is akin to *encounter groups*. Regardless of the name, the technique has strong supporters and strong detractors.

Though T-group training dates back to the 1940s, only around 1960 did interest spill out into private industry. Yet by the mid-1960s, the list of firms that had at least experimented with this radically new form of training read like a blue book of American industry.

T-group training differs from the kinds of training previously discussed in that it is concerned with real, not simulated, problems existing within the training group itself—not in the organization outside or in some hypothetical case. Rather than just teach skills and intellectual understanding, it seeks to change underlying attitudes and thus behavior on the job.

Although individual trainers may differ in emphasis, T-group training can be used to help participants:

- Learn more about themselves, especially their emotions.
- Develop insights into how they react to others and how others react to them.
- Discover how groups work and how to diagnose human-relations problems.
- Find out how to behave more effectively in interpersonal relations, and in particular, how to manage people through means other than power.
- Develop honest relations in which feelings are expressed openly.
- Confront interpersonal problems directly, so that they can be solved, rather than trying to avoid them, smooth them over, or seek a compromise that is not really a solution.

T-group training is often called *laboratory training* because T-groups are, in effect, laboratories in which people experiment on themselves and generate data for their own discussions. T-groups are really small discussion groups with no set leader. (The trainer merely raises questions and provides occasional comments.) Frequently the groups are totally unstructured; they have no set task or agenda except for a strong focus on the feelings and mutual impact of the participants. Learning takes place through analyzing one's emotions rather than intellectually through logic. The group talks about what seems important at the moment. It is felt that the lack of structure will motivate people to bring their feelings out in the open where they can be analyzed and dealt with in a more rational fashion. The OD director of a large company provided us with an example of how T-groups work in practice.

"Last week we had a session with a lot of executives at various levels, including the vice-president of one of our major divisions. After three days most people were feeling pretty open with their comments. Even the VP was talking quite freely, though it was obvious the junior people were deferring to him. Then he made a very pompous comment. A junior engineer, not in his division, snapped, 'What a bunch of malarkey!' The VP reddened a bit. I asked, 'Does that bother you?' 'Nope,' he said, 'I can take it.'

"The discussion went on to other things, but I noticed the VP wasn't saying anything. So when we had an evaluation session, I commented, 'Bob [the VP], you haven't said anything the last 30 minutes. Is your mind on other things?'

"His reply came slowly. 'If you thought I ignored Bill's comments, you're wrong. I've spent the last half-hour thinking how this is the first time anybody disagreed with me since I became VP

> five years ago. I wondered how I must react when something big comes up? How do I come over to those who work with me? I've always thought the people under me didn't have any ideas of their own. How much am I responsible for this?' "

In a well-conducted T-group, the trainees, in effect, train one another, though the trainer helps by asking skillful questions, as the above example illustrates. At times, too, the trainer provides feedback as to the interpersonal processes developing within the group.

Effective T-groups go through the three stages discussed in the early part of this chapter: unfreezing, in which participants develop, often through shock, a sense of dissatisfaction with their present behavior; change, in which they experiment with new behavior; and refreezing, in which they develop an internalized commitment to a new approach.

Though all T-group training generally takes the same over-all form, T-group trainers differ somewhat in their emphasis. One school focuses upon *individual* emotions (and the training this school offers is often called *sensitivity* training); the other is more concerned with relations *among* members of the group. Sensitivity training is in a sense the deeper form of training, and the line between it and psychotherapy sometimes becomes vague. Sensitivity training is also akin to such movements as transactional analysis, Synanon and Esalen groups, and Alcoholics Anonymous.

Both forms of T-groups have been subject to much debate. Two main arguments have been made against their use as a form of management training.

Controversies regarding T-groups

Excessive stress. Critics argue, first, that T-group trainers create stress situations for their own sake. There is a danger that training of this sort may do a better job of tearing people apart than of bringing them together. At worst, T-groups may trigger hidden psychological instabilities, leading to mental breakdown or, at best, to a frustrating experience that interferes with real learning. (In addition, it is argued that such training interferes with personal privacy, particularly in firms that make attendance at such programs almost compulsory.) [1]

Defenders counter that one of the hallmarks of skilled trainers is that they keep tensions within bounds and that they make sure that critical comments are "caring" rather than destructive. Further, the tensions generated in T-groups are no greater than those endemic to any large organization. To these arguments, critics reply that many organizations send to T-group training only those who "need" it most—frequently the most unstable. And, too often,

---

[1] Recently a federal appeals court ruled that a "race relations seminar" (designed to foster racial tolerance) might violate a federal employee's First Amendment rights if it permitted "inquiries into personal beliefs and association choices," especially if "the seminar compelled her to disclose facts about her home life, her beliefs, and her associations which had nothing to do with Air Force duties." Presumably, the same principles would apply to a requirement that an employee attend a T-group involuntarily.

groups are started by unqualified trainers who lack the skill to keep pressures at tolerable levels.

The impartial observer must note that there have been cases in which T-group training has led to personal damage. But this may be an argument chiefly for better care in selecting trainers and the restriction of organizationally sponsored T-groups to forms that stress group learning rather than sheer expression of emotion.

Carry-over difficult. It is charged that whatever changes occur in the T-group tend to fade out once the trainee returns to an unsympathetic environment where company policy and the boss's attitude may inhibit the exercise of newly-learned skills. T-group members learn chiefly to get along with other T-group members. Managers who have learned to express their emotions openly may find their honesty misunderstood by those who have not shared the managers' experiences. "Laboratory values are so different from the values of most organizations that if individuals learned well at the laboratory they would probably tend to conclude that they should not use their new learning back home except where they have power and influence." [2]

Because of this problem, acknowledged by all, there has been a trend toward "family" T-groups consisting of all those who work together. Thus, all the top people in a department are trained at once. But such grouping raises serious ethical questions, since attendance is scarcely voluntary. Further, as long as only part of the total organization has been trained, difficulties in communications may arise among those who have adopted the new values and those who adhere to the old ones. The answer may be to provide T-group training for everyone, but this may be prohibitively expensive. Even if it were possible to send everyone through T-groups, the kind of "dirt" aired in such sessions and the intense feelings often engendered by them may in fact make it harder for managers to work together after the session is over. T-group training may improve the interpersonal relations for some managers, but may be harmful for others.

Organization development

Since the mid-Sixties, in part because of the problems discussed above, many organizations have switched from T-groups to a broader, more eclectic approach to management change, now generally known as organization development.[3] As the name implies, OD seeks to change not only individuals but also the values and behavior patterns of the organizations within which they work.

As the field has grown, OD has taken on a wide variety of forms, ranging from attempts to improve relations within single departments through changes in the structure of the organization as a whole and even relations among

---

[2] Chris Argyris, "On the Future of Laboratory Training," *Journal of Applied Behavioral Sciences*, Vol. 3, No 2 (April 1967), p. 163.

[3] See Wendell French and Cecil Bell, Jr., *Organization Development*, 2nd. ed. (Englewood Cliffs, N.J.: Prentice-Hall, 1978); Robert Golembiewski, *Renewing Organizations* (Itasca, Ill.: Peacock, 1972).

organizations as a whole—for example, between unions and managements, between community leaders and representatives of minority groups, and even between countries. Among the possible outcomes of an OD program are increased individual trust, redesigned jobs, participative work groups, new approaches to reducing conflict, higher productivity, and greater organizational flexibility. Six common denominators of most OD programs are:

1. They are heavily concerned with changing attitudes and improving interpersonal relations.

2. Solutions to organizational problems are generated by organizational members, rather than imposed from above.

3. There is heavy emphasis on a self-diagnosis process, often called *action research*.

4. Problems are typically attacked at the group or work-team level first, before problems at other levels are considered.

5. Heavy use is made of the three-stage attitude change model (unfreezing, change, refreezing).

6. The change process is initiated and monitored by a *consultant*.

Compared to T-groups, OD is characterized by less deep intervention (therefore less danger of engendering excess psychological stress) and greater emphasis on carry-over and on organizational (as opposed to group or individual) factors. Some approaches to OD still make use of T-groups in a modified form, but they do this as only one step in an integrated program.

OD and T-groups

T-groups seek to increase their participants' ability to be good group members in *any* situation; OD seeks actual improvement in interpersonal relations in specific organizations. T-groups are essentially artificial groups, and they deal with tensions that arise in their own little world—tensions that in a sense are artificially created. OD, by contrast, is concerned with tensions that arise on real jobs. It takes as its bailiwick not just relations within groups, but also relations among groups and even among organizations.

Despite this major difference, the two forms of development have much in common. Their shared point of departure is the individual, rather than the constraints within which he or she works. Although OD's ultimate goal is increased organizational effectiveness—a behavioral rather than an attitudinal measure—OD programs typically start with individual attitudes and utilize confrontations and experiences within groups as their primary learning techniques (as opposed, say, to lectures, individual coaching, or structural changes introduced from the top). Both T-groups and OD share a common faith in "interpersonal trust," in facing interpersonal problems directly, so they can be solved, rather than trying to avoid, smooth over, or compromise them in a way that is not a lasting solution.

As suggested earlier, an effective OD program typically consists of a number of parts, each designed with the needs of the particular organization in

Step-by-step progression

mind. Many programs move by steps, as their focus shifts from the individual to the organization and from emotions toward structure. For convenience of exposition, let us describe one *possible* sequence of techniques, with the warning that OD rarely proceeds this smoothly and that no two consultants utilize exactly the same approaches.

Step one might be a T-group. In terms of overall OD design, the intent is to open people up and to develop problem-solving and analytic skills that will be useful at later stages.

Step two could involve a problem-solving exercise such as running a mock company or even constructing a building out of Tinkertoy pieces, followed often by some kind of feedback, then a discussion of the interpersonal dynamics at work during the exercise. The purpose of step two is to permit the application of the skills developed in step one and also to permit their testing in a different kind of reality.

Step three could then deal directly with the on-the-job problems faced by the work team. It would permit application of the generalized skills developed in step one and the specific insights acquired in step two. Here the purpose is to make actual changes in on-the-job relations and to monitor their effectiveness.

Step four might be like step three, except that it would deal with relations among work teams, departments, or groups of supervisors and subordinates or staff and line personnel. In general, the purpose here is to help groups understand one another, with the hope that improved understanding will lead to better cooperation. "Intergroup" programs might deal, for example, with the problems arising out of lateral relations, such as described in Chapter 12.

Step five could involve going beyond strictly interpersonal relations to deal with structural changes affecting the organization as a whole—changes not only in tables of organization and reporting relationships, but in job descriptions, evaluation programs, communications systems, and the like. Presumably, the interpersonal trust developed in earlier stages now permits problems at this level to be confronted more realistically. Among the solutions that might evolve from such a program as MBO (see next chapter) and matrix organization.

Very few OD programs cover all five steps. Indeed, a major criticism is that step five, organizationwide structural change, is often ignored altogether. Some programs stop at step two, without an institutional effort to obtain carry-over or application to the job.

Though the example above imperfectly reflects reality, it stresses the critical point that OD must solve three problems: confrontation (information-getting or unfreezing), change, and carry-over (action or refreezing). Let us consider these in turn.

Confrontation

Perhaps the thing that distinguishes OD from other forms of consultancy is its imaginative use of confrontation. Broadly defined, *confrontation* is a diagnostic or information-getting process in which organizational members obtain feedback on their behavior in a form that will provide insights useful for improving their performance. Thus confrontation is change-oriented feedback.

The object of this feedback normally is to induce participants to compare their (or the system's) *actual* behavior with their *idealized* concept of that behavior. The resultant "perceptual gap" may serve a combination of purposes:

1. The comparison may reveal such a discrepancy between intended (or desired) and actual behavior that it will disturb the previously stable psychological equilibrium and introduce "unfreezing"; i.e., a desire for change or a "conviction of sin."
2. By bringing problems to the surface, confrontation can define (and even dramatize) their nature.
3. It can help the organization make informed and realistic choices as to possible behavioral change.

Thus confrontation should occur not just once, but it can be repeated at every stage of the OD process. Indeed, some observers say that a major purpose of OD is to make confrontation an organizational way of life.

Feedback must be in a form that is believable and that leads to action. Note that confrontation in itself does not automatically guarantee unfreezing. For feedback to be accepted, it should be dramatic enough to induce disequilibrium but not so threatening that it leads to greater defensiveness. It should be in a form that increases rather than decreases interpersonal trust, otherwise participants are unlikely to trust or learn from each other. Neither will they feel as free to experiment with new forms of behavior.

Forms of confrontation vary greatly. T-groups, of course, provide a great deal of feedback to their members, but even so simple a device as the feedback of videotapes made in ordinary management meetings can be extremely effective in illustrating weaknesses. (In observing the video feedback of his performance at a product planning meeting, a manager learned to his dismay that he constantly interrupted his colleagues.) Simulations, such as the management game, can generate data on how a group performs. After the simulation is over, the group evaluates the effectiveness of its internal processes.

The best-known OD technique, the *management grid*, uses a series of questionnaires (as well as simulations) to force managers to confront the gap between their idealized and their present behavior. "You have to build a model," says Robert Blake, the grid's originator, "as if you had no past tradition, no past practices, cult, or ritual. Then you see how lousy you really are in comparison with where you should be. So the ideal is a searchlight for seeing the actual. You have to close the gaps once you see them. You can't live with contradictions." [4]

Other OD programs begin with an employee attitude survey or with a series of interviews with subordinates and peers. The findings of these studies are then reported to the management group with identification of source removed. If the studies are well conducted, they identify problems that require management's attention; often, these problems are ones that management had been unaware of or had ignored.

A fairly typical OD effort involved a hotel chain. Here the president was concerned with the relations between headquarters staff (such as accounting and sales) and their counterparts in individual hotels.

[4] *Business Week,* October 18, 1969, p. 159.

The consultant intensively interviewed a sample of people from all levels and then reported back to a meeting consisting of the president, the heads of the headquarters' staff groups, and the general managers of the various hotels. Sample items from his report:

Headquarters staff people: The president expects us to introduce change and upgrade quality, but the general managers won't let us into the hotels to do it.

General managers: The corporation talks decentralization but we have little voice in setting our own advertising policy.

Hotel staff people: Our rewards come entirely from the hotel managers. We have no chance of being promoted into headquarters, and no one in headquarters is interested in our future.[5]

The *survey feedback* approach makes use of employee attitude questionnaires.[6] Typically, top management is closely involved in selecting the types of questions to be asked. Usually they relate to subjects such as organizational climate, pay and benefits, supervisor/employee benefits, or opportunities for personal growth. The consultant then collects questionnaire responses from employees at all levels. Next, the overall questionnaire findings are reported back to a meeting of the top management group with the consultant present. Members of the group are asked to help interpret the data, to consider plans to deal with the problems the data reveal, and then to consider how this data may be introduced at the next lower level. Similar meetings are held at successively lower levels. Each division, department, or section meets in turn to discuss the implications of survey findings pertaining to its own unit. Thus, change starts at the top but eventually involves the entire organization.

Intergroup exercises may involve two groups that have had difficulty working together in the past. Each group is instructed to meet by itself and to write down answers to questions like the following:

How do you view the other group?
How do you think the other group views you?
What's your best guess as to how the other group thinks you view it?

The two groups meet together, and each divulges its list. Each group is permitted to ask the other to enlarge upon its answers, but argument is not permitted. Exercises such as this often reveal misunderstandings, which sometimes can be easily cleared up. In any case, the parties have obtained considerably greater insight into the sources of their difficulties.

Change

Only a fuzzy line separates the confrontation and change stages. Once confrontation has identified the key problems and persuaded the parties that

---

[5] Adapted, with slight modification, from Richard Beckhard, "An Organization Improvement Program in a Decentralized Company," *Journal of Applied Behavioral Science*, Vol. 2, No. 1 (January 1966).

[6] D. A. Nadler, P. H. Mirvis, and C. Cammann, "The Ongoing Feedback System," *Organization Dynamics*, Spring 1976, pp. 63–80.

change is necessary, the next step is to analyze the problems in greater detail, to generate alternative solutions, and then to evaluate their relative advantages and disadvantages.

Put another way, presumably the initial confrontation unfreezes *attitudes;* the change stage requires participants to unfreeze their *behaviors* and to develop and test new skills. If the confrontation periods have generated a supportive atmosphere in which resistance to change has been reduced, participants will feel free to experiment with new behaviors. They will try these on for size before adding them as permanent parts of their repertoire.

Change is handled in a variety of ways, depending on the nature of the program. Sometimes change is quite straightforward. Using data disclosed by feedback as a springboard for discussion, the OD consultant seeks to induce managers to suggest solutions to their problems. The group is challenged to develop new ways of relating to each other and to test out their choices in terms of their impact on the larger social systems. In the hotel case (discussed above), a list of recommendations was developed, many of which were implemented. For example, one of the hotel staff people was appointed to provide needed liaison between headquarters and the hotels.

The solution of other types of problems requires learning new attitudes and skills. To facilitate the learning process, OD programs utilize three main approaches. *Didactic instruction* involves lectures, exercises, readings and the like, all of which are designed to suggest new ways of handling problems identified during the confrontation period. If subordinates complain about inadequate guidance, the consultant may give a short lecture on the strengths and weaknesses of MBO as a goal-setting technique. In *modeling* (or identification) participants learn to copy the behavior of their consultant or other respected members of their group.[7] For example, the frank, open discussion in the T-group described earlier provided a model for the VP when he "opened up" himself to analyze his own reactions to criticism. Finally, there is *internalization.* Here, instead of directly copying the behavior of others, the participant experiments with new patterns of behavior on his own. Once having decided that he should change, our VP, for example, must now "try out" a variety of new approaches to encourage subordinates to express their opinions more honestly.

Refreezing

Refreezing involves both making a *commitment* to try new behavioral patterns and then some form of *maintenance activity* to prevent slipping back into earlier behavior patterns.

As we have seen in Chapter 9, a formal commitment to try out new behavior patterns, particularly if made in a public setting, helps refreeze both behaviors and the attitudes associated with them. But pledges to change job-related behavior, made in an OD setting, are often forgotten back on the job; and even if the new behaviors are tried on the job, they often fade out

---

[7] For a discussion of the difference between modeling and internalization, see Edgar Schein, "Organizational Socialization and the Practice of Management," in Barry Staw, ed., *Psychological Foundations of Organizational Behavior* (Santa Monica, Ca.: Goodyear, 1977).

as participants become discouraged. To avoid fade-out, it often helps to establish formal mechanisms providing continual feedback as to whether the new behaviors or procedures are being implemented. Managers in one company hold "sensing sessions" to diagnose interpersonal problems that may be impeding their operations. Periodic attitude surveys may also serve this feedback function.

Feedback alone, of course, is not enough. The new behaviors must be rewarded by the participants' peers and superiors, for in an unsympathetic atmosphere the new skills will soon be forgotten.

OD: a continuous process

Refreezing should not be the last step, because OD involves not just solving specific problems, but learning an entire process of action research or problem-solving.[8] While maintenance activities help ensure that participants are doing what they have committed themselves to do, yesterday's commitments may not be appropriate in today's circumstances. So, at its best, OD teaches groups to diagnose and evaluate their ever-changing problems on a continuous basis. The process as a whole may run as follows:

Problem identification → Research on nature of problem → Evaluation of alternate solutions → Commitment to one solution → Maintenance → Reevaluation

Controversies regarding OD

OD has been highly controversial. For some it is almost a religion. Others see it as a form of charlatanism. There is a continuing debate among OD's critics and supporters and among proponents of alternative OD techniques. The following are some of the points at issue:

Loss of managerial decisiveness. One charge against OD is that it makes managers so sensitive to the feelings of others that they are unwilling to make hard decisions. OD-trained managers sometimes talk for talk's sake and luxuriate in the expression of feelings rather than take action. Furthermore, they may be so "open" and honest in the expression of their feelings that their behavior approaches downright rudeness. Questions have been raised as to the value of complete openness under every circumstance. Excess honesty can often hurt a relationship, even in marriage.

OD supporters reject these arguments. They insist that OD is designed to help managers face problems, not run away from them. OD values "have within them a very real toughness: In dealing with each other, we will be open, direct, explicit. Our feelings will be available to one another, and we will problem-solve rather than be defensive."[9] OD does not "value all openness. It values openness which helps the individuals involved to learn."[10] Open-

---

[8] In other words, OD should be concerned not only with whether policies are being carried out, but also with whether they are appropriate. It should emphasize what Argyris calls double-loop learning. See Chris Argyris, "Double-Loop Learning in Organizations," *Harvard Business Review* (September 1977), 115–25.

[9] Sheldon A. Davis, "An Organic Problem-Solving Method of Organizational Change," *Journal of Applied Behavioral Science,* Vol. 3 (January 1967), p. 4.

[10] Argyris, "On the Future of Laboratory Training," p. 162.

ness, it is argued, is a relationship of trust between people, permitting them to understand each other. It is neither "diplomacy," which hides problems, nor irresponsible "honesty," which requires individuals to express their feelings without regard to their impacts on others. And it is suggested that by providing managers with a broader range of facts (including facts about how other participants feel) OD helps them to make better decisions.

Perhaps the real question is whether participants in OD can pass through the stage of concern about feelings and interpersonal relations to the stage of realistic examination of organizational problems. Nevertheless it is relevant that many organizations now offer their managers courses dealing in such topics as rational decision making, assertiveness, and bargaining—all of which are designed to increase managerial decisiveness.[11]

Attitudes vs. structure. A related objection to OD is that it places excessive emphasis on feelings and informal relationships rather than on structural elements such as job descriptions, formal responsibilities, promotion and compensation schemes, work flows, and the like. Opponents argue that OD approaches the problem of change from the most difficult end, the human personality, when changes in structure can achieve results more economically and with less pain. Lasting value changes are extraordinarily hard to induce when they are not supported by preceding or simultaneous changes in structure. By contrast, structural changes can change attitudes quite quickly and relatively permanently. "Indeed, it is now well established that one's attitudes are *determined* by the behaviors one engages in—rather than vice versa, as traditionally had been thought. This is especially true when individuals perceive that they have substantial personal freedom or autonomy in choosing how they will behave." [12]

OD supporters argue that attitudinal or value changes are necessary preconditions for either behavioral or structural change. OD not only helps managers make better decisions, but it makes decisions easier to implement. Change of any sort will be resisted if introduced by autocratic methods, and this is especially true with regard to changes in managerial skills. Participative supervision is unlikely to work as long as managers are "interpersonally incompetent." Job enrichment or MBO programs have little chance of success unless line managers are emotionally in tune with these programs' objectives.

Thus the basic question is whether one should change from within or from without. These two approaches have been called by their critics "conversionist" and "engineering." In its early days, most OD stressed attitude change. More recently, greater emphasis has been given to structural considerations. Among the forms of change introduced through OD have been a reduction in the number of organizational levels, matrix organization, job redesign, MBO,

---

[11] An implicit assumption behind much conventional OD is that the typical manager is too assertive or domineering. Conventional OD places great stress on consideration and listening. Arguably, assertiveness training implies just the opposite. Actually, consideration and assertiveness are not so much opposites as equally important aspects of the communications process.

[12] J. Richard Hackman, "Work Design," in J. Richard Hackman and J. Lloyd Suttle, *Improving Life at Work* (Santa Monica, Ca.: Goodyear, 1977), p. 102.

the installation of a Scanlon Plan, the establishment of task force work teams, and even changes in office architecture to facilitate communications. It is increasingly recognized that the attitudinal and structural approaches complement rather than contradict each other. Thus, new skills are often required to make structural change work, while structural changes help reinforce behavioral skills.

Treatment of conflict. Opponents have charged that OD programs tend to ignore the realities of power and conflict. Indeed, some early OD literature seemed to suggest that conflict was due entirely to lack of understanding and could be eliminated merely by improving interpersonal skills. Even today some versions of OD imply that once the parties are imbued with sufficient "trust" and "openness," they will renounce the use of power. Opponents of OD argue that this is highly unrealistic, that there are real differences of interest (as between subordinates and superiors or between unions and management), that these differences will persist and might increase, even after the parties get to know each other better, and that often they are resolved only on the basis of relative power advantages.

In recent years, OD consultants have begun to recognize that power is indeed one lever to effect organizational change, and some have begun to incorporate training in bargaining skills as part of their programs. There is increasing recognition that although OD may not finally resolve all conflict, it does help to bring conflict out in the open and to equip managers with skills to channel conflict in constructive directions.

Motivation for entering OD

Too often OD has been introduced for the wrong reasons. OD for a while was a fad, and many organizations experimented with it just because it was the thing to do, without understanding what OD was really trying to accomplish. Other organizations viewed it as a form of fun and games, which might boost employee morale. If OD leads to better understanding, they argued, so much the better. Better understanding never did anyone any harm; and besides, OD shows the employees that the organization cares for them.

In other instances OD has been used by top management as a means of straightening out subordinates or as a means of selling an unpopular set of changes. Under these conditions, so-called participation is merely a sham.

Many organizations have entered OD with unrealistic expectations, viewing it as a magic cure-all. When early progress proved slow, these organizations became discouraged—and thus concluded that OD would never work. Such organizations become "inoculated" against resuming OD later on.

Thus, organizational motivation is critical. It makes a big difference whether the consultant is being called in to deal with specific problems or just to provide "some OD training." It also makes a difference whether the management representative who brings the consultant in is seeking to improve his personal pattern of behavior—or (as is more common) wants to change the behavior of others. Managers should feel free to opt out of the program if they wish, and there should be clear understanding both of the process involved and the goals OD is seeking to achieve. Finally, the organization should recognize that gains through OD are slow and that it sometimes requires several years before meaningful progress materializes.

Evaluating training and OD effectiveness

Management training and OD are still in their infancy, and much of the activity in this area is done on faith, with little hard evidence of its effectiveness. Organizations seem to be following a "policy that is best characterized as spending millions for training, but not a penny for training evaluation."[13]

Evaluation of any training program is difficult. Student evaluations are somewhat suspect, since real learning is often frustrating, and the inspiration peddler may win the popularity contest over the trainer who poses difficult questions.

It is possible, perhaps with before-and-after tests, to measure changes in attitudes during training; but as we have seen, attitudes developed in class may fade away rapidly in an unsympathetic back-home environment. A more important consideration is whether training changes on-the-job behavior. The trainee's performance can be evaluated by the boss, subordinates, and fellow workers, and this evaluation may be made just before training, immediately after training, and well after training (the last series to see whether change has persisted). Unfortunately, the fact that the evaluators know that the trainee has gone through training may influence their judgments.

To many members of management, the crucial test is whether training increases efficiency and profits. In practice, it is extremely difficult to isolate the impact of training on organizational effectiveness, because so many other factors may be responsible, such as changes in technology or market conditions. Ideally, one should take a number of identical groups doing the same work under identical conditions and then train the managers of some of these groups and leave the others as controls. Yet, in real organizations (as opposed to those created in the research lab) it is difficult to find groups that will remain identical (except for the characteristics being studied) throughout the research.

Persistent current research into the lasting impact of training, particularly T-group training, is demonstrating that T-groups do change attitudes and even behavior. Whether trainees benefit seems to be related to (1) how well they react during training and their willingness to accept feedback reports (and these, in turn, seem to be related to basic personality variables such as ego strength, and flexibility) and (2) the trainee's security, power, and autonomy on the job.

Evaluating OD is even harder than evaluating individual training. In the first place, OD involves changes in an entire organization, thus making it even more difficult to select appropriate control groups. Second, most OD programs involve a variety of separate techniques. Even if we can determine that the program as a whole has been a success, we may find it difficult to isolate which portions of the program made the greatest difference.

Despite these problems it now seems clear that OD can lead to improved

---

[13] John R. Campbell, *et al.*, *Managerial Behavior, Performance, and Effectiveness* (New York: McGraw-Hill, 1970), p. 49.

organizational performance if introduced under the right circumstances, but it is also clear that a poorly planned program may do more harm than good. For OD to be successful, at least the following conditions must prevail:

- Top management must support it strongly.
- Changes must be made in structures and policies and must be consistent with any changes in attitudes which the program produces.
- All portions of the organization must change in a synchronized manner.
- Sufficient time must be allowed for all those involved to work out their problems. In practice, this appears to mean at least seven days of participation in any one program.[14]

Beyond this, the limited evidence suggests that no form of OD is uniformly best; however, OD programs using several forms of intervention (e.g., survey feedback, the Grid, and intergroup exercises) are more effective than those using one technique only. Finally, OD seems more likely to be successful in high-technology, constantly-changing organizations in which a great deal of coordination is required among work groups and rapid communication is needed up and down all organizational levels. OD may be particularly useful in countering the kinds of devisiveness that appears to be inherent in increasing specialization and professionalization. It is also appropriate if a matrix organization is to work. On the other hand, in industries with stable environments and easily routinized jobs, OD appears to be less worthwhile.

---

[14] Jerry Porras and P. O. Berg, "The Impact of Organization Development," *Academy of Management Review*, Vol. 3, No. 2 (April 1978), 249–66.

performance appraisal and management by objectives

In the typical large organization, every manager is subject to a periodic performance appraisal. As is true of other aspects of management development, the primary purpose of these appraisals has shifted in recent years. Originally a device to provide guidance to management in selecting managers for promotion or salary increases, appraisals are now also used for coaching managers to improve their performance.

An effective performance-appraisal program provides management with a rational basis for determining who should be promoted or receive salary increases. It permits each manager to be considered on the same basis as everyone else. Thus, hopefully, fewer charges of favoritism are made and better managers are selected for promotion. Long-range personnel planning (and the use of replacement charts) are also facilitated, since management can determine who should be promoted now, who should be ready after further experience and training, and who, although satisfactory on the present job, is not a likely prospect for a more difficult one. Further, management can tailor transfers to meet individual needs, and it can identify managers who need special training. Finally, performance appraisal is often needed to provide criteria for validating selection procedures or to defend against charges of discrimination.

Performance appraisal can also be used as a springboard for coaching managers and for helping them set goals for their own development. Unfortunately, the procedures that are most useful for selection purposes are less useful for self-development. As a consequence, many organizations have abandoned their *traditional* procedures, in which employees' traits were rated by their bosses, for newer less biased methods. Some organizations have abandoned ratings as such in favor of Management By Objectives (MBO) which typically involves the setting of goals by superiors and subordinates working together. Although MBO is also an important planning tool (and should not be mistakenly viewed as merely another form of performance evaluation), traditional performance evaluation and MBO are sufficiently linked together for us to consider them in the same chapter.

We shall look first at traditional performance appraisal and then at MBO. Before doing this, let us point out that performance appraisal is often conducted at the hourly-paid (especially among clerical workers) as well as the management level; for hourly-paid workers it is often called "merit rating." Further, performance appraisal is common for professional and technical employees.

Traditional performance rating

Stripped to its essentials, traditional performance rating is a matter of filling out a form (see illustration, p. 271). Normally the form is filled out by the manager's immediate supervisor and then checked by the supervisor's boss. Sometimes the rating is done by a committee:

RCA tries to minimize subjectivity by having each RCA manager rated by a group of fellow workers, generally including his immediate superior, two or three higher level managers, two or three peers, and one or two workers in lower positions.[1]

Occasionally the rating committee may also include "customers" of the individual being rated. (A maintenance manager might be rated by the production managers he or she serves.) Committee ratings have two great advantages. First, since each rater sees the person being rated from a different vantage point, the overall appraisal may be more balanced. Second, since a number of people participate, there may be greater feeling that the rating process is fair.[2]

Rating scales

A conventional rating form of the check-the-box type is sometimes called a "graphic rating" or a "rating scale." The important part here is the overall summary rating or score, which makes it possible to compare large numbers of managers. The ratings on specific factors do serve a purpose, however, in helping to pinpoint areas in which a subordinate needs further development.

In one variety of rating scale, the overall score is determined by adding up the scores given to specific factors (note the score is 35 on the form on the next page). In spite of its deceptive simplicity, this approach has severe limita-

---

[1] *The Wall Street Journal,* May 23, 1978.
[2] Some evidence suggests that in making ratings, the factors that peers emphasize are different from those their bosses do, and peers tend to be more lenient.

Rating form

	Unsatisfactory	Fair	Good	Very good	Exceptional	
Name: Wilson Olcott Position: Asst. Director, Mktg. Research Date rated: 6/25/19--						
Date hired: April 12, 19-- On position since: August 8, 19--						
Job knowledge: Extent of theoretical knowledge and practical know how as related to present job.	1	2	3	4	⑤	5
Judgment: Ability to obtain and analyze facts and apply sound judgment.	1	2	3	④	5	4
Organizing ability: Effectiveness in planning own work and that of subordinates.	1	2	③	4	5	3
Attitude: Enthusiasm shown for job; loyalty to company and superiors; ability to accept criticism and changes in company policy.	1	2	③	4	5	3
Dependability: Reliability in carrying out assignments conscientiously and with effectiveness.	1	2	3	④	5	4
Creativity: Ability to apply imagination to job, to develop new plans, cut costs, etc.	1	2	3	4	⑤	5
Dealing with people: Ability to get along with others; tact, diplomacy; ability to command and influence people.	1	②	3	4	5	2
Delegation: Ability to assign work to others and coordinate others though distribution of workload and responsibility.	1	2	③	4	5	3
Leadership: Ability to stimulate subordinates to perform their jobs effectively.	1	②	3	4	5	2
Personal efficiency: Speed and effectiveness in carrying out duties not assigned to subordinates.	1	2	3	④	5	4

Total points: 35

Evaluated by: Burt Neufane
Title: Director, Mktg. Research
Approved by: Jerry Falconner
Title: Mktg. Manager

Unsatisfactory: 10-15
Fair: 16-25 points
Good: 26-35 points
Very good: 36-45 points
Excellent: 46-50 points

tions. Consider some of the basic assumptions lying behind it: one is that each of the factors (creativity, judgment, and so forth) is of *equal* importance and that this holds true on all jobs. Yet clearly, on some jobs creativity is more important than effectiveness in dealing with people, and on others just the reverse is true. Another assumption is that these qualities are "additive"—for instance, strength in job knowledge will offset lack of leadership.

Unwilling to accept these assumptions, some companies permit their managers to give their subordinates an overall rating directly, without adding up separate factor scores. This summary rating of overall ability may be given either in numerical terms, from one to 100, or in descriptive terms, from "unsatisfactory" to "outstanding."

Both forms of ratings are often supplemented by open-ended, essay-type questions. At times the essay portion of the evaluation form takes considerably more space than does the quantitative portion. These subjective, qualitative evaluations tend to give a fuller picture than is presented by numerical ratings alone. They are also more useful for coaching, but they are of little help in comparing large numbers of people for purposes of pay increases or promotion.

Human errors in rating

Both forms of numerical ratings are subject to certain human evaluative errors. (Incidentally, these same errors distort merit rating and job evaluation.)

Ambiguity. Factors need to be described clearly, so that all raters have the same sort of behavior in mind. Further, unless all raters agree on what such terms as "good" and "excellent" mean, their final ratings simply cannot be compared.

Insufficient evidence. The boss frequently gets a limited and often a distorted view of the subordinate's performance. Particularly in jobs for which actual results are difficult to measure, the subordinate's ability to get along with the boss may have a greater impact on his or her rating than does actual performance on the job. The less contact the rater has with the ratee or the less knowledge the rater has of the ratee's job, the less useful the rating. Rating committees naturally help reduce this problem.

Differing perceptions. People differ in their standards of judgment. Even when they have no conscious prejudice, raters tend to rate subordinates similar to themselves in background, values, and style of behavior higher than they rate subordinates with dissimilar life styles (the "similar-to-me" effect). More than such obvious factors as racial discrimination are involved here. The manager who is accustomed to making quick decisions may be antagonized by the person who moves ponderously and deliberately, and vice versa. Sometimes executives who are poor managers themselves evaluate the competence of better qualified subordinates. (There is evidence that better managers also make better raters.)

Excessive leniency or strictness. As every student knows, there is a big difference between hard and easy graders. In industry, some raters rate everybody high, others are very strict, and still others play it safe by sticking to the middle. Ratings tend to be higher if the manager knows they will be revealed to subordinates. Managers often hesitate to give low ratings for fear of antagonizing their subordinates and making them less cooperative. Furthermore, supervisors fear that low ratings will reflect on their own abilities. There is always the chance that their boss will say, "If your subordinate is as bad as all this, why didn't you do something about it?" Some executives regularly rate new employees very low, then gradually raise them—thus making the employee feel good and displaying to their superiors their skill as trainers.

In many organizations there is a tendency for ratings to rise over time. During World War II nearly every soldier got the highest rating. To get the next-to-highest rating was evidence of downright incompetence.

These problems become less serious when top management stresses the importance of a wide rating spread and raises questions whenever ratings cluster at one level.

The halo effect. There is a natural tendency for raters to be influenced in rating one factor by the ratings they give on another. If a manager has a general impression that a subordinate is good, he will rate him high on all factors—and vice versa. Or his rating on the first factor listed or on the factor he thinks most important may contaminate his ratings on all others. (One way to reduce the halo effect is to rate all the subordinates on a single item before going on to the next, rather than rating one subordinate at a time.)

Influence of the job. Performance rating is designed to evaluate how well an individual does on a particular job. Although in theory performance rating is vastly different from job evaluation (which rates the job, not the manager) in practice it is common to give managers on higher-paid jobs higher ratings just because of their position.

Recency. Finally, raters tend to give recent events greater weight than those occurring at the beginning of the rating period.

All these human errors in rating can be at least partially counteracted by ensuring that the managers who do the rating are properly trained.

Traits or performance?

A more fundamental criticism of the traditional rating scale is that it places excessive emphasis on personality traits as opposed to measurable objective performance. Management development was originally introduced into many companies as a crash program designed to reveal executives who were promotable to top positions. Actual performance on the job was often considered secondary, in part because the emphasis was all on *potential* for development.

In any event, many organizations ask raters to evaluate subordinates on such factors as optimism, drive, and ability to learn. The armed services, for example, have asked for ratings of such qualities as "initiative," "force," "moral courage," and "loyalty."

What has proved wrong with this emphasis on traits? In the first place, the ratings are of little use in helping employees do a better job. It is hard for people to make real changes in their "personality," though they may put up a false front and pretend to be, in the words of one form, "radiant, confident, cheerful, courteous."

In trait rating, standards are often unclear. Exactly what is "loyalty," and how does one differentiate among various degrees of loyalty on a five-point scale? Not only is it difficult to get agreement as to what these factors mean, but their use in evaluations is particularly subject to personal or racial bias. When appraisals are used to determine who gets salary increases or promotions, they become "selection devices" and thus subject to the equal employment guidelines.³ Courts have been particularly suspicious of appraisal systems that use such vague and subjective factors as "loyalty" and "capacity for growth."

Trait-rating shares with some of personality testing the assumption that there is one psychological conformation that makes the best executive. Yet jobs differ in their psychological requirements: Sales managers may require more aggressiveness than do laboratory managers.⁴ And even where jobs are alike, people with vastly different personalities may perform equally well. Frequently, the emphasis on traits gives the advantage to the conformist who never rubs anyone the wrong way but also never has original ideas. One large company offered the following choices for the single trait, "cooperation."

1. Concedes nothing. Obstructive, antagonistic.
2. Poor mixer. Tries to run with the ball. Occasionally indulges in obstructive argument.
3. Generally adapts self to person and situations. Responsive to leadership and reasonably tactful.
4. Willing and eager to please. Works in complete harmony with group. Adaptable and courteous.
5. Adapts self very well without sacrificing standards. Goes out of his way to promote common end.

Note by favoring the manager who is "willing and able to please" over the one who "tries to run with the ball," this company is giving first priority to good human relations as opposed to decisive decision making. Yet those at the very top are often 100 percent rugged individualists. Howard Hughes would never have gotten passing marks for outgoing personality and Henry Ford, Sr., got along pretty well without too much sense of humor. Most executives are strange combinations of strengths and weaknesses.

Alternate rating methods

Because of these criticisms of traditional rating scales, personnel researchers have tried to develop new rating procedures that are less affected by raters' personal biases and less concerned with such imponderables as traits. Among the best known of these new forms of rating are *forced distribution,* the *critical incidents* technique, and *behaviorally anchored rating scales.*⁵

Forced distribution. Forced distribution is familiar to students as the old principle of "grading on the curve." The manager who uses this system

---

³ Subjective factors are also suspect when they are used as criteria, for validating tests.
⁴ One study found that an intense sense of honesty almost guaranteed failure on a particular type of sales job. John C. Miner, "Management Appraisal," in W. Clay Hamner and Frank L. Schmidt, eds., *Contemporary Problems in Personnel,* rev. ed. (Chicago: St. Clair, 1977), p. 233.
⁵ For a discussion of a variety of other techniques, including the forced choice or paired comparisons techniques, see Lawrence Cummings and Donald Schwab, *Performance in Organizations: Determinants and Appraisals* (Glenview, Ill.: Scott, Foresman, 1973).

of rating is expected to rank subordinates by group, instead of ascribing a set of rating points to each individual. In a typical system, the top 10 percent of the managers are placed in the highest class, 20 percent in the next, 40 percent in the middle bracket, 20 percent in the next-to-lowest, and 10 percent at the very bottom.

This system obviously eliminates the danger that the manager will be overly lenient. Moreover, it is easy to explain and administer. Yet this scheme has distinct drawbacks: In effect, it assumes that all groups have the same proportion of average, poor, and outstanding managers. But this is not likely to be true, particularly when there are only a few managers in a given group. Forced distribution is greatly resented by both bosses and subordinates. That is why the armed forces, which had experimented with this approach after World War II, later abandoned it.

Critical incidents. The critical incident technique of rating is also known as the "critical requirement system" and the "performance-record program."

The first step is to draw up for each job a list of *critical job requirements.* For a foreman, for instance, these requirements might include "improving equipment," "getting along with staff," "meeting schedules," and so forth. Typical job requirements for a sales manager might be "developing new customers" and "avoiding losses."

Once the critical job requirements have been determined, the next step is to train managers to be on the lookout for *critical incidents* or outstanding examples of the subordinate's success or failure in meeting the requirements. The manager lists the incidents as he or she observes them and gradually builds up a record for each subordinate, with the "debits" on one side and the "credits" on the other:

Dealing with Unions

9/21 Failed to consult with steward before making transfer.	8/6 Persuaded steward to withdraw grievance in regard to employee discharged for excessive absenteeism.
11/7 Made transfer in violation of sect. 39 (c) of contract.	12/3 Gave excellent answer to union grievance.

Normally, no attempt is made to balance the "debits" and the "credits." And yet the critical incident method does provide the raw materials for other forms of appraisal.

The great advantage of this approach is that all ratings are based on objective evidence rather than on a subjective evaluation of traits. It is no longer enough for the boss to say, "Joe has trouble dealing with people." The boss can cite specific incidents to prove this contention. To ensure objectivity, the manager is requested to record each incident immediately instead of trying to think back over, say, the last six months before making a rating.

On the other hand, care must be taken to ensure that the manager's recordkeeping does not degenerate into supervision in detail. He should emphasize *what* is accomplished, not *how* it is accomplished. Further, keeping a "little black book" in which mistakes are recorded conflicts with the philosophy that management should not overemphasize blame-finding.

Behaviorally anchored rating scales. This technique involves the development of rating scales, which are custom made for each job. In somewhat simplified form the main steps are:

1. Meetings are held with the managers who will rate the people holding the job in question. These managers are asked to list several key dimensions of proficiency on the job. (For example, a rating scale developed for college professors included such dimensions as Depth of Knowledge, Interpersonal Relations with Students, and Ability to Motivate.)[6]
2. The same or a different group provides examples of good, average, and poor performance for each dimension. (For a professor's Interpersonal Relations with Students, an example of good performance might be "When a class doesn't understand a concept, this professor could be expected to sense it and act to correct the situation," while an example of average performance might be "During lectures this professor could be expected to tell students with questions to see him during his office hours.")
3. A number of such *behaviors* are generated and each is given a value ranging from 1 (very poor behavior) to 7 (outstanding behavior).
4. Once the scale is completed, raters use it to evaluate the *expected* behaviors of each person being rated. Individual rating scores are computed on the basis of each persons' typical or expected behavior on each scale.

Behavioral scales have three main advantages. In the first place, those who do the rating can participate in developing the scale and are therefore more likely to understand and use it. Second, since the items are highly specific there is less chance of such errors as ambiguity, excessive leniency, or halo effect. Finally, this technique focuses on behavior (*how* the managers work) rather than traits (their personalities) or performance (how *much* they can put out). Normally, behavior is easier for the manager to change than either personality or performance (particularly since performance may be affected by factors not under the individual manager's control). Thus, behavioral ratings may be particularly useful for coaching or training.

A major disadvantage is the time and cost of developing rating scales for each separate job (although families of jobs may sometimes be combined). Further, since *expected* rather than actually observed behavior is rated, ratees can always deny that in fact they ever behave as the raters say they would. Finally, since this technique emphasizes methods rather than results, it may encourage the manager to overemphasize the specific behaviors rated. (To return to our previous example: to get a high rating a professor in a large class may feel compelled to answer all questions at length, thus leaving little time for the main lecture.)

---

[6] The example is from Oren Harari and Sheldon Zedeck, "Development of Behaviorally Anchored Scales for the Evaluation of Faculty Teaching," *Journal of Applied Psychology,* 58 (1973), 261–65. See also James G. Goodale, "Behaviorally-based Rating Scales," in Hamner and Schmidt, eds., *Contemporary Problems in Personnel.*

Evaluating these techniques. Each of these techniques has supporters, as do other techniques not discussed here. But no technique has been shown to be uniformly superior to traditional rating scales. Indeed, some argue that training managers to improve their effectiveness in using traditional scales may result in much greater payoff than would equal time spent in developing special techniques.[7] It can be argued that it makes little difference what appraisal system is used, provided the managers involved can understand it.

The evaluation interview

Many organizations require each manager to discuss subordinates' progress with them periodically. Evaluation interviews serve two purposes: (1) they serve as a form of feedback, which helps subordinates evaluate their progress and where they stand in the eyes of their boss, and (2) they provide an opportunity for managers to counsel subordinates on how to improve their performance.

Superiors frequently recoil at the thought of having to tell their subordinates how they stand or what they need to do to improve themselves. Too often managers fool themselves into thinking that their subordinates really know their weaknesses already, and they are often shocked when a subordinate tells them "Since you never complained, I thought I was doing OK." Well-conducted evaluation interviews can reduce such misunderstanding. As one junior executive commented, "Before this evaluation system was installed, the only time the boss would tell you how you were doing was when you were in trouble. If he'd say, 'I'd like to talk about your future,' that meant you were really going to get chewed out."

But evaluation interviews are not easy. Poorly handled they may lead to hostility and even greater misunderstanding. Consequently, many organizations spend considerable effort on training their managers to handle evaluation interviews, giving particular emphasis to listening techniques. To ensure that no essential part of the interview is left out, managers are often encouraged to follow a standardized outline. For example:

1. The superior tells the subordinate the purpose of the interview, that it is designed to help him or her do a better job.
2. The superior presents the evaluation, giving the strong points first, then the weak points, and ending on a positive note. (Sometimes this is called a "sandwich," since the meat—the criticism—is surrounded by blander material.)
3. Next the superior asks for comments. He (or she) anticipates that the subordinate may show some hostility to negative evaluations and allows him to blow off steam. The superior accepts any criticism or aggression on the part of the subordinate and does not expose unjustified excuses.
4. The superior then encourages the subordinate to give his own version of his progress and problems.
5. The interview closes with a discussion of what the subordinate can do to improve his performance in the future and what the superior can do to help.

[7] John Miner, "Management Appraisal."

Some managers start the interview by asking the subordinate, "Tell me, how do *you* think you are doing?" Then they show the subordinate the evaluation. This has the advantage of letting the subordinate tell his or her side of the story first; it is often easier for a person to criticize himself than to accept criticism from others.

Difficulties in conducting evaluation interviews

In recent years many organizations have become discouraged with appraisal programs. The rating period often turns out to be a time of apprehension and discomfort for managers and subordinates alike. Despite the publicity with which appraisal programs are typically introduced, many managers merely go through the motions of conducting interviews; others "forget" about them altogether. It is not uncommon for managers to hand subordinates their ratings without comment or to explain the rating in a rather embarrassed fashion without giving the subordinate a chance to comment or reply.

Why are managers generally so unenthusiastic about the evaluation program? Many have little skill in listening techniques; others, feeling that their primary function is "to get work out," have little interest in taking time from their "main job" to develop subordinates.

Yet even managers who are sympathetic to the principles of management development feel uncomfortable when they have to criticize people they work with on a daily basis. As one manager said, "I dread the time when I have to give ratings. Nobody appreciates them, and I get into an endless series of arguments, which makes it that much tougher to get the work out. People hold a grudge every time I tell the truth."

Subordinates tend to react to performance evaluation with defensiveness, suspicion, and hostility. They hope the boss will recognize their merits but fear that he or she will criticize them unfairly. Since many are primarily concerned with defending themselves, they resist the boss's criticisms and suggestions. In fact, evidence suggests that subordinates tend to rate their own performance higher than do their bosses (and few view themselves as below average); consequently the interview turns out to be a deflating, ego-damaging experience. Criticism may result in lower, not higher performance, particularly in the areas most criticized. Even praise may have an uncertain effect.[8]

Another explanation for the widespread resistance to conventional forms of evaluation interviews lies in two assumptions: (1) people want to be told where they stand, and (2) if they are told their weaknesses, they can change for the better. Neither assumption is universally valid, as the examples at the top of the next page suggest.

Perhaps the trouble here is that interviews serve two purposes. First, they relay the superior's judgments as to the subordinate's performance (judgments with important implications for salary increases and possible promotions), and second, they are designed to help subordinates improve their performances. Some authorities contend that these two objectives—*judgmental* and *developmental*—are so inconsistent that the details of the performance ratings should be kept secret and that performance rating and

---

[8] For a review of the evidence, see Miner, "Management Appraisal."

> A liberal arts college decided to rate faculty members on a scale from 1 (drop from faculty) to 5 (deserves substantial pay increase) and to reveal the results to each faculty member. The rating program was conducted by a joint faculty-student committee. A 65-year-old professor was given a rating of 2 on the grounds that her teaching was getting dull. The professor's grade for a lifetime of devoted service was a D! She was too old to change her ways, and in any case the college had no intention of dropping her a few years before retirement.
>
> Consider a laboratory division head who is technically brilliant but suffers from shyness and insecurity in dealing with people. Would telling him of his failure improve his dealings with people? Of course not. Certainly it wouldn't help him gain self-confidence.

evaluation interviews should be treated as separate processes. Secrecy is desirable, these authorities argue, because except in the hands of an exceptionally skilled interviewer, evaluation interviews focused on actual rating scores are likely to foster more antagonism than understanding. Furthermore, unless ratings are kept confidential they are unlikely to be candid. The evidence suggests that nonsecret ratings tend to be higher than secret ones, and there is reason to fear that managers are unwilling to give low ratings to aggressive employees who are likely to challenge them.

When to use evaluation interviews

There are no simple answers to the questions of whether an evaluation interview will be useful and what sort of interview should be used in a given situation. The choice depends on the subordinate's needs and the superior's skills.[9] The manager should use the form of interview that he or she finds most comfortable. For instance, the superior who tries to use the nondirective interview with no understanding of the approach will simply give the subordinate the impression that he is two-faced, particularly if the nondirective approach is totally inconsistent with his normal pattern of supervision. In any event, the manager should recognize that the objectives of the interview vary from one person to another. For example:

- If the fault is difficult or impossible to correct, there is no point in discussing it at all (unless the subordinate demands to know why he or she hasn't been promoted).
- If managers have faults that are correctable, it may be better to let them bring them up themselves when they see fit. Since evaluation interviews are held periodically, there is no need for supervisors to be disappointed if subordinates don't give a perfect self-analysis during the first session. The important thing is that the subordinates make gradual progress in correcting their limitations if they can and in accepting limitations if they cannot overcome them.
- In some cases individuals' performances may be so poor as to raise the possibility of their being discharged. Under such circumstances it is only fair that they be given warning, even though there is little chance of changing their behavior.

[9] Lawrence Cummings and Donald Schwab, "Designing Appraisal Systems for Information Yield," *California Management Review,* 20, No. 4 (Summer 1978), 18–25.

The appraisal interview is actually a form of coaching. So why formalize the process? After all, good managers recognize that coaching should occur more frequently than once every six months; they hold the equivalent of an evaluation interview whenever they think a subordinate will profit from it. On the other hand, poor managers will probably only go through the motions of a proper evaluation interview (which may do more harm than good) or perhaps ignore it altogether.

Thus, a companywide policy requiring periodic evaluation interviews is most useful for the *average* supervisor, for it forces him to take time off from his duties, to think through how each of his subordinates has been progressing, and then to sit down with each subordinate to talk over their long-range relationships.

Management by objectives

Designed to overcome the limitations of traditional systems, Management by Objectives (MBO), sometimes called results-oriented appraisal or Work Planning and Review, has been widely adopted by many organizations. MBO is based on concrete objectives, which are set jointly by superior and subordinate.[10] Together they establish short-term performance goals, ways the subordinate can improve his efficiency and that of his department (for example, cut idle machine time by 5 percent, reduce scrap by 3 percent, or install a new production line by January 30). At the end of a set period (six months or a year), they meet again to evaluate how well these goals have been met, to discuss what can be done better, and to set new goals for the next year.[11] Thus the subordinate is judged by standards he helped determine.

MBO consists of three important elements: goal setting, participation, and appraisal.

Goal setting. MBO goals should be objective and measurable if possible (reduce scrap by 3 percent); if not, they should at least be specific ("develop understanding of computer techniques among subordinates"). In either case, goals should be realistic but tough—tough enough to make the managers stretch a bit.

Individual goals should be consistent with organizational objectives. If top management plans to increase sales by 15 percent, it is not sufficient for manufacturing to set a goal of increasing production by only 5 percent (on the other hand, MBO may provide the mechanism by which manufacturing may signal top management that the 15 percent goal is unrealistic). Similarly, the goals of various departments should dovetail: it makes little sense for sales to commit to a new computerized credit system by March 1 if systems won't

---

[10] The concept of MBO was originally proposed by Peter Drucker in *The Practice of Management* (New York: Harper, 1954), and suggested as a performance appraisal technique by Douglas McGregor in "An Easy Look at Performance Appraisal," *Harvard Business Review*, 35, No. 3 (May 1957), 90–94. More recent studies and reviews include Stephen Carroll and Henry Tossi, *Management by Objectives*, (New York: Macmillan, 1973); Miner, "Management Appraisal"; and F. E. Schuster and Alvin Kindall, "Management by Objectives—Where We Stand," *Human Resources Management*, 13, No. 1 (September 1974), 8–11.

[11] Sometimes the subordinate writes a self-appraisal before this meeting.

have a program ready until late July. To help resolve these problems of coordination, some companies give managers overlapping responsibilities to set joint or team goals.[12]

Joint goal setting is not enough, however. An effective MBO program requires that managers anticipate snags and barriers and that they work out an *action plan* showing in detail how the goals are to be reached. Regardless of the date the new computerized credit system is to be introduced, sales personnel must be trained to use it. This means the sales manager must plan a training program, not just for his staff but perhaps for himself as well. In addition to performance objectives, subordinates may set *personal development* objectives, which will help them reach their performance objectives (and perhaps prepare them for promotion). For a sales manager, such a personnel development objective might be to spend more time with the marketing research staff so as to anticipate changes in customer preferences, or to attend a leadership program to improve relations with subordinates. Properly used, an MBO program sets the direction for both individual careers and the organization as a whole; but it requires intensive participation on the part of managers at all levels, from top to bottom.

MBO goal setting has two main advantages. In the first place, as we have seen in Chapter 3, the mere process of goal setting is highly motivating. People like to know what they are expected to do. Those with high need achievement, in particular, gain satisfaction from meeting goals, particularly tough ones. Since MBO goals are custom-made for the special characteristics of each manager's job, they are especially motivating.

Second, MBO emphasizes the future, which can be changed, rather than the past, which cannot. Applied throughout the organization, MBO becomes more than a method of appraisal: it becomes a style of management that emphasizes forward planning rather than aimless fire fighting.[13] Thus it develops into a powerful technique for nonfinancial budgeting and for communicating management's priorities. It requires management to define exactly what it wants to accomplish and to specify all important objectives, especially those commonly ignored in traditional financial budgets (such as equipment maintenance, employee and product development, and customer relations). It helps clarify responsibilities, organize the job, and iron out problems in advance. As a result it makes decision making more rational for both boss and subordinate. It facilitates interdepartmental communications and coordination. Since MBO forces management to think about improving interpersonal effectiveness, it is also a program of organization development.

Participation. In principle, MBO programs permit subordinates to set goals either by themselves or jointly with their superiors, thus facilitating inter-

---

[12] Wendell French and Robert Hollmann, "Management by Objectives: The Team Approach," *California Management Review*, 17, No. 3 (Spring 1975), 13-22.

[13] In some organizations, MBO has gone through three stages. At first it was chiefly a means of performance appraisal. Next it became a planning technique used to decide *how* the organization should reach its objectives. Finally, it began to be viewed as a strategic planning tool to help management reevaluate its objectives and determine *where* it should be going. Sometimes these objectives conflict. George Strauss, "MBO: A Critical View," *Training and Development Journal*, 26, No. 4 (April 1972), 10-15.

nalized motivation. Frequently, too, managers help set not only their own goals but also those of the larger organization. The fact that these goals are accepted voluntarily and put in writing increases the sense that a contract has been struck and helps hold individual managers to their commitment.[14]

Further, in contrast to the "closed system" implied by traditional ratings, MBO gives subordinates an active role, increases their sense of control over their environment, and reduces their dependence on the boss. Finally, by emphasizing specific performance rather than character traits, MBO permits recognition of the innovative manager who gets results by unconventional means.

Appraisal. In principle, with MBO, subordinates are evaluated against standards they helped set themselves. Usually the atmosphere is less punitive and arouses less anxiety than do conventional appraisals. The boss becomes less a judge and more a coach. The concern is not with what went wrong last period, but how can errors made last period be corrected in the next.

At its best, the MBO process is a two-way street. Both the subordinate's performance and the relationship between the boss and the subordinate are reviewed. The boss may ask the subordinate what he, as the superior, can do, refrain from doing, or do differently to help the subordinate do an even better job. This approach gives a better balance to the interview, since each party is evaluating the other and both recognize that the subordinate's efficiency is greatly affected by what the superior does.

Limitations

Despite the initial enthusiasm with which many organizations greeted this new approach, experience suggests that MBO has a number of limitations. In the first place, the theory that subordinates set goals by themselves (or jointly with their bosses) may turn out to be illusory. It all depends on whether the participative approach, which is required for goal setting by the subordinate, is consistent with the boss's ordinary management style. The boss who regularly consults with subordinates finds this new approach quite easy. Not so the boss who is decisive and directive and never takes time to listen. With such a boss, MBO, by setting highly specific goals (and usually goals that get tougher each year) merely makes the subordinate feel less secure.

In any case, knowing that his boss is the one who hands out rewards, the typical subordinate may look anxiously for some indication as to what this boss thinks are proper goals. Once these become clear, he will quickly adopt them with "enthusiasm." Indeed, some subordinates might prefer their boss to indicate a preference from the start, instead of making them go through guessing games. Further, with organization-wide goal setting, the individual's freedom to set a personal goal is sharply reduced. If top management sets a goal to increase production by 15 percent, a foreman can suggest only means of reaching that goal. At the most, individual subordinates have the freedom to *negotiate* goals, not to set them independently. At times this negotiation

[14] Gerald Salancik, "Commitment and Control of Organizational Behavior and Belief," in Gerald M. Salancik and Barry Staw, eds., *New Directions in Organizational Behavior* (Chicago: St. Clair, 1977).

process turns into a game. After all, a manager's apparent "performance" is a function of his initial goal. If his goals are set low, it is easy to look good. And so the trick, in some situations, is to set a low initial goal and sell one's boss that this goal is really hard to reach.

Because MBO places heavy stress on measurable standards, it may cause problems in dealing with intangible, unmeasurable aspects of the job. Production, which is measurable, is emphasized over employee development, which is not. Because of this difficulty, quality may be sacrificed for sheer quantity; trivial items may assume undue importance because they can be counted.

A laboratory director set as her goal the enhancement of her laboratory's professional prestige. Since prestige is difficult to measure, she set as her performance target a certain number of papers to be read at professional meetings. To fill this quota she "encouraged" individual subordinates to accept the writing of papers as goals for themselves. The result, as might be expected, was that the required number of papers were read, but they were of such poor quality that they lowered rather than raised the laboratory's prestige. (The story might have been less tragic if the director's subordinates had felt really free to reject their assignments.)

As our example illustrates, creative work, such as research, personnel, or advertising, is often difficult to measure, as indeed is most staff work (since it must achieve its results through others).

Overemphasizing measurable data also encourages covering up poor performance or actually falsifying data. A subordinate may slight long-run improvement to look good during the current evaluation period. Since each individual is encouraged to make himself look good, cooperation is discouraged. In addition, to the extent that a manager's overall performance is evaluated on the basis of a relatively few measures, there is a danger that accidental factors outside his control may distort the picture. During a period of rapid change, goals may become outmoded long before the next review period comes around. Perhaps the real test of a manager is the ability to handle the unexpected. Yet in times of crisis MBO is often ignored.

Unless an endless number of factors are considered, some significant items may be ignored or fall into chinks between measured goals. When one goal must be achieved at the expense of another, the manager has only imperfect standards for choice. He or she may easily emphasize side goals over the main show. ("I could meet all my goals in developing new accounts, but in so doing I would lose $1,000,000 in bread-and-butter sales.")

Making MBO work

MBO has been introduced into many companies, but according to one study, in fewer than 10 percent of these was the system really successful.[15] Organizations must commit a great deal of time and effort if MBO is to become a new way of organizational life. It is simply too easy to go through the motions of setting goals and then to ignore them. Frequently there is a boomerang effect: the high hopes that some managers set when MBO is first announced

[15] Schuster and Kindall, "Management by Objectives—Where We Stand."

lead to sad disillusionment when the promised participation turns out to be a sham. Successful introduction of MBO may require a full-scale Organization Development effort. Further, unless management constantly reemphasizes its commitment to MBO (especially by practicing MBO at its own level), the entire process will gradually atrophy.[16]

The main problem is that in many cases a participative system is grafted on an autocratic organization. In practice, MBO can be used for different purposes. Following the terminology introduced in Chapter 2, traditional managers can use MBO to set specific goals; human relations oriented managers may also use MBO to listen to their subordinates' gripes and to manipulate them to accept (presumably voluntarily) the goals which higher management had intended from the start. But only the managers who are convinced of the value of internalized motivation are likely to permit their subordinates to participate on an equal basis in setting goals not just for themselves but for the wider organization.

The research suggests that of the two main aspects of MBO, goal setting and participation, it is the setting of clear, concrete goals, not the sense of participation, that is important for increased performance. Concrete goals direct performance, reduce uncertainty, and serve as an instrument of communications—and they do so whether goals are introduced directly or participatively. So traditional and human relations-oriented managers may find MBO useful, particularly if they do not engender unrealistic expectations about participation. Joint goal setting is more effective than goal setting by the boss, but only if the boss uses participation on a day-to-day basis.

On the other hand, as we have seen, excessive emphasis on a few measurable goals may lead to other elements of the manager's performance being ignored. Nevertheless, used with discretion, goal setting provides a framework within which subordinates are motivated and receive specific cues about how they stand and what they should do to improve.

Promotions and salary increases

Should MBO be used for determining who should get promotions or salary increases? Here there are many uncertainties. A manager's past performance on his present job may provide only an imperfect indicator of his potential for a new job, especially if one job requires the day-to-day supervision of a work team and the higher job involves long-term planning and coordination with staff groups. Other factors besides past performance must be taken into account in making promotion decisions, including the manager's success in earlier rating periods. In addition, personality traits, as disclosed by good selection tests or in assessment centers, may be relevant.

Some organizations separate evaluation of managerial *potential* from evaluation of present *performance* (with judgments as to potential kept confidential). The evaluations occur at different times, and different forms are used for each purpose. Often the evaluation of potential is not even shown to the subordinate.

---

[16] John M. Ivancevich, "Changes in Performance in a Management by Objectives Program," *Administrative Science Quarterly*, 19, No. 4 (December 1974), 563–74.

MBO may not be appropriate for determining who should get a salary increase either, since it provides little basis to compare one manager against another. Yet any salary program that bases salary on performance must make such comparisons. Therefore, a separate procedure may have to be established for salary purposes. Thus an organization may have as many as three appraisal programs, each for differing purposes: for promotions, for salary increases, and for coaching.

Separating coaching appraisal from the other two has another advantage. It separates the boss's developmental function from his judgmental one. But having three different procedures may lead to chaos (as well as much paper work), particularly if the ratings are inconsistent with each other. A manager who regularly meets MBO goals yet is never promoted may become terribly frustrated.

Certainly salary increases should be consistent with appraisals, whether or not appraisals are based on subordinate-set goals. Salary appraisal should be a fairly explicit procedure in which individuals are (in most cases) told the basis for pay decisions. Although MBO results should perhaps be a major factor in this process, the reward system should take into account a broader set of variables than does MBO. Unmeasurable aspects of performance (for example, whether the manager is improving his relations with other departments) as well as such factors as seniority, the organization's salary position, and salaries paid by competitors should all be considered.

Perhaps in organizations with "closed" personnel systems, promotion prospects will be kept secret. It is possible, however, for a manager in an "open" system to conduct an appraisal interview that combines the three forms of appraisal:

"Joe, you've met every one of your MBO targets. Congratulations! There will be a salary increase for you, but to get a greater increase next period, you may wish to concentrate on these during the next rating period. We ought to think about the future, too. As we mentioned last time, the XYZ job requires certain skills. What kind of progress are you making in acquiring these?"

index

A

Absenteeism, 54, 62, 63, 87, 118
Acceptable behavior, groups and, 94–95
Achievement, 9, 11, 15–16, 35
Administration, 35
Advancement, 8–9, 35
Advance warning, 185–86
Advisory interdependence, 236, 237
Advisory relationships, 244–46
Affiliation, need for, 15, 44
Aggression, 30, 39, 161
Appraisal, 282
Approval, as support function, 83–84
Argot, 132
Arguing, 158–59
Argyris, Chris, 18n, 19n
Attention, 52
Attitudes, group, 99–100
Auditing, 239–40, 241
Automation, 21, 161
Autonomy, 11–12, 18, 19, 49–50, 88n

B

Ball, George, 163
Bargaining
 change and, 174–75
 implicit, 27, 36–38, 117, 169, 174
Behaviorally anchored rating scales, 276
Belongingness, 9

Blacks, discrimination against, 105, 194
Blake, Robert, 261
Blocked mobility, 4
Blue-collar workers
 competition and, 38
 expectancy theory, 44
 job redesign and, 60
 work, attitudes towards, 21, 23
Body language, 133
Bogey (standards of output), 29n, 30, 53
Brainwashing, 141n
Buffering, 59n
Built-in alarms, 210
Bureaucracy, 5, 208
Bureaucratic theory, 198

C

Case method, management training and, 253–54
Catharsis, 148
Ceremony, 178
Challenge, 18–19, 24–25
Change, 5, 41, 160–79
 causes of resistance to, 161–69
 commitment to, 162–63, 173–74
 communication and, 172
 fast vs. slow, 176–77
 group decision making and, 172–74
 organization development and, 262–63

 overall organization and, 167–69
 overcoming resistance to, 170–71
 reducing resistance to, 169–79
 types of resistance to, 160–61
 unions and, 166, 174–75
Chrysler Corporation, 67
Civil Service regulations, 29
Clothing Workers Union, 162
Cognitive dissonance, 136–37
Cohesiveness, 108–10, 117–18
Collective bargaining, 175
Command, unity of, 227
Commitment, 17, 23, 120
 change and, 162–63, 173–74
 goal-setting and, 65
 group, 101–2
 in organization development, 263–64
 to superordinate goals, 40
Communication, 130–46
 change and, 172
 discipline and, 185–86
 feedback, 142–43
 improving, 139–46
 listening, see Listening
 modes of, 132–34
 reception, 134–38
 transmission, 131–34
Companionship, as group function, 93–94
Company policy, 35
Competition, as motivation method, 27, 38–39
Computers, 166–67
Concentrated workweek, 66–67
Confidence, 150–51

287

Conformity, groups and, 100
Confrontation, organization development and, 260–62
Consideration, 32
Consistency, 207
  in discipline, 186–89
Contingency theory, 77–78
Contracting, matrix structure and, 228–29
Control Data Corporation, 70
Counseling, employee, 94, 149
Counter culture, 7
Courtesy, 83
Covert feelings, in communication, 132
Critical incidents technique, 275–76

D

Daydreaming, 53, 54
Decision making, 87, 119–27
Defensive avoidance, 137
Delegation, 203–13
Demotion, 183
Depth attention, 52
Didactic instruction, 263
Direct questions, 158
Discharge, 182
Disciplinary layoffs, 182
Discipline, 36, 180–95
  advance warning, 185–86
  avoidance of, 181–82
  communication and, 185–86
  consistency in, 186–89
  government imposed standards, 193–95
  immediate, 184–85
  impersonality in, 189–91
  progressive, 182
  red-hot-stove rule, 183–91
  types of, 182–83
  unions and, 191–93
Discrimination, 105, 194
Drucker, Peter, 280n

E

Economic incentives, change and, 171–72
Economies of scale, 222
Effort, 210
Egoistic needs, 6, 9–10, 13, 14, 18, 58–59, 88
Empathetic listening, 155–56
Empire building, 24
Employee counseling, 94, 149
Encounter groups, 255
Equity, 43, 44
Esteem needs, 13n
Evaluation, 210

Evaluation interviews, 277–80
Expectancy theory, 27, 42–45, 79–80, 119, 120
Expectations, 17, 59
  of communication receiver, 135, 139
  supervisory legitimacy and, 112–17
Expressive orientations toward work, 23–25

F

Face-to-face integration, 241–42
Failure, need to avoid, 15
Fair competition, 39
Fair Labor Standards Act, 69
Fair treatment, 37, 85–86
Fantasy, 24
Farming, 3–4
Favoritism, 85, 129, 151, 186, 187
Feedback, 51
  in communication, 142–43
  evaluation interviews, 277
  in goal-setting, 64
  job redesign and, 55–56
  in organization development, 260–61
Fixation, 31
Flextime, 66, 67–69, 71
Forced distribution, 274–75
Ford, Henry, 104
Ford Motor Company, 33, 163
Foreman training, 249
4-day week, 66–67
4-40 plan, 66–67
Free speech, 194
Fringe benefits, 8, 32
Frustration, 30–31, 82
Functional organization structure, 220–23, 231

G

Galbraith, Jay, 220
General Electric Company, 168–69
General Foods Corporation, 60, 61
General Motors Corporation, 62
Goal setting, 47, 63–66
  delegation and, 209–210
  group, 102–3
  MBO, 280–81, 284
  supervision and, 80–81
Goldplating, 99
Government imposed standards, 193–95
Grievance procedure, 87, 191–93
Group decision making, change and, 172–74
Group influence, management training and, 250
Groups, 32, 93–110

  attitudes and values, 99–100
  cohesiveness, 108–10, 117–18
  commitment, 101–2
  formation of, 96–101
  goal setting, 102–3
  impact of, 98
  informal leaders, 107–8, 127–29
  as organization, 97–98
  orientation, 100–101
  pressures to conform, 100
  reasons for formation of, 93–96
  standards of behavior, 39, 98–99, 112–13, 173, 181
  status systems, 103–7
  supervisors of, see Supervisors, as group leaders

H

Hall, Edward, 133n
Halo effect, 273
Hamaker, L. S., 39
Hawthorne studies, 32, 148–49
Herzberg, Frederick, 34n, 35, 39
Hierarchies, 196–216, 238–39
  definition of, 196
  delegation, 203–13
  first-line supervisor, 202–3
  managers and, 200–203
  nature of, 196–200
  span of control, 213–15
  supervisory styles, 200–201
  traditional vs. modern view, 198–200
Hierarchy of needs, 13–14, 15
Horizontal contacts, 198–99
Human relations, 27, 32–36, 40, 75–76
Human resources, 39n
Hybrid organization structure, 220, 221, 230–31
Hygienes, 34, 59–60
Hygienic management, 32, 34–35, 37, 41, 82

I

Identification, as group function, 94
Imagination, 12
Immediate discipline, 184–85
Impersonality in discipline, 189–91
Implicit bargaining, 27, 36–38, 117, 169, 174
Impression management, 131
In-basket technique, 254–55
Incentive system, 29n, 36, 38, 44, 53
Independence, 18, 210
Individual differences, psychology of, 74–75
Indoctrination, 210–12
Indulgency pattern, 36–37

Industrial relations, 3–4
Industrial revolution, impact of, 3–5
Informal leaders, 107–8, 127–29, 201
Initiative, 12
Input/output relations, 17
Instrumental orientations towards work, 23–25
Integration mechanisms, 238–42
Interaction styles, 133
Interdependence, 236–38
Intergroup exercises, organizational development and, 262, 268
Internalization, 263
Internalized motivation, 27, 39–42, 204
Interpersonal relationships, change and, 164–65
Interviewing
 defined, 147
 evaluation, 277–80
 See also Listening
Involvement, management training and, 250

J

Jargon, 132
Job and finish, 65
Job challenge, 18–19, 24–25
Job enlargement, 41, 54–55, 204
Job enrichment, 56–57, 265
Job legitimacy, 113–14
Job redesign, 40, 41, 47, 54–63
 evaluation of, 62–63
 feedback, 55–56
 job enlargement, 41, 54–55, 204
 job enrichment, 56–57, 265
 job rotation, 54
 motivation and, 57–60
 organizational change and, 60–61
 unions and, 61–62
 work teams, self-managing, 57
 work units, establishment of natural, 55
Job rotation, 54
Job satisfaction
 determinants of, 17–18
 extent of, 48–49
 importance of, 18–25
 mass production and, 49–54
 productivity and, 34–35
 See also Motivation
Job security, 7, 14
Job sharing, 66, 70–71

K

Knowledge, desire for, 12–13

L

Laboratory training, see T-group training
Labor unions, see Unions
Latent content, of message, 155
Lateral relationships, 217–18
Layoffs, 8, 182
Leadership, see Supervision
Lecturing, management training and, 253
Legitimacy
 supervisors and, 112–17
 support and, 82
Leisure, 21, 22, 65
Leniency, 117
Liaison specialists, 240
Listening, 147–59
 empathetic, 155–56
 establishing confidence, 150–51
 historical background, 148–50
 initiating action, 151–52
 as management tool, 150
 nondirective approach, 149, 152–53
 off-the-job problems, 152
 probes, 152, 156
 techniques, 153–57
 things to avoid, 157–59
Love needs, 13n
Loyalty, 83, 101, 103
LPC, 75n

M

McClelland, David, 15–16, 44
McGregor, Douglas, 5n, 183
Management by exception, 209
Management by Objectives (MBO), 65, 263, 265, 270, 280–85
 appraisal, 282
 goal setting, 280–81, 284
 limitations of, 282–83
 making work, 283–84
 participation, 281–82, 284
 promotions and salary increases, 284–85
Management game, 254
Management grid, 261, 268
Management training, 248–58, 267
 conventional techniques, 253–55
 forms of, 248
 historical development, 249
 organizational climate and, 251–53
 requirements for effective, 249–53
 T-groups, 249, 255–58
Manifest content, of message, 155
Maslow, Abraham, 5n, 13–14
Mass production, 49–54
Masterminding, 159
Matrix organization structure, 220, 221, 226–30, 231

Mayo, Elton, 94
MBO, see Management by Objectives (MBO)
Modeling, 263
Money
 goal-setting and, 65
 as need satisfaction, 6–7, 16–17
Morale, 34
Motivation, 27–46
 competition, 27, 38–39
 human relations, 27, 32–36, 40, 75–76
 implicit bargaining, 27, 36–38, 117, 169, 174
 internalized, 27, 39–42, 204
 job redesign and, 57–60
 traditional form of, 27, 28–32

N

Needs, relative importance of, 13–17
Need satisfaction, 5–13, 19
No attention jobs, 52
Noise, effect on communication, 137–38
Nondirective listening, 149, 152–53
Nonverbal cues, 133, 144

O

Off-the-job behavior, 6, 35, 152, 194–95
Older workers, discrimination and, 194
Open-system career paths, 40
Oral warnings, 182
Organizational change, job redesign and, 60–61
Organization charts, limitations of, 219
Organization design, 217–47
 advisory relationships, 244–46
 building work-flow teams, 231–36
 choice of, 231
 functional, 220–23, 231
 hierarchies, see Hierarchies
 hybrid, 220, 221, 230–31
 integration mechanisms, 238–42
 interdependence, 236–38
 lateral relationships, 217–18
 matrix, 220, 221, 226–30, 231
 product, 220, 223–26, 231
 role of structure, 218–20
 service relationships, 242–44
Organization development (OD), 248, 258–68
 change and, 262–63
 commitment and, 263–64
 common denominators, 259
 compared to T-groups, 259
 confrontation, 260–62

Organization development *(cont.)*
  controversies over, 264–66
  evaluation of, 267–68
  feedback, 55–56
  motivation for entering, 266–67
  refreezing, 263–64
  step-by-step progression, 259–60
Organization structures, *see*
    Organization design
Ostracism, 100, 135
Oversupervision, 78

P

Participation, 40
  developing group, 119–27
  MBO programs, 281–82, 284
Participative goal-setting, 64–65
Part-time work, 66, 69–71
Paternalism, 32–34
Path-goals analysis, *see* Expectancy theory
Peace Corps, 18
Performance appraisal, 269–80
  alternative rating methods, 274–77
  evaluation interviews, 277–80
  traditional rating systems, 270–74
  See also Management by Objectives (MBO)
Permanent dual reporting relationships, 229
Personality disturbances, 18, 19
Personal relations, as support function, 84–85
Physical needs, 5, 6–9, 13
Physiological needs, 13n
Piecework, 29n, 36, 38, 44, 53
Policies, 205, 208
Pooled interdependence, 236
Power, need for, 15
Praise, 6, 43, 83
Premature judgment, listening and, 157
Pressure, 39
  traditional motivational approach and, 28–31
Priming, 17
Probes, as communication technique, 152, 156
Productivity, 11
  goal-setting and, 64–66
  job redesign and, 63
  job satisfaction and, 34–35
  See also Supervision
Product organization structure, 220, 223–26, 231
Professional groups, 99
Progressive discipline, 182
Project groups, short-term, 227–28
Promotion, 4, 284–85
Protection, group membership and, 95–96

Proxemics, 133n
Psychosomatic illness, 18
Punishment, *see* Discipline

R

Racial discrimination, 105, 194
Rating, human errors in, 272–73
Rating scales, 270–71, 276
Reciprocal interdependence, 236, 237
Recognition, 35
Red-hot-stove rule, 183–91
Redundancy, in communication, 145–46
Reference group, influence of, 135–36
Reflective summary, 154–55
Refreezing
  management training and, 251, 257
  organization development and, 263–64
Regression, 31, 39, 161
Repression of feelings, 31
Resignation, 31
Responsibility, 35, 88
Retirement, 18, 19
Rewards, 42–45
Role-playing, 255
Roosevelt, Franklin D., 99
Routinization, 207
Rules, 205–9

S

Sabotage, 24, 30, 54, 87
Safety, 6
Safety needs, 13n
Salancik, Gerald, 5n
Salary increases, MBO and, 284–85
Scapegoating, 31
Scheduling, *see* Work schedules
Scientific management, 28, 49, 198, 227
Sears Roebuck Company, 214
Security needs, 5, 6–9, 13, 32
Self-actualization, 13, 18
Self-discipline, 180
Self-evaluation, 17
Self-managing work teams, 57, 59, 119
Seniority, 7, 8, 38
Sensitivity training, *see* T-group training
Sequential interdependence, 236, 237
Service interdependence, 236, 237
Service relationships, 242–44
Simulation, management training and, 254–55
Skill, 10–11, 50
Skinner, B. F., 5n
Slack, 242
Slowdown, 30

Smith, Adam, 4
Social comparisons, 17
Social distance, 115–16
Social games, 53
Socialization, 210–12
Social needs, 5, 9, 13, 14
Social norms, 17
Social relations, 52
Span of control, hierarchies and, 213–15
Spatial relations, communication and, 133–34
Specialization, 3–4, 12, 49
Speech, freedom of, 194
Spoilage, 30
Spontaneous cooperation, 39n
Stabilization, 240–41
Standards of behavior, group, 39, 98–99, 112–13, 173, 181
Standards of output, 29n, 30, 53
Status anxiety, 106
Status differentiation, 115–16, 151
Status inconsistency, 105–6
Status systems, group, 103–7
Stealing, 188, 189
Stereotyping, 135
Strikes, 54, 187
Structure
  definition of, 77
  goal-setting, 80–81
  guidance of employee efforts, 81–82
  relationship between support and, 90–91
  technical assistance, 82
  use of, 86–89
Sublimation, 31
Suboptimization, 102–3
Supervision, 40, 73–92
  contingency theory and, 77–78
  expectancy theory and, 79–80
  flextime and, 69
  human relations studies, 75–76
  by results, 209–10
  traits studies, 74–75
  See also Structure; Support
Supervisors, 35, 111–29
  building a work team, 117–19
  developing group participation, 119–27
  introduction of new, 177–79
  legitimacy, 112–17
  use of informal organization, 127–29
  See also Supervision
Support, 9, 82
  creating feeling of approval, 83–84
  definition of, 77
  developing personal relations, 84–85
  legitimacy and, 82
  providing fair treatment, 85–86
  relationship between structure and, 90–91
  use of, 89–90
Surface attention, 52, 53

Survey feedback, 262, 268
Suspension, 184–85
Symbols, 132–33, 139–40, 163–64, 175

T

Task identity, 50–51
Task significance, 9–10, 50
Taylor, Fredrick W., 28n, 49–50
Teamwork, developing, 118–19
Technical ability of supervisors, 114
Technology, 3–5, 212–13
T-group training, 249, 255–59, 267
Theory Y, 39n
Through-the-job satisfaction, 6
Tone, communication and, 134
Traditional form of motivation, 27, 28–32
Trait rating, 273–74
Traits studies, 74–75
Transactional analysis (TA), 134
Turnover, 54, 62, 63, 87, 118

U

Uncertainty, change and, 163
Uncertainty absorption, 107
Underprivileged workers, expectancy theory and, 44
Unemployment, 7, 18

Unfreezing, 249–50, 251, 257
Unions, 7, 8
 change and, 166, 174–75
 discipline and, 191–93
 job redesign and, 61–62
 work schedules and, 67, 71
Union steward, 129
United Auto Workers, 62
United Mine Workers, 162
U.S. Post Office, 215
Upward mobility, 8

V

Values, group, 99–100
Variety in jobs, 51–52
Vroom, Victor, 34n

W

Watson, Thomas J., Jr., 211n
Western Electric Company, 148–49
White-collar workers
 competition and, 38
 traditional motivational approach and, 29
Women
 discrimination against, 105, 194
 work schedules, 47, 66
Work, attitudes towards, 20–25

Work customs, 116
Work demands, 116–17
Work-flow teams, 231–36
Work groups, see Groups
Working conditions, 6, 35
Working supervisor, 129
Work schedules, 66–71
 flextime, 66, 67–69, 71
 4-day week, 66–67
 job sharing, 66, 70–71
 part-time work, 66, 69–71
 status and, 104
 union attitudes to, 67, 71
Work teams, self-managing, 57, 59, 119
Work-to-rule campaigns, 208
Work units, establishing natural, 55
Work week, 21, 66–67
Written communications, 144, 145
Written warnings, 182

Y

Youth culture, 29
Youth rebellion, 115

Z

Zone of indifference, 112